The Universal Vehicle Discourse Literature

(*Mahāyānasūtrālaṁkāra*)

By Maitreyanātha/Āryāsaṅga

Together with its *Commentary* (*Bhāṣya*)
By Vasubandhu

TREASURY OF THE BUDDHIST SCIENCES series
Editor-in-Chief: Robert A.F. Thurman
Jey Tsong Khapa Professor of Indo-Tibetan Buddhist Studies,
Columbia University
President, American Institute of Buddhist Studies

The American Institute of Buddhist Studies (AIBS), in affiliation with the Columbia University Center for Buddhist Studies and Tibet House US, has established the *Treasury of the Buddhist Sciences* series to provide authoritative English translations, studies, and editions of the texts of the Tibetan Tanjur (*bstan 'gyur*) and its associated literature. The Tibetan Tanjur is a vast collection of over 3,600 classical Indian Buddhist scientific treatises (*śāstra*) written in Sanskrit by over 700 authors from the first millennium CE, now preserved mainly in systematic 7th–12th century Tibetan translation. Its topics span all of India's "outer" arts and sciences, including linguistics, medicine, astronomy, socio-political theory, ethics, art, and so on, as well as all of her "inner" arts and sciences such as philosophy, psychology ("mind science"), meditation, and yoga.

The Publisher gratefully acknowledges the generous support of the Infinity Foundation in sponsoring the publication of this series.

The Universal Vehicle Discourse Literature

(*Mahāyānasūtrālaṁkāra*)

By Maitreyanātha/Āryāsaṅga

Together with its *Commentary* (*Bhāṣya*)
By Vasubandhu

Translated from the Sanskrit, Tibetan, and Chinese by
L. Jamspal, R. Clark, J. Wilson, L. Zwilling, M. Sweet, R. Thurman

Honorary Editor: Gadjin Nagao
Editor-in-Chief: Robert A.F. Thurman
Editing and Design: Thomas F. Yarnall

Tanjur Translation Initiative
Treasury of the Buddhist Sciences series

A refereed series published by the
American Institute of Buddhist Studies
at Columbia University, New York

Co-published with
Columbia University's Center for Buddhist Studies
and Tibet House US

2004

Tanjur Translation Initiative
Treasury of the Buddhist Sciences series
A refereed series published by:

American Institute of Buddhist Studies
Columbia University
623 Kent Hall
New York, NY 10027

Co-published with Columbia University's Center for Buddhist Studies and Tibet House US.

Distributed by Columbia University Press.

Printed in the United States of America on acid-free paper.

ISBN 0-9753734-0-4 (cloth)

Library of Congress Cataloging-in-Publication Data

Asaṅga.

[Mahāyānasūtrālaṅkāra. English]

The universal vehicle discourse literature = Mahāyānasūtrālaṁkāra / by Maitreyanātha/Āryāsaṅga ; together with its commentary (bhāṣya) by Vasubandhu ; translated from the Sanskrit, Tibetan, and Chinese by L. Jamspal ... [et al.] ; editor-in-chief, Robert A.F. Thurman.

p. cm. — (Treasury of the Buddhist sciences)

Translated from the Sanskrit, Tibetan, and Chinese.

Includes bibliographical references and index.

ISBN 0-9753734-0-4 (cloth : alk. paper)

I. Title: Mahāyānasūtrālaṁkāra. II. Thurman, Robert A.F. 1941– . III. Jamspal, L., 1936– . IV. Vasubandhu. Mahāyānasūtrālaṁkārabhāṣya. English. V. Title. VI. Series.

BQ2003.E5.T58 2004

294.3'85—dc22

2004052913

Contents

Note

In transliteration of Sanskrit words, we have followed the standard conventions in the italicized occurrences in parentheses and footnotes, but have departed from this in the English text, omitting diacritical vowel marks, using sh for ś, sh for ṣ, and ch for c. For the Tibetan alphabet we have adopted the following English letters: k, kh, g, ng, c (also ch in English text), ch, j, ny, t, th, d, n, p, ph, b, m, ts, tsh, dz, w, zh, z, ', y, r, l, sh, s, h, a. For most Tibetan names we have kept the unsounded pre-initial letters, capitalizing the first sounded initial consonant.

PREFACE

Homage to the Teacher Manjughosha!

The Universal Vehicle Discourse Literature (*Mahāyānasūtrālaṁkāra – MSA*) was chosen by the late Venerable Geshe Wangyal and the main translator, Acharya Dr. Lobsang Jamspal, as the founding cornerstone of the American Institute of Buddhist Studies' (AIBS) long-term project to translate and publish all the works contained in the Tibetan Tanjur (*bstan 'gyur*). Since the Tanjur is the main collection of the Tibetan translations of the Indian Buddhist Scientific Treatises (*śāstra*), we are calling the collection of English translations that will gradually emerge the *Treasury of the Buddhist Sciences.*

At the beginning of this series, it is important to acknowledge that whatever we may be able to understand about these texts we owe to our various teachers, Indian, Tibetan, Mongolian, Japanese, European, and American. Among predecessors, aside from the great Indian Pandits themselves, the "Ornaments of Aryavarta," my personal debt is great to Lama Tsong Khapa (1357–1419), from whose *Essence of True Eloquence* I glimpsed the gist of the Vijnanavada Idealism, and to the Venerable Geshes (*kalyāṇamitra*) Ngawang Wangyal (20th century), dBal mang dKon mchog rGyal mtshan (19th century), and dbYangs can dGa ba'i bLo gros (18th century), who elucidated Tsong Khapa's tradition of insight so effectively. I have a special purpose in acknowledging my gratitude to these great Lama scholars, as it is my firm conviction that the centuries of first-rate scholarship by the Tibetan and Mongolian monks during the second Common Era millennium forms a bridge from the profound scholarship of the ancient Indian masters to our contemporary Buddhological scholars. We should stop considering non-Western and non-modern scholars as mere "natives" or "informants" in comparison with ourselves as critical scholars, realize that the lines between "primary sources" and "secondary scholarship," "traditional" and "critical" or "scientific," "subjective" and "objective," and so on, are more or less arbitrary constructions, and be more rigorously self-critical and learn to give credit where credit is due. In matters textual and philosophical, we should overcome our modernistic pride that wants us somehow to invent every insight anew. We should recognize the contribution of the monastic scholarly tradition of Nalanda, Vikramashila, and so forth, that lived on to the present century in the monastic universities of Tibet and Mongolia, and we should make good use of this contribution in our scholarly work today.

Tsong Khapa wrote the story of his intellectual and spiritual education in the form of a eulogy to Manjushri (his patron celestial bodhisattva, the Buddhist deity of wisdom) entitled *Destiny Fulfilled.*[1] About the *Universal Vehicle Discourse Literature,* he says:

> Next I studied in conjunction
> The *Universal Vehicle Discourse Literature*
> and the *Bodhisattva Stages,*
> And I put their points together
> And gained the understanding
> Of the teaching of the Savior Maitreya.

Here we present our English translation of Maitreyanatha's *Universal Vehicle Discourse Literature*, as transmitted to and presented by Aryasanga in the fourth century CE, along with its verbal commentary (*Mahāyānasūtrālaṁkāra-bhāṣya – MSABh*) by Asanga's brother Vasubandhu. The *Discourse Literature* is the most foundational of the set of the famous *Five Teachings of Maitreyanatha* (*byams chos sde lnga*), within which the Tibetan tradition also includes the *Realization Literature* (*Abhisamayālaṁkāra – AA*), *Analysis of Center and Extremes* (*Madhyāntavibhāga – MAV*), *Analysis of Things and Their Reality* (*Dharmadharmatāvibhaṅga – DDV*), and the *Jewel Gene Analysis* (*Ratnagotravibhāga – RGV*) or *Further Continuum* (*Uttaratantra – UT*). These *Five Teachings* are considered the wellspring of what the Tibetans call the "magnificent deeds trend of the path," the compassion side, which balances the "profound view trend of the path," the wisdom side. Three out of five of them (*MSA*, *MAV, DDV*) are also considered works metaphysically aligned with the Idealist (*Vijñānavādin*) school of Mahayana thought. For this school, these three texts are foundational among scientific treatises (*śāstra*), as the *Elucidation of the Intention Discourse* (*Saṁdhinirmocanasūtra*) is foundational among discourses.

To accompany the *Discourse Literature*, following the advice of Lama Tsong Khapa, we also have a complete draft of the *Bodhisattva Stages* (*Bodhisattvabhūmi – BBh*), which Tsong Khapa considered to serve as Asanga's deeper commentary on the *Discourse Literature*, which, among other texts, we hope to polish and publish in the near future.

---

[1] See my *Central Philosophy of Tibet*, Introduction, wherein I translate this "Education Poem" in full.

This publication has taken a very long time to materialize, about thirty years. The blame for this glacial slowness is entirely mine: I take full responsibility for the many delays during this time, as now for having the temerity to actually release the text, when it seems we could continue endlessly with further improvements. We began in 1972 when Christopher George and I founded the first incarnation of the American Institute of Buddhist Studies (then simply the Buddhist Studies Institute) in Washington, New Jersey, under the urging of the late Venerable Geshe Wangyal, who had commanded us to undertake the translation of the "whole Tanjur!" We obtained a generous, multi-year grant from Dr. C.T. Shen's Institute for the Advanced Studies of the World Religions (IASWR) to begin by translating some of the works of Maitreyanatha, Aryasanga, and Vasubandhu. The Venerable Geshes Losang Tharchin and Jampel Thardod began to work with Art Engle and Robert Clark on the *Treasury of Clear Science* (*Abhidharmakośa – AK*) and the *BBh*. The Venerable Acharya Lobsang Jamspal soon arrived from India and began to work on the *Discourse Literature* with Mr. (now Dr.) Joseph Wilson. Chris George and I worked on the editorial side at first, though I soon began also to work with Brian Cutillo on primary translations of the *Elucidation of the Intention Discourse*, the *Discourse Literature*, and Asanga's *Clear Science Compendium* (*Abhidharmasamuccaya – AS*) and *BBh*. By 1976, these drafts were still incomplete, when the Institute moved with me, again at Geshe Wangyal's insistence, to the academic atmosphere of Amherst, Massachusetts. I was then working as an assistant professor at Amherst College, and we changed its name to the "American Institute of Buddhist Studies." Dr. Jamspal continued to work on the *Discourse Literature*, though since the IASWR funding ran out around then, things progressed slowly.

Although the *MSABh* manuscript translated from the Tibetan was in rough draft by the later 1970s, we decided we needed more thorough consultation with Sthiramati's subcommentary as well as further comparison with Sanskrit editions and the Chinese translation, not to mention a better developed choice of English terminology. In 1978, we obtained a generous grant from the National Endowment for the Humanities in order to continue to engage Dr. Jamspal, and also to bring on board Drs. Leonard Zwilling and Michael Sweet, at that time recent graduates of University of Wisconsin at Madison's Buddhist Studies program, to work through the entire text with me as editor and co-translator to finalize the manuscript. Dr. Jamspal remained part of the team; he read through Sthiramati's entire subcommentary, and he added notes and corrected the text in places where Sthiramati gave new insight. Dr. Zwilling focused on the Sanskrit and Dr. Sweet focused on the Chinese, so we were able to correct, improve, and amplify the basic translation from the Tibetan version by means of word-by-word comparison with the Sanskrit edition and occasional consultation of the Chinese translation. Note that I do not say "Sanskrit original," since the editions available are from Newari copies made much later than the versions used by the ancient Chinese and Tibetan translators. In some cases, it seems the Newari copies have changed more than the long-printed Chinese and Tibetan editions. Nevertheless, a Sanskrit edition, when available, holds considerable authority in determining best meanings, so we made great effort to use it to the full.

By 1980, then, the translation was somewhat finished, but I was still unsatisfied with numerous points and some terminological choices. I very much wanted this work, the cornerstone of the whole Tanjur project, to set a new standard in both precision and clarity. So I sent out the draft manuscript to a number of the most eminent Buddhological scholars around the world.

Among them, it was particularly Professor Gadjin Nagao, Emeritus from Kyoto University, who had the time, profound knowledge, and persistent dedication to work through the manuscript carefully and to provide detailed feedback. In fact, he took the *MSABh* manuscript we sent him and began to check it against the several Sanskrit manuscripts available to him in Japan. Throughout the 1980s, he organized an ongoing workshop at the offices of *The Eastern Buddhist* journal at Otani University in Kyoto. This workshop became a kind of institution in which a whole generation of visiting scholars studied the *MSABh* and enjoyed the careful scholarship and deep insight of Professor Nagao. I obtained a grant to spend three months in Kyoto in 1985, where I tried to incorporate Professor Nagao's critical improvements, as well as going through the entire text once again myself. Professor Nagao had only reached chapter fourteen by that time, so, though we had again "finished" the main work, I decided to wait a few more years. At a private dinner in Kyoto, I did request the eminent scholar to serve as Honorary Editor of the work, which he accepted when I explained that "Honorary" meant to honor his hard work and deep insight concerning the work, while excusing him from responsibility for errors of mine, experimental choices of English terminology, and any inevitable imperfections. A few years later, Professor Nagao wrote me that he would be able to go no further than the sixteenth chapter. He subsequently wrote a beautiful essay on the "The Bodhisattva's Compassion Described in the *Mahāyānasūtrālankāra*" published in the *festschrift* organized for him by Jonathan A. Silk,[2] where he mentions his involvement in our project with his characteristic humility.

---

[2] Jonathan A. Silk, ed., *Wisdom, Compassion, and the Search for Understanding: The Buddhist Studies Legacy of Gadjin M. Nagao* (Honolulu: University of Hawai'i Press, 2000).

In the late 1980s, we and the Institute moved to Columbia University in New York, where we were able to work out an affiliation in 1988 such that I and subsequent occupants of the newly established Jey Tsong Khapa Professorship in Indo-Tibetan Buddhist Studies would remain formally charged with the task of translating and publishing "the whole Tanjur," as the *Treasury of the Buddhist Sciences*. Fundraising was slow, and the pressing needs of the Tibetan people, whose scholars are the actively creative intellects indispensable to our whole project, seemed more urgent a use for whatever support people generously gave. The Institute went somewhat onto the back burner, while we focused on developing Tibet House US, the American institution dedicated to preserving Tibetan civilization, founded at the request and with the gracious patronage of His Holiness the Dalai Lama.

Finally, in the year 2000, the founder of the Infinity Foundation in Princeton, New Jersey, Mr. Rajiv Malhotra, saw the relevance of the *Treasury of the Buddhist Sciences* to the recovery and presentation to the world of ancient India's classic Buddhist heritage, and the Foundation awarded the Institute, in affiliation with the Columbia University Center for Buddhist Studies, a publication grant to start the actual printing. In 2001, the Infinity Foundation joined with Tibet House US in another grant to engage the scholarly, administrative, editorial, and design services of Dr. Thomas Yarnall, to advance and complete the project.

There is a landmark French translation and Sanskrit edition of the *Literature* by the late, great Professor Sylvain Lévi of France, which was very helpful to our team at every stage of the work. And during the long time in which our translation was developed, excellent scholarly work was done on the *Literature* in English by Dr. Paul Griffiths in the U.S. and by the Poona scholar, Dr. Surekha V. Limaye. Thus, another time-consuming work remains for a further edition after comparing their versions to ours in close detail, which comparison will no doubt reveal still further improvements and annotations that can be made. I do feel, however, that our current version must be published without further delay, with the open invitation to all scholars to add further correction and polish to future editions.

The task remains for me to thank all the scholars who advised and supported this work, the late Venerable Geshe Wangyal, the founder of the Tanjur translation initiative; the late Dr. V.V. Gokhale of Poona, a great Indian Buddhist Pandit of the modern era, who taught and advised us during early stages; Professor Emeritus Alex Wayman, my predecessor in Buddhist Studies at Columbia, whose works on Maitreyanatha's school were seminal in English scholarship in this field; Professor David S. Ruegg, whose related works have been a gold mine of insights and information; Professor Emeritus Gadjin Nagao, whose assistance has been so great we have placed him in tribute as Honorary Editor; Dr. Lobsang Jamspal, whose tireless, careful work has contributed so much, he being truly the main "source translator;" Geshe Jampel Thardod, who helped at the beginning; Dr. Leonard Zwilling, who did a brilliant job coordinating the Sanskrit editions with the Tibetan translations and commentaries and re-translating where appropriate; Dr. Michael Sweet, who helped centrally with those tasks and also looked at the Chinese translation and associated scholarship in that language; Dr. Thomas Yarnall, whose expert assistance on all levels from the scholarly revision, to the design expertise, to the publishing technicalities, has been indispensable; Mr. Paul Hackett, who carefully prepared the index; Mr. Rajiv Malhotra, whose insight and generosity gave us the means to complete the publication; the Board and Staff of Tibet House US, who assisted with vital support; Professor Ryuichi Abe and my other colleagues at the Columbia Center for Buddhist Studies; Wendy Lochner, Rebecca Schrader, and James Jordan of Columbia University Press, which is distributing the series; and my wife, Nena von Schlebrugge Thurman, who has put up with all this and given unstinting support over the many years. With all of this excellent assistance and support, all delays, errors, and imperfections remaining are entirely my fault.

Robert A.F. Thurman (Ari Genyen Tenzin Chotrag)

Jey Tsong Khapa Professor of Indo-Tibetan Buddhist Studies, Columbia University
President, American Institute of Buddhist Studies

Gandendekyi Ling
Woodstock, New York
June 2004

INTRODUCTION

1. The World of the Literature

As its title implies, *The Universal Vehicle Discourse Literature* is the basis of a new presentation and interpretation of the doctrines contained in the universal vehicle discourses (the *Mahāyāna sūtras*). When well elucidated, beautifully arranged, and eloquently presented, the gems of these discourses become "literature," "*belles lettres*" (*alaṁkāra*), words and ideas appealing to the connoisseur, the educated person of refined sensibilities, the aficionado of good taste.[3]

To begin by looking at the *Literature* in its historical moment, we see that this text emerges in the brilliant world of early Gupta India in the center of Eurasian civilization. Indeed, the Universalist Buddhist vision is that the great philosopher and adept Asanga (ca. 294–376 CE),[4] as directly inspired by the celestial bodhisattva, Maitreyanatha, was one of the master builders of the high culture of this brilliant civilization. The task for Maitreya as *arthajño* (one who understands the situations of beings in history)[5] and for the "Experientialist" (*Yogācāra*) brothers Asanga and Vasubandhu was to attract the cultivated public of the Gupta age to the Buddha teaching, to reveal the "works of fine art," the ornamental words and ideas, the "literature" of the universal vehicle discourses.

If we widen our historical lens to survey the broader geopolitical context of the Indian subcontinental world of the fourth and fifth Common Era centuries in which Maitreyanatha revealed the *Literature*, we see that in the West of Eurasia this was the time when the Roman empire had become officially Christian, following the rise of the Roman Emperor Constantine (288–337 CE) and the monumental labors of Augustine of Hippo (354–430 CE). In the Far East, these were the centu-

---

[3] It is in this sense that I have recently come to favor rendering *alaṁkāra* as "literature." While this is the term that will be used throughout this introduction, the translation below (completed and typeset in an earlier phase) still contains the more literal rendering of *alaṁkāra* as "ornament."

[4] Our dating follows Stefan Anacker's well-reasoned dating of Asanga's younger half-brother, Vasubandhu (316–396), along with the tradition that Asanga was 22 years older and died 20 years earlier. (Tibetan tradition has it that he lived a mere one hundred and fifty years, from approximately 300 to 450 CE.)

[5] For a discussion of the many connotations of *arthajño*, see below, p. xxiv *ff.*

ries wherein Buddhism entered China on a large scale, serving important spiritual and social needs for the non-Chinese rulers and their subjects in the Northern kingdoms and also for the post-Han indigenous Chinese dynasties in the south. In Iran, the Sassanians were establishing their Zoroastrian empire, borrowing both from the Kushan and Gupta cultures to their east, and also from the newly Christianized Byzantine Roman culture in the West.

In India, the Kushan empire of "Indo-Scythians," or Shakas, which had stretched for centuries from Central Asia down into the Gangetic heartland, had lost its hold, while the newly energized Gupta dynasty was reviving a powerful north Indian imperialism centered in the old Mauryan capital of Pataliputra. The powerful southern dynasty of the Shatavahanas was still going strong based in the Deccan, while other eastern and southern Indian polities flourished independently.

These are the summary geopolitical facts. If we focus our historical lens to highlight the social dimensions of the world at this time, we see that a Eurasia-wide chain of stable imperial capitals – Rome, Alexandria, Constantinopolis, Babylon, Pataliputra, Ayodhya (and many others in north and south India), the Silk Route city-states, Chang-An, and so on – had connected the early Common Era millennium Eurasian world in a network of flourishing trade. Central to this network had been the far-flung empire of the Turkic Kushans (Indo-Scythians), who had encouraged the trade and communication that had improved the wealth of the city-state units of the empires. Warfare, wealth, education, and literacy had significantly enlarged and enriched the urban populations of these cities. Quite a number of people enjoyed sufficient leisure to taste the delicacies of sensual pleasure and the agonies of existential anxiety and therefore wanted greater meaning for their lives than simply getting and spending. Such people, as always until the last five hundred years of European "modernizing" imperialism, were more numerous, powerful, wealthy, educated, and literate in the imperial cities of the Indian subcontinent than elsewhere. Contemporary Western people are much more familiar with Roman culture, so well documented and reconstructed by Peter Brown and other scholars of late antiquity. Still, there is sufficient information about societies from Rome all the way to China to extrapolate what life was like in India, the central subcontinent of Eurasia.

In India, this was the century of the world-class master poet and playwright, Kalidasa, who, over a millennium later, was proclaimed rather extravagantly by Goethe to have been the greatest poet ever to have lived. The linguistic, logical, mathematical, medical, economic, literary, architectural, religious, and philosophical traditions of this Gupta civilization were of great brilliance and sophistication, far ahead of anything elsewhere in the Eurasian world. The Greco-Judaic-Roman

West, with the burning of the Alexandrian Library, was settling down into a long dark age under an imperial Roman Christianity. In the East, the pluralism of the post-Han Chinese world was allowing considerable social, spiritual, and cultural progress to build up toward the eventual brilliance of the great Tang dynasty – a build-up, it must be added, largely fueled by the wholesale importation of Buddhistic spirituality and civilization from India via Central Asia.

With this brief historical survey, we can see how the Gupta civilization emerging at the end of the fourth century would come to set the standard of "classical" in Indian art and culture. Highly cultured writers are composing brilliant plays and poems, while the painters and sculptors of the era envision and create the most sublime buddha, bodhisattva, and deity images. The newly, Indian-secured empire, liberated from the Central Asian Kushans, gives the merchant classes a protected range within which to produce and trade and flourish, and the numbers of urban, cultivated, thoughtful people have vastly increased since the days of the discovery of the Mahayana and the profound philosophizing of Nagarjuna.

Nagarjuna had re-discovered the universal vehicle discourses for everyone, but his philosophical works, except for the "path" works for his royal friend, Udayi, reflected a primary concern to liberate individual vehicle monastic intellectuals from the knots of their conceptual confusions. His successor, Aryadeva, expanded his scope and applied Nagarjuna's therapy to a number of Brahmin theories, refuting their dogmatic tendencies as well as those of other Buddhists. Only Ashvaghosha and Aryashura had written in cultivated Sanskrit literary forms for the educated middle classes.

Returning now to the revelation of *The Universal Vehicle Discourse Literature* itself, the legend runs that Asanga withdrew from society to propitiate the future Buddha Maitreya out of intense dissatisfaction with the prevailing interpretations of Buddha Dharma in his day, seeing the individual vehicle scientific treatises of Abhidharma as too realistic and dualistic, and the Centrist treatises of Nagarjuna and Aryadeva as too nihilistic and frightening, for many of his contemporaries. He felt he could not evolve a middle way between these extremes merely by tinkering with interpretations. He needed a whole new inspiration, a complete new synthesis. So he sought the aid of Maitreyanatha, the spiritual savior of Tushita's Joyous Mind Dharma Center.

Maitreyanatha's inspiration (*pranetṛtva*) was forthcoming, and Asanga became the "medium" or "channeling speaker" (*vaktṛ*) for his "Five Teachings": the "*Two Literatures*" (*alaṁkāra*) – the *Discourse Literature* (*MSA*) and the *Realization Literature* (*AA*); the "*Two Analyses*," one unpacking the three realities (*MAV*) and one the two realities (*DDV*) ; and the *Jewel Gene Analysis* (*RGV*) , a treatise on the most positive Buddhology elaborated, following the *Lotus* and *Great Ultimate Nirvana* discourses in emphasizing the ultimate immanence of the perfection of enlightenment. To further elaborate these seminal, inspired works, Asanga added the more technical *Bodhisattva Stages* (*BBh*) to his Abhidharmic *Disciple Stages* (*SBh*), with the *Five Condensations* (*saṁgrahaṇī*) as subcommentaries; he wrote his own commentary on the *Jewel Gene Analysis*, grounding himself on the newly rediscovered *Elucidation of the Intention Discourse*; and he wrote his two compendia, *Universal Vehicle Summary* (*MS*) and *Clear Science Compendium* (*AS*). In addition, Asanga's lectures to his circle are reflected in the commentaries and subcommentaries of Vasubandhu, Sthiramati, Arya Vimuktasena, Gunaprabha, Dignaga, and other luminaries of the school.

From all this work inspired by Maitreyanatha emerged the full elucidation of the "magnificent" (*udāra*) stage of the bodhisattva path, systematically presenting the socially and cosmologically positive implications of the universal vehicle discourses to the cultured Gupta public. Coming from the frontier crossroads town of Takshashila, Asanga and Vasubandhu were as well-versed in Vedist culture as in Buddhist culture, and also perhaps the international culture of the Central Asian kingdoms. Thus, just as their contemporary, Augustine of Hippo, was able to articulate the Christian vision of sin and salvation in mainstream terms for Greco-Roman culture, so they, under Maitreyanatha's charismatic inspiration, articulated the Buddha's universal vehicle messianic vision in mainstream terms for Gupta Vedist culture.

2. The Author of the Literature

Maitreyanatha and Aryasanga

There has been much argument about the author of the *Literature.* In the Buddhist scholarly tradition, including in India, Tibet, and East Asia, the work is accepted as authored by the celestial bodhisattva Maitreya, called Natha, meaning "spiritual intercessor," or more simply "savior," channeling his summary of the universal vehicle teaching by the yogi and scholar, Aryasanga (ca. 294–376 CE).[6] The book is thus considered a kind of "divine revelation," yet it is not included in the

[6] See above, p. xiii, note 4.

"Scripture" collection (Kanjur) in Tibet, along with the discourses of Shakyamuni Buddha; rather, it is included in the "Scientific Treatise" (Tanjur) collection. This is because the tenth-stage bodhisattva Maitreya, though embodied in his last pre-buddhahood life as a divine teacher in the Tushita heaven of the desire realm, is still not quite a perfect buddha, not completely enlightened, and so he draws on Shakyamuni's discourses, extracts literary gems from them, and elucidates them in the same manner as all the human philosopher yogin sages, such as Nagarjuna and Asanga himself.

In more modern times, Eastern and Western scholars debated the subject of the *Literature*'s authorship at length. Professor Sylvain Lévi, our distinguished predecessor who translated the *Literature* and its commentary into French from Sanskrit and published it in 1911, considered that the Maitreyan inspiration story was good enough to be accepted as indicating Asanga's own report of his source of divine inspiration. Subsequently, the great Japanese philologist Ui Hakuju disagreed and argued that Maitreyanatha was an otherwise unknown human person, the personal teacher of Asanga and a human author in his own right. Professor Paul Demiéville came to the defense of Lévi, arguing that the Maitreyanatha story does fairly indicate Asanga's source of inspiration, but that Asanga himself is the author. The colophons of the extant Sanskrit edition and of the Tibetan translation give the author's name as Vyavadatasamaya (Chin. *ji-ging-jing shi* = very pure time; Tib. *rtogs pa rnam par byang ba* = pure realization, as in Skt. *abhisamaya*, Tib. *mngon rtogs*), which is probably the name of Maitreya as a divinity in Tushita (as Shakyamuni Buddha, named early in his human life as Siddhartha Gautama, was known as Shvetaketu in his immediately previous life as a Dharma king among the Tushita deities).

We agree that nothing in history can be known with absolute certainty. We do uphold the principle, however, that if there is no clear evidence to the contrary, one cannot discount a traditional attribution merely as a metaphysical ideology. Thus, the modern prejudice that a celestial being named Maitreyanatha, renowned as the bodhisattva who is the next buddha on Earth, waiting in Tushita heaven, could not exist since there are no celestial beings, there are no heavens in the desire realm, there is no such thing as a genuine revelation, and so on, is nothing but a prejudice, a bit of modernist, materialist, secularist ideology, no more and no less rational than the belief in all of the above. After all, in our very modern age, in the world of roaring printing presses and bookstore chains, there are quite a few books believed to be "channeled" by a human writer, the authorship of which is attributed to various sorts of celestial beings, including Atlantean warriors, angels, Jesus Christ, mystics, guides, deceased Tibetan Lamas, even "God" himself, and so forth.

Among these books, there are no doubt both genuine and spurious examples, but they are not that unusual. Why should there not be many such traditions in a yogic, spiritual culture such as that of classical India? Therefore, it is my position that the traditional account is the best working hypothesis, until someone comes up with solid evidence to disprove it. Maitreya the bodhisattva is thus considered to be the author, Asanga the channel medium and writer, and Vasubandhu, Asanga's younger brother, the author of the "word commentary" we translate herein. Putting it this way allows us to put forth a new theory of the first few verses – that they are a preface written by the medium, Asanga, with the actual work beginning from the chapter on the "Authenticity of the Universal Vehicle." Asanga's own commentary to the *Discourse Literature* seems to me to be the *Bodhisattva Stages*.

So, how does the story go of this unusual revelatory composition of the *Discourse Literature*?

Maitreyanatha is a celestial bodhisattva, one of the "eight close children" of the Buddha Shakyamuni. He is believed to be next in line to emanate an incarnation on Earth some thousands of years in the future. The second part of his name, "Natha," means "protective intercessor" in the spiritual sense, meaning one who protects beings from rebirth in hells, pretan, or animal realms. Since this is a much greater sort of protection than mere defense against mundane dangers, I translate it by the Western spiritual term, "savior."

Maitreya is referred to as the "Regent" of the Buddha Shakyamuni, ruling in his stead in the Tushita heaven wherein all buddhas live their last lives as divine bodhisattva teachers, at the mid-point of their descent from the highest heaven Akanishtha into the world of human beings on the planet Earth. He will continue that regency until such time as evolution brings our world to the point of readiness to receive his buddha-mission. According to legends, this will be many centuries in the future, when the human lifespan has increased again to many thousands of years, and when the planet will be entirely dominated by a benevolent "Wheel-Turning" Sovereign named Shankha. Maitreya will be born the son of a Brahmin priest, unlike the warrior-class Shakyamuni. The world in his time will be politically centralized, and, therefore, the warrior caste and its virtues will be obsolete. He will renounce the world and attain enlightenment in a single day, not requiring six long years of meditative asceticism, as did Shakyamuni. His teaching will not deviate from that of previous buddhas.

Maitreya also often figures among the great bodhisattvas in the assemblies gathered around Shakyamuni to listen to his teachings in the universal vehicle discourses. In fact, he and Manjushri are often paired there in dialogues, or in alternating interlocution of the Buddha. While the individual vehicle discourses are collected by Ananda, Shariputra, and so forth, the universal vehicle discourses are collected by Maitreya, Manjushri, and Vajrapani. Furthermore, although presently considered to reside in Tushita heaven, the fourth heaven up among the six desire realm heavens, Maitreya does not fail to work by miraculous means in this world to mature living beings toward enlightenment and prepare Earth for his eventual mission.

It is considered (especially in the Tibetan tradition, with the Chinese and Japanese traditions agreeing in general, although differing in particulars) that Maitreya authored five great treatises, using the Noble Asanga as a scribe, three of which expand on the *Elucidation of the Intention* and the *Visit to Lanka Discourses* of Shakyamuni to establish them as the basis of the idealistic school of universal vehicle philosophy, the Idealist (*Vijñānavādin*) or Experientialist (*Yogācārin*) school.

One of the most common icons in Tibet is called the "Refuge Tree," which presents the Buddha Shakyamuni in the center of a host of Indian, Tibetan, and supernatural teachers. To Shakyamuni's left is Manjushri, at the head of the lineage of the "profound view" trend of the path of enlightenment, and to his right is Maitreya, at the head of the "magnificent deeds" trend of the path of enlightenment. Beneath Manjushri sit Nagarjuna and Aryadeva, at the head of all the earthly, historical teachers who maintained the unbroken succession of this tradition of critical philosophy. Beneath Maitreya sit Asanga and Vasubandhu, at the head of the succession of the lineage of ethically oriented philosophers. Of course, Buddha in the center of this icon represents the unification in perfection of both these lineages, so no ultimate dichotomy is intended by the separation of the two. There are, however, different persons on different stages of the path at different times; there are, therefore, different teachings elaborated for their benefit that emphasize either wisdom or compassion.

Tibetan sources allege that Asanga's mother was a Buddhist nun who despaired of the state of Buddhism in the India of her time and decided she must bear sons who would renew its energies. First, from a warrior-class father, she gave birth to Asanga; then, from a Brahmin-class father, Vasubandhu; and third, from a merchant father, a son called Virincavatsa. The Chinese accounts have all three born from the same father, a Brahmin of the Kaushika clan, but the Tibetan account gives this rather more charming version of the mother's efforts to tap all aspects of the gene pool. Asanga first joined the Vatsiputriya branch of the Sarvastivada school and became a great teacher of the individual vehicle. He then heard of the universal vehicle discourses and soon became fascinated by their teaching of universal compassion and transcendent wisdom. He recognized therein the liberating teaching that could bring Indian Buddhism into its glory. He received initiation into the

Mayajala Tantra and then set forth to contemplate great compassion, seeking to enlist the mystic aid of the supernal bodhisattva Maitreyanatha. He reasoned that, since the teaching of the late Shakyamuni Buddha was already so poorly understood and practiced throughout the land, the future buddha, believed to reside in the Tushita heaven of the desire realm, should be requested to make an anticipatory visit to the planet to revive the Dharma in Asanga's own day and age.

Leaving his home monastery in Takshashila, near present-day Peshawar, Asanga meditated for twelve long years on universal compassion and on the invocation of Lord Maitreya. At last, frustrated by the failure of his invocation, he abandoned his quest. His faith and his sense of self-worth utterly shattered, he wandered forth from the cave a broken man. He stopped near the first town at the sight of an old female dog who was suffering terribly from suppurating wounds all over her hindquarters. He became absorbed in the relatively simple task of trying to help at least this one sentient being. If only he could bring even temporary relief to one other being, perhaps his life would have served some purpose. As he was about to clean her wound, he noticed her live flesh was already crawling with maggots, so he could not help her without harming them. After several moments' thought, he took a sharp shard and cut a piece of flesh from his own emaciated thigh, shrunken by long asceticism, and placed it on the ground next to the dog. He planned to pick off the maggots one by one and place them on the fresh flesh. Unable to grasp them with his fingers, he put out his tongue to lick them off. As he neared the foul-smelling dog's wound, he was overwhelmed by revulsion, and, closing his eyes, had to force himself to go through with the operation. Suddenly there was a kind of soft explosion in front of his face, and when he started back and opened his eyes, he beheld the bodhisattva Maitreya standing before him, radiant in a rainbow aura. Overwhelmed with faith and joy, he prostrated himself at the Lord's feet over and over again.

All too quickly recovering his composure, he complained to Maitreya and asked him why he had been so slow to respond to his ardent invocations. Maitreya replied that he had always been right in front of Asanga, but that, as the yogi himself had persistently been caught up in self-involvement and had not yet generated great compassion, he had been unable to see him. After all, Maitreya is the incarnation of love, and only those capable of great compassion can perceive love, even when it is right before them. Asanga was not utterly convinced by this explanation, so Maitreya shrunk himself into a small globe of light and permitted Asanga to carry him through the town to show him to the populace. Asanga, heedless of his gaunt appearance and even his bleeding thigh, did as he was told and ran joyfully through the town proclaiming the advent of the future buddha. The townspeople looked wonderingly at what they saw as a crazed yogi from the forest, bleeding and tattered, running around with a contemptible, sick dog on his shoulder, shouting about the future buddha. They drove him promptly from the town. Fortunately, the bodhisattva used his supernatural power to take Asanga with him up to the Tushita heaven, where he instructed him in the universal vehicle teachings. These teachings were brought back to the human plane in the form of the *Five Maitreya Treatises* (as mentioned above, the *MSA*, *MAV*, *DDV*, *AAA*, and *RGV*).

I like to think of Asanga as the Augustine of India. Each took respectively the Buddhist or Christian universalist countercultural tradition he championed and reformulated and reinvigorated it to suit the civilizational needs of his Indian or Roman cosmopolitan culture. To build such a culture, of course, each had to resort to divine inspiration, Asanga from the bodhisattva Maitreya, the future buddha, and Augustine from his Savior Jesus Christ.

In the rougher world of Roman North Africa, Augustine had a wild youth and had to hear the voice of God and feel the saving grace of Jesus to pull himself together and subsequently provide the synthesis of Christian spiritual culture and Roman material civilization that founded the Western world that lasts until today. Unlike Augustine, Asanga was not a libertine in his youth but was rather a Buddhist monk-scholar, reinforced by a spiritual mother from an early age and by his more developed culture and institutions to pursue the meaning of life, attain enlightenment, and save the world of fellow beings. However, in the middle of his life, he reached a vale of despair reminiscent of that plumbed by Augustine, a vale from which only divine intercession could extract him. Augustine went into the garden and followed divine command to read from the Scripture. Asanga left his comfortable monastic academic community, went twelve years into the wilderness to contemplate, and encountered Maitreya, the great celestial bodhisattva. Maitreya took Asanga with him to his home base in Tushita heaven, The Joyous Mind Dharma Center, where he taught him the *Five Maitreya Treatises*. I know of no tradition specifying which of the five texts was given in what order. Considering the contents of the five, *The Universal Vehicle Discourse Literature* (*MSA*) is probably basic to the others, as it gives an overview of the Mahayana cosmos, path, and buddhaverse, summarizing the magnificent universalist vision from the Idealist/Experientialist perspective. The *MAV* and the *DDV* logically follow, as they expand and refine the metaphysical implications of the Idealist vision. The *AA* turns the attention away from the wisdom side of metaphysical systems to the art (*upāya*) side of the path, articulating in a beautiful system the hidden meaning of the *Transcendent Wisdom Discourses* (*PPS*), the basic texts of the entire Mahayana, namely the path of development of the compassionate bodhisattva devoted to Transcendent Wisdom.

Like the *PPS* texts themselves, the *AA* therefore is interpretable in either an Idealist or a Centrist fashion. Finally, the *RGV* reformulates in a brilliant synthesis the entire cosmos of enlightenment, opening the door to the vision of the infinite magnificent deeds of the bodhisattvas and buddhas, interpretable metaphysically from a number of perspectives, most clearly that of the peerless Dialecticist Centrists.

Bringing these teachings back to earth in India, Asanga went to work to elaborate the texts into a new synthesis of the Buddhist vision with the sophisticated culture of the nascent Gupta empire. He built a new monastery at the sacred grove Veluvana, at Rajagrha in Magadha, and a circle formed around him to learn the new synthesis of the universal vehicle teachings. It is even said that he was at first unable to explain fully some of the more abstruse doctrines of the new idealistic system that Maitreyanatha had taught, so he persuaded the bodhisattva to come down in person to the great lecture hall of the monastery during the nights. There, invisible to all but Asanga, the bodhisattva himself would directly teach his own doctrines, duly channeled by Asanga. In time, Asanga himself went on to write a compendium of the new teachings, a massive and comprehensive synthesis of Buddhist doctrines and practices known as *The Stages of Yoga Practice* (*Yogācārabhūmi – YBh*) together with five analytic commentaries on that work, the *Compendia* (*saṁgrahaṇī*). The Mahayana portion of the *YBh*, the *Stages of Bodhisattva Practice* (*Bodhisattvabhūmi – BBh*), closely parallels the structure of the *MSA* and can very plausibly be considered Asanga's own "meaning commentary" (Tib. *don 'grel*) on the *MSA*. In fact, the *Bodhisattva Stages* follows the *Literature* so closely that it was considered by Chinese Buddhist scholars to have been authored by Maitreya himself. These parallels are shown in the following table:

MSA (adhikāra)	***BBh (paṭala)***
1. Authenticity of Mahayana	-----
2. Taking Refuge	-----
3. Gene	1. Gene
4. Spiritual Conception	2. Spiritual Conception
5. Practice	3. Self-interest and Altruism
6. Truth	4. Meaning of Truth
7. Power	5. Power
8. Maturity	6. Maturity
9. Enlightenment	7. Enlightenment
10. Faith	8. Faith

11. Dharma Quest	Dharma Quest
12. Teaching	Teaching
13. Practice	Practice
14. Advice and Instruction	Genuine Instruction
15. Artful Evolutionary Action	Artfulness
16. Transcendences [1–17]	9. Generosity
Justice	10. Justice
Patience	11. Patience
Enterprise	12. Enterprise
Contemplation	13. Contemplation
Wisdom	14. Wisdom
Social Graces [72–79]	15. Social Graces
17. Measure of Worship and Service	16. Measure of Worship and Service
18. Enlightenment Accessory	17. Enlightenment Accessory
19. Excellence	18. Excellence
20–21. Signs of Practice and Attainment [1–2]	19. Bodhisattva signs[7]

Asanga also provides another work parallel to the *Literature* in his *Universal Vehicle Compendium* (*MS*), wherein he quotes forty-one verses from the *Literature*, yet mentions it by name only once. This work differs from Maitreya's work in several points of explanation, most importantly in details of his description of the Buddha bodies and the bodhisattva stages. There is also evidence that Asanga knew parts of his brother Vasubandhu's commentary, since he quotes it on occasion. This does not seem to me a problem for the attribution of the commentary to Vasubandhu, if we understand the way in which these works were composed. Asanga lectured on the *Literature* to a number of disciples including Vasubandhu, and the explanations were noted down and made into various commentaries. Since they were originally Asanga's own comments (perhaps channeled from Maitreya himself), they may turn up in various later written redactions. They reflect, thus, the prevalent opinions of the school rather than the bright ideas of different individuals. Similarly, when Arya Vimuktasena (6th century) refers to a quote from the *Literature Commentary* as "by Acharya Asanga," he is referring to the well-known source of a statement, not necessarily the authorship of a textual quote.

---

[7] Close correspondence continues in the final sections. See Ui, Hakuju, *Studies in the Yogācārabhūmi* (*Yugaron-kenkyu*) (Tokyo: Iwanami Shoten, 1958).

Maitreyanatha, knower of import (*arthajño*)

In the historical setting outlined above, Aryasanga communicates the intervention of Maitreyanatha. *The Universal Vehicle Discourse Literature* begins with the following Sanskrit words:

> *Arthajño 'rthavibhāvanāṁ prakurute vācā padaiścāmalair*
> *Duḥkhasyottaraṇāya duḥkhitajane kāruṇyatas tanmayaḥ* /

Working on this text on and off for some time, I have always felt that if I could just understand the meaning of the first word of the text, the rest would be easy. I still feel that way, and I am still trying to understand that word. To read the *Literature* intelligently, we need insight into that first word, the expression *arthajño*, "knower of import," remembering that *artha* also can mean value, substance, and purpose.

Combining our own interpretations with what numerous scholarly commentators on the text have given us, we come up with a number of different schemas for organizing the material of the *Literature.*

In analyzing *arthajño*, we can discern three important levels according to which to pursue its meaning: 1) the level of understanding, which involves hermeneutics, philosophy, or "views" (*darśana*), wherein "meaning" is something more than the words of the text; 2) the level of relating the study of the text to the practice of the path to enlightenment, the level of path or meditation, a level always important in any Buddhist scientific treatise; and 3) the level of application, fruition, or action, which I will argue always involves sociological and historical issues, both in the original constitution of the text and in the re-elucidation of its import in contemporary times. These three levels (to be discussed in three subsections below) correspond to the traditional Buddhist categories of "view" (*dṛṣṭi*), "meditation" (*bhāvanā*), and "action" (*caryā*), or even the most ancient "wisdom" (*prajñā*), "mind" (*citta*) (or "concentration" [*samādhi*]), and "ethics" (*śīla*), the three spiritual educations (*adhiśikṣā*).

Before going into these three levels in more depth, we should read our translation of the first two verses of the text to provide the context for the analysis. In the first verse, I have put in ordinary brackets the interpolations arising from my interpretation of the authorship of the text, and in square brackets what we would have to write if we took this as coming from the same author as the main text.

> 1. (Our Lord Maitreyanātha) [(or) I, the Lord Maitreya,]
> Knowing the (supreme) import (*arthajño*)

(Of the universal vehicle scriptures),
Creates an exhibition of that import
With flawless language and expressions,
In order to save beings from suffering;
He [I] being compassion incarnate.
To those beings who seek the Dharma,
The Truth as taught in the supreme vehicle,
He reveals [I reveal] this fivefold interpretation,
An elegant way to the unexcelled.

2. The Dharma here disclosed gives the utmost joy,
Like gold hand-beaten, like a lotus fully bloomed,
Like a delicious feast when famished, like good news read in a letter,
Or like a casket of jewels thrown open.

These first stanzas, and four more I will quote below, serve as a preface to the work. They are separated as such in Tibetan and Chinese translations, though not in Lévi's Sanskrit Ms. In my opinion, therefore, the first stanza is most conveniently read as a salutation by Asanga to Maitreyanatha; those two being the persons whom Vasubandhu, in his *Analysis of Center and Extremes Commentary* (*MAVBh*), calls "speaker" (*vaktṛ*) and "author" (*pranetṛ*), respectively. This preface contains the traditional prefatory matters: salutation; reason for composition; qualifications of author; and immediate and ultimate relevances to readers. Granting that the Tibetan and Sanskrit texts make no distinction between authors of the preface and the main text, my justifications in considering the preface to be by Asanga about Maitreyanatha is that the main verb is in the third person, and so awkward in referring to oneself, and also that it may seem immodest of Maitreyanatha to refer to himself as *kāruṇyatas tanmayaḥ*, "made of compassion." Finally, the second verse sets forth a fivefold structure for the work, using a set of five similes.

Philosophical and Hermeneutical Level

Let us analyze these verses on the hermeneutical and philosophical levels. It is significant that Maitreyanatha is called a "knower of import" (*arthajño*) rather than a "knower of Dharma (teaching)" (*dharmajño*), as would be expected for a great Dharma Teacher. "Import" is prominent in the famous "four reliances" (*pratisaraṇa*): rely on the teaching (Dharma), not the person (*pudgala*); rely on the import (*artha*), not the letter (*vyañjana*) (of the teaching – this second relating inversely to the two kinds of teaching, textual and realizational [*āgama-adhigama-dharma*]); rely on the definitive meaning (*nītārtha*), not the interpretable meaning (*neyārtha*); rely on (non-dual) intuition (*jñāna*), not on (dualistic) consciousness (*vijñāna*). Asanga discusses these issues of "import" at some length in the *Bodhisattva Stages*. He is strongly interested in hermeneutical issues from his long exposure to and esteem for the *Elucidation of the Intention Discourse*, a basic work for him and the archetypal "hermeneutical" *Discourse*. So, one of the functions here of the epithet *arthajño* is to signal the ability of an enlightened person to re-interpret the teaching in terms that will keep them vital to the understanding and practice of contemporary disciples.

A second set of categories standard in Buddhist philosophies concerns the "four intellectual knowledges" (*pratisaṁvid*): knowledges of teachings, meanings (imports), parts of speech, and eloquence. dBal mang mentions that the Pandit Parahitabhadra discerns these four as attributed to Maitreyanatha by the first verse, with "knower of the import fashions an exposition of that import" indicating teaching- and meaning-knowledges; "with impeccable language and expressions" indicating grammatical knowledge; and with "a fivefold access to that import, a practical way that leads to the unexcelled" indicating the knowledge of eloquence. Parahitabhadra also comments that "*arthajño* refers to Maitreya who knows the import of the universal vehicle according to the intention of the Victor," glossing "import" here as "intentional import" (*abhisaṁdhyartha*).

To go more deeply into the philosophical processes involved, we need the help of Vasubandhu's and dBal mang's elucidations. The first stanza refers to a "fivefold access to that import," and the second stanza describes the aesthetic process of coming to an understanding in terms of a fivefold joy. Vasubandhu relates these similes to five types of "realizational meaning" (*adhigamārtham*): "This verse uses five examples to explain the Dharma in terms of its fivefold import: its provability, understandability, conceivability, inconceivability, and perfection – this last being its experiential import, its interior realizability, its actuality as the accessories of enlightenment." Following these famous categories, we equate them with the five similes as follows:

1) hand-beaten gold ornament = joy = the provable
2) blossomed lotus = joy = the understandable
3) fine feast when famished = joy = the conceivable
4) good news received = joy = the inconceivable
5) opened jewel casket = joy = the perfection

On the hermeneutical level, the level of philosophical view, these five joys are unpacked by dBal mang, following Sthiramati, in terms of the three realities (*svabhāva*) – the imaginatively constructed (*parikalpita*), relative (*paratantra*), and perfect (*pariniṣpanna*) realities – as follows:

> The three realities (*trisvabhāva*) are the constructed reality, and so on, divided into five as: 1) the constructed; 2) the apprehended object relative; 3) the subjective subject relative; 4) the unchanging perfect; and 5) the unerring perfect. (These can be aligned with five similes, as follows:)
>
> 1) The superior joy of freedom from that fear (constantly present) when one perceives the constructed reality as if real, achieved by means of realizing the unreality of all constructed things (is like the joy of beholding ornaments of beaten gold).
>
> 2) The great joy of understanding the relativity of particular objects such as form and sound (is like the joy of seeing the blossomed lotus).
>
> 3) The great joy of conceiving the constructed as illusory is like the third (joy of a fine feast when famished).
>
> 4) The great joy of the dualism-free realization of the intellectually inconceivable, changeless perfect is like the fourth (joy of the surprise of good news in a letter).
>
> 5) The great joy of the realization of the ultimate unerring perfect (that is, the relative devoid of the imaginatively constructed) is like the fifth (supreme joy of beholding the opened casket of precious jewels).

We note that the philosophical view changes here with different stages, and we see clearly the Idealist's central way, avoiding the extremes of the absolutist reification of the constructed and the nihilistic repudiation of the relative, balancing relativity and emptiness in perfect, nondual harmony.

A second way of unpacking the five joys and five meanings bridges from our philosophical level to our meditational level and involves relating the five to the "five categories" of the Idealists: name; process (*nimitta*); conceptual thought; thatness; and non-conceptual intuition. dBal mang brilliantly elucidates:

> 1) Here "name" is the constructed reality. When one proves or determines that the "form itself" appearing in the form of its designative base is not established to be present as it appears, one has the joy of realizing objective selflessness, like the joy of wearing an ornament of beaten gold.
>
> 2) As for the process of applying names, which is the external relative reality of form, and so on, when you realize relativity by noting the specifics or particulars of cause and effect, there is the joy of realizing the inexorability of evolutionary causality, like the joy of seeing a lotus blossom.
>
> 3) When you see the illusion of imaginative constructedness by considering or analyzing with the four reasonings whether or not the construction of the unreal is illusory or not, there is the joy of tasting the elixir of the teaching, like the joy of a fine feast when famished.
>
> 4) When you reflect on the inconceivability to the speculative mind of the actuality of thatness, reality devoid of substantial subject-object dichotomy, you generate the joy of the holy intuition wherein dualistic perception declines, like the joy of having surprise news of a good friend in a letter.
>
> 5) And when you attain or understand the non-conceptual intuition of the Buddha's samadhic equanimity, the thatness that is the object only for a buddha's introspective insight, there is a great joy, like the joy of opening a casket of precious jewels.

Here, the philosophical view bridges over into meditation, with the insight (*vipaśyanā*) reflection combining with one-pointed concentration (*śamatha*) to result in nondual intuition of the ultimate perfect as the relative devoid of the imagined.

Meditational and Realizational Level

Perhaps the relation of the text of *The Universal Vehicle Discourse Literature* to the path, its presentation of the stages of practice, is best accomplished according to yet another system of interpretation, which dBal mang claims comes from the oral tradition of his mentors, and which he therefore values most highly of all. The following is my summary translation of his exposition of this oral tradition:

> 1) The verbal universal vehicle is the means of expression and must be established as the unerring word of Buddha, as in the "Proof of Authenticity of the Universal Vehicle" (first) chapter, and so the joy of understanding that well is like the joy of beholding beaten gold.
>
> 2) The universal vehicle as expressible object has the path as means of attainment and the fruition as goal. The basis of the path is the "Taking Refuge" (second chapter), the "Spiritual Gene" (third chapter), and the "Spiritual Conception" (fourth chapter), and the actuality of the path is the "Practice" (fifth chapter), and when these are realized as far excelling the individual vehicle path, the great joy generated is like that of seeing the blossomed lotus.
>
> 3) Now the "Thatness" taught in the seventh (our sixth) chapter and the "Power" in the eighth (our seventh) are the distinguishing characteristics of the path, the means of attainment; it is unfitting to think erroneously about the import of thatness, and if it is considered unerringly, faults are abandoned and excellences attained, and so it is the "to be considered," and the joy thereby generated is like the joy of a fine feast when famished.
>
> 4) The characteristics of "Power" and the (eighth) chapter's enlightenment endowed with "Evolutionary Maturity" refer to the person, the embodiment of the traveler on the path; these two are hard to measure for the disciples and hermit buddhas and so are inconceivable to them. As this text so explains them, the joy (of understanding them) is like the joy of getting good news from a letter.

> 5) The unexcelled enlightenment of the goal, the fruition of the universal vehicle, is to be realized by attaining the perfect intuition of the Lord Buddha in individual introspective insight, and the joy of seeing this explained as the meaning of the (ninth) chapter is like the joy of beholding the opened casket of precious jewels. The rest of the chapters are the expansion of this tenth (our ninth) chapter. This is the context in which to explain this great treatise, *The Universal Vehicle Discourse Literature*, the way its explanations are understood connected to the ways of generating joy – it is a wondrous explanation, so my Lama, the very actuality of Manjushri, used to say.

dBal mang gives still one more way of understanding the five understandings and five similes in terms of the "three persons," the persons who: 1) do not know the meaning of the universal vehicle; 2) who entertain doubts about it; and 3) who entertain wrong notions about it:

> 1) The first simile illustrates the joy of the person who thinks the universal vehicle is not the Buddha's teaching – as well as (the joy of) the person who doubts about it – when they understand the proof that the universal vehicle is the Buddha's teaching.
>
> 2) The second illustrates the joy of the person who doesn't know the meaning of the universal vehicle when she comes to know specifically or in detail the meaning of the universal vehicle.
>
> 3) The third illustrates the joy of all three types when by means of (global) learning, and so on, they enter into the topics of the universal vehicle that can be considered carefully and come to develop the proper mindful attitudes about evolutionary causality.
>
> 4) The fourth illustrates the joy of all three when they no longer conceptualize the inconceivable topics and thereby do not repudiate evolutionary causality.
>
> 5) The fifth simile illustrates the joy of considering the conceivable, aggregates, elements, media, and so forth, and of abandoning the erroneous attitudes toward the four inconceivable topics, thereby

> achieving perfect enlightenment abandoning all obscurations. This fifth joy is that of the person who understands the meaning of the universal vehicle.

In these explanations, the "import" known by Maitreyanatha is as much "path" or meditation as it is "view" or wisdom. The text leads the bodhisattva through the stages of a process of mental cultivation (*yogācāra*) into an awareness of the perfect reality, being the inconceivable, nondual perfect-relative reality, inexorable in evolutionary causality while free of all taint of substantial subject-object dichotomy.

Actualization and Socio-historical Level

Coming to the third level, the socio-historical level, there is little help in the commentaries, concerned synchronically as they are with the authentic view and practice of the bodhisattva. We need to add from a modern perspective the sociological/historical dimension of *arthajño*, relating meaning to context.

In Maitreyanatha/Aryasanga's enterprise as master builders of the high culture of the Gupta civilization, the third level of significance of *arthajño* emerges, *artha* here in its mercantile connotation of "value" or "worth." This level, at which *arthajño* gains almost the flavor of "connoisseur," a person of discerning taste and fine discrimination, is the level on which the universal vehicle message is presented in aesthetically satisfying terms to a bourgeois intelligentsia. As discussed above, it was our authors' task to attract such people to the Buddha's ornamental words and ideas, to reveal his "works of fine art," the "literature" (*alaṁkāra*) of his universal vehicle discourses. The similes contained in the remaining four verses of the Prologue reinforce this aesthetic atmosphere.

> 3. Just as a well-adorned face of naturally outstanding beauty gives people even more intense delight when they behold it in a mirror, so this Dharma, always outstanding in its natural brilliance, gives a still more distinct satisfaction to the wise when its meaning is critically elucidated.

This third verse argues for the tertiary adornment of highlighting the already beautiful, already well-adorned universal vehicle teaching in the mirrors and lenses of critical elucidation, using a simile perfectly understandable to merchants with their knowledge of marketing and display.

> 4. Like a medicine foul in smell yet sweet in taste, this Dharma should be understood to have two dimensions, its (sometimes hard-to-take) literal dimension, and the always-beneficial dimension of its import.

This fourth verse shows Maitreya/Asanga's difficulty in selling the universal vehicle to the cultivated, urban elites. The monastic teaching seems foul to them by its emphasis on the impurity and ugliness of life, suffering, impermanence, and so forth. The previous systematization of the universal vehicle, that of Nagarjuna and sons, also had the foul smell of nihilism in its constant harping on emptiness, highlighting the superficially frightening aspect of the *Transcendent Wisdom Discourses*. The sweet taste of its beneficial import, therefore, had to be revealed by the Idealistic hermeneutic, critiquing the exaggerated dualistic realism of the individual vehicle by means of its Idealistic reduction to the reality of mind-alone, and critiquing the exaggerated nihilism of the Centrists by its Experientialist grounding of the viability of relativity in the ineffability of the nondual relative reality.

> 5. This Dharma, expansive, tough, and deep, is like a monarch, very hard to please; and yet, also like a monarch, once pleased, it is the bestower of the treasure of the highest excellence.

> 6. Just as the priceless, classic jewel gives no satisfaction to the undiscriminating person, this Dharma is wasted on the unintelligent; in the opposite cases, each gives due satisfaction in the same way.

The fifth verse promises the rich reward of propitiating the majestic energy of the universal vehicle, evoking its sustaining grace, by means of the simile of a king. And the sixth challenges the readers to take some trouble educating themselves to cultivate their ability to appreciate the precious gems of universal vehicle teachings.

This third, socio-historical, level is not simply scholastic and irrelevant, as some may think, inasmuch as it is this level, in fact, that could enable modern interpreters to relate the universalist teaching to the present day, creating the sound basis for making it intelligible to modern people.

So, we have here three levels, philosophic, meditational, and historical, all the same in one sense as mutually implying one another, clearly distinct in another sense, as one can focus on one level at a time. Perhaps by means of these reflections, we can better understand the intention of the authors and better translate this beautiful text into our modern languages.

A concluding point, perhaps quite relevant to the historical issue, is that the first chapter provides the ground of the whole "yoga" or systematic experiential program the text inculcates. This is the chapter "Proof that the Universal Vehicle is the Buddha-Word." For the bodhisattva's path of refuge, recognition of genealogy, conception of the spirit of enlightenment, and practice, the essential point of departure is the sense of the historical presence and ultimate competence of the buddhas. Since "modern" historicism categorically rejects Shakyamuni Buddha's authorship of the universal vehicle discourses, essentially agreeing with the ultra-conservative, contemporary Theravada position, it is difficult in the contemporary universe of scholarly discourse to present the arguments of that chapter with any persuasive force, yet perhaps it is not impossible. But this goes beyond the scope of our task here, and I only mention it to illustrate the importance of the historical reality for the historically entangled action of development of the bodhisattva's practice.

Toward the end of his life, Asanga wrote a commentary on the *Jewel Gene Analysis* (*RGV*), which, according to the Tibetan tradition, affirmed his own personal Centrist viewpoint. His elaboration of the Idealist system had been in terms of the needs of the disciples of his day, opening for them a "centrist" way between the extremes of individual vehicle realism and Centrist nihilism. It was not really an expression of his own personal understanding, namely, Dialecticist Centrism, which would be identical to that of Nagarjuna or any of the enlightened masters. Leaving this Tibetan view aside for the moment, let us now describe Asanga's achievement in philosophical terms, how it is that he is regarded as one of the two "Great Champions" (*mahāratha*), systematizers of the "magnificent deeds" (*udāracaryā*) aspect of the universal vehicle.

3. The Source Texts of the Literature

There are three known Sanskrit texts of the *MSA* – a Nepali manuscript, a copy of which was utilized by Sylvain Lévi for his first edition of 1907, and two other manuscripts in the possession of the Ryukoku University in Kyoto.[8] Lévi's

[8] The Ryūkoku University manuscripts are described in TAKEUCHI (1956). These two additional Skt. manuscripts were not available for us to consult; however, Professor Nagao used them extensively in making his *MSA* index (see our bibliography herein) and in working over our translation.

published text contains quite a few errors, many of which were corrected by Lévi himself in the notes to his French translation published in 1911. On the basis of a list of corrections to Lévi's text provided by Professor Nagao, only a few new readings have been added, at I.1, XI.5, XII.7, and XVI.48. From comparison with the Tibetan, we have read the commentary to X.9 as constituting another verse in that chapter; the first half of XI.35 as commentary on the preceding verse; and the first sentence of the following commentary as the last half of that verse; and we have added one additional verse after XVI.53, and another after XVIII.1.

Lévi's Sanskrit text contains eight hundred and sixty-four verses interspersed with the prose commentary. It is divided into chapters, the first fifteen being serially numbered, followed by four unnumbered chapters and a final chapter designated the twenty-first. Lévi resolves the discrepancy in enumeration by calling the last chapter XX–XXI, though it is made up of two parts with a break at verse 43, with a final section of nineteen verses in praise of the Buddha. The Tibetan Tanjur, however, contains a translation of the verses under the title *Mahāyānasūtrālaṁkāra-kārikā* (Peking 5521), and of the verses and commentary together (which almost exactly corresponds to the divisions of the Sanskrit text) under the title *Sūtrālaṁkāra-bhāṣya* (Peking 5527). Both Tibetan translations were first prepared during the 8th–9th century royal translation project at Samye monastery by the pandit Shakyasimha and the translator Dpal brtsegs, and they were revised in the 11th century by the Pandit Parahita, the Great Brahman Sajjana, and the famous Tibetan monk-translator, Ngog Loden Sherab. The first Tibetan translation cannot be dated exactly, but a final limit is set by its inclusion in the Ldan kar catalogue of 812, of which Dpal brtsegs was one of the compilers. The Chinese translation was prepared between 630 and 632 by the Indian Prabhakaramitra, who had studied under Shilabhadra at Nalanda, as Xuan-zang was to do later.

The Chinese translation by Prabhakaramitra breaks up the text into twenty-four chapters by taking verses 1–6 of Sanskrit I as a separate chapter, dividing Sanskrit XVIII into three chapters, and Sanskrit XXI into two. The Tibetan translation also divides Sanskrit I into two parts (a seven-verse preface; and a twenty-one-verse second chapter, "Proving the Authenticity of the Universal Vehicle"), but it combines the Sanskrit chapters XX–XXI into a single twenty-first chapter.

The Chinese translation calls verses 1–6 *nidāna*, and the Tibetan translation uses *dang-po*; both terms have the sense of introduction or preface. The following table shows the correspondences between the Sanskrit, Tibetan, and Chinese versions, together with the number of verses in each chapter:

Sanskrit	**Tibetan**	**Chinese**
I. mahāyānasiddhi (21)	1. ādi (6)	1. nidāna (8)
	2. siddhi (15)	2. siddhi (17)
II. śaraṇagamana (12)	3. śaraṇagamana (12)	3. śaraṇagamana (12)
III. gotra (13)	4. gotra (13)	4. gotra (13)
IV. cittotpāda (28)	5. cittotpāda (28)	5. cittotpāda (21)
V. pratipatti (11)	6. pratipatti (11)	6. pratipatti (11)
VI. tattva (10)	7. tattva (10)	7. tattva (11)
VII. prabhāva (10)	8. prabhāva (10)	8. prabhāva (10)
VIII. paripāka (22)	9. paripāka (22)	9. paripāka (22)
IX. bodhi (86)	10. bodhi (86)	10. bodhi (80)
X. adhimukti (15)	11. adhimukti (15)	11. adhimukti (15)
XI. dharmaparyeṣṭi (78)	12. dharmaparyeṣṭi (78)	12. dharmaparyeṣṭi (74)
XII. deśanā (24)	13. deśanā (24)	13. deśanā (24)
XIII. pratipatti (29)	14. pratipatti (29)	14. pratipatti (29)
XIV. avavādānuśāsanī (51)	15. avavādānuśāsanī (51)	15. avavādānuśāsanī (51)
XV. upāyasahitakarma (5)	16. upāyasahitakarma (5)	16. upāyasahitakarma (5)
XVI. pāramitā (79)	17. pāramitā (80)	17. pāramitā (59)
XVII. pūjāsevāpramāṇa (66)	18. pūjāsevāpramāṇa (66)	18. pūjā (5)
		19. sevā (7)
		20. brahmavihāra (49)
XVIII. bodhipakṣa (104)	19. bodhipakṣa (104)	21. bodhipakṣa (87)
XIX. guṇa (80)	20. guṇa (80)	22. guṇa (65)
XX–XXI. caryāpratiṣṭha (61)	21. caryāpratiṣṭha (61)	23. caryāpratiṣṭha (27)
		24. buddhapūjā (19)

In our English translation we have followed the Tibetan and Chinese, taking the first six verses as a "Prologue." However, to keep the numbering of the main chapters in consonance with the well-known numbering of the Sanskrit and French translations, we count the *Mahāyānasiddhi* chapter as the first. Then, we split the XX–XXI chapter into two, called "Practice" and "Culmination," to end with the total number of twenty-one chapters.

The *BBh* follows the pattern of the *MSA* very closely, which is why I consider it to be Asanga's own "meaning-" or "depth-commentary" (Tib. *don 'grel*) on the text. Lévi reproduces a table from M. Wogihara that shows the correspondences:

MSA	***BBh***	
adhikāra	*paṭala*	*yogasthāna*
3. gotra	1. gotra	I: ādhāra
4. cittotpāda	2. cittotpāda	
5. pratipatti	3. pratipatti	
6. tattva	4. tattvārtha	
7. prabhāva	5. prabhāva	
8. paripāka	6. paripāka	
9. bodhi	7. bodhi	
16a. pāramitā	8–14. balagotra + six pāramitās	
16b. saṁgrahavastu	15. saṁgrahavastu	
17. pūjāsevāpramāṇa	16. pūjāsevāpramāṇa	
18. bodhipakṣa	17. bodhipakṣa	
19. bodhisattvaguṇa	18. bodhisattvaguṇa	
20. caryā, v. 1–2	1. bodhisattvaliṅga	II: ādhāraṇudharma
v. 3–5	2. pakṣa	
v. 6	3. adhyāsaya	
v. 9–32	4. vihāra	
v. 8	1. upapatti	III: ādhāraṇiṣṭha
v. 7	2. parigraha	
v. 32–41	3. bhūmi	
v. 42	4. caryā	
v. 49	5. lakṣaṇānuvyañjana	
v. 43–61	6. pratiṣṭha	

The gap in correspondence between *MSA* chapters 10–15 and the *BBh* is highly intriguing. If *BBh* is Asanga's "meaning commentary," as I have surmised, then why not unpack those chapters? I leave this question to the future, when we complete and publish the *BBh* translation.

Professor Lévi was interested in the peculiarities of the language of the *MSA*, which he considered not adequately accounted for if taken merely as adjustments to metre. He considered the author to be one "qui manie le sanscrit avec autant de richesse et de souplesse" (handled the Sanskrit with so much richness and agility.) Thus, he found some of the irregularities (from the Paninian point of view) in the text to be somewhat surprising. He hypothesized that the irregularity of Buddhist Sanskrit came from the Buddhist interest in moving away from rigid grammatical rules toward the common speech of the times. In the Sanskrit text there are some words we have not found in the dictionaries of either Monier-Williams or Edgerton. Whether these words are "Buddhist Hybrid Sanskrit" vocabulary, are unique to our text, or are simply scribal errors, is impossible to decide with certainty. Both Lévi and Bagchi have listed these words, oddities of both "euphonic combination" (*sandhi*) and omission of such combination, and the varieties of metres used in the text.

As we would expect from its title, *The Universal Vehicle Discourse Literature* and its *Commentary* by Vasubandhu contain both direct and indirect references to the discourses (*sūtras*) comprising the universal vehicle literature, and also to the Sanskrit scriptures (*āgama*) that correspond to the Pali *nikāyas*. For the most part, the indirect references pertain to the latter body of works from which the author has mainly drawn upon the *Saṁyuktāgama* (= *Saṁyutta Nikāya*) and the *Ekottarāgama* (= *Anguttara Nikāya*). Both Lévi and Bagchi already have listed these sources, but it may be useful also to list them here.[9]

Direct references (our numbering):

Akṣarāśi-sūtra III.2
Āryākṣayamati-sūtra IV.20
Kṣāranadī-sūtra XIV.23–26
Guhyakādhipati-nirdeśa XII.9
Gocarapariśuddhi-sūtra V.9
Daśabhūmika-sūtra VII.4; XIV.4–6; XVIII.55
Pañcaka XVIII.93–104
Pañcasthāna-sūtra XVI.17–18
Paramārthaśūnyatā XVIII.93–104
Parijñā-sūtra XVIII.93–104
Prajñāpāramitā I.6; V.11; XI.77
Brahmaparipṛcchā-sūtra XI.76; XII.5
Bhārahāra-sūtra XVIII.93–104
Māṇḍavya-sūtra XXI.54
Ratnakūṭa (corresponds to Kāśyapaparivarta) XIX.28–29
Śrīmālā-sūtra XI.59

[9] Chapter and verse numbers in all tables below correspond to our numbering (for which, see above, pp. xxxiv–xxxv). Unless otherwise noted, the specific names of discourses and scriptures appear in the *Commentary* to the chapter and verse mentioned in these tables.

The commentary also refers to another of Maitreyanatha's works, the *Madhyāntavibhāga* (*MAV*) at XVIII.44–45, and to the *MSA* itself at P.2 (Prologue 2). The commentary to X.1 may contain a reference to the *BBh*. The passage from the *Śrīmālāsūtra* is not found in any extant version of that work.

Indirect references (our numbering):

āgama XVIII.83–84
āha XII.18
iti XII.19–23; XVI.19–20
uktaṁ XIII.12
uktaṁ bhagavatā XI.30; XIII.11; XVI.76; XVIII.83–84, 93–104
yathoktaṁ XI.53; XVI.21–22; 23–24; 25–26; 27–28; XVIII.68ab, 83–84
vacanāt XVII.19; XX.33ab
sūtra XVI.21–22, 68–69
sūtrokta X.14 (verse)

The following works not cited in the *MSA* are mentioned by Sthiramati and/or Asvabhava as sources of the *MSA*.

Gayāśīrṣa-sūtra IV.2; XVII.36
Tathāgatotpatti-saṁbhava-nirdeśa IX.69, 71, 72, 75
Daśadharmaka-sūtra III.5
Pitāputra-samāgamana-sūtra P.5 (Prologue 5)
Buddhabhūmi-sūtra IX.34, 52, 56–59, 67–74, 82
Laṇkāvatāra-sūtra XI.44
Vajracchedikā-prajñāpāramitā-sūtra IX.4
Saddharma-puṇḍarīka-sūtra IX.7, 41 (verse)
Sarvabuddha-viṣayāvatāra-Jñānālokālaṁkāra-sūtra IX.4, 52
Vimalakīrti-nirdeśa IX.54
Sāgaramati-paripṛcchā-sūtra IX.36
Yang dag pa'i rtsa ba'i lung (?) XII.1

The sources for V.6 and XVII.19 are unidentified.

4. The Philosophy of the Literature

At the time Asanga lived, Nagarjuna's teachings had spread in India for about two hundred years. The individual vehicle Abhidharma teachings also were still studied and practiced in many parts of India. It was a time of uncertainty and creativity in Indian civilization; a prescient thinker easily may have foreseen a resurgence of Indian nationalistic feeling and wished to formulate Buddhist thought in such a way as to enable it to take its place near the center of the coming "classical" culture. The major forms of Buddhist thought then available were not suited to fulfill that function. Both individual vehicle monasticism (with its refined psychological scholasticism) as well as central way critical thought (with its razor-sharp dialectic) were too remote from the needs of the rising middle classes, having little explicit emphasis on social philosophy, little inspiring devotionalism or ritualism to involve the masses, and few connections with the Brahminical culture other than critical opposition. The universal vehicle discourses of course were there, and possibly quite well ensconced in the popular imagination of especially the southern kingdoms that still enjoyed the prosperity and peacefulness inherited from the slowly waning Shatavahana dynasty that had so well supported Nagarjuna. But on the intellectual level, the philosophy of Nagarjuna was perhaps a bit too abstruse and difficult for many educated thinkers, its uncompromising central doctrine of voidness too easily confused with nihilism sanctioning complete withdrawal from social concerns, in spite of the radical and well-argued social doctrines in Nagarjuna's *Jewel Rosary*.

Some new synthesis of Brahminical culture and the universal vehicle teachings – a synthesis that could give Buddhism accessibility as a lay religion, with philosophical appeal for the educated elites – was what was required. There was no need to depart from the spirit of Nagarjuna's own incomparable breakthroughs in epistemology and metaphysics, as well as his practical systematization of the trove of discourses he discovered. Rather, there was a need to shift the emphasis from the profound aspect, the teaching of the nature of absolute reality, to the magnificent aspect, the evolutionary conception of the spirit of enlightenment, the will to evolve body and mind over incalculable eons of lifetimes to the exalted evolutionary state of buddhahood for the sake of all beings, the elaboration of the far-reaching paths of bodhisattva practices, and the unfoldment of the magnificent panorama of the activities of the supernal bodhisattvas in the far-flung pure buddhaworlds throughout the universes of the multiverse. This was Asanga's mission, and it was to fulfill this mission that he sought the supernatural aid of the bodhisattva Maitreyanatha.

Nagarjuna had discovered the universal vehicle Scriptures, wherein the nonduality of transcendent freedom and immanent involvement were explicitly stated by the Buddha. He related that most profound teaching to the doctrines of the Abhidharmic "mind scientists." In their rigid scholasticism, they had banished the absolute into a neat little set of categories, off with space, somewhere "beyond" the formless realms of trance. Nagarjuna exploded this rationalistic dualism with his "critique of pure reason," as it were, and he returned the absolute to its place as the very fabric of the ineluctable relativity of the conventional world. His philosophical tool *par excellence* came from the *Transcendent Wisdom Discourses*, the schema of the two realities (*satyadvaya*), the absolute and the relative (or conventional), or the ultimate and the superficial. These two are only superficially opposite; ultimately, they are not different. The absolute is equated with transcendent wisdom (*prajñāpāramitā*), and the superficial with great compassion (*mahākaruṇā*). Thus, the most thoroughgoing transcendentalism, instead of robbing the relative world of value, emerged to reinforce the relative commitment to great compassion in its quest to benefit beings and transform their world into a pure land of enlightenment.

Asanga saw the difficulty of this teaching for his contemporaries, since they lived too far away from Shakyamuni and Nagarjuna. The two-edged sword of binary reality's wisdom and compassion cut so devastatingly through all pretensions of the conceptual mind, it left lesser minds feeling as if they had no ground to stand on whatsoever, prone to the trap of nihilism. Indeed, the stance of the *Transcendent Wisdom Discourse* itself was that the ground of the bodhisattva is groundlessness. So, Asanga, to provide a more solid footing, developed a system of scriptural hermeneutics that could reconcile the new urge for grounding with the scriptural basis. He discovered the key he needed in the *Elucidation of the Intention Sutra*, with its historical theory of the "three wheels of Dharma" and its metaphysical theory of the "three realities." This enabled him to provide the ground he felt people needed, and that ground was ultimately the mind.

The three wheels of Dharma teaching provided a way to elaborate the new doctrine without giving up allegiance to the *Transcendent Discourse*, the "Mother of All Buddhas." According to the *Elucidation of the Intention Discourse*, Shakyamuni taught the four noble truths as the "first turning of the wheel of Dharma," a teaching that took for granted the apparent reality of both "samsara" and "Nirvana." In the second wheel of Dharma, he taught the teaching of transcendent wisdom, stressing the universal voidness of all things to remove the disciples' attachment to the existence of all things, introducing them to their ultimate non-existence as intrinsic realities. Finally, in the third wheel of Dharma, for those disciples of sharp discrimination, he taught the existence of some things and the non-existence of other things. This third wheel of Dharma taught the three-reality theory, as a refinement of the two-reality theory taught in the second wheel, adding a central "relative reality" to serve as a ground of the absolute and the superficial realities.

The most important philosophical strategy of Maitreya's idealism, then, is the three-reality theory, which he derives from the *Elucidation of the Intention Discourse*. The beneficiaries of this teaching were puzzled about the apparent discrepancy between the Buddha's apparently realistic teaching of the *Abhidharma*, that everything in samsara and Nirvana exists in some sense as it appears to, and the apparently nihilistic teaching of the *Transcendent Wisdom*, that nothing really exists, all being universally void. For the main third-wheel disciples, the Centrist way of reconciling this – by saying that this means that all things do not exist in the ultimate sense yet still do exist in the superficial sense – was not considered satisfactory. So, there are instead *three* senses to be understood.

There are three realities: the reality of imaginative construction; the reality of the relative; and the reality of the perfect, or absolute. When the Buddha says that all things do not exist – that, as the discourses record, "There is no eye, no faculty of eye, no visible objects, and no eye consciousness… no samsara, no Nirvana, no attainment, and no non-attainment either" – he means that these things do not exist as they are conceived to exist by imaginative construction, as they are ascriptively and descriptively designated to exist and to function. He does not mean that they do not exist in the relative reality, the reality of causes and conditions. And, he does not mean that they do not exist in the absolute reality, as the pure realm of enlightenment. All things are relative to one another and to their own causes and conditions. When this relative reality is misconstrued by the imaginations of ignorant sentient beings to exist as a world of disparate subjects and objects, then it is experienced as samsara, the miserable life-cycle. When, on the other hand, it is perceived as devoid of the real existence of those imaginative constructions, as the ineffable, pure play of the mind, it is Nirvana, the absolute reality. Thus, the three realities can be succinctly understood by means of the formula "the perfect reality is the relative devoid of the imagined."

The relative reality thus becomes the basis, the ground, that the less daring contemplator of voidness felt was needed, the basis of both samsara and of Nirvana. It serves from the outset to reassure the yogin in quest of the absolute reality that the ultimate reality is not dualistic, not in some far-off abstract realm of voidness, but right before her, nondualistically in the actual, relative world, somehow overlaid by mental constructions that prevent her from seeing it effortlessly.

But what, then, is this relative reality, this ground of all? How can it be overlaid and so utterly distorted by mere mental constructions? The answer is that it can be thus radically affected by the mind if its very substance is also mind, indeed only mind. Thus, Shakyamuni in this phase of his teaching, Lord Maitreyanatha in three of his five books, and Asanga in his great compendia, elaborated the theory of "Idealism" (*Cittamātra* or *Vijñānavāda*), or "Experientialism" (*Yogācāra*). This theory stresses the mental nature of reality, resolves the mind-matter duality in favor of the mind, and, most importantly, gives the introspective yogin the confidence that, in probing into the innermost reaches of the mind in order to understand its world-constructive powers and to transcend its fettering mental habits, he is in no danger of losing touch with reality in the great expanse of empty void, since the absolute and relative realities in their pristine radiance do, indeed, lie within the individual's inner experience – hence, the other major name of the school, "Experientialism" (*Yogācāratva*). Once this problem of reality is settled, and the pure basis established from the outset, as it were, the yogin can turn her attention to the cultivation of compassion, to the deeds of the bodhisattva by means of the five paths and ten stages, with the six transcendences and the four political practices.

Thus, Asanga elaborated in breathtaking detail the magnificent action stage of the path, and he did not repeat Nagarjuna's exhaustive focus on the profound stage of the path. Of course, it must not be thought that Asanga's teaching is ultimately any less profound than Nagarjuna's. That would be to do him an injustice and to miss the greatness of his contribution. Ultimately, even the mind, the deepest relative and absolute mind that anchors both samsara and Nirvana, is also realized directly to be the shining emptiness beyond any dualities of mind and non-mind. It is just a question of emphasis, of staving off the starkness of that realization while the richness of the paths is fully felt and experienced.

Maitreyanatha and Asanga emphasized the paths of the bodhisattva, the magnificent deeds of great compassion and universal love that move the universe and bring sensitive beings to perfection in the course of time. They further provided the religious ground on which the universal vehicle became accessible to the nascent "classical culture" of India, the culture that was flowering in the Gupta era with its great artists, poets, playwrights, and religious and philosophical geniuses. Asanga followed Maitreyanatha's inspiration and made the universal vehicle literarily, philosophically, and religiously integral to classical Indian culture, bringing the Buddhist teaching out of the rarified monastic atmosphere in which it had existed from its beginnings into the mainstream of the society. Such greater availability was not won at the cost of any compromise of the universal vehicle insistence on the necessity of transcendence and the inevitability of compassionate commitment to the welfare of beings. It remained a spiritually evolutionary as well as socially revolutionary doctrine, teaching a vehicle of simultaneous personal development and social transformation.

Historically, it seems that Asanga and Vasubandhu presided over a sizeable expansion of the Buddhist movement in Gupta-dominated India of the 5th and 6th centuries CE. The idealistic interpretation of the universal vehicle that they so powerfully advanced has long been looked at as mainly a philosophical, or ideological, doctrine, expounding primarily an intellectual worldview. Its religious dimension has not been as well elucidated. A clue can be taken from the Tibetan tradition, in which the hierarchy of theories is arranged in such a way that the Idealistic/Experientialist theory represents the philosophical entry point of the universal vehicle. Some Tibetan thinkers followed the Indian philosophers Shantarakshita and Kamalashila (8th–9th centuries) in considering that Idealism (*Vijñānavāda*) was a good precursor to Centrism (*Madhyamaka*). Though I have not yet seen this mentioned explicitly in an Indian or Tibetan text, my hunch is that this is connected to the spiritual decisions involved in the bodhisattva vow, the central undertaking of the bodhisattva that marks the beginning of the Mahayana path, wherein she or he takes the formal vow to liberate every single being without exception from suffering and to lead them all into the bliss of buddhahood, turning the entire universe into a buddhaverse. How difficult it seems to make such a vow in the mind and heart if one is thinking of the "universe of beings" as an infinite, substantial, external, dense, and heavy bunch of objects! How overwhelming the prospect of transforming all of it into a buddhaverse! But, if the nature of all beings and things is mental, mind-constituted, and mind-created, then a radical transformation of the inner mind, in intersubjective interconnection with other minds, could very well be able to effect a total transformation of everything that exists with a semblance of greater ease. One could then take up the bodhisattva vow with a sense of possibility empowering the compassionate emotion and the messianic determination.

I grant that a majority of Tibetan scholars think this is all equally possible for a person open to the Centrist viewpoint, and they do not think the Idealistic stage is essential for such vow taking. But Centrism itself is an "idealistic" point of view, too, in comparison to materialistic realism, for example. The sophisticated epistemology and linguistic insight of the Buddhist Idealists are not at all discarded by the Centrists. Rather, they build upon it, turning from focus on the power of the mind in world-construction to articulating the power of language in that enterprise.

In any case, it is not necessary to go into a detailed philosophical study of Asanga's and Vasubandhu's theories in this introduction. The *Literature* is an inspired work presenting the gems of the universal vehicle discourses on many topics other than the mental nature of things. It does not announce any sort of affiliation with a school or ideology, presents a plausible interpretation of the *Discourses*, and deserves to be read on its own terms as a work of inspiration and insight.

May all experience "the joys of beholding an ornament of beaten gold, eating a fine feast when famished, seeing a lotus in full bloom, receiving good news in a letter from afar, and throwing wide open in bright sunlight a casket filled with priceless jewels!"

Prologue[1]

OM! Reverence to all buddhas and bodhisattvas!

1.[2] (Our Lord Maitreyanātha),[3] knowing the (supreme) import[4] (of the universal vehicle scriptures), creates an exhibition[5] of that

---

[1] Lévi's Sanskrit and the Chinese texts combine this section with the following chapter, while the Tibetan makes it a separate chapter 1. To compromise, we have set it as a prologue.

[2] Verses 1–3 are paralleled in the discussion on the composition of treatises in the twenty-third section of the *VS* (P Zi 205a8–206b3). The composition of treatises is divided into worship, the six reasons for composing a treatise, the four virtues of an author, and the reason why a treatise is called an "ornament of scripture." Our verse 1 resembles a summary of the six reasons and four qualities. The six reasons for composing a treatise are: to propagate the Truth, to inculcate it, analyze it, synthesize it, explain it, and ornament it with a literary style. The four virtues are: respect for past teachers, compassion for living beings, love for one's fellows in religion, and modesty. Our verses 2 and 3 contain the five similes used to explain why "a commentary representing accurately the discourses of the Transcendent Lord is called an 'ornament of scripture.'" See LII, vs. 2, n. 1; also Nishio, Kyō, "Daijō Sōgenkyōron Bodaihan no Motozuku Shokyō ni tsuite," *Ōtani Gakuhō* 17 (1935): 171.

[3] By this bracket, we are suggesting that this verse, and the prologue itself, is not part of the body of the *MSA*, which is composed or revealed by Maitreyanātha himself (see Introduction), but rather a prologue addressed by Asaṅga to Maitreyanātha – a kind of salutation. It is clear that it cannot be written by the composer of the work, due to the *kāruṇyatastanmayaḥ* (LI, p. 1.5), which could not be used by an author about himself.

This distinguishing between Maitreyanātha and Asaṅga holds even if we take the position, as we do in the Introduction above, that, while Asaṅga is the human author of both Maitreyanātha's and his own works, he writes the former as a medium for Maitreyanātha, and not of his own volition. See Introduction.

[4] *Arthajño* (LI, p. 1.4), (lit. "Knower of Things/Matters/Meaning") is a rather unusual epithet of a buddha or bodhisattva. It is, to our knowledge, unattested elsewhere in Mahāyāna literature. *Sarvajño* ("Omniscient") and *Dharmajño* ("Knower of Truth") are the more usual epithets for an enlightened one. Indeed, *artha* has a worldly connotation in the classical Sanskrit of the fourth century, as used in the *Arthaśāstra*, or "Science of Political Economy," or in the merchants' "aim of life" (*varga*), where it means "wealth." In the latter scheme it is contrasted with *kāma*, *dharma*, and *mokṣa*. A working hypothesis about the choice of this epithet has already been discussed in the Introduction. See LII, n. 1.

[5] *Vibhāvanā* (LI, p. 1.4). The use of terms from literary criticism in this verse and comment, such as *yukta*, *sahita*, *śliṣṭa*, and *paura*, suggests an intentional play on a technical meaning of *vibhāvanā*, as the poetic device "suggestion" (see *Kāvyādarśa*, II.199, and *Kāvyālaṁkāra*,

(cont'd)

> import with flawless language and expressions, in order to save beings from suffering; he being compassion incarnate. To those beings who seek the Dharma, the Truth as taught in the supreme vehicle, he reveals this fivefold[6] interpretation, an elegant way to the unexcelled.[7]

Here, (we) begin with (a verse that anticipates the standard eightfold) inquiry[8] (at the outset of a work of "ornament of scriptures"). Who creates such an ornament? One who discerns the (essential) import. What ornament does he create? He creates an exhibition of that import. With what means does he create it? By means of flawless language and flawless expressions; in more detail, "flawless language" is language that is cultured[9] and so forth, and "flawless expressions" are ex-

---

I.47). Although this verse does not explicitly contain this device (i.e., a description of an effect where the usual cause is absent or denied, or where some special cause is credited) the author may have wished to suggest that an understanding of the universal vehicle (the effect) may be gained through his work (special cause), without the necessity of studying the voluminous mass of universal vehicle scriptures (the usual cause). This generally fits well with the aesthetic and literary atmosphere of the context set up by this prologue.

[6] See the comment on verse 2 below (LI, p. 2.7).

[7] dBal Mang (8a *ff.*) mentions that the Paṇḍit Parahitabhadra discerns that the four intellectual knowledges (*pratisaṁvid*) are attributed to Maitreyanātha by the verse: "knowing the (supreme) import (of the universal vehicle scriptures), fashions an exposition of that import" indicates the knowledges of teaching (*deśanā*) and meaning (*artha*); "with impeccable language and expressions" indicates grammatical (*nirukti*) knowledge; and "this fivefold interpretation, an elegant way to the unexcelled" indicates the knowledge of eloquence (*pratibhānapratisaṁvid*).

Parahitabhadra also comments that "*Arthajño* means Maitreya, who knows the import of the Mahāyāna according to the intention of the Victor," glossing "import" here as "intentional import" (*abhisaṁdhyartha*).

[8] The next eight paragraphs respond to these standard questions; about the author, the work, the means of expression, etc.

[9] *Paura*, literally "urbane," with an interesting connotation recorded in the Chinese (T.31.590b13): *neng zhi nie-ban cheng*, in Sthiramati's commentary (P Mi 7a8) and in *VS* (P Yi 58a5–6): *de la grong khyer pa ni mya ngan las 'das pa'i grong khyer gyi dbang du byas pa yin pa'i phyir.* Thus, the civilizing influence of the cultured lifestyle, language, and sensibility of the urban middle classes is associated in these works by these monastic philosophers with the liberation that is the goal of all their teachings. The socially liberating function of the city is of course well known to social scientists, along with its obverse of alienation from rural, traditional norms.

pressions that are reasonable and beautiful. Without phonemes, words, and expressions, it is impossible to exhibit meaning.

For what purpose? To save beings from suffering. From what motive? From his compassion for suffering people; that is, from that compassion for suffering people which is natural for him, he being compassion incarnate.

Of what does he create this ornament? Of the Dharma as it is taught in the supreme vehicle; that is, of that noble Dharma wherein the supreme vehicle is taught.

For whom does he create this ornament? For those beings who seek that (truth). Here we have a locative of benefit,[10] meaning that this ornament is for the benefit of those beings who seek the universal vehicle.

How manifold is this ornament he creates? It is fivefold. He reveals an interpretation which is elegant, conducive to the unexcelled (transcendent wisdom), and of a fivefold nature, (i.e., provable, understandable, conceivable, inconceivable, and perfect). "Elegant" here means suitably composed, and "conducive to the unexcelled" means conducive to the unexcelled intuitive wisdom.[11]

> 2. The Dharma here disclosed gives the utmost joy, like gold hand-beaten, like a lotus fully bloomed, like a delicious feast when famished, like good news read in a letter, or like a casket of jewels thrown open.

This verse uses five examples to explain the truth in terms of its fivefold import: its provability, understandability, conceivability, inconceivability, and perfection. The latter is its experiential import, its interior realizability, and its actuality as the accessories of enlightenment. When this is revealed by this *Ornament of the Scriptures of the Universal Vehicle*, it gives the utmost joy, like the joys derived from beaten gold and so on, respectively.[12]

---

[10] See J.S. Speijer, *Sanskrit Syntax* (Delhi: Motilal Banarsidass, 1973), paras. 147–148.

[11] The Tibetan here reads *theg pa* (*yāna*) for *ye shes* (*jñāna*), which reading of "vehicle" is confirmed by Sthiramati (P Mi 9a5–6), and by the variant reading given in the Bagchi edition, p. 1. However, one reaches the vehicle only by means of transcendent wisdom, so we follow the Sanskrit here as less redundant.

[12] To understand more concretely the philosophical processes involved, we need the help of Vasubandhu's and dBal Mang's elucidations. The first stanza refers to a "fivefold access to that import," and the second stanza describes the esthetic process of coming to understanding in terms of a fivefold joy. Vasubandhu relates these similes to five types of "realizational

(cont'd)

But how can that noble truth, naturally endowed with the highest excellence, be any further adorned? The third verse aims to refute such an objection:

> 3. Just as a well-adorned face of naturally outstanding beauty gives people even more intense delight when they behold it in a mirror, so this Dharma, always outstanding in its natural brilliance, gives a still more distinct satisfaction to the wise when its meaning is critically elucidated.

What does this teach? Just as a face, beautiful both by adornment and by nature, gives especially intense delight when reflected in a mirror, so this truth, always beautiful both by nature and by its true eloquence, gives a distinctive satisfaction to the intelligent when its import is elucidated. Therefore, since this Dharma gives such a distinctive satisfaction, it is as if adorned still further (by a work such as this *Ornament*).

Now, the next three verses teach the threefold benefit of this Dharma, in order to instill reverence for it:

> 4. Like a medicine foul in smell yet sweet in taste, this Dharma should be understood to have two dimensions, its literal dimension and the always-beneficial dimension of its import.

> 5. This Dharma, expansive, tough, and deep, is like a monarch, very hard to please; and yet, also like a monarch, once pleased, it is the bestower of the treasure of the highest excellence.

> 6. Just as the priceless, classic jewel gives no satisfaction to the undiscriminating person, this Dharma is wasted on the unintelligent; in the opposite cases, each gives due satisfaction in the same way.

---

meaning" (*adhigamārthaṁ*, LI, p. 2.8), called provability, understandability, conceivability, inconceivability, and perfection. Following these famous categories, we equate them with the five similes as follows: 1) hand-beaten gold ornament = joy = provable; 2) blossomed lotus = joy = understandable; 3) fine feast when famished = joy = conceivable; 4) good news received = joy = inconceivable; 5) opened jewel casket = joy = perfection. For further analysis of these five see the Introduction.

The benefits of the Dharma are threefold. It is compared to medicine, since it causes the removal of the obscurations. It has the dual arrangement into literal and meaningful. It is compared to a monarch since it is the cause of power, bestowing the sovereignty of the highest excellences, such as the superknowledges. It is compared to a priceless, classic jewel, since it is the cause of the enjoyment of the wealth of the noble ones. The person of true discrimination here is understood to be a noble saint.

Chapter I

Authenticity of the universal vehicle[1]

Now, some misguided persons think, "This universal vehicle is not the authentic word of the Buddha, so how does it confer any benefit?" This verse lists the reasons to prove to them that (the universal vehicle) is indeed authentic buddha-word:

> 1. (The universal vehicle is the word of the buddha) because it was not previously predicted (as a danger); because the (vehicles) began together; because it is beyond the scope (of theology); because it is self-evident; because it must be since it exists, and there would be no such thing if it did not; because it has medicinal power; and because it has more to it than words.

"Because it was not previously predicted;" if the universal vehicle was fabricated by someone at a later time in order to interfere with the true Dharma, why did the Lord not predict it, as he did predict other future dangers?

"Because (the vehicles) began together;" it is obvious that the universal vehicle began at the same time as the disciple vehicle and not later. So why should one imagine it is not the word of the buddha?

"Because it is beyond the range (of theology);" this magnificent and profound Dharma is not within the range of theology (*tārkikāṇāṁ*), since such a (Dharma) is not found in the theological treatises of the religious (*tīrthikas*). It is quite impossible that they should have taught this, since they do not believe in it even (now) when they hear it taught.

---

[1] From here on each chapter in the Sanskrit text concludes with a phrase conforming to the following pattern: "This concludes the first chapter of the *Mahāyānasūtrālaṁkāra*, on 'The authenticity of the universal vehicle.'" We are placing the chapter numbers and titles at the beginning of each chapter, following contemporary publishing convention.

"Because it is self-evident;" even if the universal vehicle was taught by some enlightened being other (than Śākyamuni Buddha), that also proves it to be buddha-word, since a buddha is anyone who becomes perfectly enlightened and then teaches such (a vehicle).

"Because it must be since it exists, and there would be no such thing if it did not;" since there is a universal vehicle, its very existence proves it to be the word of the buddha, since there is no other universal vehicle. Or, if there were no universal vehicle, its nonexistence would entail the nonexistence of the disciple vehicle as well. It is unreasonable to insist that the disciple vehicle is the word of the buddha and the universal vehicle is not; for without a buddha-vehicle, buddhas could not originate, (and could not teach any disciples).

"Because it has medicinal power;" if one practices the universal vehicle, it serves as the ground of all nonconceptual intuitions, thereby becoming the medicine for all the mental addictions. It is therefore the word of the buddha.

"Because it has more to it than words;" its import is not just its literal meaning. Therefore, adherence to its literal meaning cannot support the notion that it is not the word of the buddha.[2]

With regard to (the reason of) "no previous prediction," one might object that the Lord did not predict the occurrence (of an artificial universal vehicle) out of neglect. The (following) verse shows the inappropriateness of (assuming) such indifference:

> 2. The buddhas' eyes see directly, they are the guardians of the teaching, and time does not impede their knowledge. Thus it is unreasonable that they should be indifferent.

What does this show? (The Buddha's) indifference to a great future calamity for his teaching is unreasonable for three reasons. The intuition of the buddhas functions effortlessly through their directly perceiving eyes. They spare no effort to

---

[2] This argument tacitly admits that the negational expressions of the *Transcendent Wisdom Scriptures*, if understood literally, have a nihilistic flavor; it anticipates Asaṅga's refutation of the Mādhyamikas as nihilistic in their doctrine of ultimate nonexistence and conventional existence, and their failure to use the hermeneutical device of the three realities which he develops. See Robert A.F. Thurman, *Tsong Khapa's Speech of Gold in the Essence of True Eloquence* (Princeton: Princeton University Press, 1984; reprinted as *The Central Philosophy of Tibet*, 1991), translation chapters 1–2.

protect the teaching. They are able to know the future with their unimpeded knowledge of all times.

Concerning the reason "because it must be since it exists, and there would be no such thing if it did not," one might object that the disciple vehicle itself is a universal vehicle, since through it great enlightenment is achieved. There is, therefore, a verse on the inappropriateness of regarding the disciple vehicle as the universal vehicle:

> 3. This (teaching of the) disciple vehicle is not (properly) called the "teaching of the universal vehicle" because it is incomplete, would be contradictory, lacks liberative art, and does not give such instructions.

"It is incomplete" in (its) instruction on altruistic concerns, since altruism is not taught in the disciple vehicle; for the disciples are only taught the techniques for their own disillusionment, detachment, and liberation. Nor can individualism become altruism just by being taught to others.

"It would be contradictory" since those devoted to their own interest apply themselves only for their own individual benefit, and it is contradictory that those striving only for the sake of their own ultimate liberation will realize unexcelled, perfect enlightenment. Nor can one become a buddha by seeking enlightenment through the disciple vehicle alone, even by striving for a long time.[3]

"It lacks liberative art" – the disciple vehicle lacks the art for buddhahood, and without the (right) art, one never attains a desired goal no matter how long one strives; just as one cannot get milk from a (cow's) horn, even with a pump.

But is the way a bodhisattva should strive taught here in some other manner? "It does not give such instructions," so the disciple vehicle itself cannot become a universal vehicle, since one encounters no such instructions therein.

It has been said that the disciple and universal vehicles are mutually contradictory; thus there is a verse on mutual contradiction:

---

[3] The disciple vehicle has a methodology for attaining the personal Nirvāṇa of a saint, but because it does not have the "magnificent" teaching of the bodhisattva's compassion and stages, it has no methodology for developing the form body essential to the attainment of buddhahood.

> 4. That individual (vehicle) is just individual (in its aim), since it contradicts (the universal vehicle) in terms of aspiration, instruction, practice, support, and time.

How are they contradictory? Through the five contradictions, those of aspiration, instruction, practice, support, and time. In the disciple vehicle, aspiration is only for the individual's ultimate liberation, instructions are for that purpose only, and practice is for that purpose only. It has only a limited support of gathered stores of merit and wisdom, and its goal is attained in little time, even in three lifetimes. But in the universal vehicle, the opposite holds in every case. Thus, there is mutual contradiction; that individual (vehicle) is just (for the) individual, and cannot become a universal vehicle.

Someone might think that, since there is the (following) definition of the word of the buddha, "it arises in the discourses, is evident in the discipline, and is not inconsistent with actual reality,"[4] the universal vehicle does not fit. For it teaches that all things lack intrinsic reality, and so cannot be the word of the buddha. Hence this verse on the universal vehicle's non-contradiction with the definition:

> 5. It too arises in its own discourses, is evident also in its own discipline, and it does not run counter to actual reality, due to its magnificence and profundity.

What does this verse show? It shows that this (universal vehicle word of the buddha) arises in its own universal vehicle discourses and is evident in its own discipline for (treating) the mental addictions of the bodhisattvas, which, the universal vehicle teaches, (mainly) consist of conceptual thoughts.[5] Due to its characteristics of magnificence and profundity it is not inconsistent with actual reality, since the actual reality that makes possible the attainment of the great enlightenment is just

---

[4] LII, p. 10, n. 10.1, quotes a phrase from the *Dīghanikāya*, XVI, 4, 8 (from the Pāli *Mahāparinibbānasutta*) which is quite close: *tāni ce sutte otāriyamānāni vinaye sandissayamānāni sutte c'eva otaranti, vinaye ca sandissanti, niṭṭham ettha gantabbam: addā idam tassa bhagavato vacanaṁ....* Lévi also confirms that Vasubandhu (he refers to the author as Asaṅga; see Introduction) quotes exactly the Sanskrit *Dīrghāgama*, which Lévi confirms from the Chinese (Tōk. XII, 9, 15a).

[5] There are universal vehicle discourses which specifically present a Discipline (*Vinaya*) for bodhisattvas; for example, the *Bodhisattva vinaya sūtra* of the *ratnakūṭa* collection.

this (universal vehicle teaching of the freedom from intrinsic reality).[6] Thus, it does not contradict the definition.

It was stated in the first verse (of this chapter) that the universal vehicle "is beyond the scope;" hence, this verse is on its non-inclusion in the scope of theology:

> 6. Theology is dependent, indefinite, non-comprehensive, superficial, tiresome, and the resort of the naïve. Thus, this (universal vehicle) is not within its scope.

Theology rests upon the failure to experience the truth (personally); that is, it is dependent upon certain sacred traditions. It is indefinite because it understands (reality) differently at different times. It is non-comprehensive because its scope does not include all objects of knowledge. Its object is the superficial reality and not ultimate reality. It is tiresome because it completely confines the human genius.

The universal vehicle, however, is none of these, from dependent to tiresome. It is taught in the discourses such as the *Transcendent Wisdom Hundred Thousand.* So it is not within the scope of theology.

It was said (in verse three of this chapter) that buddhahood is not attained in the disciple vehicle, since that (vehicle) lacks liberative art. How then is the universal vehicle endowed with the art (for attaining buddhahood)? This verse is on its fitness as liberative art:

> 7. From the magnificent and the profound come evolutionary development and nonconceptual (wisdom). (The universal vehicle) teaches both, and therein lies its art (for realizing) unexcelled (enlightenment).

What does this verse show? Teaching the magnificence of (the buddhas') power makes beings progress in evolution, since they strive through their faith in that power. Teaching the profound (selflessness develops) nonconceptual (wisdom). Hence both are taught in the universal vehicle, serving as the liberative art for (attaining) unexcelled wisdom, since those two respectively bring about the evolution-

---

[6] LI, p. 5.8 ...*athaiva hi dharmatā mahābodhiprāptaye tasmānnāsti*.... The Tibetan (D Phi 132a3–4) *byang chub chen po'i 'thob par 'gyur pa'i chos nyid ni 'di kho na yin no* clarifies this corrupt text, which would better read *tad eva hi dharmatā mahābodhiprāptaye.* See the Chinese version (T.31.591c16).

ary maturity of (other) beings and the evolutionary perfection of one's own buddha-qualities.

There are those who become frightened by this (teaching). For their sake there is a verse on the causes and the dangers of such unwarranted fear:[7]

> 8.[8] Groundless fear causes people suffering, for it has long occasioned the growth of a great mass of evil. Who has no spiritual gene, who has bad friends, whose mind is uncultivated, and who has no previously gathered virtues, fears this teaching, misses the great purpose, and wanders in this world.

Groundless fear is fear of what is not a cause for fear, and it causes suffering for beings in the bad migrations. Why? Because it causes the growth of a great mass of evil. For how long? For a long period. Next, the dangers are shown, along with their causes and duration. What is the cause of such fear? He shows four causes; lack of the spiritual gene, lack of good friends, having a mind uneducated in the reality of the universal vehicle, and not having previously stored up virtue. To miss the great purpose (of life) is to miss gathering the stores for the great enlightenment. He shows here yet another danger, from the loss of the not yet obtained.

Having shown the causes of fear, the reasons for not fearing the universal vehicle should be shown; hence a verse on the reasons not to be afraid:

> 9. There is no (universal vehicle) other than it. It is supremely hard to fathom. It is contemporary. It teaches a variety. It uses a consistent explanation, with many approaches. Its meaning is not literal. The Lord's intention is mysterious.[9] The wise do not fear this teaching since they examine it properly.

---

[7] The Tibetan (D Phi 132b2–3) reads *nyes dmigs dang rgyu nyid,* hence invalidating the Sanskrit (LI, p. 6.2): ...*ādīnave kāraṇatvena*..., which should translate, "a verse concerning the causes in the case of the danger...." If the Tibetan is right, and it makes better sense, the two should be compounded, ...*ādīnavakāraṇatvena.*

[8] From here the meter changes, moving from predominantly 16-syllable, two-line verses, to 17-syllable four-line verses, until the end of this chapter. (See LI, p. 6, n. 1.)

[9] The Sanskrit (LI, p. 6.17) *bhagavati ca bhāvātigahanāt* seems less good than the Tibetan (D Phi 132b7) *bcom ldan dgongs pa shin tu zab,* i.e., **saṁdhyātigahanāt.*

"There is no other different from it" – this can mean either that there is no universal vehicle other than it, or that, if the disciple vehicle were itself the universal vehicle, there would be no disciple or hermit sage vehicles apart from it. In fact, all (practitioners) would become buddhas.

"It is supremely hard to fathom" – the path to omniscience is very hard to fathom. It is "contemporary" because it arose at the same time (as the individual vehicle).

"It teaches a variety," teaching the variety of the paths of the stores (of merit and wisdom),[10] and not just voidness alone. Therefore, this (teaching of voidness) should be taken as intentional. "It uses a consistent explanation with many approaches," as voidness is repeatedly taught in various discourses with many approaches. Its necessity then is very great, otherwise the negation (of intrinsic reality) would have been made just once. Its meaning is not literal, not being explicit in the words.

Therefore, one should not fear (the universal vehicle). The intention of the Lord is (very hard to fathom), because the intentions of all buddhas are very deep and hard to understand. So, we should not fear (the universal vehicle teaching) just because we do not (easily) understand it. And thus the wise do not fear it, for they investigate it properly.

This verse on (the universal vehicle) as the sphere of far-reaching wisdom:

> 10. Relying in the beginning on study, the appropriate conscientious attitude emerges, and from that conscientious attitude arises that wisdom whose object is the meaning of thatness. That generates the attainment of the truth (body), and therein lies real genius. Since (truth) is (only known) personally,[11] without (such wisdom), how can you decide (that the universal vehicle is not the word of the buddha)?

Relying in the beginning upon study, the appropriate conscientious attitude arises; the word *yo* (in the first line) means "appropriate" (*yoniśa*). From the appro-

[10] The Sanskrit (LI, p. 6.22) is corrupt here: *saṁbhāramārga* has no case ending. The Tibetan *tshogs kyi lam* instead of *tshogs lam* makes it clear that the two stores of merit and knowledge are mentioned here, as suits the meaning of "variety," and not just the accumulation path of the five paths.

[11] Following the Tibetan (D Phi 133a7): *de ltar gang gi tshe blo gros de ni so so rang gis rig pa yin na de med na 'di ji ltar nges te.*

priate conscientious attitude arises wisdom whose object is the meaning of thatness; that is the transcendent realistic view. Then comes the attainment of the truth (body), the fruition of that (wisdom). When that is attained, the (true) genius arises which is the intuition of liberation. When that intelligence is interior, it is (only personally) determined. Without it, how can there be a decision or determination that the universal vehicle is not the word of the buddha?

Another verse on (the universal vehicle's being) nothing to fear:

> 11. "Neither I nor the Buddha understand the profound. Why is that profound not accessible to theology? Why is liberation only for those who understand the import of the profound?" Such a fearful position is irrational.

If one were to say, "I don't understand the profound; it is frightening," it would be wrong. Or, "A buddha also does not understand the import of the profound, so why does he teach it? It is frightening," it would be wrong. Or, "Why is liberation only for those who understand the import of the profound, but not for the theologians? It is frightening," it would be wrong.

One verse on the (universal vehicle) being proven by lack of faith:

> 12. (The superiority of the universal vehicle) is proven by the fact that those of petty aspiration, those of very lowly elements, and those surrounded by narrow-minded friends do not have faith in this Dharma which teaches magnificence and profundity so well.

One whose aspiration is petty develops on that account a lowly element which permeates his fundamental consciousness. He (tends to) surround (himself with) narrow-minded friends whose aspiration and elements are similar to his own. If such a person has no faith in the teaching of the universal vehicle, wherein magnificence and profundity are well taught, that in itself proves the excellence of that universal vehicle.

One verse on the irrationality of rejecting discourses which one has not heard:

> 13. One who has gained knowledge through one course of study and then reviles (another) which he has not studied, is a fool. How can he be certain (it is worthless) when a boundless variety of learning still remains?

Granting a lack of faith in the universal vehicle, the indiscriminate rejection of unstudied discourses is irrational. That person is a fool who gains knowledge through one course of study and then reviles another study just in general. How can one be certain that the universal vehicle is not the word of the buddha, when a boundless variety of learning still remains? One has no strength other than learning, so it is wrong to reject what has not been learned.

What has been studied should be properly incorporated in conscientious attitudes; hence this verse on the drawbacks of inappropriate conscientious attitudes:

> 14. The meaning (of the discourses) being (too) literally construed, self-conceited understanding leads to the ruin of intelligence. One rejects the well taught and so suffers a defeat, confused by hostility toward the teaching.[12]

"Self-conceited understanding" is complacent attachment to one's own view, not seeking the (true) import from the wise. It leads to the ruin of intelligence, due to the loss suffered from failure to attain the intuition attuned with reality. Such a one rejects the well-taught explanations of the teaching, thereby gaining great demerit and so suffering a defeat. The confusion of hostility toward the teaching leads to the (harmful) evolutionary action of abandonment of the teaching; this is its major drawback.

Hostility (toward the teachings) is irrational, even when one does not know that their meaning is not literal; hence this verse on the inappropriateness of resentment:

> 15. A hostile mentality is naturally deficient, not fit to apply even to the faulty, not to mention the teaching, even when in doubt. Therefore, simple impartiality is preferable, for it is free of fault.

Naturally deficient means naturally reproachable. Thus, simple impartiality is preferable. Why? It is free of fault, while hostility is faulty.

---

[12] The Tibetan (D Phi 134a2): *chos la khong khro sgrib* indicates an emendation of the Sanskrit from (LI, p. 8.7): *dharme pratighāvatīva* (*pratighātameva*) to *dharme pratighāvṛtīva*, which is more in accord with the commentary's *pratighātamāvaraṇaṁ*.

Chapter II

Going For Refuge

First, this verse summarizing the (bodhisattva's) distinctive going for refuge:

> 1. One who has gone for refuge in this vehicle should be known as supreme among refugees, due to a substantial distinctiveness with four aspects: universality, commitment, attainment, and supremacy.

Why is only the one (who goes for refuge in the universal vehicle) foremost among those who go for refuge? Because of a substantial distinctiveness with four aspects, known as: universality, commitment, attainment, and supremacy. The meanings of universality, commitment, attainment, and supremacy will be explained below.

Nevertheless, some are faint-hearted, because refugees have many difficult duties. This verse is to encourage their going for refuge:[1]

> 2. The resolution is difficult in the beginning, and difficult to practice even for hundreds of thousands of eons. Yet when accomplished it has great value in promoting the welfare of beings. Therefore, it is here in the supreme vehicle that refuge has the supreme value.

This shows that the determination to go for refuge causes fame, because of the distinctiveness of its vows and practices. Its great value is shown by the distinctiveness of its attainment of fruition.

A verse on the meaning of the "universality" mentioned above:

> 3. One who is engaged in saving all beings, who is skilled in both vehicle and intuition as universal, who has in Nirvāṇa an equal ex-

---

[1] Following the Tibetan (D Phi 134b2): *skyabs su 'gro bar spro bar bya ba'i phyir.*

> perience of life-cycle and of peace – that one should be recognized as a genius, and truly universal.

This shows the fourfold meaning[2] of "universality." Its significance with reference to beings is shown by the fact that one undertakes to save all beings. Universality of vehicles is shown by one's skill in the three vehicles. Universality of intuitions is shown by one's knowledge of the selflessnesses of subjects and objects. Universality of Nirvāṇa is shown by one's equal experience of life-cycle and of peace; that is, there life-cycle and liberation are not differentiated as evil and good.

A verse on the significance of commitment:

> 4. That genius is to be recognized as foremost in commitment who aspires with many joys to the supreme enlightenment, who tirelessly undergoes hardships, and who, once enlightened, becomes the equal of all the buddhas.

The distinctive quality of commitment is shown here by way of a threefold distinctiveness. The distinctive vow is the aspiration to the actual state of that buddha only to whom one goes for refuge out of one's abundance of joy from knowing the excellence of his virtues. The distinctive practice is the tireless performance of difficult tasks. Distinctive attainment is that one becomes the complete equal of all the buddhas by attaining highest perfect enlightenment.

Distinctiveness of commitment is shown by another verse on the excellent birth as the foremost of the buddha-children:[3]

---

[2] From here there is a gap in the Sanskrit text up to the end of the commentary on vs. 11 in this chapter, which is made up from the Tibetan translation (D Phi 134b4–136b5).

[3] The expression *Jinaputra* refers to either a male or a female bodhisattva in general. In the plural it also refers to both. The gender inflections in Sanskrit create a problem when translating into English, which has separate words for male and female children, and a general term for both collectively. Thus, if we mechanically translate *putra* as "son" in this compound, we add more sexism to the text than it naturally has. Therefore, we have consistently chosen to translate this epithet for bodhisattva as "child of the buddha," or in plural, "buddha-children." The variability of the word *putra* is shown by Pāṇini in the *Aṣṭādhyāyī* 1.2.68: *bhrātṛputrau svasṛduhitṛbhyām*. An example from Sanskrit literature of *putra* in its sense of "children" is found in the *Āśvalāyana Gṛhyasūtra* (quoted in Lanman, C.R., *A Sanskrit Reader*, Harvard University Press, Cambridge, MA, 1978, p. 98.19–21): *...aṅguṣṭhameva gṛhṇīyādyadi kāmayīta pumāṁsa eva me putrā jāyeranniti* "...the thumb only should grasp, if he wants to give birth to male children."

> 5. That genius is to be recognized as foremost in commitment who is wonderfully born as foremost of the buddha-children, with the peerless spirit as seed, peerless wisdom as mother, the wealth of the stores as womb, and peerless compassion as gentle nurse.

Excellent birth is shown by the distinctive excellence of such noble birth, through peerless seed, mother, womb, and nurse. The conception of the spirit (of enlightenment) is the bodhisattva's seed, transcendent wisdom the mother, endowment with the stores of merit and wisdom the womb that nurtures, and compassion the nurse that takes care.

Another verse shows that such wonderful birth, a distinctiveness of (the bodhisattva's) commitment, is itself distinguished by physical excellence:

> 6. Her body is beautiful with all the various marks. She has gained the strength to develop all beings. She has found the peace and infinite great bliss of a buddha. She knows how to manifest great liberative arts to protect all beings.

Her physical excellence is shown by four distinctivenesses: distinctive physical beauty because of adornment with the marks (of the great person), the word "various" implying their superiority to those of the universal monarch and so on; distinctive strength because she has gained the strength to bring all beings to evolutionary perfection; distinctive happiness because she has found the peace and infinite great bliss of a buddha; and distinctive intuition because she knows how to manifest great liberative arts for giving full refuge to beings. It can thus be understood that a buddha-child is called "wondrously" born for her consummate perfection in four areas: physical form, strength, happiness, and knowledge of her own arts.[4]

Another verse shows the excellence of (a bodhisattva's) birth through the fact that it carries on the buddha's lineage without interruption:

> 7. Coronated by all buddhas with great rays of light, he truly possesses all authority over the teaching, he knows how to manifest the

---

[4] Here, there is an interesting connection between the Tibetan (D Phi 135a5): *sems can kun bskyab thabs chen bsham pa shes* and the commentarial gloss (D Phi 135b1): *rang gi bzo shes pa phun sum tshogs pa*, thus associating the "liberative art" notion of *upāya* with the actual crafts of artistic creativity (*śilpa*).

> maṇḍala of a buddha's retinue, and, applying the precepts, he strives to administer punishment and reward.

There are four causes of a crown prince's noble birth which enable him not to be cut off from the family lineage: his receiving coronation, the unimpededness of his authority, his critical skill in adjudicating disputes, and his administering punishment and reward. In a parallel manner, the bodhisattva receives consecration with rays of light, has universal authority of the teachings because of his unobstructed intuition, knows how to manifest the maṇḍala of the retinue of the buddha, and is skilled in applying the precepts to punish the faulty and reward the virtuous.

The distinctiveness of (the bodhisattva's) commitment is further shown by another verse, comparing him to a prime minister:

> 8. Like a prime minister, (the bodhisattva) enters among the transcendences, always watches over the far-flung accessories of enlightenment, always properly guards the three secrets, and always ceaselessly accomplishes the welfare of many beings.

One is appointed prime minister for four reasons: (he is) entrusted to go among the queens, he moves in the inner circles; he watches over all the treasures; he is entrusted with all secret intelligence; and he controls all disbursements. In the same way, the bodhisattva enters among the transcendences, always watches over the accessories of enlightenment scattered throughout various discourses without forgetting them, always keeps the three secrets of body, speech, and mind, and always ceaselessly accomplishes the welfare of many beings, as he wills the benefit of infinite beings.

One verse on the significance of realization:

> 9. She attains a great mass of merit, preeminence in the three worlds, mundane happiness, alleviation of a great mass of suffering, the bliss of highest insight, a body of many teachings, supreme and eternal, a store of virtues, the elimination of the instincts, and deliverance both from worldly pressure and from peace.

When she venerates the teaching, she gains a great mass of merit. When she conceives the spirit of enlightenment, she attains mundane happiness. At the time of realization she accepts all beings as herself and thereby alleviates a great mass of suffering; that is, she attains the power to alleviate the sufferings of all beings. When she can tolerate the nonproduction of all things, she attains the bliss of highest insight.

At the time of perfect enlightenment, she wins the body of many teachings; a buddha's body of truth is a mass of many teachings because it is the source of the infinite teachings found in the discourses and so on. (That body) is supreme because it has the best of all qualities, and eternal because it is inexhaustible. It is a store of virtues because it is the collection of the excellences of the powers, confidences, and so on. With such a body, negative instincts are eliminated, and she attains deliverance both from pressure and from peace, since it does not stand in either the life-cycle or in liberation. These are the eight aspects of the significance of realization.

A verse on the significance of supremacy:

> 10. The genius triumphs over the host of disciples through his virtue, which is magnificent, great in value, immeasurable, eternal, constant, and inexhaustible. His virtue is mundane, transmundane, evolutionary, and lordly; it is inexhaustible through ceasing the life-systems.

There are four reasons why a bodhisattva surpasses the disciples: his root of virtue is magnificent, great in value, immeasurable, and inexhaustible. These four types of virtue have been explained as the mundane, transmundane, evolutionary, and lordly; that is, worldly, transcendent, leading to perfection, and masterful. These are the four excellences of (a bodhisattva's) virtue. Lordly virtue is inexhaustible through its ceasing of the life-systems, for it is not exhausted even in that Nirvāṇa in which there is no residue of the systems.

A verse on going for refuge:

> 11. As she makes the commitment out of a will to (enlightened) reality, she is recognized through her compassionate love. Thereby she becomes all-knowing, and tireless in helping, bringing happiness, and undergoing hardships. She has all excellences cultivated by all vehicles in pursuit of transcendence. Attained conventionally and actually, such a genius' taking refuge is the best.

This teaches the subjects of nature, cause, result, activity, endowment, and typology, in the context of taking refuge. The nature of taking refuge is its commitment of the will to attain buddhahood. Its cause is compassion, from which it springs. Its result is omniscience, which proceeds from it. Its activities are tirelessness in giving help, bringing happiness, and in the performance of difficult deeds. Its endowment is the possession of all excellences cultivated in all vehicles in their pursuit of transcendence. Its types are differentiated into coarse and subtle depending on whether refuge is taken conventionally or actually.

A verse on the distinction of the accomplishment of taking refuge:

> 12. One who goes to this refuge of great import increases the host of excellences beyond measure, fills the world with compassionate thoughts, and spreads the teaching of the peerless noble ones.

This shows the great import which lies in taking refuge from the point of view of its realization of individualistic and altruistic aims. One's personal goals are realized through the increase beyond measure of many kinds of excellences. "Beyond measure" should be understood here as being beyond measurement by speculation, calculation, or chronology; that is, the increase of excellences cannot be measured by any of these because it is too great. Altruistic aims are realized spiritually through the diffusion of compassion and practically by the spread of the teaching of the universal vehicle. The universal vehicle is the teaching of the great noble beings.

Chapter III

The Spiritual Gene

A summary verse on the divisions of the spiritual gene:

> 1. Existence,[1] superiority, nature, marks, genetic types,[2] dangers, benefits, and a double comparison; (all) fourfold.

This (verse) summarizes the (main topic) divisions of the spiritual gene: existence, superiority, nature, marks, types, dangers, benefits, and a double comparison, each of which is fourfold.

A verse on the particulars of the existence of the spiritual gene:

> 2. The existence of the spiritual gene is demonstrated by the differences in (beings') elements, faith, achievement, and the acquisition of different results.

According to the *Heap of Faculties Scripture*[3] the classes of elements are infinite because of the diversity of beings' elements. Therefore, since just such kinds of

---

[1] The Sanskrit (LI, p. 10.7 *ff.*) *satva* should be amended according to the commentary's *astitva*.

[2] *Gotra*. On the doctrine of *gotra* in the Vijñānavāda, see Ruegg, *La Théorie*, pp. 73–107. Also, *VKN* pp. 425–430, and Dayal pp. 51–53. The meanings associated with this word may be seen from its equivalents in *BBh* p. 2: support or basis (*adhara*, *upastambha*, *niśraya*, *nilaya*); cause (*hetu*, *upaniṣad*, *pūrvaṁgama*, *bīja*), and in the YBh p. 26: essence (*dhātu*, *prakṛti*). In the *MSA* the line of interpretation is *gotra* = *kula* = *dhātu* = *bīja* = *hetu*. See J. Takasaki, *A Study on the Ratnagotravibhāga (Uttaratantra)*, 1966, pp. 21–22. The English equivalent of *gotra* is very hard to settle, as the word has biological, geneological, mineral, and even vegetable connotations. Takasaki chooses "germ," others "lineage," both of which seem inappropriate; the former because of its connotation of disease, the latter because of its narrowness.

[3] The Chinese (T.31.594b9, n. 2) has *Bahudhātukasūtra*. See Sthiramati (D Mi p. 46bl) and Asvabhāva (D Bi p. 60a6). On the *Akṣarāśi* and *Bahudhātukasūtras* see LI, p. 10, n. 2 and LII, p. 25 n. 2.1, *Siddhi* p. 102, and the *Kośa* I, p. 27.

elements must be acknowledged, (people on) the three vehicles differ in spiritual genes. Beings are seen to differ in faith. Some from the very outset have faith in one vehicle or the other, which would be impossible were it not for a difference in spiritual genes. Even where faith is brought about by a cause, achievement is seen to differ; some are successful and some are not, which would be impossible were it not for a difference in spiritual genes. Results are seen to differ, (that is, there are) inferior, middling, and superior enlightenments (of the disciples, the hermit sages, or bodhisattvas, respectively), which would be impossible were it not for a difference in spiritual genes, for the fruit conforms to the seed.[4]

A verse on the particulars of superiority:[5]

> 3. The spiritual gene (of the bodhisattva) is reckoned the superior because it is the cause of her excellence, completeness, universal value, and the inexhaustibility of her virtue.

The superiority of the (bodhisattva's) gene is shown to lie in a fourfold causality: the (bodhisattva's) gene is the cause of surpassing excellence, completeness, universal value, and inexhaustibility of the roots of virtue. The disciples do not have such surpassingly great virtues, nor do they have such a number of them because they lack the powers,[6] fearlessnesses,[7] and so forth. Nor are they of universal value

---

[4] See also V.4–5, XI.37, XVII.34. It is due to the differences in spiritual genes that all the buddhas are not one identical buddha; see IX.77.

The doctrine of three "fruits," i.e., the three enlightenments, would appear to contradict the doctrine of a "unique vehicle." See XI.53–54.

[5] Compare *BBh*, p. 2.

[6] Parallel to the ten powers of a *Tathāgata* (see XX–XXI.51) are the ten powers of a bodhisattva. According to *MVy* 760–769 they are: the power of 1) aspiration (*āśaya*), 2) high resolve (*adhyāśaya*), 3) practice (*prayoga*), 4) wisdom (*prajñā*), 5) vow (*praṇidhāna*), 6) vehicle (*yāna*), 7) practice (*caryā*), 8) incarnation (*vikurvaṇa*), 9) enlightenment (*bodhi*), 10) turning the wheel of the Dharma (*dharmacakrapravartana*). On the powers see *Le Traité* pp. 1606–7, 1611–2 and Dayal pp. 148–149.

[7] Like the *balas*, bodhisattvas have a set of four fearlessnesses parallel to those of the Tathāgatas; (see XX–XXI.52.) The following list from the MVY. 782–785 is obscure in meaning. Tentatively, they are: 1) retaining the spells one has studied, one is fearless in explicating their meaning (*dhāraṇīśrutodgrahaṇārthanirdeśavaiśāradyaṁ*); 2) due to understanding selflessness there naturally does not occur conduct which would be the grounds for injuring others and there is the fearlessness which is the consummate great protection of the three pure actions, and deportments (*nairātmyādhigmāt paraviheṭhanānimitta-samudācāra-sahajānadhigateryā-*

(cont'd)

because they are not altruistic. And they are not inexhaustible for they come to an end in the Nirvāṇa without residue.[8]

A verse on the particulars of the nature (of the bodhisattva's gene):

> 4. Natural, developed,[9] support, supported, existent, and nonexistent; it is to be understood in the sense of "delivering excellences."

This shows the spiritual gene to be fourfold: existing by nature, being developed, having the nature of a support, and having the nature of the supported, respectively. It exists as a cause, it does not exist as an effect. The spiritual gene is to be understood in the sense of "delivering excellences";[10] because excellences are delivered – that is, emerge – from it.

A verse on the particulars of the marks (of the bodhisattva's gene):[11]

---

patha-triṣkarmapariśuddham-ahārakṣa-saṁpannavaiṣāradyaṁ); 3) Never forgetting the teaching memorized, arriving at the culmination of wisdom and liberative art, there is unimpeded fearlessness in liberating beings, faith, manifestation, and virtue (*sadodgṛhītadharmāvismaraṇa-prajñopāyaniṣṭhāgata-sattvanistāraṇaprasāda-saṁdarśana-śubhānantarāyika-vaiśāradyaṁ*); 4) Without loss of omniscient mind or transcending through another vehicle, there is fearlessness in fully realizing complete mastery and all forms of the aims of beings (*sarvajñātācittāsaṁpramoṣānyayānāniryāṇa-saṁpūrṇavaśitā-sarvaprakāra-sattvārtha-saṁprāpaṇa-vaiśāradyaṁ*). See *Le Traité* pp. 1607, 1613.

[8] *Anupadhiśeṣanirvāṇa* (LI, p. 11.8). The highest Nirvāṇa in the Hīnayāna, as opposed to the *apratiṣṭhitanirvāṇa* (LI, p. 41,20), or the unlocatable Nirvāṇa of the Mahāyāna. See IX.45, IX.70, XVIII.69–70, XIX.61–62, and LII, p. 27, n. 4.

[9] *Paripuṣṭaṁ* (LI, p. 11.10). The *MSABh* glosses it as *samudānīta* (acquired). Compare *BBh* p. 2.4. The term *dhātupuṣṭiṁ* appears in *MSABh*. VIII.8 (LI, p. 29.20), XI.61 (LI, p. 71.7), and XVII.19 (LI, p. 122.2). *BBh* p. 56.23 explains *dhātupuṣṭiṁ* as the production and maintenance of greater and greater nourishment of the seeds of virtue subsequent to the habitual practice of virtue based on the natural excellence of the seeds of virtue (*yā prakṛtyā kuśaladharmabījasaṁpadaṁ niśritya pūrvakuśaladharmābhyāsāduttarottarāṇāṁ kuśaladharmabījānāṁ paripuṣṭatarā paripuṣṭatamā utpattiṁ sthitiṁ*). Compare *AAA* 307.14–16, and *AAV* p. 76.23–77.2.

[10] *Guṇottāraṇārthena gotraṁ veditavyaṁ* (LI, p. 11.13). Compare *AAA* p. 307.25: *niruktaṁ tu guṇottaraṇārthena dharmadhāturgotram.*

[11] In the *Dam Chos Yi bZhin Nor Bu Thar Pa Rin Po Che'i rGyan* 7b1, sGam Po Pa quotes the following verse from the *Daśadharmakasūtra* on the marks: *byang chub sems dpa' blo ldan gyi / / rigs ni mtshan ma dag las shes / / du ba las ni mer shes dang / / chu skyar las ni chu bzhin no.* "The spiritual gene of the wise bodhisattva is known from marks as fire is known from smoke, or water from water fowl." See the *Āryadaśadharmakanāmamahāyānasūtra*, Dkon brtsegs, Dsi 187a4–5. Paraphrased in Sthiramati (D Mi 48a8–48bl). See also *BBh* pp. 3–6.

5. From the very outset of practice, compassion, faith, tolerance, and dedication to beauty are declared the marks of the (bodhisattva's) spiritual gene.

The marks of the bodhisattva's gene are fourfold: from the very commencement of practice (the bodhisattva has) compassion for beings, faith in the teaching of the universal vehicle, tolerance – that is, endurance in the undergoing of ordeals – and dedication to the virtues comprised by the transcendences.

A verse on the analysis of the types (of spiritual gene):

6. In short, there are four types of spiritual gene: the determined, the undetermined, the conditionally unalterable, and the alterable.

In brief, there are four types of spiritual gene: determined and undetermined, respectively unalterable and alterable by causes.[12]

A verse on the analysis of the dangers[13] (to one who has the bodhisattva's spiritual gene):

7. Briefly, the dangers to the spiritual gene are to be known as four: habituation to the mental addictions, bad companionship, deprivation, and dependency.

In brief, there are four dangers to the bodhisattva's gene which cause one who is of that genealogy to engage in evil: obsession with the mental addictions, evil companions, lack of what is necessary (to the practice of virtue), and dependence (on others).

A verse on the analysis of the advantages[14] (of the bodhisattva's gene):

---

[12] Those who are definitely of the disciple, hermit sage, or universal vehicle families are destined to realize the fruit of their own vehicle regardless, whereas those who are not definitely of one family or another will achieve the goal to which they are led by a spiritual friend; see Sthiramati (D Mi 49a4–49b6).

[13] *Ādīnava* (LI, p. 11.24). Compare *BBh* p. 7.8 where they are called *śukladharmavairodhikā upakleśāṁ*.

[14] *Anuśaṁsa* (LI, p. 12.2).

> 8. He only visits the bad migrations once in a long while, and he is liberated from them quickly. While there, his suffering is slight, and his anguish spurs the evolution of the beings there.

The bodhisattva's gene has four advantages: he visits the wretched births once in a long while and is quickly liberated from them. Even when born there he suffers little, yet is deeply moved and out of compassion for beings there, he brings them to evolutionary maturity.

A verse on the comparison of (the bodhisattva's) spiritual gene to a great gold mine:

> 9. (The bodhisattva's gene) should be recognized as like a mine of gold, the source of immeasurable beauty, of (brilliant) intuition, of immaculate (purity), and of (the bodhisattva's) powers.

A great gold mine (*gotram*) is the source of four types of gold: abundant, shining, pure, and useful.[15] In the same way the bodhisattva's gene is the source of immeasurable roots of virtue, the source of her intuitive wisdom, the source of her immunity to mental addictions, and the source of the powers such as the superknowledges. Thus it should be recognized as like a great gold mine.

A verse on the comparison of the (bodhisattva's) gene to a great jewel mine (*gotram*):

> 10. (The bodhisattva's gene) should be recognized as like a mine of great jewels, since it causes the great enlightenment and is the source of great intuitive wisdom, the concentrations of noble beings, and the great fulfillment of all beings.

A great jewel mine is the source of four types of jewels: jewels of perfect authenticity, color, shape, and size. The bodhisattva's gene is similar, because it is the cause of the great enlightenment, the great intuitive wisdom, the concentrations of the holy ones – concentration being the shape of the mind – and the cause of the universal evolution of beings, bringing many beings to evolutionary perfection.

A verse on the analysis of (those who are) lacking the spiritual gene:

---

[15] Compare the canonical attributes of naturally luminous mind (*cittaprabhāsvarāṁ prakṛti-viśuddhaṁ*). See Ruegg (1969) pp. 79–80, 411.

> 11. (Temporarily lacking the gene,) some are exclusively given over to misconduct; some have destroyed their good qualities; some lack the virtues conducive to liberation; some have slight virtues. And there are others (who forever) lack the cause.

Here the term "lacking" in the spiritual gene designates those who lack the destiny for ultimate liberation. In brief, they are of two kinds: those who temporarily lack that destiny for ultimate liberation, and (those who lack it) forever. Those who temporarily lack the destiny for ultimate liberation are of four types: those who are exclusively given over to misconduct, those whose roots of virtue have been severed, those who lack the roots of virtue conducive to liberation, and those whose roots of virtue are feeble and whose stores are incomplete. But those who forever lack the destiny for ultimate liberation forever lack the cause for they do not have the gene for ultimate liberation.[16]

A verse on the greatness[17] of the natural and developed spiritual genes:

> 12. Although ignorant of the far-reaching teaching taught to bring help to others by showing the profound and the magnificent (truths), if one has all-embracing faith and is persevering in practice, finally one attains perfections greater than (those of) the (worldlings and disciples). One can know that this results from the bodhisattvas' spiritual genes, one natural and one developed in excellent qualities.

The teaching of the universal vehicle proclaims the magnificent and the profound; it was taught at length to bring help to others. Although ignorant of the subject matter of the magnificent and profound (teachings), if faith is all-embracing and one is indefatigable in practice, one attains perfection in the end. Great enlightenment is superior to the perfection of the (enlightenments) of the other two. This

---

16 It would appear that the idea that there are individuals incapable of ever attaining enlightenment would contradict IX.37. Sthiramati (D Mi 53b8–54a5) explains that *agotra* designates both those who will attain enlightenment after a period of time, and those who will never attain it. In the first case the privative *a-* has a pejorative connatation, and in the second it indicates the utter nonexistence (of *gotra*). These latter are *hetuhīna* (LI p. 13.1), lacking the cause (of enlightenment), i.e., *gotra*. See Ruegg (1969), p. 80, n. 3.

17 The Tibetan (D Phi 138b5) has *rang bzhin dang rgyas pa'i rigs rnam par dbye ba nyid du* instead of *che ba nyid du*, for the Sanskrit *māhātmye* (LI, p. 13.2).

is the greatness of the bodhisattva's genes, one which is naturally endowed with excellences, and one which is developed. "The other two" are worldlings and disciples. "Superior" means supreme.

A verse on the preeminence of (the bodhisattva's) gene due to its result:

> 13. For the growth of the tree of enlightenment with its overabundance of excellences, to attain great bliss and the conquest of (great) suffering, and for the sake of its fruit which gives help and happiness to self and others, that supreme spiritual gene is truly like a wondrous root.

This shows the bodhisattva's gene to be the wonderful root of the tree of enlightenment whose fruit brings benefit and happiness to self and others.

CHAPTER IV

Conception of the Spirit of Enlightenment

A verse on the characteristics of the conception of the spirit (of enlightenment):

> 1. The bodhisattvas' conception of the spirit is a will of great enthusiasm, great initiative, great purpose, great outcome, and a dual objective.[1]

It is a "great enthusiasm" because it is enthusiastic to attain[2] the profound (realization) and to perform difficult tasks for a long time, due to its armor-like energy.[3] It is a great initiative due to the application-energy, which follows on the armor-like (energy). It has great purpose because it is concerned with the benefit of self and others. It has a great outcome because it results in the attainment of the great enlightenment. This highlights the three types of virtue: the (first) two expressions indicate heroic virtue,[4] and the next two expressions, the virtue of working for the benefit (of others) and the virtue of reaping the fruit. It has a double objective because its objectives are great enlightenment and working for the fulfillment of others. Therefore the conception of the spirit is defined as a will having three virtues and a double objective.

---

[1] Quoted in *AAA* p. 283.22.

[2] *Pratipakṣotsahanāt* (LI, p. 13.21) is clearly corrupt, and should be edited, according to the Tibetan (D Phi 139a4) *sgrub pa la spro ba'i phyir*, to *pratipattyutsahanāt*, as Lévi partially does (LII, p. 32 n. 1.2).

[3] *Saṁnāhavīrya* (LI, p. 13.21). See *BBh* p. 138.10: *sannāhavīryaṁ kuśaladharmasaṁgrāhakaṁ sattvārthakriyāyai ca.*

[4] *Puruṣakāra* (LI, p. 14.1). The Tibetan (D Phi 139a4) is *skyes bu byed pa'i yon tan*, virtue, perhaps merely "character-forming."

A verse on the varieties of the conception of the spirit:[5]

> 2. The conception of the spirit is held to function on the (bodhisattva) stages as faith, a pure universal responsibility,[6] evolutionary impetus, and freedom from the obscurations.

The bodhisattvas' conception of the spirit is of four types:[7] it resembles faith on the stage of action through faith, pure universal responsibility in the first seven stages, evolutionary impetus in the eighth and the rest, and freedom from the obscurations at the buddha stage.[8]

Four verses defining the conception of the spirit:

> 3. Its root is compassion, its aspiration is the constant benefit of beings, its faith is in the teaching, and its objective is the quest for intuition of that (truth).
>
> 4. Its vehicle is zeal for the higher, its support is the vow of morality, its impediments are the resistances and insistence on the opposite.
>
> 5. Its advantage is the increase of the beautiful, consisting of merit and wisdom, and its renunciation lies in constant practice of the transcendences.
>
> 6. It terminates at each stage by application to that stage. This should be understood as the identification of the bodhisattvas' conception of the spirit.

---

[5] The following verse and the first two *pāda*s of verse three are quoted in *AAA* p. 285.23.

[6] On the connection between *bodhicittotpāda* and *adhyāśaya* see *VKN* pp. 405–407.

[7] Four types of *bodhicittotpāda* are taught in the *Gayāśīrṣasūtra*, Nu 315b7–317a4.

[8] The first two types of *cittotpāda*, i.e., *ādhimokṣika* and *śuddhādhyāśayika* (LI, p. 14.7), correspond to the first two types of bodhisattvas according to *BBh* pp. 59.27–60.2: *adhimukticaryābhūmisthito bodhisattvo 'dhimukticārī śuddhādhyāśayabhūmisthito bodhisattvaṁ śuddhādhyāśayaṁ*.

This is its definition. What is the root of the bodhisattvas' fourfold conception of the spirit? What is its aspiration? What is its faith? What is its objective? What is its vehicle? What is its support? What is its danger? What is its advantage? What is its renunciation?[9] What is its termination? Its root is compassion, its aspiration is the constant benefit of beings, and its faith is in the teaching of the universal vehicle. Its objective is the intuition of (enlightenment), in the form of a quest for that wisdom. Its vehicle is zeal for the higher, its support is the bodhisattva vow of morality, and its impediment is its danger. What is that impediment? Arousal of or insistence upon the aspiration for any other contrary vehicle. Its advantage is the increase of virtuous qualities consisting of merit and intuition, its renunciation lies in constant practice of the transcendences, and its termination at each stage results from application to that stage. It terminates with each stage after being applied there.

A verse on the conventional conception of the spirit through a formal undertaking:[10]

> 7. Through the power of a friend, of a cause, of a root, of learning, or from cultivation of beauty, it is said that the conception of the spirit through persuasion by another can have stable or unstable beginnings.

The conception of the spirit from another's persuasion – that is, from another's instruction – is called a conventional undertaking. It may come about through the power of a friend: from agreement with a spiritual friend. It may come about through the power of a cause: through the efficacy of the spiritual gene. It may come about through a root of virtue: from the development of that spiritual gene. It may come about from the power of learning – for many conceive the spirit of enlightenment where the formulations of the teaching are recited. It may come about through cultivation of the beautiful, from constant study, understanding, and retention in this life.[11]

---

[9] In the Chinese translation (T.31.595c17), verses 3–6 are summarized in two verses.

[10] *Samādānasāṁketikacittotpāda* (LI, p. 14.26). The first of ten varieties of *cittotpāda* according to *VS* (Zi 300a7).

[11] Read *dṛṣṭa eva* (or *dṛṣṭaiva*) for *dṛṣṭa iva* (LI, p. 15.4). See Ui, p. 599.

It should be understood that when it comes about through the power of a friend its occurrence is unstable; and when it is from the power of a cause, and so on, its occurrence is stable.

Seven verses on the ultimate conception of the spirit:[12]

> 8. When a perfect buddha has been well served, when the stores of merit and wisdom have been well amassed, when nonconceptual intuition of things has been born, (the spirit of enlightenment) has ultimacy.[13]
>
> 9. When equal mindedness has been acquired toward things and beings, towards their requirements and highest buddhahood, its joyfulness is outstanding.
>
> 10. One should know its birth, magnificence, enthusiasm, purity of aspiration, skill in the remainder, and renunciation.
>
> 11. Faith in the Dharma is its seed. It is born from the transcendences, the best of mothers,[14] from her blissful womb of meditation; and compassion is its sustaining nurse.
>
> 12. It should be known as magnificent, for it accomplishes the ten great vows. It should be realized as enthusiasm, for it is indefatigable in numerous ordeals over a long time.
>
> 13. Purity of aspiration comes from awareness of the nearness of enlightenment and from the acquisition of knowledge of its liberative art as well; but skill comes on the other stages.

---

[12] *Pāramārthikacittotpāda* (LI, p. 15.6). The second of ten varieties of *cittotpāda* according to *VS* (Zi 300a7).

[13] In the Chinese (T.31.596a11) verses 8–14 are rearranged into five verses. The Sanskrit *paramatāsya* (LI, p. 15.8) does not correspond well to the Tibetan (D Phi 140a3) *de ni dam par 'dod.* We have followed the Tibetan and the commentarial gloss, editing the Sanskrit to read *paramārthatā.*

[14] Compare *VKN* p. 293 (*HTV* p. 67).

14. Its renunciation is to be known through its conscious attitude attuned to the structure (of reality), through its intuition of the constructed nature (of the stages), and through the nonconceptuality of that (intuition).

The first verse shows the ultimacy of the conception of the spirit through distinctive instruction, practice, and realization. The conception of an ultimate spirit of enlightenment is at the first stage, the joyful. It is shown to be the cause of an outstanding joy there. In this context, there is equanimity towards all things due to the understanding of objective selflessness, and there is equanimity towards the doings of beings due to the wish to end their sufferings, as if they were one's own. There is equanimity towards buddhahood, due to the understanding that (a buddha's) ultimate element is indivisible from oneself. In addition one should know the six areas in which the conception of the spirit is ultimate: birth, magnificence, enthusiasm, purity of aspiration, skill in the remainder, and renunciation. Birth should be understood in terms of a distinctive seed, mother, womb, and nurse. It is magnificent because it accomplishes the ten great vows.[15] It is enthusiasm because it does not weary of ordeals of long duration. It is purity of aspiration for it knows the nearness of enlightenment and has found knowledge of the art for reaching it. It is skillful in the rest because it is skillful in the other stages. It is renunciation because of an attitude attuned to the structure of the stages. How is it that renunciation is due to an attitude? Because it knows the real structure of those stages to be mental constructions, nothing but constructions; and then again, one does not conceptualize that intuition of constructedness.

Six verses on similes of its greatness:[16]

15. One conception is like earth; another resembles fine gold; another resembles the white new moon; another is like a blazing fire.[17]

---

[15] The Chinese (T.31.596b7) adds: "as explained in the *Daśabhūmikasūtra*." See *DBhS* pp. 9.30–11.4.

[16] The same twenty two similes of *cittotpāda* are found in *AA* I.20–21, although differently expressed.

[17] Although Lévi amended the Sanskrit *'parocchrāyaṁ* (LI, p. 16.6) to *'paro jñeyaṁ* (LII, p. 37, n. 15.1) after the Tibetan translation (D Phi 140b5), on the analogy of verses 17 and 18,

(cont'd)

16. Another resembles a great storehouse; another is like a jewel mine; another is like an ocean; another like a diamond; another like the immovable king of mountains.

17. Others resemble the king of medicines; or are like a great friend. Another is like a wish-granting gem; and another is like the sun.

18. Another is like a gandharva's sweet voice; another resembles a king. There are others like a treasury and like a great highway.

19. One should know that there are conceptions of the spirit like a vehicle, a fountain, a delightful sound, and the current of a great river.

20. Among the children of the victors, the conception of the spirit is spoken of as (being) like a cloud. This spirit, so rich in virtues, should be conceived with joy.

For the bodhisattvas, the initial conception of the spirit is like the earth because it becomes the foundation for all the excellences of a buddha and for the increase of their stores of merit and wisdom. Conception of the spirit accompanied by aspiration is like fine gold, for the strong aspiration towards help and happiness is not liable to alteration. Accompanied by application it resembles the waxing new moon, for virtuous qualities increase. Accompanied by universal responsibility, it is like fire, for it attains greater and greater intensity as does a fire fed by special fuel; universal responsibility is the aspiration to the intensity of realization. Accompanied by the transcendence of generosity[18] it resembles a great storehouse, for it satisfies countless beings with material enjoyments and is inexhaustible. Accompanied by the transcendence of morality[19] it resembles a mine of precious stones, for from it all precious virtues issue forth. Accompanied by the transcendence of tolerance[20] it

---

the manuscript reading is confirmed by the Chinese (T.31.596b15), which has *zen* (*ucchrāya*) *huo*.

[18] *Dānapāramitā* (LI, p. 16.21). See XVI.17–18.

[19] *Śīlapāramitā* (LI, p. 16.23). See XVI.19–20.

[20] *Kṣāntipāramitā* (LI, p. 16.23). See XVI.21–22.

resembles an ocean, for it is not disturbed by any calamity which might befall it. Accompanied by the transcendence of effort[21] it resembles a diamond, for it is firm through being unbreakable. Accompanied by the transcendence of contemplation[22] it resembles the king of mountains, for distraction does not move it. Accompanied by the transcendence[23] of wisdom it resembles the king of medicines, for it cures the illness of all the addictive and objective obscurations.[24] Accompanied by the immeasurables[25] it is like a great friend, for in no circumstances is it indifferent to beings. Accompanied by the superknowledges[26] it is like a wish-fulfilling gem, for it gives whatever results are willed. Accompanied by the social practices[27] it resembles the sun, for it brings a harvest of disciples to evolutionary perfection. Accompanied by intellectual knowledges[28] it resembles a gandharva's sweet voice, for it teaches the Dharma which inspires disciples. Accompanied by the reliances[29] it resembles a great king, for it is the cause of nondeprivation. Accompanied by the stores of merit and wisdom[30] it resembles a treasury, for it is the repository of a great store of merit and wisdom. Accompanied by the accessories of enlightenment[31] it resembles a great royal road, for on it all the noble ones have gone. Accompanied by serenity and insight[32] it is like a vehicle, for it easily transports (beings where they want to go). Accompanied by retention[33] and eloquence[34] it resembles a fountain, for it retains and pours out without diminution the meaning of the teachings, whether

---

[21] *Vīryapāramitā* (LI, p. 16.24). See XVI.23–24.

[22] *Dhyānapāramitā* (LI, p. 16.25). See XVI.25–26.

[23] *Prajñāpāramitā* (LI, p. 16.26). See XVI.27–28.

[24] *Kleśajñeyāvaraṇa* (LI, p. 16.26). On the eight blocks see XII.19–20.

[25] *Apramāṇa* (LI, p. 16.27). See XVII.17–28.

[26] *Abhijñā* (LI, p. 16.28). See VII.1,9.

[27] *Saṁgrahavastu* (LI, p. 16.29). See XVI.72–78.

[28] *Pratisaṁvit* (LI, p. 16.29). See XVIII.34–37.

[29] *Pratiśaraṇa* (LI, p. 16.30). See XVIII.31–33.

[30] *Puṇyajñānasaṁbhāra* (LI, p. 16.31). See XVI.19–20, XVIII.38–41.

[31] *Bodhipakṣa* (LI, p. 16.32). See XVIII.57–63.

[32] *Śamathavipaśyanā* (LI, p. 17.1). See XVIII.66.

[33] *Dhāraṇā* (LI, p. 17.2). See XVIII.25–26.

[34] *Pratibhāna* (LI, p. 17.2). One of the *pratisaṁvit*. See XVIII.34.

studied or unstudied, as a fountain retains and pours out water without diminution. Accompanied by epitomes of the Dharma[35] it resembles a delightful sound, for it is delightful for disciples who desire to hear about liberation. Accompanied by the path of the unique way[36] it is similar to the current of a river, for when tolerance of nonproduction is attained it flows of its own accord. The way is unique for bodhisattvas who are at that stage, since they make no difference in the performance of their duties. Accompanied by skill in liberative art[37] it resembles a cloud, for just as all the wealth of the material world comes from the clouds, so all accomplishments of the aims of all beings, through manifestations such as dwell in the Tuṣita heaven, are based on (the conception of the spirit of enlightenment).[38] One should understand that the twenty two similes of the conception of the spirit accord with its inexhaustibility, as stated in the *Akṣayamati Scripture*.[39]

A verse in criticism of not conceiving the spirit of enlightenment:

> 21. Beings who lack the supremely valuable conception of the spirit attain peace, but lack the happinesses of the consideration of others' aims, of the perfection of its liberative arts, of the insight into the meaning of the great intimation, and of seeing the excellent truth.

Beings who are without the conception of the spirit do not attain the four kinds of happiness that bodhisattvas have: the happiness which comes from consideration of others' aims; the happiness which comes from perfecting the liberative arts (that accomplish) others' aims; that (happiness) which comes from seeing the

---

[35] *Dharmoddāna* (LI, p. 17.3). See XVIII.80–81.

[36] *Ekāyana* (LI, p. 17.4). See XVI.78, XX–XXI 12, 37.

[37] *Upāya* (LI, p. 17.6). See XVIII.69–70.

[38] *AAA* pp. 284.13–285.11 and *AAV* 16.20–22.8 agree with our text. On the relation between the twenty two forms of *cittotpāda* and the *Pañcaviṁśatisāhasrikāprajñāpāramitā*, see *AAA* 284.1–10. (Also, see Edward Conze, *The Large Sūtra on Perfect Wisdom* (Berkeley: University of California Press, 1975), p. 46 *ff.*) Note the mention of Maitreyanātha's heaven as an example of benefitting living beings, the "gentle rain of mercy" dropping on the world from his great spirit of enlightenment.

[39] The inexhaustibility (*akṣagata*, LI, p. 17.9) of the twenty two types from the initial conception of the spirit of enlightenment down to liberative art forms the greater part of the subject matter of the *AMN* in its Tibetan version. On the similes in the Chinese versions of this and allied sūtras (e.g., *Akṣayabodhisattvasūtra*) see LII, p. 17, n. 1 and Ui p. 600.

meaning of the great intimation – that is, understanding the implied meaning of the profound scriptures of the universal vehicle; and the happiness which comes from seeing the highest truth, which is the selflessness of objects.

A verse praising the conception of the spirit for its immunity from (either) bad migrations or exhaustion:

> 22. As soon as the genius has conceived this supreme spirit, her mind is well protected from endless evil; ever increasingly virtuous and compassionate, she rejoices in happiness and suffering.

As soon as she has conceived this best spirit, a bodhisattva's mind is immune from the evil habits which control infinite numbers of beings. Thus she has no fear of hellish rebirths. In increasing both her virtuous actions and compassion she comes to be always virtuous and compassionate. Due to this she is always rejoicing. She rejoices at happiness because she is virtuous, and she rejoices at (her own) suffering, when it is occasioned by accomplishing the aims of others, because she is compassionate. Thus she is immune from becoming overexhausted by the many things which she has to do.

A verse on attaining the vow of restraint:

> 23. Disregarding his own body and life, he embraces great tribulations for the sake of others. How, (even) though being harmed by another, could such a one engage in acts of evil-doing?

The quintessence of this is: how could one who loves others more than himself to the point of disregarding his own body and life for their sake engage in evil actions for his own sake when harmed by others?

Two verses on the non-reversal of the spirit:

> 24. Understanding that all things are like a magician's illusions and that rebirth is like a garden stroll, she fears neither mental addictions in times of prosperity nor suffering in times of adversity.

> 25. For those who are always compassionate, their virtues are their adornment, delight in helping beings their food, deliberate[40] rebirth their favorite place, and magical manifestation their sport.

Since a bodhisattva sees all things as like a magician's illusions, he does not fear the addictions in times of prosperity. Since he sees rebirth as like taking a stroll in a garden, he has no fear of suffering in times of adversity. What fear can then reverse his spirit of enlightenment? Further, the ornament of the bodhisattvas is their own virtue; the joy of helping others is their food; deliberate rebirth their pleasure park; and magical manifestations their sport. This is only for bodhisattvas, not for non-bodhisattvas. How then could their spirit be reversed?

A verse to reverse fear of suffering:

> 26. Since even Avīci hell becomes a realm of delight for one of compassionate nature who exerts herself for the sake of others, how in the world could such a one fear sufferings incurred for the sake of others?

If, in her exertion for the sake of others out of her compassionate nature, even Avīci hell is a realm of delight, how in the world could she allow herself to be intimidated by the occurrence of suffering occasioned by altruistic deeds? Were one to have such fear of suffering, her spirit would be reversed.

A verse to reject callousness toward beings:

> 27. Since he constantly relies upon the teacher of great compassion and his mind is tormented by others' sufferings, he feels ashamed to be exhorted by others when there is something to be done for others.

Since it is his nature to always rely on the teacher of great compassion and since his mind is tormented by the sufferings of others, when there is something to be done for other beings, it is shameful indeed if he must be exhorted by other spiritual friends.

A verse in criticism of laziness:

---

[40] *Saṁcintya* (LI, p. 18.12). As the bodhisattva no longer has the karmic factors necessary for rebirth, he voluntarily takes birth for the sake of others.

> 28. The foremost among beings, who carries on her head the great responsibility for beings, does not look well if her pace is slack. Tightly bound with various bonds, her own and others, she should put forth a hundredfold initiative.

For a bodhisattva who has taken the great burden of responsibility for beings on her own head, it is unseemly to advance lazily. She ought to make an effort one hundred times greater than that of a disciple. She is thus strongly bound with various bonds of her own and others, consisting of the mental addictions, evolutionary actions, and births.

CHAPTER V

Practice

A verse on the characteristics of practice:[1]

> 1. The practice of the victor-children consists of a great foundation, great initiative, and a great fruitful outcome. It is always a great effort, involves great endurance, and does what must be done to carry out the great purpose.

It has a great foundation, for it is founded upon the conception of the spirit (of enlightenment). It has a great initiative, for it undertakes the aims of self and others. It has a great fruitful outcome, for its result is the attainment[2] of great enlightenment. Therefore it is, respectively, a great effort because it embraces all beings, a great endurance because it endures all sufferings, and it does what must be done to carry out the great purpose: thoroughly accomplishing the aims of countless beings.

A verse on the lack of difference between (the bodhisattva's) individualism and her altruism:

> 2. When she attains the attitude of the equality of self and others or of caring for others more than for herself, then she feels that others' aims outweigh her own. What then (for her) is individualism? And what is altruism?

The attitude of the equality of self and others is attained through faith when (a bodhisattva) achieves the conception of the conventional spirit (of enlightenment), and (it is attained) through knowledge when she achieves the conception of

---

[1] *Pratipatti* (LI, p. 19.10). This is also the title of the thirteenth chapter. On the term *pratipatti*, see LII, p. 44 n. 1.1.

[2] On the basis of the Tibetan (D Phi 143a3–4) and the Chinese (T.31.597b23–24), we conclude that the original probably read *mahābodhiphalaprāptatvāt*.

the ultimate spirit (of enlightenment).[3] Again, once she arrives at the state of caring for others much more than for herself, a bodhisattva (naturally) feels that the aims of others outweigh her own in importance. What then are her individual aims? And what are her altruistic aims? This means that for her there is no longer any difference between the two.

A verse on the superiority of altruistic aims:

> 3. A worldly person, as merciless as he may be, does not inflict torment upon an enemy in the way that a compassionate one inflicts terrible sufferings upon himself for the sake of others.

The intense torment that he brings upon himself for the sake of others proves that (for the bodhisattva) altruistic aims are superior to individual aims.

Two verses analyzing the practice of altruism:

> 4. Concerning those who live in lowly, mediocre, and superior realities, (the bodhisattva) teaches (them) well, attracts (them), introduces (them), elucidates the import for them, develops them in beauty, advises them, steadies them, and liberates their intellects.

> 5. She endows them with distinctive excellence, exalts them in the clan, (confers upon them) the prophecy, the consecration, and the unexcelled exaltation of the wisdom of the transcendent lords. These are the thirteen altruistic (practices).

There are three categories of beings: those who live with an inferior, middling, or superior spiritual gene. In this context, there are thirteen altruistic (practices) for the bodhisattva. She teaches them well with the miraculous powers of instruction and demonstration. She attracts (them) through the miraculous powers of magical manifestation.[4] She introduces (them) by causing them to embrace[5] the

---

[3] On the conventional and ultimate *bodhicittotpāda*, see IV.7–14.

[4] Correct *pratihārya* (LI, p. 20.12–13) to *prātihārya*. On the three *prātihārya*s see *Kośa* VIII. pp. 110–112, and Edgerton, *BHSD*, p. 392.

[5] The Tibetan *bstan pa khas len du gzhug pa'i phyir 'jug pa* (D Phi 143b4) indicates an emendation of the Sanskrit *śāsanābhyupagamanāt* (LI, p. 20.13) to the causative *abhyupagamayanāt*.

teaching. She elucidates the import for them; that is, (she) resolves the doubts of those who have been introduced. She develops them in virtue, advises, and steadies their minds, liberates their wisdoms, and endows them with distinctive excellences such as the superknowledges. She (exalts them) by birth into the family of the transcendent lords. On the eighth stage, (she confers) the prophetic revelation (of their eventual buddhahood). On the tenth stage, she anoints them with the wisdom of the transcendent lords. (In sum,) for the sake of those who possess the three spiritual genes, the bodhisattva's altruistic practices are of thirteen kinds.

A verse on the perfection of altruistic practice:

> 6. The supreme practice of the victor-children is unerring instruction attuned to beings, without arrogance, unselfish, skillful, patient, restrained, far-reaching, and inexhaustible.

Here it is shown how altruistic practice becomes perfect. How does it become perfect? Instruction is correctly attuned to the beings endowed with (various) spiritual genes.[6] Attraction is not arrogant and introduction is unselfish, without insensitivity in action;[7] that is, there is no pride in the working of magic and no possessiveness of the beings introduced. The practice of elucidation of the meaning is skillful. The practice of development in beauty is patient. The practice of advising and so on is restrained, as without restraint one cannot advise others and so forth.[8] The practice (for exalting beings by bringing them to) birth in the (buddha-) family is far-reaching, since practice which is not far-reaching is unable to exalt by birth in the (buddha-) family and the like. And, for bodhisattvas, all altruistic practice is

---

[6] Sthiramati (D Mi 69a6) cites the following passage from the *Āryaratnakūṭa*: *nyan thos dang rang sangs rgyas kyi theg pa rnams la zab cing rgya che ba'i chos 'chad pa ni / byang chub sems dpa'i 'khrul pa'o /* (It is a bodhisattva's mistake to teach the profound and magnificent Dharma to those of the disciple or hermit sage vehicles). This corresponds to the *Kāśyapaparivarta* 11.

[7] The Tibetan translation reads *mi mthun pa mi byed pas* (D Phi 144a2), which is lacking in the Sanskrit and the Chinese.

[8] Sthiramati (D Mi 69b7) cites the following passage from an unidentified sūtra: *bdag ma grol na sems can grol bar mi nus / bdag ma zhi na sems can zhi bar bya bar mi nus / bdag ma dul na sems can gzhan dul bar bya bar mi nus so /* (If one is not liberated oneself, one will be unable to liberate other living beings. If one is not at peace oneself, one will be unable to bring peace to living beings. If one is undisciplined oneself, one will be unable to discipline other living beings).

inexhaustible, because the beings embraced by the bodhisattvas are inexhaustible. One should know then that (such altruistic practice) is perfect.

Two verses on the distinctive superiority of (a bodhisattva's) practice:

> 7. People in the desire (realm) enter into great danger, those delighting in existence enter into an unstable and aberrant pleasure, and those delighting in peace enter the eradication of their private pains; but those who are compassionate enter the eradication of all pains.
>
> 8. Foolish people always exert themselves for the sake of their own pleasure; (not only do they) fail to obtain it, they always find suffering. But the intelligent always exert themselves for the sake of others and, achieving both (individualistic and altruistic) aims, arrive at freedom.

There is great danger in desires, for they cause great physical and mental suffering as well as hellish rebirths. Aberrant pleasures are unstable and, because the delights of the form and formless realms are impermanent and because of the (overall) miserable nature of creation, they are ultimately suffering. It should be understood that "pains" means "mental addictions" because they produce suffering. Foolish people who always act for the sake of their own pleasure fail to obtain it, obtaining only suffering. But a bodhisattva who practices for the sake of others accomplishes her own and others' aims and attains the bliss of Nirvāṇa. This is another distinctive excellence of her practice.

A verse on dedicating the sphere of activity:

> 9. Whenever the victor-child is involved with the various sense-realms during his activities, he is motivated by appropriate and harmonious ideals in order to benefit beings.

In whatever way a bodhisattva becomes involved with the various sense-realms, such as the visual, while engaged in activities manifesting the behaviors (of sitting, lying, standing, walking, etc.), he is motivated in all his actions with relevant and seemly ideals for the benefit of beings, as is set forth at length in the *Purity of the Realms Scripture*.[9]

A verse criticizing intolerance of beings:

> 10. An intelligent person does not blame someone whose mind is always helplessly victimized by faults. Thinking, "this person's wrong conduct is involuntary," his mercy increases.

A bodhisattva does not pick out the faultiness in a person who never had an independent will – (being subjugated) by the mental addictions. Why? He knows that such a person's wrong conduct is involuntary and his compassion for him increases.

A verse on the greatness of (the bodhisattva's) practice:

> 11. This practice[10] triumphs over all realms and migrations. It is endowed with supreme peace. It increases with masses of various virtues, and it always embraces beings with a loving mind.[11]

The greatness (of practice) is shown to be of four kinds. It has the greatness of triumph, because it triumphs over all three realms and five migrations. As (the Buddha) explains in the *Transcendence of Wisdom*: "Subhūti, as form is that which is, and not that which is not, this universal vehicle triumphs over the world with its gods, humans, and titans and entirely liberates it." It has the greatness of Nirvāṇa, for it is endowed with the unlocated Nirvāṇa. It has the greatness of virtue and the greatness of not forsaking beings, because it increases virtue and embraces all beings.[12]

---

9 *Gocarapariśuddhisūtra*.

10 *Prapatti* (LI, p. 22.3). Compare *saṁprapatti* in III.12.

11 The Tibetan reads *byams pa'i sems pas* (D Phi 144b6).

12 Following the Tibetan *yon tan gyi che ba nyid dang / sems can yongs su mi gtong ba'i che ba nyid ni yon tan gyis 'phel ba pa dang 'gro ba sdud pa'i phyir ro /* (D Phi 145a1–2).

Chapter VI

Thatness

A verse on the analysis of the characteristics of the ultimate:

> 1. The nature of the ultimate[1] is that which is purified though not purified, not existent, not nonexistent, not such and not otherwise, not produced and not destroyed, not decreased and not increased.[2]

"Ultimate" has the meaning of "nondual." This nondual meaning is illustrated in five ways. It is not existent from the point of view of the imagined and relative identities.[3] It is not nonexistent from the point of view of the perfect identity.[4] It is not such, for there is no oneness of the perfect with regard to the constructed and the relative. Neither is it otherwise, for it has no otherness from those two. It is neither produced nor destroyed, for the ultimate realm is not creational. It is neither increased nor decreased, for it remains as it is amid the cessation and generation of the two tendencies of mental addiction and purification. It does not become purified, for it is naturally unaddicted. Yet it is not the case that it is not purified, for it is free of incidental addictions. It should be understood, then, that these five characteristics of the nondual constitute the nature of the ultimate.

A verse refuting the error of the view of self:

---

[1] *Paramārtha* (LI, p. 22.11). See also XI.50–51, and XX–XXI.60–61.

[2] For the Sanskrit *nāpi viśudhyate punarviśudhyate* (LI, p. 22.13) the Chinese has simply *fei jing fei wu-jing*; not pure, not impure (T.31.598b22).

[3] *Parikalpitaparatantralakṣaṇa* (LI, p. 22.14). See *Siddhi,* pp. 514–515, 526, and *La Somme,* pp. 17, 18.

[4] *Pariniṣpannalakṣaṇa* (LI, p. 22.15). See *Siddhi,* p. 527 and *La Somme* p. 17.

2. The self-notion[5] itself does not have the identity of a self, nor does the (selfish being's) deforming habit; their natures are different. Apart from these two there is no other (self), so it arises only as an error; liberation is therefore the termination of a mere error.

The self-notion itself does not have the nature of a (substantial) self, nor does the (selfish being's) deforming habit. Their nature differs from the (absolutist's) imaginatively constructed self.[6] (The deforming habit) consists of the five appropriative bodymind systems, for it is produced from the mental addictions and negative instinctual conditionings.[7] Nor is there (any self) found apart from those two (with the) nature of an (absolute) self. Therefore, there is no self, and the self-notion is born of error. Moreover, it should be understood that because there is no self, liberation is merely the termination of error, and there is no (substantial person) at all who has been liberated.

Two verses on the criticism of such error:

3. How is it that beings rely on what is merely an error and do not realize that the nature of suffering is constant? How is it they are unaware and aware, suffer and do not suffer, and are objective and not objective?

4. How is it that beings, directly aware of the relativistic origin of things, still resort to some other creator? What kind of darkness is this through which the existent goes unseen and the nonexistent is observed?

---

[5] *Ātmadṛṣṭiviparyāsa* (LI, p. 22.20). The fourth of the four mistaken ideas; see XVIII.43–44. See also *Kośa* V, p. 21. It is synonymous with *ātmagrāha* and *satkāyadṛṣṭi*. On the latter see *Kośa* V, pp. 15–17.

[6] Whereas the view of a self being a mental derivative (*caitta*) is a relative entity; see Sthiramati (D Mi 76a2).

[7] *Dauṣṭhulya* (LI, p. 23.2). The seeds (*bīja*) or causes, and the instinctual traces (*vāsanā*) or effects of action (*karman*). See *Siddhi* pp. 608–609.

How is it that people rely on the view of a self which is nothing but an illusion and do not see that the nature of suffering is always connected to creations?[8] They are not intellectually aware of this intrinsic suffering (although) they are experientially aware of suffering. They suffer because suffering has not been eliminated; but, because of the nonexistence of a self which possesses that suffering, they do not (really) suffer. They are objective, since there is no self in persons; there are only objects. Yet again they are not objective, for there is objective selflessness.

When people directly perceive the relational occurrence of things, (in the form) "There occur such and such things in dependence upon such and such conditions," how is it then that they resort to the view that seeing and the like are created by some other creator[9] and are not contingent occurrences? What kind of darkness is this which makes people not see the relationally occurrent which exists, and see the self which does not exist? Darkness could make it possible for the existent to be unseen, but not for the nonexistent to be seen!

A verse on the viability of both peace and life[10] without a self:

> 5. There is no difference whatsoever between the two, peace and life, in an ultimate sense. Nevertheless, those who perform beautiful acts are acknowledged to have attained peace by terminating their (involuntary) rebirths.[11]

There is no differentiation whatsoever between the life-cycle and Nirvāṇa, for they are equally without self in the ultimate context. Nevertheless, for those who perform beautiful actions, who cultivate the path to liberation, there comes an attainment of liberation due to the termination of (involuntary) lives. The error (of the self-notion) has thus been criticized.

Four verses on entering into the ultimate intuition, the remedy (for the error of the self-notion):

---

[8] *Saṁskāra* (LI, p. 23.11). On the three kinds of suffering see the commentary to the *Kośa* VI, vs. 3.

[9] That is, a self or agent: *byed pa po* (Sthiramati D Mi 77b2).

[10] The Tibetan (D Phi 145b7) lacks *skye ba* for the Sanskrit *janma* (LI, p. 23.19).

[11] In the Chinese version (T.31.599a1), *pāda*s c and d are rendered: "By well remaining without self, birth is terminated and Nirvāṇa obtained."

> 6.[12] Once she has gathered the limitlessly fulfilling stores of merit and wisdom, a bodhisattva becomes decisive in her judgment about things; thus, she realizes that the objective realm is caused by verbalization.[13]
>
> 7.[14] And once aware that objects are mere verbalizations she securely dwells in the realm of mind alone with such (objective) appearance. Then she realizes intuitively that the ultimate realm is (immanently) present, free of the nature of duality.
>
> 8. Realizing intellectually that there is nothing apart from mind, she understands then that mind (itself) has no (ultimate) existence. Understanding that duality has no existence, such a genius dwells in the ultimate realm which has no (duality).
>
> 9. The power of the genius' nonconceptual knowledge, always and everywhere accompanied by equanimity, clears away the dense thicket of faults projected upon (relative reality), just as a powerful antidote dispels a poison.

The first verse shows the entrance into (ultimate realization); for it shows the accumulation of merit, the decisive judgment about things developed from concentrative meditation, and the realization that the objective perception of these things is due to mental verbalization. In the compound "limitlessly fulfilling," "fulfilling" signifies "completion," and "limitlessly" a length of time whose periods are incalculable.

The second verse shows that once she understands that objects are merely mental verbalizations, (a bodhisattva) dwells in mind alone appearing as that. This

---

[12] Verses 6–10 are found at the conclusion of the third chapter of *MS* where they are quoted from the *MSA* by name. Also compare verses 1–3 at the beginning of the fourth chapter of that same work.

[13] The Tibetan version has *chos la sems pa shin tu rnam nges phyir / don gyi rnam pa brjod pa'i rgyu can rtogs* (D Phi 146a3), in Sanskrit *dharmeṣu cintāsuviniścitatvājjalpahetvarthakaraṁ*, instead of the manuscript *dharmeṣu cintāsuviniśritatvājjalpānvayāmarthagatiṁ* (LI, p. 23.27). Note here the *arthagatiṁ*, which means "understanding" in the opening verse.

[14] Compare this verse and the preceeding with XI.5–7.

is the bodhisattva's stage of (achievement of) the aids to penetration.[15] Subsequently she realizes the ultimate realm with direct (nonconceptual) intuition, free of the nature of duality, the nature of subject and object. This is the stage of the path of insight.

The third verse shows the manner in which (a bodhisattva) realizes that the ultimate realm is manifestly present. How does she realize that the ultimate realm is manifestly present? She has already realized intellectually that there is no perceived object apart from mind. She then realizes that the "mind alone" as well does not exist, for where there is no apprehended object there is no apprehending subject. Once she understands that this duality does not exist, she stands in the ultimate realm which has no (duality), free of the nature of subject and object; and this is how she realizes the ultimate realm to be manifestly present.

The fourth verse shows that, due to a foundational transmutation[16] in the condition of the (bodhisattva on the) path of meditation, she experiences the entry into ultimate intuition. Through the power of her nonconceptual intuition which is always and everywhere equal, she clears away, as a powerful antidote dispels poison, the long-persisting mass of the faults (of the imaginary nature) – negative instinctual conditionings themselves based upon the relative reality wherein (nonconceptual intuition) persists in equality.[17]

A verse on the greatness of the intuition of ultimate reality:

> 10. He who is well established in the holy Dharma proclaimed by the Sage,[18] having directed his intelligence to the ultimate realm

[15] *Nirvedhabhāgīyāvastha* (LI, p. 24.10). These aids to penetration are heat, peak, tolerance, and triumph, the moments of the path of application leading to the path of seeing.

[16] On *āśrayaparivartana* (LI, p. 24.17) see IX, 12–17 and XI, 17–18, 42.

[17] At the end of this passage the Tibetan version has the phrases */ de gang la mnyam pa nyid du song zhe na / gzhan gyi dbang gi ngo bo nyid la'o* (D Phi 146b4), which nearly correspond to the Sanskrit *yatra tatsamatānugataṁ cet paratantre svabhāve* (LI, p. 24.18). However, instead of *kutra* the Sanskrit has the relative *yatra*, which is placed in the sentence next to *tadāśrayasya dūrānupraviṣṭasya doṣasaṁcayasya* (LI, p. 24.18–19), indicating that the relative is the ground of even the imaginary, faulty nature of subject-object dichotomy. Here we have followed the Sanskrit, as it better explains the *tadāśrayasya* of the verse as well.

[18] The Tibetan translation (D Phi 146b4) seems to read Sanskrit *vyavasthau* here, agreeing in case with *dharmadhātau* (LI, p. 24.21), as in the commentary "well established Holy Dharma proclaimed by the Buddha" modifies the "ultimate realm," proceeding from the object to which the bodhisattva directs his mind. They are not really that far apart in meaning, but in this case the Sanskrit seems preferable.

> which is its root, realizes that the drive of awareness is merely mental construction. Such a brave one swiftly travels to the far shore of the ocean of excellences.

Well established in the excellent teaching proclaimed by the Buddha, the bodhisattva who has entered the intuition of ultimate reality directs his intelligence to the ultimate realm of the root mind, (a mind) which has the quintessential teaching for its object. He thereupon realizes all activity of awareness, the functions of mindfulness, to be mere mental constructions. Thus he travels swiftly to the far shore of the ocean of excellences, which is buddhahood. This is the greatness of the intuition of ultimate reality.

Chapter VII

Power

A verse enumerating the characteristics of "power":[1]

> 1. The power of the bodhisattva who has achieved bravery lies in his intuitive knowledge of lives, speech, minds, the sum of good and evil, proper destinations, and transcendence – (such psychic powers being) unobstructed throughout the universe regarding all varieties (of beings).

Knowledge of others' lives is the superknowledge of (beings') deaths and future lives. Knowledge of speech is the clairaudience of the divine ear; it is the knowledge of the speech spoken by beings reborn in such[2] and such lives.[3] Knowledge of mind is the superknowledge of (others') modalities of mind. Knowledge of the past sum of good and evil is the superknowledge of (beings') former lives. The knowledge of the proper destinations where disciples (or buddhas) are situated is the superpower of the domain of telekinesis. Knowledge of transcendence is the superknowledge of the termination of contamination; (it) being knowledge of the way in which living beings transcend (involuntary) rebirth. Such knowledge of those six kinds of objects in all varieties, manifestly present without obstruction in all universes, constitutes the power of the bodhisattva, consisting of (his distinctive

---

[1] *Prabhāva* (LI, p. 25.1), *mthu* (D Phi 146b7), *shen tung* (T.31.599b14). dBal Mang (42b1) introduces this chapter as follows: "In the aftermath-attainment following the intuitive experience of thatness in *samādhi*, the bodhisattva must achieve the aims of others by his extensive power, ..." hence the chapter on power.

[2] Following G. Nagao, editing *tatra gatvopapannā* (LI, p. 25.5) to *tatra tatropapannā*, according to Ryūkoku University Ms. A.

[3] Here the six clairvoyances are *cyutopapādābhijñā*, *divyaśrotrābhijñā*, *paryāyābhijñā*, *pūrvanivāsābhijñā*, *ṛddhiviṣayābhijñā*, and *āsravakṣayābhijñā* (LI, p. 25.4 *ff.*). The same list is found in the *BBh* p. 40 and *AS* p. 98. However, in many places *divyacakṣu* (or *divyaṁ cakṣuṁ*) is found instead of *cyutopapādābhijñā*, e.g., *MVy* 202; see *Kośa* VII pp. 98–100 and Edgerton p. 50.

form of) the six superknowledges. This analysis of the characteristics of power gives its actual nature.[4]

A verse on the topic of the cause (of the bodhisattva's power):

> 2. Having reached the full purity of the fourth contemplation,[5] through maintaining nonconceptual intuition and conscious attention to the structure of reality (revealed by the teachings),[6] (the bodhisattva) attains the supreme accomplishment of power.

This verse indicates in which state, by which intuition, and through which thoughtful attitude (the bodhisattva) achieves power.

A verse on the topic of fruition:

> 3. (The bodhisattva) always lives with the incomparable and magnificent, holy, divine and sublime stations; (simultaneously) visiting

---

[4] The hexad of *svabhāva*, *hetu*, *phala*, *karman*, *yoga*, and *vṛtti* are found frequently employed in the *MSA* as an analytical device (e.g., IX.56–59, XVI.17–28, XX–XXI.60–61) as in the *YBh*, *RGV*, and *AS*. On the hexad see J. Takasaki, "Description of Ultimate Reality," *The Journal of Indian and Buddhist Studies* IX., no. 2, 1961, and reprinted in Takasaki, *A Study on the Ratnagotravibhāga*, Appendix III.

[5] The fourth contemplation is the last and highest of the four concentrations of the form realm, containing eight heavenly regions, all called in general the "pure station of infinite equanimity," *upekṣāpramāṇabrahmavihāra*.

[6] The terms for the two means of attaining the bodhisattva powers from the state of the fourth contemplation – i.e., nonconceptual intuition and adaptive attention to reality – are in different cases, instrumental and ablative (*...graheṇa* and *...manaskriyātaṁ*, LI, p. 25.11–12), which might lead one to miss their need of combination, taking the former as a means of attaining the contemplation, and the latter as the means of gaining power therein. The Tibetan connects the two compounds by *dang* (D Phi 147a4), effectively putting them in the same case and thereby eliminating this ambiguity.

dBal Mang (43a4 *ff.*) points out that all three – the state, the intuition, and the conscious thought – are required. The translation of *manaskāra* by "attention" all alone is inadequate, as it connotes mere concentration on one point; this misses the structured, discursive nature of its "mental activity." Quoting scriptures, dBal Mang points out that the contemplation and the intuition are the general prerequisites, but the powers themselves only follow thoughtful adaptation to the revealed nature of things. Thus, to develop clairvoyance, one must systematically think of boundless space as filled with light and transparent forms; to develop clairaudience, one must think of the limitless variety of sounds; to develop telepathy, one must focus on the workings of beings' minds; to develop telekinesis, one must focus on the lightness of the body; and so forth.

> all universes, she worships the buddhas and leads beings to perfection.[7]

This shows the fruits of power to be threefold: (the bodhisattva remains) herself in the blissful, holy, divine, and sublime stations which are unequalled and excellent, and, when she visits other universes, she worships the buddhas and purifies beings.[8]

Four verses on the topic of activity, which is sixfold. A verse on the (bodhisattva's) visionary[9] and manifestational activities:

> 4. He sees all universes, along with their sentient beings, evolutions, and dissolutions, as just like a magician's illusions; and, having his (tenfold) mastery, he manifests such (cosmic events) in various forms, according to his wish.[10]

(A bodhisattva) sees all universes along with their sentient beings, evolutions, and dissolutions as just like a magician's illusions. He manifests these (cosmic processes) to others as he wishes, in various forms such as quaking, blazing, and so on.

---

[7] According to *BBh* p. 63.20, the holy (*ārya*) states are the three "doors of liberation," *tatra śūnyatānimittāpraṇihitavihārā nirodhasamāpattivihāraścāryo vihāra ityucyate*, i.e., the *samādhis* of voidness, signlessness, and wishlessness, and the cessation equipoise (*nirodhasamāpatti*); the divine (*divya*) states are the four *dhyānas* of the *rūpadhātu* and the four *samāpattis* of the *ārūpyadhātu*; and the sublime (*brāhma*) states are the four immeasurables (*apramāṇas*). See Barbara Stoler Miller, *Journal of Indian Philosophy* (1979), pp. 209–221, for a discussion of these categories.

[8] In this sentence, both the Sanskrit (LI, p. 25.17) and the Tibetan (D Phi 147a6) leave out most of the verbs, assuming them to be supplied from the verse. From the dual activity in other locations – worshiping buddhas and helping beings – dBal Mang took his cue to expand the interpretation of the "location-knowledge" (*tatsthāna…jñānaṁ*) mentioned in VII.1 above.

[9] The Tibetan version (D Phi 147a7) reads *mthong ba'i lam*, i.e., *darśanamārga*, instead of *darśanakarma* (LI, p. 25.19), or P *mthong ba'i las*.

[10] G. Nagao interprets this as "according to the wishes of beings for whom he manifests such forms," following the indication of the Chinese *ta suo yu* (T.31.599c11). dBal Mang (44a5) reads it "as he wishes," indicating the degree of his mastery (*ji ltar 'dod pa bzhin gyi dbang dang ldan pa'i phyir*).

For he has attained the ten masteries taught in the *Discourse on the Ten Stages* in the context of the eighth stage.[11]

A verse on the activity of radiance:

> 5. Emitting radiant light rays, she causes those who suffer violently in the hellish states to migrate to the heavens, and, causing the lofty,[12] elegant palaces of Māra's followers to shake, she terrifies the demons.

The activity of the radiance (of the bodhisattva's radiance) is shown to be of two types: it causes those born in hellish states to develop faith and to take rebirth in the heavens, and it brings anxiety to the demons and their stations by causing them to shake.

A verse on the activities of play and emanation:[13]

> 6. In the midst of a supreme assembly, (the bodhisattva) manifests the play of innumerable concentrations, while at all times carrying out beings' purposes through artistic, incarnational, and supreme emanations.

Amid the assemblies of a buddha's circle, (the bodhisattva) manifests his play with immeasurable concentrations. He always accomplishes the purposes of beings by means of three kinds of emanations. The three types of emanation are: the emanation of artistic creativity, the emanation of whatever incarnation he wishes for the sake of his disciples, and the supreme emanation, dwelling in the station of Tuṣita, and so forth.[14]

---

[11] The ten masteries (*vaśitā*) according to the *DBhS* p. 46.6–14 are mastery over lifespan (*āyur-*), mind (*ceto*), property (*pariṣkāra-*), action (*karma-*), rebirth (*upapatti-*), faith (*adhimukti-*), vow (*praṇidhāna-*), magic power (*ṛddhi-*), Dharma, and intuition (*jñāna-*).

[12] For the Sanskrit *kṣubdha* (LI, p. 26.6), G. Nagao prefers the Ryūkoku Ms. A reading *ucca*. The Tibetan (D Phi 147b3) agrees, reading *mtho* (*ucca*) which is confirmed by Sthiramati (D Mi 86a2; P Mi 98a5–6).

[13] Following G. Nagao's reading of Ryūkoku Ms. A, which adds *nirmāṇakarma* after *vikrīḍanakarma* (LI, p. 26.9), as does the Tibetan (D Phi 147b4) *sprul pa'i las*.

[14] According to Sthiramati (D Mi 86b3–4; P Mi 99a1) "supreme emanation" (*uttama-nirmāṇa*, LI, p. 26.11) refers to the acts of the buddha-life; see *RGV* II.53–56. These three emanations are identical to the threefold function of the emanation body (*nirmāṇakāya*) of a

(cont'd)

A verse on the activity of purifying the (buddha) land:

> 7. Through his mastery of intuitions he realizes a pure land so that he may manifest whatever he wishes (to benefit beings). For those who have never (heard) the name "buddha," he makes the name "buddha" known and thereby sends them on to other realms (not lacking buddhas).

The purification (of the buddha land) is twofold.[15] It is purified by the purification of the material environment; for as (a bodhisattva) has mastery of intuitions he creates at will a buddha land made of crystal or of sapphire, and so on. (It is also purified) through the purification of the inhabitant beings; for he causes those who have been born in realms where the name "buddha" does not exist to hear the name "buddha." Through this they are caused to have faith and to take (eventual) rebirth in universes where that (name) is not absent.

A verse on the topic of the endowment (of power):

> 8. (The bodhisattva's) ability to develop living beings is like (the power to fly) of a bird whose wings are fully grown. She receives exceptional praise from the buddhas, and her speech is authoritative for beings.

A threefold endowment is shown: endowment with the ability to develop living beings, endowment with praise, and endowment with acceptable speech.

A verse on the topic of operation:

---

buddha. See below, IX.58–64, 75. dBal Mang remarks here (44b4) that Vasubandhu's use of *tuṣitabhavanavāsā* as an example of the supreme emanation is purposeful, ruling out any opinion that the Bodhisattva Maitreya, author of the work and inspirer of the cult, is merely an "incarnational emanation body."

[15] Following G. Nagao's reading of Ryūkoku Ms. A *dvividhayā pariśodhanayā*, in preference to Lévi's text, which awkwardly introduces the notion of "sin" (*pāpa*, LI, p. 26.18).

> 9. The power of the brave one consists of six superknowledges, three knowledges,[16] eight liberations,[17] eight sovereignties,[18] ten totalities,[19] and innumerable concentrations.

The bodhisattva's power operates in six ways: through the superknowledges, the knowledges, the liberations, the sphere of sovereignty, the sphere of totality, and innumerable concentrations.

Having thus expounded (the bodhisattva's) power through six topics which display its characteristics, there is a verse in order to emphasize its greatness:

> 10. He whose intelligence has attained the highest mastery always establishes powerless beings in independence, and always single-mindedly enjoys himself in benefiting others. The good, brave (bodhisattva) roams through his lives just like a lion.

Three varieties of greatness are shown here: the greatness of mastery, for, having himself acquired mastery over supreme intuition, he establishes beings in their own independence who previously had no independence due to their mental addictions; the greatness of enjoyment, for his sole delight is always to bring benefit to others; and the greatness of utter freedom from fear of life.

---

[16] The three knowledges (*vidyā* LI, p. 27.7) correspond to the first, fourth, and sixth clairvoyances as enumerated above. See *Kośa* VII. p. 108.

[17] On the eight *vimokṣa* (LI, p. 27.7), see *Kośa* VIII pp. 203–211, and *AS* p. 95; also *Le Traité* III pp. 1281–1299.

[18] On the eight *abhibhvāyatana* (LI, p. 27.9), see *Kośa* VIII pp. 211–213, and *AS* p. 96; also *Le Traité* pp. 1299–1304.

[19] On the ten *kṛtsnāyatana* (LI, p. 27.8) see *Kośa* VIII 213–215, and *AS* p. 96; also *Le Traité* pp. 1304–1307.

Chapter VIII

Evolutionary Maturity[1]

A summary verse on the evolutionary maturity of the bodhisattva:

> 1. Delight, faith, serenity, sympathy, tolerance, intelligence, strength, unassailability, completeness – (the bodhisattva is endowed with) all of these to a high degree. This is the definition of the evolutionary maturity of a victor-child.

(The bodhisattva is endowed with) delight in the Dharma which teaches the universal vehicle, faith in its teacher, serenity of the addictions, sympathy for beings, tolerance in undergoing hardships, intelligence in apprehension, retention, and penetration, strength in practical realization, unassailability by demons or rivals, and completeness[2] of endowment with the factors of abandon.[3] "To a high degree" indicates the magnitude of delight and so on. It should be understood that the bodhisattva's own evolutionary maturity is summarized in these nine aspects.

A verse on evolutionary maturity as delight:

---

[1] dBal Mang (46a3) introduces this chapter usefully: "Once a (bodhisattva) has intuitively experienced the actual condition of things, not only does he need to accomplish the purposes of others in the aftermath (wisdom), but also his own character matures by realizing thatness, and others become mature through faith that arises when they see his extensive power. Hence there is the chapter on evolutionary maturity."

[2] The Sanskrit (LI, p. 28.3) and Chinese (T.31.600b9) commentaries do not repeat the verse's *samupetatā* (LI, p. 27.20), though the Chinese does have the abbreviation *zhi* for *zhi zhu.*

[3] As in the case of the four *samyakprahāṇa,* exertion and abandonment are closely related. This ambiguity is reflected in the Tibetan *yang dag rtsol ba* (true exertion), and the Chinese *zheng jing jin* (true abandonment). Our translation "abandon," referring to the energy derived from intense letting go toward a desired aim, seeks to preserve this ambiguity. See below verse 10, and XVIII.45–49.

> 2. The nature of the compassionate (bodhisattva's) true maturity in her embrace of the holy Dharma is (delight in) three, (serving, learning from, and consciously attending to) a spiritual friend, (delight) in intense efforts in and successful accomplishment[4] (of inconceivable sciences), and (delight in) upholding the supreme teaching.

The three (serving, and so on) of the spiritual friend are service to a holy person, learning (from him) the holy Dharma, and the proper thoughtful attitude (in the light of what one has learned). Intense energy is a boundless energetic initiative. Successful accomplishment is lack of doubt about any of the inconceivable sciences.[5] Upholding the supreme teaching is the guarding of the teaching of the universal vehicle, by protecting those who practice it from persecutions. This should be understood as the nature of the bodhisattva's maturity as joy in the context of her embrace of the Dharma of the universal vehicle.

What is the cause of this maturity? The three (actions), such as (serving) the spiritual friend. What is its (actuality in) maturity? Its actuality is endowment with intense energy and successful accomplishment. What is its action? The upholding of the supreme teaching. This (verse) therefore illustrates those (three, cause, actuality, and action).

A verse on maturity as faith:

> 3.[6] Acknowledgement of excellence, swift attainment of the concentrations, experience of the fruit, and also imperturbability[7] of

---

[4] The Sanskrit *parārdhaniṣṭho* should read *paramaniṣṭho* as the Tibetan *dam pa'i mthar phyin*.

[5] *Ācintyasthāna* (LI, p. 28.9). The *Acintitasutta* of the *Aṅguttaranikāya* (II, 80) deals with four inconceivables: the sphere of a buddha (*buddhavisaya*), the sphere of one in meditative absorption (*jhānavisaya*), the ripening of actions (*kammavipāka*), and cosmological speculation (*lokacinta*). In place of cosmological speculation, Sthiramati (D Mi 91a1; P Mi 103b3–4) has the power of medicines and mantras (*sman dang sngags kyi mthu*). dBal Mang (46b6) describes the four inconceivable sciences as those of evolution, of medicine and mantras, of buddha-wisdom, and of the sphere of yoga. Sthiramati (P Mi 103b2) agrees.

[6] The Chinese translation (T.31.600b19) reads: The characteristics of the maturity of faith are a Tathāgata's stores of merit and intuition, a pure mind which cannot be defiled, and swift reception of the intuition (which is) the definite result.

[7] For the Sanskrit *adhyabhedatā* (LI, p. 28.15) read *apy-*, following the Tibetan (D Phi 149a2) *kyang*.

> mind; this is the nature of the true maturity of a victor-child who trusts the teacher.

This maturity is indicated in terms of its cause, actuality, and action. Its cause is knowledge of his excellences, that he is the lord, the transcendent,[8] and so on at length. Its actuality is imperturbability of mind, since faith has been gained through such knowledge.[9] Its action is the swift attainment of the concentrations and the personal experience of their fruits, the superknowledges, and so on.

A verse on maturity as serenity:

> 4. The nature of true maturity for a victor-child who dispels addictions consists of thorough restraint, freedom from afflicted calculations, and unobstructedness and pleasure in virtue.

For a bodhisattva, serenity is dispelling the addictions. As a maturity, it is again demonstrated via cause, actuality, and action. Its cause is thorough restraint of the sense faculties through mindfulness and vigilance. Its actuality is the freedom from addicted calculations. Its action is unobstructedness in the cultivation of remedies and intense delight in goodness.

A verse concerning the nature of maturity as compassion:

> 5. The nature of (the bodhisattva's) maturity as sympathy for others consists of natural compassion, sensitivity to the sufferings of others, determined rejection of inferior thoughts, progress in excellence, and birth as foremost in the world.

The causes developing (maturity as compassion) are the natural spiritual gene, sensitivity for the sufferings of others, and the determined rejection of inferior vehicles. Its actuality is progress in excellence, since it progresses in increase of ma-

---

[8] The Tibetan (D Phi 149a3), mis-spells *gshegs pa* as *gshess pa*.

[9] The Tibetan (D Phi 149a3) reads the Sanskrit as *āvedyā*, translating it as *shes nas*, instead of the manuscript *avetya* (LI, p. 28.18), a variant of *abhedya*. The meaning is much better, as it provides the reason for the imperturbability of mature faith, i.e., that it is grounded on knowledge. As the Ms. reads it is more or less redundant. The Ms. *prabhāva* (LI, p. 28.18) seems corrupt; cf. the Chinese translation (T.31.600b19 *ff.*).

turity. Its evolutionary action on the stage of nonregression is (to produce) an embodiment superior to that of any other being.[10]

A verse on the nature of maturity as tolerance:

> 6. The nature of maturity as tolerance consists of natural steadfastness, cultivation of critical discernment, constant endurance[11] of the miseries of cold and the like, progress in excellence, and intense delight in virtue.

Steadfastness, endurance, and tolerance are synonyms. In its maturing, the causes are the spiritual gene and the cultivation of critical discernment. Its actuality is the endurance of the terrible sufferings of cold and the like. Its action is progress in excellence of tolerance and intense delight in virtue.

A verse on maturity as intelligence:[12]

> 7. The nature of maturity as excellent intelligence consists of purity of development, mindfulness not to forget one's learning and so forth and to gain insight into the well-said and ill-said, and adeptness in generating great understanding.

Its cause is purity of development consistent with intelligence. The actuality of maturity as intelligence is that mindfulness (both) does not forget what was long ago learned, considered, and contemplated, or what was long ago explained, and gains insight into the meaning of good explanations and bad explanations. Its action is adeptness in generating transcendent intuitive wisdom.

A verse on maturity as the acquisition of power:

> 8. The nature of maturity as acquisition of power consists of the development of two elements by means of two virtues, supreme fit-

---

[10] See II.6. The Sanskrit *ātmabhāvatā* (LI, p. 29.7) is possible for Tibetan *lus*, but does not fit so well with the Tibetan (D Phi 149b1), *lus mchog tu 'gyur pa*, which accords with the Tibetan translation of *jagadagra janmatā* by *'gro ba'i mchog 'gyur lus* in the verse.

[11] The Tibetan (D Phi 149b2) *rtag mi mjed* seems to read *avivarjana* for *adhivāsanā* (LI, p. 29.9), while *sahanaṁ* in the commentary is also translated *mi mjed.*

[12] Compare *BBh* p. 56.6.

> ness of embodiment[13] for a fruitful outcome, the consummation of one's heart's desire, and the achievement of leadership in the world.

The cause of such maturity is the growth of the seeds of both merit and intuition. The actuality of such maturity is the fitness for realization of one's embodiment. Its action consists of the consummation of desires and the achievement of leadership in the world.

A verse on maturity as unassailability:

> 9. Maturity as unassailability consists of aspiration for the good Dharma after its rational investigation, freedom from demonic obstructions,[14] attainment of excellence, and refutation of opposing positions.

The cause of such maturity is the aspiration to the holy Dharma when examined by reason. Its actuality is freedom from demonic obstacles, since Māra is unable to create obstacles on the path. Its action consists of the attainment of excellence and the refutation of all opposing positions.

A verse on maturity as endowment with the factors of abandon:[15]

> 10. The maturity of a victor-child as endowment with the factors (of abandon) consists of her gathering of the good, fitness of her life for making efforts, and her great delight in solitude and in the highest virtues.

The cause of such maturity is the gathering of the roots of virtue. Its actuality is her body's tolerance for undertaking efforts. And its action consists in her prizing of solitude and her delight in the highest virtues.

---

[13] *Āśraya* (LI, p. 29.20; D Phi 149b6–7). Cf. Sthiramati (D Mi 94b4; P Mi 110b6).

[14] The Tibetan (D Phi 150a1) reverses the order of the second and third quarters of the verse, which better suits the commentarial arrangement into cause, actuality, and action.

[15] *Prāhāṇikāṅga* (LI, p. 30.3; D Phi 150a3). According to Sthiramati (D Mi 96a2; P Mi 109a3–4) abandonment here refers to the abandonment of subjectivity and objectivity upon the cognition of the *dharmadhātu* on the first bodhisattva stage. The five factors which accompany it are faith (*dad pa*), honesty (*g-yo med pa*), guilelessness (*sgyu med pa*), physical health (*lus la nad med pa*), and wisdom (*shes rab*). For the canonical list of the five factors see LII, p. 62, n. 10.1, and *PTSD* p. 411 s.v. *padhāniya.*

A verse on the greatness of (the bodhisattva's) ninefold maturity:

> 11. (The bodhisattva), himself mature in these nine areas, (naturally) gains the ability to bring others to maturity. Himself an embodiment of Dharma constantly on the increase,[16] he always becomes the dearest relative of all the world.

Its greatness is twofold: it is the recourse for the evolutionary development of others, and it constantly increases the body of Dharma. For that reason (the bodhisattva) becomes the best relative of all the world.

Eleven verses expounding the evolutionary maturing of beings:

> 12. Boils when ready to be drained and food when ready to be enjoyed, both are considered mature; in the same way, in this life-form, evolutionary maturity is shown in the two tendencies, the eradication (of the resistances to virtues) and in the enjoyment of (the remedies of addictions).[17]

This verse shows the actuality of maturity. The maturity of a boil is its readiness to be drained, and that of food is its readiness to be enjoyed.[18] In the same way, in the life-habits of beings there are (resistances) like boils and (remedies) like food; so eradication of resistances is like draining (the boils) and enjoyment of remedies is like enjoying (food). Such readiness is called the evolutionary maturity

---

[16] Reading *dharmamaya* instead of *śubhamaya* (LI, p. 30.10) which is supported by Sthiramati (D Mi 96b4; P Mi 110a2) and Vasubandhu (D Phi 150a5) *dharmamaya* (*chos kyi rang bzhin*). The Chinese (T.31.600c29–601a1) has *zeng shan zeng fa shen* (*śubhadharmakāya-pravardhita*).

[17] This verse is so compressed, it is confusing. The Sanskrit is especially muddled in the second line (LI, p. 30.14), which reads *tathāśraye 'smindvayapakṣaśāntatā tathopabhogatva suśāntapakṣatā*. The Tibetan reads (D Phi 150a7) */ de bzhin rten 'dir phyogs gnyis zhi ba dang / de bzhin dpyad pa nyid du smin pa bstan /*, giving a basis to emend the end of the Sanskrit line from *...bhogatvasuśāntapakṣatā* to *...bhogatvaṁ ucyante pakvatāṁ*.

The commentary (LI, p. 30.18) gives the gloss of *vipakṣapratipakṣa* for *pakṣadvaya*, which clarifies the similes of boil-draining and food-enjoying for eradicating resistances and enjoying remedies. But it is better to split the similes and maturities in the verse, as English cannot capture the play on *pakṣa*.

[18] Compare *BBh* p. 55.3 *ff.*

of the life-form. Here the two tendencies can be recognized as the resistances and the remedies.

The second verse:

> 13.[19] Beings are considered to have (dissociative) dis-maturity, pleni-maturity, para-maturity, (adaptive) ad-maturity, (polite) socio-maturity, super-maturity, (constant) auto-maturity, and ultra-maturity.

This shows the subdivisions of maturity. Dis-maturity is maturity through dissociation from the addictions. Pleni-maturity is complete maturity through the three vehicles. Para-maturity is excellent maturity because it is superior to the maturity of the religious. Ad-(aptive) maturity is maturity in tune with the disciples by teaching the Dharma as adapted to them. Socio-maturity is respectful maturity. Super-maturity is maturity in realization. Auto-maturity is constant maturing through not mistaking the aim. Ultra-maturity is gradually developing higher and higher maturity through not losing the aim. These are the eight subdivisions of the evolutionary maturing of others.

The third and fourth verses:

> 14. Neither mother nor father nor relative lives as devoted to son or kin, as a spiritual victor-child, with her will to help here and now, lives intent upon the evolutionary benefit of the whole world.

> 15. Likewise beings do not feel a love even for themselves, not to speak of for beloved others' lives, anything like the love the compassionate (bodhisattva) feels for other beings; for (her love) brings them help and happiness, (which selfish love never does).

---

[19] In this verse the eight types of maturity are formed through the addition to *pācana* of the prefixes *vi-*, *pari-*, *pra-*, *anu-*, *su-*, *adhi-*, *ni-*, and *ut-*. Compare IX.14 in which the ten varieties of transmutation are formed by the addition of *pra-*, *ut-*, *a-*, *ā-*, *ni-*, etc. to *vṛtti* and the six types of *vāda*, in *AS* p. 104. In order to convey this playfulness, we have used parallel English prefixes, adding explanatory adjectives in brackets where not obvious in meaning: i.e., *vi-* = dis-, *pari-* = pleni-, *pra-* = para-, *anu-* = ad-, *su-* = socio-, *adhi-* = super-, *ni-* = auto-, *ut-* = ultra-.

What is shown by these two verses? They show the kind of aspiration through which a bodhisattva brings beings to evolutionary maturity. It is an aspiration superior to that of parents and relatives, and (even) superior to mundane beings' love of themselves. For it truly brings beings help and happiness, while the self-love of mundane beings brings them neither help nor happiness.[20]

The remaining verses show that the perfection of the transcendences is the practice that brings beings to evolutionary maturity.

A verse on what manner of generosity brings living beings to evolutionary maturity in what way:

> 16.[21] A bodhisattva has absolutely no body or property which are not to be given to others. He matures others with two types of assistance and is never satisfied with the virtues of equal giving.

He matures (beings) with three types of generosity: giving all his body and property, giving impartially,[22] and giving insatiably. How does giving mature beings? Through assistance in this life and in future lives. He fulfills their desires (in this life) without reservation, and having thereby[23] gathered (beings) together (in subsequent lives), he establishes them in virtue.

A verse on what manner of morality brings living beings to evolutionary maturity in what way:

> 17. (The bodhisattva's morality) is constant, natural, surpassingly nonviolent, automatically delightful, and consciously vigilant. She establishes others in it and, rendering them assistance in two ways,

---

[20] The Sanskrit is completely inaccurate here, omitting two privative *a-* particles before *hite* and *sukhe*. Following the Tibetan (D Phi 151a2) *bdag nyid phan pa ma yin pa dang / bde ba ma yin pa la sbyor ro /*, we read *'hite 'sukhe caiva....*

[21] The Chinese version (T.31.601b2) reads: Body and wealth are all given up, equally without resentment. The impoverished are fulfilled and established in roots of virtue.

[22] *Aviṣamadānena*, (LI, p. 31.15). The Tibetan (D Phi 151a4) reads: *mi mnyam pa med par sbyin pa*, and in Sthiramati's commentary *mi mtshungs pa med pa'i sbyin pa* (D Mi 99b6).

[23] Reading editor's suggested *tena* for awkward *anāgatena* (LI, p. 31.17).

> she brings others to maturity through the succession of evolutionary and dispositional excellences.[24]

(She brings living beings to maturity) by means of five types of morality: firm morality,[25] natural morality,[26] and morality fulfilled through its surpassing nonviolence. Fulfilled nonviolence is surpassingly nonviolent due to the fulfillment of the ten paths of virtuous actions, stated (to take place) on the second (bodhisattva) stage.[27] (Fourth and fifth are) the morality of realization, through her automatic delight (in the ten virtues), and uninterruptedly unerring morality, through her conscious vigilance. How does (such morality) bring beings to evolutionary maturity? By installing them in morality. She renders assistance in two ways, in this life and in future lives. She renders others assistance continuously in the succession of future lives by means of the succession of evolutionary and dispositional excellences, for as the (positive) evolution and (moral) disposition of this (being's future lives) are mutually reinforcing, they are uninterrupted.

A verse on what manner of tolerance brings living beings to maturity in what way:

> 18. If another injures him he takes him for a benefactor enduring
> even the greatest violation; through enduring injury with thoughts
> of liberative art he leads those who do harm to accept virtue.

If another injures (the bodhisattva), he matures him through tolerance in enduring the most terrible injuries with the idea that (his tormentor) is a benefactor. This idea of benefactor should be understood to operate in accord with the fulfill-

---

24 Evolutionary excellence (*vipākaguṇa*) arising from morality is rebirth in the higher states of humans and gods. The dispositional excellence (*niṣyandaguṇa*) is the propensity for further practice of morality in those lives. See dBal Mang (51b5).

25 *Dhruvaśīla*, (LI, p. 31.21). Sthiramati (D Mi 100b3) explains firm morality as morality which lasts from the time it is taken up until death or enlightenment. Sthiramati uses *rtag pa'i tshul khrims* (D Mi 100b2 *ff.*; P Mi 114a3–5) in place of Vasubandhu's *bstan* (sic for *brten*) *pa'i tshul khrims* (D Phi 151a5).

26 *Prakṛtiśīla*, (LI, p. 31.21). Sthiramati (D Mi 100b4; P Mi 114a5–7) explains natural morality as the practice of morality in the present life due to its practice in previous lives, or morality which leads to pleasure in the smallest of virtues regardless of what kind of life is obtained in the future.

27 The Chinese translation (T.31.601b14) reads: in the *Daśabhūmikasūtra*.

ment of the transcendence of tolerance. How does it mature beings? Through assistance in this life in enduring injury, and through assistance in future lives. Knowing the liberative art, he leads offenders to accept virtue by winning them over through endurance of injuries.

A verse on what manner of effort brings living beings to evolutionary maturity in what way:

> 19. She, the spiritual victor-child, relies on highest striving to bring hosts of beings to a superior maturity; she does not lose heart in ten million aeons in order to bring about even a single virtuous thought in one other (being).

This is due to effort of great magnitude which does not tire even over a long period of time. Since she brings infinite living beings to maturity, she does not lose heart over long periods of time. She does not lose heart even in ten million aeons, (striving) for the sake of a single virtuous thought in another (being). How does she bring them to maturity? Through assistance in this life and in future lives by leading the mind toward virtue.

A verse on what manner of contemplation brings living beings to evolutionary maturity in what way:

> 20. Having attained unexcelled mastery of the mind, he wins over others to this teaching; and having relinquished all desire for being honored by others, he causes them to increase in virtue.

He brings (beings) to maturity through contemplation which has attained unexcelled mastery, through non-exploitiveness and through the relinquishment of all desire to be honored by others. He brings others to maturity by winning them over to the buddha's teaching and causing those who have been won over to increase virtuous qualities.

A verse on what manner of wisdom brings living beings to evolutionary maturity in what way:

> 21. Having become fully decisive about the system of ultimate and intimated meaning,[28] he easily dispels the doubts of beings; and

---

[28] *Bhāvārtha*, (LI, p. 32.23). The Tibetan (D Phi 152a3) reads *dgongs don*. See XII.16–17.

> thus from their reverence for the teaching of the victor, he and others increase with excellent virtues.

A bodhisattva brings about (beings') maturity through wisdom which is utterly decisive about the principles of the definitive and interpretable meanings. How does it bring (beings) to maturity? Through dispelling the doubts of living beings. Thus, because they develop great reverence for the teaching, they increase good qualities in themselves and in others.

A concluding verse:

> 22. In that way a bodhisattva, out of compassion migrating in the same realms as all beings, leads the whole world to a happy migration or to the three virtues in lesser, middling, and superior ways.

Where does she lead them? To progress in the happy migrations or to the three vehicles. Who does she lead? All beings. With what does she lead? With compassion. Who leads? The bodhisattva. Through what type of action? Through lesser, middling, and superior types. For how long a time? By elucidating these (topics), (the author) briefly shows the greatness of evolutionary maturity. It should be understood that the lesser type of action takes place on the bodhisattva's stage of action through faith, the middling type on the (first) seven stages, and the superior type takes place on the eighth, (ninth and tenth) stages. Her migrating in common with beings as long as the world exists means (that she stays with them) forever.

Chapter IX

Enlightenment[1]

There are two verses on omniscience,[2] with a third to explain them:

> 1–2. Through countless hundreds of ordeals and countless gatherings of virtue, destroying countless obscurations over immeasurable periods of time, omniscience is attained: unspoiled by any obscuration, it is celebrated as buddhahood, like a casket of jewels thrown open.

> 3. Having undergone the awesome ordeal with a hundred labors, having gathered all beauty, having destroyed all obscurations after the great period of time of the longest eon, and having eradicated even the subtle obscurations encountered on the stages, buddhahood appears like an opened casket of jewels, magnificent in splendor.

Buddhahood is presented in the context of its realization, its reality, and a simile. It is realized by however many hundreds of ordeals, by however huge stores of virtues, for however long and due to the abandonment of however many addictive and objective obscurations. This is its realization. Its reality is the attainment of omniscience unspoiled by any obscuration. Its simile is a casket of jewels thrown open.

---

[1] dBal Mang (53b5) locates this chapter in the flow of the text: "As one will attain enlightenment by maturing the characters of oneself and others, there is the chapter on 'Enlightenment.' Its main parts are three: 1) the structure of the great enlightenment; 2) the conduct engaged in practicing it; and 3) the reasons to reinforce the motivation to achieve it, emerging from expressing the greatness of the great enlightenment."

[2] *Sarvākārajñatā*, (LI, p. 33.12). The first of the three types of omniscience according to the *AA*; see Obermiller, *Analysis of the Abhisamayālaṁkāra*, p. 2 *ff.* According to Sthiramati, (D Mi 107a1; P Mi 121a2–3) it is the unmistaken knowledge of all phenomena as suffering, impermanent, empty, and selfless.

Two verses on the nonduality[3] which characterizes that same buddhahood, and on its power:[4]

> 4. Although all things are buddhahood,[5] there exists no thing whatsoever; it consists of virtuous qualities but they do not define it.
>
> 5. Because it is the cause of the jewel of the Dharma it resembles a mine of jewels; because it is the cause of a harvest of beauty it resembles a raincloud.

All things are buddhahood because suchness is without differentiation and because buddhahood manifests through its purity. Yet in buddhahood there is no thing whatsoever which exists in terms of the imaginatively constructed reality of things. Buddhahood consists of good qualities, for its presence transforms[6] the virtues, the transcendences, and so forth. And yet they do not describe it (adequately), because the transcendences and so forth are not absolutely established as transcendences by any intrinsic reality.[7] This is its nondual nature. Its effectiveness is like a mine of jewels and like a raincloud, because it is the origin of (both) the jewels of the Dharma teaching and the harvests of virtue (that grow) in the fields of the lives of the disciples.

---

3 *Advaya*, (LI, p. 34.1). For references see *VKN* pp. 301–2 n. 1.

4 *Sānubhāve*, (LI, p. 34.1). This seems to be a corruption of *saprabhāve*, as the Tibetan (D Phi 152b6) reads *mthu dang bcas pa*, although the commentary glosses both *anubhāva* and *prabhāva*.

5 *Sarvadharmāśca buddhatvaṁ* (LI, p. 34.3). Sthiramati (P Mi 122a5–7): all phenomena *sub specie aeternitatis*, i.e., empty, unborn, undying, etc., are not different from the *dharmakāya* of a buddha. In this connection he cites the following two *pāda*s from the *Sarvabuddhaviṣayāvatārajñānālokālaṁkārasūtra*: *mi skye chos ni rtag tu de bzhin gshegs / thams cad chos kyang bde bar gshegs dang dra /* "Unborn phenomena are always the Tathāgata, all phenomena are also like the Sugata." For references to parallel passages in other sūtras see *BBS*, vol. II, p. 24.

6 *Parīvṛtti* (LI, p. 34.9). See below vs. 12–17.

7 Sthiramati (P Mi 122b6–8). That is, the perfections do not inherently exist as perfections.

> 6. Buddhahood includes all things, or otherwise excludes all things.[8] It is like a mine of Dharma jewels, because it produces the jewels of the Dharma so great and vast. It is like a raincloud, showering upon beings a rain of great, well-explained, and inexhaustible Dharma, because it is the cause of the vast growth in beings of the harvest of virtues.

This third verse explains the same topic.[9] Because it is the cause of the production of the jewels of the Dharma, so great and vast, it is like a jewel mine. Because it is the cause for beings' great abundance in the harvest of virtue, it is like a raincloud, showering beings with the Dharma which is great, well-explained, and inexhaustible. So should the words be construed here.

Five verses on this same buddhahood as the unexcelled refuge:

> 7.[10] Buddhahood is the constant deliverance from all the hosts of addictions, from all evil actions, and even from birth[11] and death.

This succinctly shows that it is a refuge in serving as deliverance from defilement by the addictions, actions, and (sufferings of) birth (and so forth).[12]

> 8. It is thus the best of refuges from all injuries, from hellish rebirths, from unliberating arts, from materiality,[13] and from the individual vehicle (alone).

---

[8] *Sarvadharmavyapetaṁ* (LI, p. 34.13). Sthiramati (P Mi 123b2–3): "neither phenomena in general, nor the perfections in particular, are characterized as either subject or object." dBal Mang (55a4) explains that *sarvadharmaṁ samuditam* explains verse 10.4 in detail, that all things are included in the selfless truth body of thatness. *Sarvadharmavyapetaṁ* explains verse 10.5, because the truth body excludes all things in their imagined nature. Alternatively, *dharma* here can be understood as "qualities," buddhahood including the powers and fearlessnesses and so forth, and excluding all conceptualizations of subject and object.

[9] The Tibetan (D Phi 152b6) also has this phrase just before verse 10.4.

[10] Compare *Saddharmapuṇḍarīkasūtra* III 86, 87.

[11] The Tibetan (D Phi 153a6) reads *rga ba* "old age" instead of *skye ba* "birth," which latter is supported by the commentary.

[12] *Kleśakarmajanmasaṁkleśa* (LI, p. 34.23). See *Siddhi* pp. 215–218.

This second verse shows in detail that it delivers beings from injuries and so forth. It is a deliverance from all injuries; since through the buddha's power the blind recover sight, the deaf hearing, the mentally disturbed a healthy mind, and the sick a cure, and so on.[14] It is a deliverance from hellish rebirths; since through a buddha's radiance those who have been reborn there are liberated and (others) are granted immunity from being born there.[15] It is a deliverance from unliberating arts; for it raises (beings) up from the views of the religious. It is a deliverance from materiality; for it leads to final freedom by means of the two vehicles. It is a deliverance from the individual vehicle (alone); for it makes the universal vehicle the inclusive vehicle for those of indeterminate genealogy.

> 9. Supreme buddhahood is accepted as the incomparable refuge. It grants protection amidst births and deaths, amidst all addictions and hellish migrations, for all those who have fallen into various dangers, materiality, (inferior) vehicles, unremitting suffering of various kinds, hellish rebirths, and unliberating arts.[16]

This third verse shows by that same meaning that this refuge is supreme, peerless and incomparable.

---

[13] *Satkāya* (LI, p. 34.25). Here the equivalent of *satkāyadṛṣṭi*; Sthiramati (P Mi 125bl–2). It is the false view that affirms the transitory body of the five psycho-physical systems to be the self or the property of a self. In XVIII.92 it is identical to *saṁkleśa*. (See LII, p. 70, n. 8.1).

[14] The traditional miracles produced by the presence of a buddha. (See LII, p. 70, n. 8.2).

[15] *Tadagamane ca pratiṣṭhāpanāt* (LI, p. 35.3). See VII.5.

[16] The Tibetan (D Phi 153b3) reads differently, yet closely enough to indicate the jumbled state of Lévi's Sanskrit manuscript: */ sangs rgyas nyid de skyabs ni dpe med mchog tu 'dod / / sna tshogs 'jigs 'gyur 'jig tshogs kun dang theg pa dang / / ngan song rnam mang sdug bsngal thabs min song ba rnams / / skye dang 'chi dang nyon mongs ngan song kun las srung /* Line 1 of the Sanskrit text (LI, p. 35.6) is alright: *śaraṇamanupamaṁ tacchreṣṭhabuddhatvamiṣṭhaṁ*, but line 2 should be emended (emendations underlined): *jananamaraṇasarvakleśāpāyeṣu rakṣā*, and line 3: *vividhabhayagatasarvasatkāyayānānaṁ*, and line 4: *pratatavividhaduḥkhāpāyānupāgānāṁ* /. This follows the Tibetan exactly, the emendations fit well with the orthography, and it makes much better sense in keeping with the commentary and the previous verse.

> 10. Buddhahood is accepted[17] as the best of refuges in this world, with a body utterly fulfilled with the buddha-qualities, (with a mind) knowing how to guide beings in the holy Dharma, (with deeds) transcendent out of mercy towards all beings.

This fourth verse shows the reasons why this is such an unexcelled refuge. It is the ultimate success in individualistic aims, since its nature is perfect fulfillment with all buddha qualities such as the strengths and fearlessnesses. It is also the ultimate success in altruistic aims, since it is the knowledge of the arts of guiding beings in the holy Dharma and since it is compassion that has become transcendent.[18]

> 11.[19] For as long as the world may last, buddhahood is accepted as the great refuge of all beings, as it eliminates all evil and brings forth all perfections.

This fifth verse (on buddhahood as refuge) shows in summary for how long a time, for how many beings, and for what purpose it is a refuge. For what purpose? For eliminating all evil and bringing forth all perfections.

Six verses on the foundational transmutation:[20]

---

[17] Lévi's alternate *iheṣṭhaṁ* (LII, p. 71, n. 10.1) for *ihatyaṁ* (LI, p. 35.10) is supported by the Tibetan *'dod* (D Phi 153b5). See also LI, p. 35, n. 4: *ihaiṣyaṁ*.

[18] *Karuṇāpāragamanāt* (LI, p. 35.13). This provides another instance reinforcing the translation "transcendence" for *pāramitā*, as "perfection" is proper for *niṣṭhā*, *susaṁpūrṇa*, *sampanna*, and so forth, terms relating to completion and fulfillment, expressions not chosen as equivalent with *pāragamana*.

[19] Quoted at the conclusion of the nine similes in the chapter "Bondage by the Infinity of Passions" in the 6th chapter of the Chinese translation of the *RGV* (Ui, p. 606).

[20] *Āśrayaparāvṛtti* (LI, p. 35.17). Literally, "revolution of the support." In the *BBh* p. 253–4 Asaṅga explains the term as the expulsion from the *āśraya* of all depravity (*dauṣṭhulya*) as a result of which the bodhisattva's *āśraya* is transformed (*pravartate*) so that he never more commits any sin which would result in a bad rebirth. Compare *MS* 43b3–4. However, like the *BBh*, our text is silent on exactly what it is which undergoes the transmutation. On the term *āśraya* in the *MSA*, see G. Nagao, "Connotations of the Word *Āśraya* (Basis) in the *Mahāyāna-Sūtrālaṁkāra*," ch. 7 in *Mādhyamika and Yogācāra* (Albany: SUNY Press, 1991). According to Sthiramati (P Mi 127b8–128a2), *āśraya* is here the group of five psychophysical systems. For the literature on this term see *La Somme*, II p. 16, and pp. 609–612.

> 12. When the seed of the addictive and objective obscurations, which has been continuously persistent from primordial time, is destroyed by all kinds of very extensive abandonments, then buddhahood is attained as a transmutation of the vital foundation, endowed with the superior excellence of virtuous qualities, by means of the path of utterly pure nonconceptual (contemplative) intuition and of (aftermath intuition) extremely great in scope.

This verse shows that the foundational transmutation comes from freedom from the seed of the resistances and from possession of the perfection of the remedies, and is attained by means of two types of path; an utterly pure path of transcendent intuition, and a path of an aftermath intuition whose scope is the infinity of objects.[21] "Primordial" means from beginningless time. "By all kinds of very extensive abandonments" means by the kinds (of abandonments practiced) on the bodhisattva stages.

> 13. Standing there, a transcendent lord surveys the world as if he stood upon the great king of mountains. As he feels compassion for those who delight in peace, what need to speak of other persons who delight in existence?[22]

This second verse shows the superiority of such foundational transmutation over other (transmutations).[23] Standing there (in suchness, a buddha) gazes out over the world, distant, middling, and near as if he were standing upon the great

---

[21] Sthiramati (P Mi 129a3): the intuition whose object *siddhi* is the infinity of knowables is mundane. Compare *RGV* p. 88.13–14: *dvividhaṁ jñānaṁ lokottaraṁ avikalpaṁ tatpṛṣṭha-labdhaṁ* (*laukikaṁ*, after the Tibetan) *ca / laukikalokottarajñānaṁ āśrayaparivṛttir hetuṁ*. "Intuition is of two kinds, transmundane, which is non-differentiative, and mundane, which is acquired after it. The mundane and transmundane intuitions are the cause of the foundational transmutation." See Obermiller, *The Sublime Science*, pp. 241–2.

[22] Reading, according to Lévi's suggestion (LII, p. 72, n. 13.1), *bhavābhirāme* for *janamaghābhirāme* (LI, p. 36.5).

[23] Following the Tibetan (D Phi 154a5), *gnas yongs su gyur pa de gzhan las khyad par du ston*, in Sanskrit *āśrayaparāvṛtir anyebhyastadviśeṣaṁ darśayati* instead of Lévi's manuscript (LI, p. 36.6): *anyāśrayaparāvṛtibhyastadviśeṣaṁ darśayati*, which would pose the awkward problem of trying to imagine what "other foundational transmutations" Vasubandhu might have had in mind.

king of mountains. Upon gazing he feels compassion even for disciples and hermit buddhas. How much more so towards others?[24]

> 14. The foundational transmutation of the transcendent lords is accepted as a "pro-mutation," a "super-mutation," a "dis-mutation," a "de-mutation," a "per-mutation," a "dual" (mutation), a "nondual" (mutation), an "equal" (mutation), a "special" (mutation), and a "universal (mutation)."[25]

This third verse shows (transmutation) in its ten varieties: the transcendent lords' foundational transmutation is a "pro-mutation" because it mutates for the sake of others. It is a "super-mutation," that is, the greatest mutation, because of its superiority to all other things. It is a "dis-mutation" with regard to the cause of addictions. (These are all) foundational, shown to be foundational transmutations. It is a "de-mutation" because it ceases addictions. It is a "per-mutation" since its mutation persists until eternity. It is a "dual mutation" because it mutates to show both perfect enlightenment and ultimate liberation. It is a "nondual mutation" as it is unlocatable either in the life-cycle or in liberation, created or uncreated. It is an "equal mutation" because it is equal with disciples and hermit buddhas through the commonality of their liberations. It is a "special mutation" because the buddha qualities of the strengths, fearlessnesses, and so on are uncommon. It is a "universal mutation" because it is present in the teachings of all vehicles.

> 15.[26] As space is considered always omnipresent, so this[27] (transmutation) is considered always omnipresent: as space is omnipresent in the multitude of forms, so this (transmutation) is omnipresent in the multitude of beings.

---

24 Sthiramati (P Mi 129b2): ordinary beings.

25 This play on mutation (*vṛtti*) is achieved by adding the prefixes *pra-*, *ud-*, *a-*, *ni-*, *ā-*, *dvaya-*, *advaya-*, *samā-*, *viśiṣṭā-*, *sarvagā-*.

26 Quoted slightly differently in the commentary to *RGV* I.147. See Johnston's edition (*RGV*), p. 71.2–5.

27 Sthiramati (P Mi 130b8) equates the foundational transmutation here with the *dharma-dhātu*, and buddhahood as the ultimate reality of all things.

This fourth verse shows the omnipresence of buddhahood whose reality is that (of the foundational transmutation). The analogy to space is set forth in the first half and explained in the second. It should be understood that buddhahood's omnipresence in the multitude of beings is due to the perfection of (a buddha's) acceptance[28] of all living beings as himself.

> 16.[29] Just as the reflection of the moon cannot be seen in a broken water pot, so the buddha's reflection is not seen in evil beings.

This fifth verse proves by means of an example that despite omnipresence, the image of a buddha is not seen in beings who are not fit vessels.

> 17. Like a fire which blazes in one place but goes out elsewhere, so should appearance and disappearance be understood in the case of buddhas.

This sixth verse shows by the example of a fire which blazes and goes out that buddhas appear, because a buddha is born when there are good people fit to be cultivated by a buddha, and that buddhas disappear, because they pass into ultimate liberation when beings have become civilized.

There are four verses on the activities of a buddha being spontaneous and uninterrupted:

> 18.[30] Like the emergence of sounds from unstruck drums,[31] so, for a victor, the emergence of teaching is free of conscious effort.

---

[28] *Upagamana* (LI, p. 36.23). See also II.4 on *abhyupagama.*

[29] Compare this verse and the following with *MS* X.31–32 (47a3–4): *sems can nyes pas mi snang ste / snod chag pa yi zla ba bzhin / / 'jig rten kun la nyi bzhin du / de dag chos 'od khyab par mdzad / / la lar rdzogs par byang chub ston / la lar me bzhin mya ngan 'das / / nam yang med pa ma yin te / de bzhin gshegs pa rnams kyi sku / /* "Due to the faults of living beings it does not appear, like the moon in a broken pot; yet the dharma-rays pervade all the world like the sun. Like a fire, perfect enlightenment is shown to some and Nirvāṇa to others; eternal is the body of the Tathāgatas."

[30] Compare this verse and the following with *MS* IX.23 (40b7–8): *ji ltar nor bu sil snyan dag / rtag pa med pa rang las byung / / de ltar rtag tu rtog med par / sangs rgyas phrin las sna*

(cont'd)

19. Just as a jewel effortlessly radiates its luminosity, so the buddhas manifest their deeds without any conscious effort.

These two verses prove the spontaneity of buddha-activities by analogy with the sound of an unstruck drum and the luminosity of a jewel.

20. Just as the activities of people appear uninterruptedly in space, so the activities of the victors appear uninterruptedly in the uncontaminated realm.

21. Just as activities (of people) continually arise and cease in space, so also the activities of buddhas arise and cease in the uncontaminated realm.[32]

These two verses show that a buddha's activities are without interruption; for a buddha's activity is incessant. It is like the activities of the people in space; although they are without interruption, some arise and others come to an end.

There are sixteen verses on the profundity of the uncontaminated realm:

22. Although not different before and after, it is unspoiled by any obscuration. Suchness is accepted as buddhahood, neither pure nor impure.

It is not pure because it is not different before and after.[33] It is not impure because it is subsequently unspoiled by any obscuration, free of any taint.

---

tshogs byung / / "Like a jewel or gongs which appear of themselves without thought are the various buddha deeds which appear without conceptual thought."

[31] *Tūrya* (LI, p. 37.8). Tibetan: *rnga* (D Phi 155a1). Chinese: *tian gu* (heavenly drum) (T.31.602b16). Although *tūrya* is properly cymbals or a gong (*MVy* 5021, *sil-snyan*), it also customarily denotes the heavenly drum (*devadundubhi*) which hangs in the palace of Indra and which, without being struck, summons the gods to hear the Dharma. See *RGV* IV.31–37 (p. 102.5–19), quoted from the *Jñānālokālaṁkārasūtra*; for a translation of this *RGV* passage see Obermiller, *The Sublime Science*, p. 273.

[32] *Anāsravadhātu* (LI, p. 37.19). See below vs. 21–37. On the various theories concerning the "outflows," see *Siddhi* pp. 694–702. In our *śāstra* the unpolluted realm is identical to *dharmadhātu*, *dharmakāya*, *tathatā*, the "noble lineage" (*āryagotra*, XI.43), and liberation (*vimukti*, XI.44).

> 23.[34] In pure voidness buddhas achieve the supreme self of selflessness,[35] and realize the spiritual greatness of the self by discovering the pure self.

This shows the supreme self of the buddhas[36] in the uncontaminated realm. Why? Because hers is the self of supreme selflessness. Supreme selflessness is completely pure suchness, and that is a buddha's "self," in the sense of "intrinsic reality." When this is completely pure, buddhas attain superior selflessness, a pure self. Therefore, by attaining a pure self buddhas realize the spiritual greatness of self.[37] Thus it is with this intention that buddhas are declared to have a supreme self in the uncontaminated realm.

> 24.[38] That is why buddhahood is said neither to exist nor not to exist. When such inquiries are made about a buddha, the way of impredicability is preferred.[39]

For that reason,[40] buddhahood is not said to exist, for suchness[41] is characterized by the (ultimate) nonexistence of persons and things. Since buddhahood

---

33 Sthiramati (P Mi 138b2–4): before and after refer to pre- and post-buddhahood. The body of truth, that is, Thusness, is empty and luminous by nature at both times. As there is nothing in itself to be purified it is "not pure"; but since its adventitious defilements have been purified at the time of buddhahood it is not "impure."

34 According to Ui, p. 607, this verse is quoted in the Chinese version of the *RGV.*

35 Following the Tibetan (D Phi 155a6), *bdag med mchog gi bdag thob pas*, and emending the Lévi manuscript from *nairātmyānmārgalābhataḥ* (LI, p. 37.25) to *nairātmyātmāgralābhataḥ*.

36 *Buddhānāṁ paramātmā* (LI, p. 39.1). Here we see in unmistakable terms the Upaniṣadic formula applied to the buddha, preceding by centuries the Vedantic renaissance led by Śaṅkarācārya and his followers, whose philosophical and soteriological debt to the Buddhist experientialists cannot be appreciated without a thorough knowledge of the Maitreyanātha corpus and its attendant literature.

37 Compare *RGV* p. 31.10–16. See Obermiller, *The Sublime Science*, pp. 168–9.

38 This verse is quoted in prose in the commentary to vs. 23 in the Chinese version of the *RGV* (Ui, p. 607).

39 *Avyākṛtanaya* (LI, p. 38.7). On the "unanswered questions" see Jayatilleke, *Early Buddhist Theory of Knowledge*, para. 807, and Murti, *Central Philosophy of Buddhism*, p. 34 *ff.*

40 That is, because the buddha's self is selflessness.

has such a nature, it is also not said that it does not exist, for it exists in the nature of suchness. Therefore, when inquiries are made about the existence or nonexistence of a buddha, such as whether or not a transcendent lord exists after death, impredicability is preferred.

> 25. Like the fading of heat in iron and of shadows in vision is (the fading of delusions) in the buddha's mind and intuition; it cannot be declared as either existent or nonexistent.

The fading of heat in iron and shadows[42] in vision is not existent, for its characteristic is the nonexistence of heat or shadows; yet it is not nonexistent, for it exists through its nature of fading. In the same way, the fading, in the mind and intuition of buddhas, of attachment and ignorance which correspond to heat and cataracts, is not declared to be existent, as it manifests as nonexistence, and yet is not (declared to be) nonexistent, as the liberations of mind and intuition exist through their respective natures of liberation.

> 26. For buddhas, in the immaculate realm there is neither unity nor plurality, because they are incorporeal like space and yet still accord with their previous bodies.

In the uncontaminated realm, buddhas have no unity due to their accord with their previous bodies, nor have they plurality, for, like space, they are incorporeal.

> 27. Enlightenment is thought to resemble a jewel mine of the buddha qualities such as the powers, and to resemble a great raincloud (that nourishes) the crops of virtues of beings.

> 28. It is thought to resemble the full moon, full of merit and intuition, and to resemble a giant sun, radiating the light of intuition.

---

[41] The Tibetan *de bzhin nyid ni* (D Phi 155b2) translates *tathatāyāṁ*, which is lacking in Sanskrit. Compare LII, p. 69, n. 1.

[42] Read *timirasya* (LI, p. 38.13).

These two verses comparing (enlightenment) to a jewel mine, a great rain-cloud, the full moon, and a giant sun are self-explanatory.

> 29. Countless rays of light merge together in the disc of the sun and always perform a common function and illuminate the world.
>
> 30. Just so, it is considered that innumerable buddhas merge together in the uncontaminated realm and work together in their deeds and radiate the sunlight of intuitive wisdom.

The first verse shows the common function (of the buddhas) through their analogy with the common function of merged rays of sunlight. The common activity of light rays should be understood through the uniform activities of ripening, drying, and so forth. The second verse shows that in the uncontaminated realm their common activity merges in their deeds such as emanations.[43]

> 31. When a single ray of sunlight is emitted all the sun's rays are emitted; and so should one recognize the emission of the intuitive wisdom of the buddhas.

This shows, by means of (the analogy of the sun's) simultaneous emission of all its rays, the simultaneous function of the intuitions of all the buddhas.[44]

> 32. As there is no possessiveness in the operation of the sun's rays, so there is no possessiveness in the operation of the buddhas' intuitions.
>
> 33. As the world is illumined by the rays from the sun's single emission of light, so the buddhas' intuitions simultaneously illumine all objects.

---

[43] G. Nagao here points out that Sthiramati seems to regard this as a technical description of the functions of sunrays, their "merging function" *'dres pa gcig tu 'jug pa* (**miśrakāvṛtti*; *MVy* 4195) and their "uniform operation function" *bya ba gcig tu 'jug pa* (**ekakāryavṛtti*).

[44] The manuscript *sa ca* (LI, p. 39.11) should not be emended to *saha*, as Bagchi suggests (Bagchi 42.11), but rather to *sarva*, following common sense and the Tibetan *thams cad* (D Phi 156a4).

These two verses on, respectively, the (buddha-intuitions') absence of possessiveness and simultaneous illumination of all objects,[45] are self explanatory.

> 34. Just as clouds and so forth are thought to obscure the rays of sunlight, so the deficiencies of beings obscure the buddhas' intuitions.

Just as clouds and so forth obscure the rays of sunlight by not allowing them to shine,[46] so the deficiencies of beings obscure the buddhas' intuitions, those beings not being receptive[47] (to the buddha wisdom) due to their deficiencies of excessive involvement in the five corruptions.[48]

> 35. Just as it is on account of knotting[49] that coloring is brilliant or faint on variegated cloth, so it is on account of evolutionary momentum that intuition is brilliant or faint in liberation.

Just as it is through a particular knot that color on cloth will be brilliant in one place and faint in another place,[50] in the same way it is due to a particular instinctual storing of the strength to carry out a previous aspiration that intuition is brilliant in the liberation of buddhas, but faint in the liberations of the disciples and the hermit buddhas.

---

45 The Tibetan (D Phi 156a6) reads *sakṛt* (*cig car*) for *jagat* (LI, p. 39.15), which is preferable in this context.

46 The Sanskrit (LI, p. 39.20) and Chinese (T.31.604b15) read *aprabhāsena*, but the Tibetan (D Phi 156a7) and Sthiramati *pratibhāsane*.

47 See *BBS* I, sec. 3.10.

48 The five "degeneracies" (*kaṣāya*, LI, p. 39.21) are 1) lifespan, 2) living beings, 3) affliction, 4) wrong views, and 5) aeon. See *BBh* p. 173 *ff.*

49 The Sanskrit (LI, p. 39.22) gives *pāṁśu* "dust," as in *pāṁśukūla*, the rags from a dust heap out of which the monk makes his robes. See Edgerton, p. 338, s.v. *pāṁśukūla*. The Chinese (T.31.604b17) renders it as *tzu-hui*, muddy ashes, which Ui (p. 68) takes to be a kind of dye. The Tibetan (D Phi 155a7), however, gives *mdud*, "knot," which suggests a possible *pāśa*. Sthiramati (P Mi 138b5–6) confirms the Tibetan translation in describing the process referred to in the verse as tie dying: "When a white cloth is knotted up and subjected to a dye the unknotted portion takes the color forming a pattern with the knotted part."

50 Omitted in Sanskrit; see the Tibetan translation (D Phi 156b1).

36. The profundity of the buddhas in the immaculate realm has been expressed in terms of characteristic, place, and actions; yet it is like painting the sky with colors.

The three types of profundity of the buddhas in the uncontaminated realm have been explained as follows: four verses (22–25) on the profundity of characteristics, a fifth (26) on the profundity of place due to being unlocatable as a unity or as a diversity, and ten verses (27–36) on the profundity of actions. In addition the profundity of characteristics has been spoken of in terms of the characteristic of complete purity (22), the characteristic of the highest self (23), the characteristic of the impredicable (24), and the characteristic of liberation (25). Profundity of actions has been spoken of from the point of view of actions based on the jewels of the accessories of enlightenment, and so forth (27ab), actions of bringing living beings to maturity (27cd), the action of arriving at culmination (28ab), the action of teaching the Dharma (28cd), the action of creating emanations and so forth (29–30), the action of the function of intuition (31), the action of nonconceptuality (32), the action of intuition with various aspects (33), the action of non-functioning intuition (34), and the action of distinctive intuitions within similar liberations (35). It should be understood that since it is unfabricated,[51] the uncontaminated realm is like space, and therefore teaching about the varieties of its profundity is like painting the sky with colors.[52]

---

[51] *Niṣprapañca* (LI, p. 40.11). Sthiramati (P Mi 139a8): without the duality of subject and object.

[52] Asvabhāva (P Bi 78b8) gives the *Sāgaramatisūtra* as the authority for the examples of the variegated cloth (*gos bkra ba nyid*) in vs. 35 and figures in the sky in vs. 36. In the *Ārya-sāgaramatiparipṛcchāsūtra* (mDo Pu 90a8–90b6) the followers of the disciple vehicles, hermit sage vehicle, and the buddha vehicle are compared to pieces of paper (*ras sog bu yug*), cheap fabric (*ras phran yug*) and fine fabric (*ras bcos bu*) respectively, which, when placed into a vat (*snod*) containing blue, red, and gold (i.e., the disciple vehicle, etc.) pick up one color or the other depending upon how they are twisted (*de dag snod gcig gi nang du bcug ste bscu* (sic., see Jäschke's Tibetan Dictionary, p. 144 s.v. *gcud, lcud*) *bas na ji ltar kha bsgyur ba'i bye brag bzhin du tshon 'dzin te*), that is, according to the disposition (*bsam pa*) of the disciple, etc. As for the example of painting of the sky, we have been unable to locate a parallel in the above named sūtra.

37.[53] Although suchness is in all beings without distinction, when it has become pure it is transcendent buddhahood: therefore all beings have its embryonic essence.

There is suchness in all beings without distinction, while a transcendent lord has it as his nature in pure form. Hence it is said that all living beings have the embryonic essence of a transcendent buddha.[54]

There are eleven verses on the analysis of mastery:[55]

38.[56] The mastery of disciples surpasses that of ordinary persons, and that of the hermit buddha stage[57] surpasses that of the disciples;

39. (but) that does not approach even a fraction of the mastery of bodhisattvas, and that does not approach even a fraction of the mastery of transcendent lords.

These two verses show the mastery of the buddhas through the distinctiveness of their outstanding powers.

40. The buddhas' mastery is accepted as immeasurable and inconceivable, in terms of for whom, where, how, to what extent, and for what length of time it is exercised.

---

[53] Quoted in the commentary to *RGV* I.48; compare also *RGV* I.27.

[54] *Tathāgatagarbhā* (LI, p. 40.16). Sthiramati (P Mi 139b 1–4): identical to *tathatā* and *nairātmya*. As there is no difference in *nairātmya* between ordinary beings and saints, except that for the latter it has been purified of adventitious defilements, in which case it is called "*Tathāgata*," all beings are *Tathāgata* in embryo.

[55] See *DBhS*, p. 63.16–21. Quoted in Sthiramati (P Mi 140a5–140b1).

[56] *Vibhutva* (LI, p. 40.17). It is defined below in vs. 48 as the "accomplishment of inconceivable actions." The commentary to XVI.16 classifies it as being of three types: body (*kāya*), conduct (*caryā*), and preaching (*deśanā*). The first is the province of the intrinsic reality and beatific bodies, the second of the emanation body. The third consists of unimpeded preaching of the six transcendences in all their aspects.

[57] Lévi's suggested emendation of *pratyekabuddhebhyo manaṁ* (LI, p. 40.18) to *pratyekabuddhabhaumena* (LII, p. 80, n. 38.1) suitably accords with the Tibetan *rang sangs rgyas kyi sa pa yis /* (D Phi 157a2).

This third verse shows how it is immeasurable through a division into types and through the specifications of its profundity. How is it inconceivable? In terms of the person for whose sake, of the universe where, of how in what manner, of what degree, little or great, and for how long a time it is exercised.

The remaining verses show the types of mastery according to differences in transmutation.[58]

> 41.[59] Highest mastery is attained in the transmutation of the five sense faculties, in the operation of all (faculties) upon all objects, and in the arising of twelve hundred virtues.

Two kinds of supreme mastery are attained when the five faculties are transmuted: mastery over all five sense faculties in their operation upon all five objects[60] and mastery over the arising of twelve hundred virtues for each.

> 42. Highest mastery is attained in the transmutation of the (addicted) mentality,[61] and in the perfectly immaculate, nonconceptual intuition[62] which accompanies such mastery.

When the mentality is transmuted, highest mastery is attained in that intuition which accompanies mastery, which is nonconceptual and very pure, together with which all knowledge of mastery operates.

> 43. In the transmutation of perception[63] with its object, highest mastery is attained in a pure land, wherein one manifests enjoyments at will.

---

[58] Sthiramati (P Mi 140a7) takes transmutation in the sense of purification.

[59] See for example the eighteenth chapter of the *Saddharmapuṇḍarīkasūtra*.

[60] Sthiramati (P Mi 140a8): after purification, any of the senses will be able to exercise the function of all, the eye will hear, and so on.

[61] Sthiramati (P Mi 142a2–4): here *manas* stands for the *kliṣṭamanas*. See also XI.45 on the transmutation of the *manas*.

[62] Sthiramati (P Mi 142b3): this intuition is either the transformed *ālayavijñāna* or (142b7) the transformed *kliṣṭamanas* which is the *samatājñāna*. The reasons for its being the former are obscure, since its transmutation is described in verse 45 below.

In the transmutations of the object and of perception, highest mastery is attained in purifying the (buddha) land, wherein one freely manifests enjoyments.

> 44. In the transmutation of discriminative thought, highest mastery is attained, while all intuitions and actions are unimpeded at all times.

In the transmutation of discriminations, highest mastery is attained, intuitions and actions being entirely unimpeded at all times.

> 45. In the transmutation of the foundation,[64] highest mastery is attained, which is the unlocated[65] Nirvāṇa in the immaculate state of buddhas.

In the transmutation of the foundation, highest mastery is attained which is the unlocated Nirvāṇa in the buddhas' uncontaminated realm.

> 46.[66] In the transmutation of (sensation, even in) sexual union, highest mastery is attained in the station of the buddhas' bliss, while in the unaddicted vision of the consort.

In the transmutation of (sensation even in) sexual union, both (partners) stand in the buddhas' bliss and in the unaddicted vision of the consort.

---

63 *Udgraha* (LI, p. 41.12). The group of five sense consciousnesses; XI.41.

64 *Pratiṣṭhā* (LI, p. 41.19). Sthiramati (P Mi 143b5–7): the *ālayavijñāna*. See also XI.44 on the transmutation of the *ālaya* which is also called "seed" (*bīja*).

65 *Apratiṣṭhita* (LI, p. 41.20).

66 This verse has been taken by some scholars, such as Lévi and Bagchi, to be a reference to tantric practices. This view was rejected by Winternitz who understood *parāvṛtti* (LI, p. 41.23) in this context to mean "turning aside, discard." See S.B. Dasgupta, *An Introduction to Tantric Buddhism*, pp. 53–54. See also XIII.11–13 for another possible allusion to tantric practice by Asaṅga, as well as *AS* p. 108. The tantric allusion here could not be clearer, replete with *buddhasaukhyavihāre* (LI, p. 41.24). However, dBal Mang does not give the verse a tantric interpretation, stating that this verse refers to the transmutation of sensation (*vedanā*), and that the ability to remain dispassionate even in sexual union is an illustration of the enlightened person's mastery.

> 47. In the transmutation[67] of the conception of space,[68] highest mastery is attained, in the wealth of obtaining any object desired and in the opening up of motion and matter.

In the transmutation of the conception of space, highest mastery of two types is attained, in that objects are obtained just by wishing for them, through which space becomes a treasury, and in the opening up of motion and matter because one moves (through anything) and creates space as one wishes.

> 48. Thus mastery is considered immeasurable through immeasurable transmutations, as it can accomplish inconceivable works in the stainless station of the buddhas.

Thus, from this perspective, the transmutations are immeasurable. Here it should be understood that the highest mastery is the accomplishment of inconceivable deeds in the buddhas' uncontaminated realm.

Seven verses on such a (masterful) buddha as the cause for bringing beings to maturity:

> 49. Everywhere the world progresses, thanks to the good instructions of the victors: those advanced in virtue reach supreme perfection, while those backward in virtue advance to the greatest increase; thus there is steady progress for both mature and immature, although it never attains totality.[69]

This shows the kind of maturing of which (a buddha) is the cause. Those who have amassed the roots of virtue (are caused to) advance to a high degree of liberation. Those who have not amassed the roots of virtue (are caused) to amass the roots of virtue. The immature become mature in advancing to a high degree of

---

[67] The Sanskrit reads *vyāvṛttau* (LI, p. 42.2) instead of *parāvṛttau* here, though the Tibetan reads *gzhan gyur* as usual.

[68] *Ākāśasaṁjñā* (LI, p. 42.2). Sthiramati (P Mi 144a7–8): the idea that wherever there is obstruction there is form, and wherever there is no obstruction there is space.

[69] The Tibetan clearly translates a variant Sanskrit, calling for moving our Lévi manuscript (LI, p. 42.11–14) line 3 to line 1 and emending the last line, *apakvaḥ pakvo vā (na) ca punaraśeṣaṁ dhruvamiha* to something like *tathāpakvaḥ pakvo vā vrajati dhruvamapi nāśeṣaṁ*. The Tibetan (D Phi 158a1) reads *de ltar ma smin smin pa rtag 'gro ma lus min.*

growth in virtue. The mature advance to a high degree of perfection. Thus does the world constantly progress; and yet it never becomes a (perfect) totality, since it is infinite.

> 50. It is a great wonder of this world that everywhere the brave (bodhisattvas) constantly attain on all occasions the great enlightenment, so hard to gain, so marvelous in endowment with supreme excellence, such a sure and constant refuge for the refugeless; and yet it is not a wonder, since they have practiced the excellent way.[70]

This second verse shows the wondrous and non-wondrous character of the maturity of mature bodhisattvas. "(They attain) constantly and on all occasions" means (that they attain) always and without interruption, and (that they) "have practiced the excellent way" means (that they have) practiced the path consistent with (great enlightenment).

> 51. Simultaneously[71] through many hundreds of doors, (a buddha) displays the (turning of the) wheel of Dharma in one place, in an-

---

[70] Sthiramati (P Mi 146b6–7): they are reaping the fruit of that which they have sown and cultivated. dBal Mang comments (63b–64a) that it is not so wonderful from one point of view, since they have practiced the excellent way of the six transcendences and so on, and so their buddhahood, the perfection of their individualistic and altruistic drives, follows naturally, just as a Shala tree grows naturally from the Shala tree seed.

Again the Sanskrit of this verse is in poor shape, as Lévi seems aware from the many parenthetic emendations he makes. According to the Tibetan, which is quite clear, it should be emended as follows:

> *tathā kṛcchrāvāpyāṁ paramaguṇayogādbhutavatīṁ*
> *mahābodhiṁ nityāṁ dhruvamaśaraṇānāṁ ca śaraṇaṁ /*
> *labhante yaddhīrā diśi diśi sadā sarvasamayaṁ*
> *tadāścaryaṁ loke suvidhacaraṇānāścaryamapi / /*

> *de ltar 'jig rten phyogs phyogs brtan rnams rtag par dus kun du (tu) /*
> *byang chub chen po thob dka' yon tan mchog ldan rmad byung can /*
> *rtag brtan skyabs med rnams kyi skyabs gang yin pa thob pa de /*
> *ya mtshan che la tshul bzang spyad phyir ya mtshan che ba'ang med / /*
> (D Phi 158a3–4).

[71] The Tibetan reads *cig car* (D Phi 158a5), *yugapat*, which should be placed at the end of the third line in place of the *asakṛt* (LI, p. 43.5), which has the opposite, and contextually less desirable meaning. The commentary also has *yugapadbahumukha*.... The end of third

(cont'd)

> other invisible rebirth,[72] in still another various activities of beings, in another total enlightenment, and in still another liberation in Nirvāṇa: and he does all these without moving from that (ultimate) place.

This third verse shows (that a buddha) through many doors causes simultaneous implementation of arts for maturing (beings), how and in what place he dwells, and that he civilizes beings. "Various activities of beings" (refers to) the different *Former Life Tales*. "Without moving from that place" (refers to) the uncontaminated realm.

> 52.[73] Buddhas do not consider "This being have I matured," "This one will (I) mature,"[74] "(This one I) presently mature"; rather, beings (are caused to) advance towards evolutionary maturity without premeditated action, through (leading them into) constant, universal virtuous practices through the doors of the three (vehicles).

This fourth verse shows (a buddha) without premeditated action causing (beings) to implement their evolutionary maturity automatically. "Through the doors of the three" (refers to) the three vehicles.

> 53. Just as the sun effortlessly ripens the harvests of crops by universally emitting its bright and profuse rays of light in all directions, so the sun of Dharma accomplishes the evolutionary maturity of beings by universally emitting in every direction the light rays of the Dharma, which lead to peace.

This fifth verse shows a simile to illustrate the unpremeditated maturing (of beings).

---

line should so be emended to *nirvāṇaṁ yugapat*, or *nirvāṇaṁ sahakṛt* to stay closer to the orthography.

[72] *Janmāntardhiṁ* (LI, p. 43.4), glossed by dBal Mang as *'pho ba*, transmigration, or voluntarily assuming rebirth through the Between state, invisible to ordinary beings.

[73] This verse and the following one are consistent with the Chinese translation in the *Jñāna-ālokālaṁkārasūtra*; see *BBS* II, pp. 14–15.

[74] Reading with the Tibetan (D Phi 158a7), the Chinese (T.31.605c10), and Sthiramati, *rab tu smin bya* (*prapācyo*), rather than the Sanskrit manuscript *aprapācyo*.

> 54.[75] Just as a single lamp kindles an immeasurable, incalculable mass of many other lamps and yet does not become exhausted, so a single (buddha's) maturity kindles a measureless, incalculable host of many other (beings') maturities and yet never becomes exhausted.

This sixth verse shows evolutionary maturing through a process of transmission.

> 55. Just as the great ocean neither becomes saturated nor increased through the profusion of clear waters flowing into it, so the realm of the buddhas is neither saturated nor increased by a constant, continuous flow of pure (beings): and this is the greatest wonder of the world.

This seventh verse shows through a comparison with the great ocean that the ultimate realm is never saturated by the entrance of mature (beings) into liberation, for there is always room, nor does it increase, for there is nothing greater (than it).

Four verses on the perfection of the ultimate realm:[76]

> 56.[77] Its (negative) nature is the suchness of all things, purified of the two obscurations, and its (positive) nature is the inexhaustible mastery over the intuition into reality and (over the intuition) into it as (filled with relational) objects.[78]

---

[75] See *HTV* p. 39 quoted in Sthiramati (P Mi 148b7–149a2). Vimalakīrti, in the account given by the bodhisattva Jagatīṁdhara, cites this simile to Māra's goddesses when, after having instructed and delighted them with the Dharma, he consoles them before sending them back to Māra's heaven to serve there as inexhaustible lamps of Dharma.

[76] According to the *BBS*, which provides the basis for the rest of the chapter, the stage of buddhahood consists of five dharmas: the pure *dharmadhātu* and the four intuitions; see Sthiramati (P Mi 149b8).

[77] The original of this verse is found in *BBS* I, pp. 22–23.

[78] *Vastujñānatadālambavaśitākṣayalakṣaṇaṁ* (LI, p. 44.9). Sthiramati (P Mi 150a6–150bl): *vastu* = *ālayavijñāna*, and *vastujñāna* = pure mundane intuition. This intuition represents the transmutation of the *ālaya* as the support of "bad conditionings" (*dauṣṭhulya*). *Tad* = *dharmadhātu*. The *dharmadhātu* as the object of nonconceptual intuition represents the transmuta-

(cont'd)

This first verse is concerned with the topic of the reality (of the ultimate realm). Its (negative) nature is the suchness of all things, completely purified of the two obscurations, the addictive and the objective. And its (positive) nature is inexhaustible mastery over the two intuitions into (ultimate, unitary) reality and into that (reality) as (a plenum filled with) objects.

> 57. The understanding of suchness and its comprehensive meditation (lead to) total realization, whose fruition is inexhaustibility in providing the two (stores) to all beings in every possible way.

This second verse is concerned with the topics of cause and effect (in regard to the ultimate realm). Comprehensive meditation on the understanding of suchness is the cause of the perfection of the ultimate realm. "Comprehensive" means "through the doors of all the various formulations of the teaching." Its effect is (the buddhas') inexhaustibility in providing the two (stores) of (wisdom and merit that bring) benefit and happiness to all beings in every way.

> 58.[79] (The ultimate realm) has the action of technique in deployment of the (buddha) magical emanations of body, speech, and mind, and is endowed with the doors of concentration and retention,[80] and of the two immeasurable (stores).

This third verse is concerned with (the ultimate realm in terms of) the topics of activity and endowment. Its activity is the threefold magical emanation of body and so forth. Its endowment is possession of the doors of concentration and retention, and of the two immeasurable stores of merit and intuition.

---

tion of the path (*mārga*). On *dauṣṭhulya* and *mārgaparāvṛtti*, see *Siddhi*, p. 665. dBal Mang (64b–65a) clarifies, tacitly correcting Sthiramati's (or the translator's) equation of *vastujñāna* with mundane, aftermath intuition: "...because he has attained inexhaustible mastery of nonconceptual, equipoised intuition that realizes the reality (of source consciousness) and inexhaustible mastery of the aftermath intuition that realizes the object in that reality." Thus, he equates *vastu* with *ālaya*, *vastujñāna* with *samāhitajñāna*, and *tadālamba(jñāna)* with *pṛṣṭhalabdhajñāna*, much better in context.

[79] Quoted from *BBS*, loc. cit.

[80] On the "doors of concentration and retention" see XVIII.25–26, and on "retention," see XVIII.71–73.

> 59.[81] Its function differs in terms of (the bodies of) intrinsic reality, spiritual beatitude, and magical emanation. It is celebrated as the perfection of the ultimate realm of the buddhas.

This fourth verse is concerned with (the ultimate realm in terms of) the topic of function. Its function varies due to the functioning of the (buddha-) bodies of intrinsic reality, beatitude, and emanation.

There are seven verses on the analysis of the body of a buddha:[82]

> 60. The varieties of the body of buddhas are the intrinsic reality body, the beatific body, and the emanation body; and the first is the ground of the other two.

The body of the buddhas is threefold: The "intrinsic reality body" is the body of truth, whose nature is the foundational transmutation. The beatific body is that through which (a buddha) causes the circle of assemblies to enjoy the Dharma. And the emanation body is that through which they emanate (into the worlds) to fulfill the purposes of beings.

> 61. In all universes, the beatific body is distinguished by its gathering of hosts, its buddha-lands, its names, its bodies, its spiritual beatitudes, and its activities.

The beatific body differs in all universes due to its gathering of hosts, (sometimes consisting of (the bodhisattvas) Akṣayamati and so on, sometimes of Avalokiteśvara, Samantabhadra, and so on), in its buddha lands, (such as Akaniṣṭha and so on, made of jewels and gold and so on), in its names (such as Vairocana, Amitābha, and so on), in its bodies (endowed with auspicious marks and with different sizes and capacities), its enjoyment of the teachings (of the universal vehicle and so forth), and its activities (such as accomplishing the aims of beings).[83]

---

[81] Quoted from *BBS,* loc. cit.

[82] For a detailed discussion, see *Siddhi* II, pp. 762–813.

[83] The elucidations in brackets of these six attributes of the beatific body come from G. Nagao's reading of Sthiramati, and from dBal Mang's commentary (66a).

62. The reality body is considered equal, subtle, and integrated with that (beatific body); it is also considered the cause of the mastery of beatitude, (when buddhas) manifest beatitudes at (their) pleasure.

The intrinsic reality (body) of all the buddhas is equal because it lacks differentiations.[84] It is subtle because it is difficult (for the disciples and hermit buddhas) to understand. It is inter-related with the beatific body and is the cause of (the buddhas') mastery of beatitude in displaying at will the enjoyments (of such as buddha-lands and universal vehicle teachings and so forth).[85]

63. The emanation body is considered to consist of the innumerable emanations of a buddha; the fulfillment of the two aims (of self and other) is grounded in all forms on these two (beatific and emanation bodies).

The emanation body of the buddhas consists of the buddha emanations which are of immeasurable variety. The beatific body has the nature of the fulfillment of one's individual aims. The emanation body has the nature of the fulfillment of others' aims. Thus the (emanation body as the) fulfillment of the two aims rests, respectively, on the two, the truth body and the beatific body.[86]

---

[84] Sthiramati (P Mi 153a6): it being none other than the *dharmadhātu*.

[85] Material in brackets in this paragraph is from G. Nagao and Sthiramati.

[86] According to the Sanskrit Ms. (LI, p. 45.20), the Chinese translation (T.31.606c28), and Sthiramati, but the Tibetan (D Phi 159b4) has *rang bzhin gyi sku* (*svābhāvikakāya*) for *sāṁbhogika* following Asvabhāva (P Bi 82bl–3), according to which the fulfillment of one's own aims rests on the *dharmakāya*, whereas that of the aims of others rests on both the beatific and emanation bodies.

dBal Mang comments in a complex and interesting way here (66a6 *ff.*): "Consider the fulfillment of the two aims: it is grounded on the two form bodies of universal forms; fulfillment of individual aims grounded on the beatific body, in enjoying perfect station, company, and teaching, and fulfillment of altruistic aims grounded on the emanation body, manifesting bodies attuned to the inclinations of disciples. So, the text says, 'fulfillment of the two aims is grounded on the two, universal in their forms.' In one sense, the emanation body is grounded on the beatific body, and that beatific body is grounded on both truth and emanation bodies. Or else, the emanation body, universal in its forms, accomplishing the aims of self and other, itself is grounded on the other two bodies."

(cont'd)

64. Through its constant manifestation of art, incarnation, great enlightenment and Nirvāṇa, the emanation body of a buddha is the great art for the deliverance (of beings).

The emanation body always manifests for disciples as art, such as a performance upon the vīṇā and so forth, incarnations (as humans, animals, useful objects and so forth), and (the deeds of a supreme emanation body such as) utterly perfect enlightenment and Nirvāṇa. Therefore, it is the great art for deliverance (of beings). It should therefore be understood as having the nature of fulfillment of the aims of others.

65. The body of the buddhas should be understood as consisting of these three bodies; these three bodies make manifest the ground (of reality) and (fulfill) the aims of self and other.

All of the bodies of the buddhas are subsumed under these three bodies. These three bodies make manifest the aims of self and others, along with their ground. Two are revealed in (fulfilling) the aims of self and other, and (those) two are dependent on (the third), as previously stated.

66. These (three bodies) are considered equal in ground, intention,[87] and action; they have permanence by nature, by constancy, and by continuity.

The three bodies of all buddhas are without distinction in three ways, respectively: in ground, for the ultimate realm is undifferentiated; in intention, for no buddha has any peculiar intention; and in action, for their deeds are common. In these three bodies there are, respectively, a triple permanence, because of which it is said that the transcendent lords have eternal bodies. (They have) permanence by nature, because the intrinsic reality (body) is eternal by nature. (They have permanence) by constancy, through uninterruptedness, because the beatific body enjoys

So, we can conclude that either reading is possible, since truth and form bodies traditionally correspond to self- and other-fulfillment, but within form body, beatific and emanation bodies correspond self- and other-fulfillment modalities.

[87] Although the Sanskrit has *āśaya* (LI, p. 46.8), the Tibetan (D Phi 160a1) has *dgongs pa* (*saṁdhi*), preferable in context.

the Dharma without interruption. (And they have permanence) through continuity, because the emanation body manifests emanations again and again, even after disappearing (into Nirvāṇa).

There are ten verses on the analysis of buddha intuition:[88]

> 67.[89] The mirroring intuition is unmoving, and three (other) intuitions are dependent upon it, namely, equalizing, distinguishing, and all-accomplishing (intuitions).

The intuition of the buddhas is fourfold: the mirroring intuition, the equalizing intuition, the distinguishing intuition, and the all-accomplishing intuition. The mirroring intuition is unmoving, and the three intuitions based upon it move.[90]

> 68.[91] The mirroring intuition appropriates nothing as "mine," poses no divisions, always coheres, is without confusion amid all objects, and never confronts them.

The mirroring intuition is always free of "mine," it is without restriction from spatial location, it always coheres temporally, it is without confusion about all

---

88 For a detailed account of the various theories concerning the four intuitions, see *Siddhi* pp. 684–692.

89 The first two *pāda*s are based on *BBS* I.3.2, quoted in Sthiramati (P Mi 155b3–5), and the remaining *pāda*s on *BBS* I.3.4.

90 The Chinese translation of the commentary (T.31.606c25 *ff.*) adds that the four intuitions are the results of the transmutation of the 8th, 7th, 6th, and the group of five *vijñāna*s, respectively. This is also the view of Sthiramati (P Mi 128a2–5). According to Ui, p. 611, the doctrine of the attainment of the intuitions through the transmutation of the consciousnesses is unknown in the *YBh* and the *MS* simply states that the intuitions are attained through the transmutation of *vijñāna*.

dBal Mang comments (67b) that "moving" and "unmoving" indicate that the former is a nonconceptual, concentrated intuition, and the latter three are conceptual, aftermath intuitions.

91 The first two *pāda*s are based on *BBS* I.3.5 quoted in Sthiramati (P Mi 155b8–156a2), and *BBS* I.3.7 through *'gyur te*, quoted in Sthiramati (P Mi 156a4–5). The second two *pāda*s are based on *BBS* I.3.3., quoted in Sthiramati (P Mi 156a7–a56bl), and *BBS* I.3.6, in Sthiramati (P Mi 156b4–6).

objects because it is always free of obscurations, and it never confronts those (objects as a separate subjectivity), being imageless (in itself).[92]

> 69. It resembles a great mine of intuitive wisdoms, since it is the cause of all intuitions. It is beatific buddhahood itself,[93] (called "mirroring intuition") since the (other) intuitions arise as reflections within it.

As it is the cause of the equalizing and other intuitions in all their forms, it is like a great mine of all intuitions. And because beatific buddhahood and its intuitions arise in it like reflections, it is called the "mirroring intuition."

> 70. The equalizing intuition regarding beings is considered immaculate due to the purity of the meditation (equalizing self and other). Immersed in unlocalized peace, it is accepted as the equalizing intuition.[94]

At the time of direct realization,[95] the equalizing intuition towards beings that the bodhisattva acquires from purity of meditation (on) that (equality of self and other) is just the immersion in the unlocalized Nirvāṇa at the attainment of enlightenment: such intuition is called "equalizing intuition."

> 71.[96] It is considered always accompanied by great love and compassion, and it manifests the buddha image to beings according to their faith.

---

[92] dBal Mang explains here the five characteristics of the mirroring intuition (67a6–b2): "It has no 'I' and 'my' habits, poses no restrictions of east and west and object and subject, is continuous and uninterrupted, untroubled, clearly reflecting the images of all objects like a mirror, and not confronting any object, lacking conceptualization."

[93] Sthiramati (P Mi 157a2–3): *ālayavijñāna* = *saṁbhogakāya*.

[94] The source of the last two *pāda*s is the eighth characteristic of *samatājñāna* as found in *BBS* I.4.8, quoted in Sthiramati (P Mi 157b2).

[95] Sthiramati (P Mi 157a7): at the first of the bodhisattva levels.

[96] The source of this verse is the fourth, fifth, (both quoted in Sthiramati, P Mi 157b6) and sixth characteristics of *samatājñāna* in the *BBS* I.4.46. Sthiramati (P Mi 157b5) also cites a

(cont'd)

It is accompanied by great love and compassion at all times and it shows the buddha image to beings in accordance with their faith. It is for this reason that some beings see blue transcendent lords, some see yellow transcendent lords, and so on.[97]

> 72.[98] The distinguishing intuition is always unobstructed regarding objects, and it is just like a treasury of retentions and concentrations.

> 73.[99] It manifests all masteries in the circle of the hosts, and it rains down the great teaching which resolves all doubts.

Such is the distinguishing intuition according to the verse.

> 74.[100] The all-accomplishing intuition fulfills the aims of all beings in all realms through varied, inconceivable, and innumerable emanations.

---

passage from the *TOSN*: *sangs rgyas bcom ldan 'das rnams ni ye shes kyi zla ba chen po yin te / sems can thams cad la zhi ba nye bar ston pa'i phyir ro.* "The Lord buddhas are a great moon of intuition for they reveal peace to all living beings."

[97] Sthiramati (P Mi 157b8–158al) cites the following passage from the *Tathāgatācintya-guhyanirdeśa*: *sems can la las ni de bzhin gshegs pa'i kha dog sngon por / la las ni ser por mthong ba.* "Some living beings see a blue transcendent lord, some see a yellow." This passage is not to be found in the Tibetan version of that work, but compare *Dkon brTsegs* P Tshi 144b7–145a5. This is an intriguing suggestion of the presence of tantric visionary experiences even at the time of Vasubandhu.

[98] The source of the first two *pāda*s is the tenth characteristic of *pratyavekṣaṇājñāna* in *BBS* I.5.10 cited in Sthiramati (P Mi 158a4–5), and the source of the second two *pāda*s is the first characteristic in *BBS* I.5.1 cited in Sthiramati (P Mi 158b2–3). Sthiramati (P Mi 158a7–8) also cites a passage from *TOSN*: *sangs rgyas bcom ldan 'das rnams ni ye shes kyi nyi ma chen po yin te / shes bya thams cad la ye shes kyi snang bar byed pa'i phyir ro.* "The buddhas, the bhagavans, are a great sun of gnosis for they cause the light of intuition to shine upon all objects of knowledge."

[99] The source of the first two *pāda*s is the fifth characteristic of *pratyavekṣaṇājñāna* in *BBS* I.5.4 quoted in Sthiramati (P Mi 158b5–6). The source of the next two *pāda*s is the eighth characteristic in *BBS* I.5.8 quoted in Sthiramati (P Mi 158b8–158a1).

The all-accomplishing intuition fulfills the aims of all beings in all universes through innumerable and inconceivable emanations of various kinds.

> 75.[101] That buddha emanation (body) should be understood as always totally inconceivable with respect to its varieties of accomplishments, its numbers, and its universes.

The buddha emanation body should be known as always and in every way inconceivable, due to its varieties of accomplishments, its numbers, and its universes.

> 76. The four intuitions originate from retention, equal-mindedness, elucidation of the authentic teaching, and accomplishment of tasks.

In this verse, "from retention" (refers to) teachings which have been learned, "from equal-mindedness"[102] (refers to) the equalizing of self and other among all beings, and the rest is self-explanatory.

There is a verse on there being neither a unity nor a plurality of buddhas:

> 77.[103] There is no oneness of buddhas, because of different spiritual genes, because of not being useless, because of completeness, because of lack of a primordial; nor is there a plurality (of buddhas), because there is no differentiation in the immaculate ground.

---

100 This verse and the following verse appear to be a summary of the section on *kṛtyānuṣṭhānajñāna* in *BBS* I.6.1–10 which is explained in terms of the establishment of the *nirmāṇakāya* as emanations of body, speech, and mind.

101 Sthiramati (P Mi 159b4) cites the following passage from the *TOSN*: *sangs rgyas bcom ldan 'das rnams ni ye shes kyi sman chen po dang ldan pa sems can thams cad kyi nyon mongs pa'i nad zhi bar byed pa'i phyir ro.* "The buddhas, the bhagavans, possess the great medicine of intuition for they cure the illness of the addictions of all living beings."

102 Read *samacittāt* vs. Ms. *samacittatā* (LI, p. 48.1) with the Tibetan *sems mnyams pa'i phyir* (D Phi 161a1).

103 This verse also appears in the tenth chapter of *MS*.

It is unacceptable to say there is but one buddha. Why? "Because of different spiritual genes" (refers to the fact that) there is no end of beings who have the buddha genealogy: So how can it be said that from among them only one has become perfectly enlightened and that others will not become perfectly enlightened? For then the other bodhisattvas' stores of merit and intuition would be useless, as they would not become perfectly enlightened, and it is unreasonable they become useless. Therefore, "because of usefulness" it is not the case that there is but a single buddha. Further, the carrying out of the aims of others would be incomplete if there was anyone that the buddha did not establish in buddhahood; and this is unreasonable. Again, there is no such thing as a primordial buddha, for without the stores, buddhahood is impossible, and the stores are impossible without another buddha. Therefore, because there is no primordial buddha, it is unreasonable that there be only one buddha. (On the other hand,) a plurality (of buddhas) also is not accepted, for the buddhas' body of truth is undifferentiated in the uncontaminated realm.

There are four verses on entrance into the liberative art of buddhahood:

> 78. The reality of the (conceptually) not existent is actually the supreme existent; that not perceived in any way is considered the supreme of all perceptions.

What is not existent as an imaginatively constructed reality is actually the supreme existent as a perfected reality. The total nonperception of any constructed reality is itself the highest perception; that is, (the perception) of the perfect reality.

> 79. Meditation is considered supreme for those who do not discern any meditation; and those who do not perceive any realization are considered to have supreme realization.

Supreme meditation is the nonperception of meditation (on the second to the tenth bodhisattva stages). Supreme realization is the nonperception of the realization (of the buddha bodies, the powers, confidences, and so forth, on the buddha stage).[104]

---

[104] Material in brackets from G. Nagao, reading Sthiramati.

80. Bodhisattvas who consider their own mastery, length (of practice), sign (perceived), and heroic effort (undertaken), are arrogant, and their enlightenment is said to be far away.

Those arrogant bodhisattvas who consider (themselves as having) buddhahood as mastery endowed with miraculous qualities, who consider (themselves) to have spent a long time in its realization, who consider its sign as an object of mind, and who consider their own heroic effort, thinking, "We who have made heroic effort will attain buddhahood" – of such, since they rely on (dualistic) perception, it is said that enlightenment is far away.

81. It is said of the nonconceptualizing bodhisattvas, who consider what has been mentioned to be mere imaginative construction, that enlightenment has been attained.

"Who consider that everything is 'mere imaginative construction'" (refers to the fact that) they do not conceptualize what is merely conceptually constructed. It is said of such nonconceptualizing bodhisattvas that it is actually as if they have attained enlightenment when they attain the tolerance of the nonproduction of all things.

There are four verses on the mutual unity of the activity of the buddhas:

82.[105] When rivers, even though they have not gone underground, have separate beds and separate waters, they have but little water, carry out separate tasks, and can sustain but few water creatures;

83. But once they enter the ocean, they are all together in one place, they become a single, great water, they merge into a single activity, and they become a great and constant sustenance for the host of water animals.

84. The brave (bodhisattvas) who have not entered buddhahood have separate grounds and different ideas, they have little realization, their activities are separately their own, and they always sustain the needs of but a few beings;

[105] The source for this verse is *BBS* I.7.5.

> 85. But once they have entered buddhahood, they all have a single great ground and a single great realization, they merge in united activity, and they become a great and constant sustenance for an immense host of beings.

Rivers have different beds due to the difference in their channels. They carry out separate tasks because they perform tasks separately. "Sustain but few" (refers to their ability to) sustain but tiny numbers. The rest is self explanatory.

There is a verse on enthusiasm for buddhahood:

> 86. Thus, it is fitting for the beautiful-minded to take up the spirit of enlightenment, because it is endowed with incomparable virtues, because its buddha stage is the cause of benefit and happiness, and because it is the inexhaustible source of supreme bliss and beauty.

Due to (buddhahood's) endowment with incomparable virtues, one's individual aims are fulfilled. Because buddhahood is the cause of help and happiness, others' aims are fulfilled. Because it is a mine of irreproachable, supreme, inexhaustible bliss, one comes to dwell in a distinctive bliss. It is therefore fitting[106] that the intelligent person should embrace the vow for buddhahood and so take up the magnificent spirit of enlightenment.

---

[106] The Tibetan *rigs so* (D Phi 162a4) corresponds, as in the verse, to the Sanskrit *arhati*, corrupted as *ahīna*.

CHAPTER X

Faith

Summary:

> 1.[1] Introduction, authentication, refuge, spiritual gene, conception of the spirit, concerns of self and other, truth, power, evolutionary maturity, enlightenment.[2]

It is to be understood that the Introduction up to the Enlightenment chapter correspond to the sections of the *Bodhi(sattvabhūmi)*.[3]

Two verses analyzing the varieties of faith:[4]

---

[1] The Chinese omits this verse (T.31.608b10).

[2] Sthiramati comments on this summary as if it came at the end of the Enlightenment chapter. He also indicates that the prologue is treated as a separate chapter. He gives the following numbers of verses for each of the ten sections. Prologue - 5, Proof - 15, Refuge - 12, Gene - 13, Conception - 27, Self interest - 3, Other-interest - 6, Truth - 10, Power - 10, Evolution - 20, Enlightenment - 87, Total = 208.

[3] *Eṣa ca bodhyādhikāra ādimārabhya yāvat bodhipaṭalānusāreṇānugantavyaṁ* (LI, p. 50.4). This seems to refer to the *BBh* chapter of the *YBh*. The translation follows Sthiramati (P Mi 164a8–164bl): *dang po'i skabs nas brtsams te byang chub kyi skabs gyi bar du bshad pa 'di dag rnal 'byor spyod pa'i sa byang chub sems dpa'i sa las rim pa skad* (*paṭala*, but *MV* 1471 *rim par phye ba*) *du 'byung ba de bzhin du 'dir yang sbyar bar bya'o*. There are no formally corresponding *paṭalas* in the *BBh* for the *Prologue*, *Mahāyānasiddhyadhikāra*, and *Śaraṇādhikāra* of the *MSA*, but otherwise the correspondence seems to obtain. See the Introduction on the relationship between these two texts.

[4] The Sanskrit reads *prabhedalakṣaṇavibhāge* (LI, p. 50.5), but the Tibetan translates only *vibhāge*, which indeed implies the other two terms.

We translate *adhimukti* here as "faith," instead of "orientation," "aspiration," "interest," as in other contexts, since, according to Sthiramati (P Mi 165a2–3), here *adhimukti, śraddhā*, and *saṁpratyaya* are equivalents.

> 2. (Faith is) arisen, not arisen, subjective, objective, from a teacher's authority, from inner authority, erring, unerring, revelational, non-(revelational), literal, wishful, and visionary.

Arisen (faith) is in the past or present. Unarisen (faith) is in the future. Subjective (faith) is internal, having faith in an object. Objective (faith) is external, (deriving from) the object of faith itself. (Faith) from a teacher's authority is coarse, and from one's inner authority is subtle. Erring (faith) is inferior, because it is misplaced. Unerring (faith) is excellent. Revelational (faith) is in the immediate, from the presence of its conditions. Non-revelational (faith) is in the remote, in the opposite case. Literally expressible (faith) is born from study. Wishful (faith) is born from reflection. And visionary (faith) is born from meditation, through inner experience.

> 3. Faith is subvertible, adulterated with resistances, unadulterated, individual, magnificent, obscured, unobscured, energetic, unenergetic, provisioned, unprovisioned, firmly engaged, and far-reaching.

(Faith which is) subvertible is feeble; adulterated with resistances is middling; unadulterated with resistances is great. Individual (faith) is faith in the other vehicle; magnificent (faith) is in the universal vehicle. Obscured (faith) is prevented from improvement, and unobscured is unobstructed. Energetic (faith) is constant and dedicated in application;[5] unenergetic is the opposite. Provisioned (faith) is ready for realization; unprovisioned is the opposite. Firmly engaged (faith) is engaged in the stages; and far-reaching is faith on the remaining stages.

Three verses on the hindrances to faith:

> 4. (The hindrances to faith are) abundance of negative attitudes,[6] laziness, erroneous practice, bad friends, weakness of virtue, and improper attitudes.

The hindrance to an already arisen (faith) is a predominance of negative attitudes. The hindrance to the not yet arisen (faith) is laziness. The hindrance to sub-

---

[5] *Sātatyasatkṛtyaprayoga* (LI, p. 50.18). See LII, p. 94, n. 3.1.

[6] The Chinese (T.31.608c16) has *duo wang*, "much forgetfulness."

jective and objective faith is erroneous practice, since there is addiction to just those (states of faith). The hindrance to faith on a teacher's authority is bad teachers, because they lead one to misplace one's faith. The hindrance to faith on inner authority is weakness of the roots of virtue. The hindrance to unerring faith is improper attitudes, because they negate it.

> 5. (More hindrances to faith are) carelessness, little learning, complacency with little learning and reflection, pride in mere serenity, and non-cultivation.

(The hindrance to) revelational (faith is) carelessness, because (faith) is created through vigilance. (The hindrance) to literal (faith) is little learning because the scriptures of definitive meaning are not studied. (The hindrance) to wishful (faith) is complacency just with study and with little reflection. (The hindrance) to visionary (faith) is complacency just with reflection and pride in mere serenity. And the hindrance to subvertible (faith) and unadulterated (faith) is non-cultivation.

> 6. (More) hindrances to faith are non-discontent, discontent, obscuration, non-dedication, and non-gathering of stores.

(The hindrance) to the individual (faith) is lack of discontent with the life-cycle. (The hindrance) to the magnificent (faith) is discontent (with it). (The hindrance) to the unobscured (faith) is obscuration. (The hindrance) to the energetic (faith) is non-dedication. And (the hindrance) to the provisioned (faith) is non-gathering of the stores (of merit and wisdom).

Five verses on the benefits of faith:

> 7–8. The benefits of faith are great merit, freedom from regret, happiness, great joy, nondeprivation, firmness, improvement, direct realization of the teaching, supreme attainment of the aims of self and other, and swift superknowledge.

The benefits of arisen or present (faith) is great merit. (The benefit of) past faith is freedom from regret, because there is no remorse. (The benefit) of the subjective and objective (faith is) great happiness due to endowment with meditative concentration. (The benefit) of (faith) developed by a spiritual teacher is nondeprivation. (The benefit) of autonomous (faith) is firmness in faith. (The benefit) of unerring, revelational, study-produced (literal, wishful, visionary, subvertible, and adulterated faiths) is excellent progress. (The benefit of) the great (unadulterated faith) is direct realization of the teaching. (The benefit) of individual (faith) is attainment of one's own aims. (The benefit) of magnificent (faith) is highest attainment of the aims of others. And the benefit of the good tendencies of the unobscured, energetic, and provisioned (faiths) is swift superknowledge.

> 9. In the greedy, (faith) is like a dog; in meditators it is like a tortoise; in the self-preoccupied it is like a servant; and in the altruistic it is like a king.

> 10.[7] (A greedy person) is never satisfied, like a sick and hungry dog. (A meditator is) like a tortoise which retracts (into its shell) in the water. (The self-preoccupied is) like a servant, who always proceeds with the posture of terror of his master. (And the altruistic is) like a king, ruling his country with his edicts.

> 11.[8] Thus the differences between the desirous, the stable, those who work selfishly, and those who work altruistically should always be understood from the differences of their faiths. Having considered that the best (of faiths) is properly found here in the universal vehicle, the brave (bodhisattva) should always choose that here.

For the desirous, faith is like a dog. For those who have attained mundane meditative concentration it is like a tortoise. For those preoccupied with their own concerns it is like a servant. And for those concerned with the aims of others it is like a king. This meaning is exemplified by the next (verse). (And the last shows) that it leads to faith in the universal vehicle.[9]

---

[7] As printed in Lévi's Sanskrit; in the Chinese (T.31.609a21) this forms the commentary to the preceding verse. The Tibetan (D Phi 163a6–7) and the *Kārikās* (D Phi 12b7–13a1), supported by Sthiramati (D Mi 151a *ff.*) who quotes these metrical verses with *zhes bya ba smos te*, read this as another verse, making 9–11 run together as three verses. If a *daṇḍa* is added after *kṣudhitako* in the Ms. (LI, p. 52.7), there are four lines of exactly seventeen syllables each, which also reads like a verse, rather than prose commentary.

[8] The Chinese (T.31.609b) omits.

[9] This paragraph confirms the Tibetan reading of verse ten as a verse, not as a commentary: 1) it would be redundant, if the former were commentary also; 2) the *etamevārthaṁ pareṇopapādya* (LI, p. 52.15) would not make good sense.

A verse to prevent despair about faith:

> 12.[10] Since infinite human beings attain enlightenment at every moment, one should not sink into despair.

There are three reasons why despair is improper; because human beings attain enlightenment, because they continually attain it, and because infinite numbers attain it.

Two verses on the distinctive merit of faith:

> 13–14.[11] Just as merit grows in giving food to others, but not in eating it oneself, so it is with the great production of merit spoken of in the scriptures. It is obtained by teaching the altruistic Dharma, but it is not obtained by teaching the individualistic Dharma.

When food is given, merit is produced, since it is related to the aims of others; but not if one eats it oneself, because that is related to one's own aims. Likewise, the great outcome of merit spoken of in various scriptures of the universal vehicle is obtained from teaching the Dharma of the universal vehicle which has the aims of others as its basis, but not through teaching the Dharma of the disciple's vehicle which has the individual's aims as its basis.

A verse summarizing the fruits of faith:

> 15. When the (bodhisattva) genius constantly generates great faith in the magnificent Dharma of the great noble ones, she develops the continual increase of vast merit and of (faith) itself, gaining (her own) spiritual greatness by means of such incomparable excellences.

Where? By what kind of faith? Who? What fruit does she get? The (bodhisattva) genius acquires a triple fruit by means of undiminishing superior faith in the magnificent Dharma of the universal vehicle. She attains an increase of immense

---

[10] This verse is also found in the third chapter of the *MS*.

[11] The Chinese (T.31.609b11) reduces this verse and the following to a single verse.

merit, an increase of faith, and, having those as a cause, the greatness of incomparable good qualities which is buddhahood.

CHAPTER XI

Investigation of the Dharma[1]

In the chapter on the investigation of the Dharma there are four verses on the investigation of the (teaching as) objective:

> 1. Whether the baskets are three or two, they are accepted (as "baskets"), because they collect things, for nine reasons. They cause liberation through (positive) instinctual conditioning, understanding, pacifying, and realization.

The three baskets are the (collections of) discourse, discipline, and clear science texts.[2] Divided into the individual and universal vehicles, the three become two, the disciple collection and bodhisattva collection. Again, for what reason are the three or the two called "baskets"? It is because they collect things; that is, because they collect all things to be known. Why are they three? There are nine reasons (as follows).

---

[1] dBal mang, 70b3 and 73b6, places this chapter in context: "The second part (from the "Faith" chapter on) is the way of how to practice (the first having been what is to be practiced), which has four parts: the way to practice with thought, the way to practice with application, the technique of intensifying the impact of those, and the way to combine all of that with skill in liberative technique. The first of these consists of two, the way to develop faith in the universal vehicle teaching, and the way to seek the teaching, once one has faith....

In the way to seek the teaching, there are four sections: the way to seek the universal vehicle teaching, having found it, the way to impress it in attitude, the types of quest, and the expression of its greatness.

In the first of these there are three, the way to seek the three baskets in general, the way to seek the intended meaning in the expansive teaching in particular, and the factors of the perfect quest.

The first of these has three again, the way to seek the teachings of the discourses, the objective, the way to seek the discovery of the object, and the way to seek conscious attitudes."

[2] The discussion of the *tripiṭaka* in *MSABh* 1–4 is identical to that in the commencement of Vasubandhu's *Bhāṣya* on the *Mahāyānasaṁgraha*; see *La Somme* pp. 2–5.

The discourse (collection) is the remedy for doubt, since it teaches a decisive solution to one who has doubt about the meaning. The discipline is the remedy for the pursuit of the two extremes, since it rejects reproachable enjoyments, (and thus treats) the extreme of attachment to sense pleasures, and since it allows irreproachable enjoyments, (and thus treats) the extreme of self-mortification.[3] The clear science is the remedy for fanaticism about one's ideology, since it elucidates unerringly the natures of things.[4]

Further, the discourse (collection) teaches the three educations.[5] The discipline (collection) makes possible the accomplishment of the first two, supreme morality and supreme mind, since one who has morality gradually becomes free of remorse and so achieves meditative concentration.[6] The clear science (collection) makes possible the accomplishment of supreme wisdom, since it analyzes things unerringly.

Further, the discourses expound the teaching and its meaning;[7] the discipline brings about the realization of the teaching and its meaning,[8] since one who

---

[3] *Antadvaya* (LI, p. 53.21). The two extremes of attachment to sensual pleasure (*kāmasukhallikānuyoga*) and attachment to self mortification (*ātmaklamathānuyoga*) were condemned by the Buddha in his first discourse; see *Saṁdhinirmocanasūtravyākhyā* 112, *Lalitavistara* p. 303.

[4] Compare *AS* p. 79 on the functions of the three "baskets."

[5] *Śikṣātraya* (LI, p. 54.1). These are: 1) *Adhiśīla* (or simply *śīla*), exceptional morality; 2) *adhicitta* or *samādhi*, exceptional mind or meditative concentration; and 3) *adhiprajñā* (or simply *prajñā*), exceptional wisdom. The first refers primarily to the *pratimokṣasaṁvara* or code of monastic rules, the second to the four meditative concentrations of the form realm (*rūpadhātu*), and the four absorptions (*samāpatti*) of the formless realm (*arūpyadhātu*), and the third to exact knowledge of the four holy truths; see Sthiramati (P Mi 174b7–175a1). dBal mang, 74b1 *ff.*, calls the above interpretation that of the "common" (with the individual vehicle) three educations, elucidating the uncommon three as "the three moralities, the concentrations such as sky-treasury, and the nonconceptual wisdom." The discourses orient the intelligence to these three. The discipline mainly enables practice of morality, but also assists practice of exceptional mental education through attaining *samādhis* gradually by means of vigilance and alertness and loss of remorse and so on, and the clear science enables achievement of the exceptional wisdom education by extensively teaching techniques for discerning unerringly the meanings of the teachings.

[6] Reading *avipratisārādikrameṇa* with the Tibetan translation and Sthiramati.

[7] About "doctrines and meanings" here, dBal mang has the following interesting analysis (74b5): "As for 'doctrine and meaning,' these can mean the pairs name/word/letter *vs.* systems/elements/media, or systems/elements/media *vs.* intention and implication (*dgongs pa*

(cont'd)

has practiced the discipline of the addictions realizes both; the clear science (collection) bestows skill in settling hermeneutical discussions, connecting teachings and meanings.[9]

For these nine reasons the collections are accepted as three.

They have liberation from the life-cycle as their aim. How do they liberate? "They cause liberation through (positive) instinctual conditioning, understanding, pacifying, and realization." The mind is instinctively conditioned through learning (the collections). One gains understanding through thoughtful reflection. One becomes pacified through serenity meditation. And one gains inner realization through transcendent insight.

> 2. In summary, the discourse (*sūtra*), discipline (*vinaya*), and clear science (*abhidharma*) are considered to have fourfold meaning. When he understands them, the genius achieves omniscience.

In brief, discourse, discipline, and clear science are each fourfold in meaning. The bodhisattva who understands them[10] attains omniscience. Also, the disciple who knows the meaning of even a single verse attains the exhaustion of the contaminants.

> 3.[11] "Discourse" (*sūtra*) is so called because it informs (*sūcanāt*),[12] through context, nature, teaching, and meaning. "Clear science" (*abhidharma*) is so called because it confronts (*abhimukhato*),[13] is

dang ldem dgongs), or the ten virtues, cause of ascendance *vs.* the enlightenment accessories, cause of liberation."

8 *Dharmārthaniṣpattir* (LI, p. 54.3).

9 The Tibetan translation (D Phi 164b1), reads *sāṁkathya* (LI, p. 54.4) as *'brel ba'i gtam. Sāṁkathya* is usually translated *'bel gtam*, meaning only religious or philosophical discussion, and dBal Mang uses *bel gtam*.

10 That is, discourse, discipline, and clear science.

11 The Chinese (T.31.609c28) reads: "Sūtra-Discourse is so called according to its fourfold significance as support, characteristic, phenomenon, and meaning."

12 *Sūcanātsūtraṁ* (LI, p. 54.15). On this etymology see *La Somme* p. 3 n. 2.

13 *Abhimukhata* (LI, p. 54.16). On this etymology see LII, p. 99, n. 3.2.

> repetitive (*abhīkṣṇyād*), is triumphant (*abhibhavagatito*), and leads to understanding.[14]

How is each one understood to have a fourfold meaning? The "discourse" (collection) is so called because it shows context, nature, teaching, and meaning. Here "context" signifies the place wherein, the person by whom, and the audience to whom a discourse was taught. "Nature" means the natures of superficial and ultimate realities. "Teaching" refers to the systems, media, elements, foods, dependent origination, and so on. "Meaning" means the intended implication.[15]

The clear science is so called because it confronts, is repetitive, is triumphant, and leads to understanding. The teaching which clearly confronts Nirvāṇa is the clear science, since it is that which teaches the truths, the accessories of enlightenment, the doors of liberation, and so forth. The teaching which is clearly repetitive is the clear science, because it displays each thing in many ways, as formful, formless, comparable, and so on. The (teaching which is) clearly triumphant is the clear science, since it triumphs over opponents' criticism and (successfully) addresses controversial issues, and so forth. And it is "clear science" because it leads to the clear understanding of the meaning of the discourses.

> 4. "Discipline" is so called because of offense, origin, remission, and absolution; and also with regard to person, proclamation, interpretation, and determination.

Discipline should be understood with regard to offense, origin, remission, and release. "Offense"[16] refers to the five categories of offense. The origin of offenses is ignorance, recklessness, excess of addictions, and disrespect. Remission[17] comes about from aspiration (to reform), and not from punishment. Absolution is

---

[14] Following the sense, the context, and the Tibetan (D Phi 164b4–5) */...yang yang dang / / zil gnon rtogs phyir mngon pa'i chos /*, we read in Sanskrit *'bhīkṣṇyādabhibhavābhigatito* in place of the Ms. *abhīkṣṇyādabhibhavagatito* (LI, p. 54. 15).

[15] *Anusaṁdhiṁ* (LI, p. 54. 18). See XII.16–17. The Chinese (T.31.610a7) inserts the following verse here: "Abhidharma is so called according to its fourfold significance as confrontation, repetition, victory, and understanding." The Tibetan states the same content in prose as commentary on 3cd above. We do not restore as verse as it would be redundant with 3cd.

[16] *Āpattinikāya*. The five categories of offenses common to the *vinaya*s of all schools. In Pāli they are: 1) *pārājika*, 2) *saṁghādisesa*, 3) *pācittiya*, 4) *pāṭidesanīya*, 5) *sekhiya*.

[17] *Vyutthāna* (LI, p. 54.24). On this term see LII, p. 100, n. 4.2.

due to seven kinds (of circumstances): (by) confession; (by) acceptance of the punishments for postulants and so forth; (by) relaxation (of) a rule, though already laid down, through authorizing (its relaxation) by a subsequent instruction; (by) suspension, when the community unanimously consents to let a regulation drop; (by) physical transmutation, resulting from the change of the masculine or feminine sex organs of a monk or a nun, in a case when the offense is not common (for both monks and nuns);[18] (by) realistic insight, a special kind of discernment guided by the epitomes of the teaching;[19] and (by) experience of ultimate reality, the understanding of reality by insight into the truths, in the absence of minor or very minor offenses.

Again, the discipline is to be understood in four senses: with regard to the person, that is, the person regarding whom the regulation is proclaimed; with regard to proclamation, that is, the occasion in regard to which the Teacher, informed of an individual fault, gathers together the community and proclaims the regulation; with regard to interpretation, that is, a regulation having been stated, there is a (detailed) analysis of what has been stated in brief; and with regard to determination, that is, the judgement as to how, and in what case there is or is not an offense.

Three verses on the investigation of the (process of) discovery of (the teaching as an) objective:

> 5.[20] The objectives are accepted as the Dharma (itself), the internal, the external, and the two together. The two are discovered

---

[18] *Āśrayaparivṛtti* (LI, p. 55.5). On the theme of change of sex in Buddhist literature see *VKN* pp. 280–281 n. 37. "If the sin is not common" (*asādhāraṇā vedāpattiṁ*): if a monk or a nun commits an act which is not regarded as an infraction by the rules for both monks and nuns, that infraction does not require expiation in the event of a change of sexual organs where that individual's former state would have required such; see Sthiramati (P Mi 178a4–8) and LII, p. 100 n. 4.7.

[19] *Dharmoddāna* (LI, p. 55.6). See XVIII 80–81.

[20] The translation here follows the text as restored by Lévi on the basis of the Tibetan. The third *pāda*, however, is problematical. As restored by Lévi it reads: *dvayor dvayārthena lābho* (LII, p. 102, n. 5.1) which was apparently the reading before Sthiramati, but as restored by Mr. Takenai Shoko on the basis of a further manuscript of the *MSA* the *pāda* reads: *lābho dvayadvayārthena* which agrees with the Chinese (T.31.610b5) *de er wu er yi*. See Ui p. 614.

> through two realities, and (their suchness is realized) through non-apprehension of their duality.[21]

The teaching as objective has already been explained (above). "The internal" refers to the body, and so forth (the six sense-faculties). "The external" (refers to the six objects). Concerning that, the body as cognizer is internal and the cognized is the external. "Both" refers to the suchness of cognizer and cognized. Both internal and external objects are discovered through two realities; when one sees that the cognizer is not different from the cognized, and the cognized is not different from the cognizer, respectively. Then, the reality of all internal and external objects is realized through the non-apprehension of either (as substantially distinct).

> 6–7.[22] The teaching as objective is discovered by the three wisdoms, (born of) learning, (reflection, and meditation, respectively,) when one with faith focuses on its stated meaning (learned) through mental verbalization, when one recognizes the fact that its objective appearance is because of mental verbalization, and when one fixes the mind itself (exclusively) upon the nominal (life-

---

[21] dBal mang, 75b3 *ff.*, explains this verse and its context most helpfully: "In the second there are two, investigation of discovery of objective object, and investigation of discovery of subjective subject. First, consider that objective: it is threefold or fourfold; on the preparation path it is the teaching in three baskets, on the application path it consists of the inner things of the body, etc., and the outer things such as form, and on the insight path the two suchnesses of inner and outer things – these are the bases for eliminating reifications or the objectives.

The discovery of the objective in teaching is explained later. Consider the two objectives, inner and outer: there is a process of discovering them; because they are discovered by the force of discovering the realities of them both.

Consider the two meanings of suchness: there is a process of discovering them; on the application path, first one sees many apprehended objects as distinct from the subjectivity, and then one sees those apprehended objects as not different from the subjectivity – in short, they are discovered by the process of not perceiving any substantial subject-object dichotomy."

[22] The Chinese (T.31.610b15) reads: "The three objects attain the three knowledges; purely holding the domain of mental verbalization, having clarified the specified meaning, the pacified mind only has name."

systems).[23] And this discovery of the threefold objective is based upon the previously mentioned (three baskets of the teaching).

The teaching as objective is discovered by means of the three wisdoms born from learning, reflection, and meditation. When the mind is faithful and concentrated,[24] focused upon a stated sense using mental verbalization, that (objective teaching) is discovered through the wisdom born of learning. "Mental verbalization" means "conceptual consideration." "Faithful" means "having a decisive trust." To be "focused" means "to discern." When one focuses on the fact that the appearance of the object is only because of verbalization, one discovers the teaching as objective through the wisdom born of reflection. When one sees that objects appear solely from mental verbalization and that there is nothing other than mental verbalization – comparable to what has been said in connection with the discovery of the two objects (in the preceding verse) – that is, when one fixes the mind upon the nominal, the teaching as objective is discovered through the wisdom born of meditation, since there is no (longer any) apprehension of duality – as has been said in connection with the discovery of the dual object in the non-apprehension of duality (in the preceding verse). Consequently, the discovery of the above three objectives (i.e., the internal, the external, and both together) is based upon the discovery of the teaching (of the three baskets) as objective.

Five verses on the investigation of conscientious attitudes:[25]

---

[23] This interpretation of the process of generating the three wisdoms is beautifully set forth by dBal Mang (76a). He quotes Sthiramati as glossing *nāmni* as referring to the four mental systems, as in its usage in the *nāmarūpa* branch of dependent origination.

[24] dBal Mang gently disagrees with this interpretation of Vasubandhu's, in that he does not consider the wisdom born of learning to be "concentrated" (*samāhita*), saving the *pradhāraṇāt* for usage with the wisdom born of reflection, whereas Vasubandhu uses the verse's *pradhāraṇāt* twice.

[25] Sthiramati (P Mi 193a7) gives the following equivalents of *manasikāra*: *ekāgra* (one-pointedness), *dhyāna* (contemplation), and *samādhi* (meditative concentration). *Amarakośa* 291 gives the following equivalents of *manaskāra*: *cittabhoga* (lit. "mental inflection" or attention), *saṁkhyā* (deliberation), and *vicāraṇa* (reflection). We use the new translation "attitude" as the base for various usages of *manasikāra*, since it describes a structuring of consciousness which is both fixed in a certain orientation "unconsciously," and also consciously deliberative and selective. "Attention" only conveys the fixated aspect, and "mentation" or "thought" only the deliberative aspect.

8–12. Such is the (eighteenfold) conscientious attitude of the yogis, composed of all (conscientious attitudes): triply genealogical; dutiful; in lifestyle bound or free; settled in faith; intensely enthusiastic; (contemplative) life twofold, incomplete or fulfilled; (in realms still) verbal or nonverbal; endowed with (conceptual) wisdoms or with the (wisdom) associated with meditative experience;[26] five kinds (of attitudes) with objects combined and seven kinds with isolated objects; five kinds of thorough realization; four and thirty-seven (attitudes) associated with meditation on the aspects (of the holy truths); (attitudes whose) nature is the two paths, (insight and meditation); (attitudes) with two benefits; and (attitudes) with receptivity; functional (attitudes); (ultimately there are) masterful (attitudes); (with regard to vehicles, there are) limited and unlimited (attitudes).

Attitudes are of eighteen kinds: (attitudes which are) definite as to spiritual gene; engaged in duty; distinguished by life(style); settled in faith; intensely enthusiastic; dependent on meditation; endowed with knowledge; with objects combined; with objects isolated; guaranteed by thorough knowledge; intent upon the form of meditation; consisting of the paths of serenity and transcendent insight. (They are) beneficial attitudes, receptive (attitudes), applicational attitudes, masterful attitudes, limited attitudes, and unlimited attitudes.

(Attitudes are) definite as to spiritual gene, as when one is definitely of the disciples' genealogy. They are engaged in duty, when one has gathered the stores. They are distinguished by life(style), with the householder's life with its bonds or the monk's life free from all bonds.[27] They are settled in faith, accompanied with recollection of the buddhas.[28] They are intensely enthusiastic, accompanied by confidence in the buddhas. They are dependent on meditation, accompanied by preliminary and actual meditation, with both consideration and judgement, with no consideration but only judgement, and with neither consideration nor judge-

[26] *Upaniṣad* (LI, p. 56.15). On this term see Ruegg, *La Théorie*, p. 87 n. 3.

[27] *Saṁbāddha* (LI, p. 56.27). The characteristic of the householder's estate; see our note to XX.5, and LII, vs. 8–12 n. 3.

[28] *Buddhānusmṛti* (LI, p. 56.28). *MS* chapter 10 discusses a sevenfold recollection of the buddha; see *La Somme* pp. 314–317 and p. 61 for references. *Buddhānusmṛti* is counted as one of six recollections; see *MVy* 1149–1154.

ment.[29] They are endowed with wisdom, associated with meditative experience, that is, accompanied by application – in this instance it consists of learning, reflection, and meditation respectively.

With objects combined, (attitudes are) of five kinds according to whether objects are summarized or taught in discourse, epitome, verse, and anthology; with objects dispersed they are of seven kinds according to whether objects are word, sentence, letter, selflessness of persons, selflessness of things, formful things, or formless things – formful things being physical objects, the formless things being sensual and mental objects.

(Attitudes are) guaranteed by thorough knowledge with regard to the objects and the facts to be thoroughly realized, with regard to thorough realization itself, its fruit, and its intense experience. The object to be thoroughly understood is suffering. The facts to be thoroughly understood are suffering's impermanence, pain, voidness, and selflessness. Thorough realization is the path; the fruit of thorough realization is liberation. Its intense experience is the intuitive vision of liberation.

(Conscientious attitudes are) intent upon the kinds of meditation, whether four or thirty-seven. Meditation is of four kinds, as it concerns the selflessness of the person, selflessness of objects, vision, or intuition. Meditation also has thirty-seven kinds.[30]

In the case of the four foci of mindfulness one meditates on ugliness, suffering, impermanence, and selflessness. In the case of the four realistic abandons one meditates on achievement, cultivation, elimination,[31] and remedy.

In the case of the four bases of magic powers, when generating zeal one cultivates the attitude that remedies complacency. When one is exhausted and renews one's efforts, one cultivates attitudes that remedy distraction and doubt, respec-

---

[29] Vasubandhu refers here to the four contemplations, the first of which has both approach and actual states. The first has both consideration and judgement, the second has no consideration but still has judgement, and the third and fourth have neither. The Tibetan text is clear here. The Sanskrit (at LI, p. 57.2) should read: *savitarka-savicāra-nirvitarka-savicāra-mātrāvitarkāvicāra-sahagataḥ*.

[30] The thirty seven factors of enlightenment; see XVIII 42–65.

[31] The reading of the text here is open to question. In Lévi's edition the word is *vinirdhāvana* (LI, p. 57.16) which in n. 7 to vs. 8–12 of his translation he corrected to *nirvidhāvana*, the original form seemingly being a typo. However he suggests in the same footnote that *nirvighāṭana* be read instead on the basis of the Tibetan *bsal ba*. Since *vi-dhū*, *nir-dhū*, *vi-han* and *nir-han* all have the same general meaning of removal or expulsion, which is the sense of the Tibetan and the Chinese *duan* (T.31.610c27), our translation is certain although the form of the original text is not. See Ui, p. 614.

tively. When one controls the mind, one cultivates the meditative concentration that remedies elation, and when one intensifies the mind one cultivates the concentration that remedies depression.

In the case of the spiritual faculties one meditates with mind fixed on faith in transcendental perfection and, as with faith, so with resolution, retention of the teaching, mental stability, and analytic discernment. In the case of the five spiritual powers, the resistances are abolished by these same five attitudes.

In the case of the seven factors of enlightenment one cultivates adeptness in enlightenment, analytic discernment, enthusiasm, happiness, fitness, mental stability, and equality.

In the case of the branches of the path one meditates the certainty of achievement, the conservation of the stage of purification, the instilling of realization in others, the engagement in morality dear to the saints, the getting along with a minimum of possessions, the cultivation of the path achieved in previous practice, the retention of the signs of living by the Dharma, and the foundational transmutation which is stability in signlessness.

There is no instruction in the path consisting of the meditation of serenity and transcendent insight (as it is unnecessary). Beneficial attitudes are twofold: one removes bad conditioning, and the other the signs of views. The receptive attitude takes the counsels of buddhas and bodhisattvas in the Dharma-stream (*samādhi*).

Applicational attitudes are fivefold in the domain of meditative concentration. The applicational attitude concerned with numbers counts the numbers of words, sentences, and letters in the scriptures, and so on. The applicational attitude concerning occurrence observes two types of occurrence, the measurable occurrences of letters and the immeasurable occurrences of words and sentences. The applicational attitude concerned with construction observes dualistic constructions depending on dualism, (wherein) words are constructed depending on objects, and objects are constructed depending on words, while letters are not constructed.[32] The applicational attitude concerned with order observes the process of cognition of objects preceding the cognition of words.

The penetrative applicational attitudes are elevenfold, according to whether they penetrate the incidental, the signs of discourse, the non-apprehension of content, the non-apprehension of apprehension, the ultimate realm, subjective selflessness, objective selflessness, inferior aspirations, aspirations to magnificent greatness,

---

32 *Aparikalpamakṣaraṁ* (LI, p. 58.7). What is probably behind this notion is that letter (*akṣaraṁ*) means "indestructible" (*akṣaraṁ*).

the arrangement of the teachings in the order of realization, and the teachings themselves so arranged.

Masterful attitudes are of three kinds: well purified of the addictive obscurations, well purified of the addictive and objective obscurations, and well purified in the realization of excellence. The "limited" attitude refers to the first purification, and the "unlimited" attitude refers to the last two purifications.[33]

Two verses on the investigation of the reality of things:

> 13. Reality is that which is always free from duality, is the ground of error, and is absolutely inexpressible, naturally free from fabrication. It is considered as what should be known, what should be abandoned, and also what should be purified, (even though) naturally immaculate. In its purification of addictions, it is considered as resembling space, gold, and water.

The reality which is always free from duality is the constructed reality, for it is absolutely nonexistent in terms of its subject-object nature. (The reality which is) the ground of error is the relative reality, since therein imagination constructs (subject-object duality). The inexpressible, naturally unfabricated (reality) is the perfect reality. Of these (three realities), the first, (the nonexistent imagined), is to be thoroughly understood, the second, (the relative as erroneously imagined), is to be abandoned,[34] the third is both (the perfect as the relative free of the imagined) to be purified of incidental defilement and (the perfect as pure object, to be realized as) naturally pure. In its natural purity, it is like space, gold, and water insofar as it purifies addictions. For space and so on are not naturally impure, nor is their purity not considered the result of the removal of incidental defilements.

> 14. Indeed, nothing other than this (triple) reality is found in the world, and yet the whole world is confused about it. How has such an amazing folly overtaken people, where the real is completely forsaken and the unreal is persistently maintained?

---

[33] Following the Chinese *xiao zuo yi zhe, wei chu qing jing. da zuo yi zhe, wei hou er qing jing* (T.31.611a24), which is lacking in the Sanskrit and Tibetan.

[34] Sthiramati (D Mi 174a5) remarks that "while it is said 'to be abandoned,' the second reality, the relative, is not to be abandoned, since it is the taint of the subject-object duality that exists in the relative that is to be purified."

In fact, no world other than this reality realm thus defined is found to exist, since the ultimate realm is not something separate from things.[35] The rest is self evident.

Fifteen verses investigating the illusoriness in reality:

> 15.[36] Unreal imaginative construction is declared to be just like magical illusion, and the error of duality to be just like a magical creation.

Unreality construction, the form of the relative reality, should be understood as like sticks and clods and so on, the sources of error, which are manipulated by the magician's spells. And the form of the imaginatively constructed reality, the appearance in that (relative) of the unreal construction of subject and object through the error of duality, should be understood as like the magician's creations, such as the shapes of elephants, horses, or gold, and so on which appear in the magical illusion as if they existed.

> 16. It is accepted that the ultimate reality is like that (imagined) not existing in that (relative); and the superficial reality is like that (imagined) being perceived in that (relative).

Just as the (imagined) elephant and so on does not exist in that (relative) magical creation, so the ultimate reality is accepted as the nonexistence of the dualistic imagined reality in that relative reality. (And) just as there is a perception of the (imagined) elephant and so on existing in that (relative) magical creation, so the superficial reality is the perception of the unreality (imaginary) construction (in the relative).

> 17. Just as in the absence of that (illusory effect), one perceives the manifestation of its cause, so when there is the foundational transmutation, one perceives the manifestation of the unreality-construction.

---

[35] See XIII.9.

[36] Vs. 15–23 with *MSABh* are quoted by Jñānaśrīmitra in his *Sākārasiddhiśāstra* pp. 484–486.

In the absence of that magical creation the manifestation of its cause, a stick and so on, is perceived as a real object. In the same way, once (one attains) the foundational transmutation,[37] one perceives unreal construction as an actual object, the error of duality being absent.

> 18. People, when no longer deceived, act freely in relation to (what had previously been) the cause of that (illusion); in the same way, upon foundational transmutation, the ascetic,[38] no longer deluded, acts as he pleases.

When people are no longer deceived, they can interact freely, independently, with such things as sticks of wood (previously used by magicians) as causes (of deception). Similarly, upon foundational transmutation, the saint, no longer deluded, has freedom of action and independence.

> 19. On the one hand its form is here, and on the other its existence is not found. That is why both existence and nonexistence are ascribed to magical illusion, and so on.

This verse is self evident.

> 20. Therein, existence is not exactly nonexistence and nonexistence is not exactly existence; the nondistinction between existence and nonexistence is attributed to illusion and so on.

Existence in this case is not exactly nonexistence; inasmuch as there is existence of a certain form, it is not nonexistent. And the nonexistent is not exactly existent; the nonexistence of the elephant and so on is not an existent.[39] Nondistinction of existence and nonexistence is attributed to illusion and so forth. The existence of such an (illusory) form (of an elephant and so on) then is precisely the

---

[37] That is, the transmutation of the fundamental consciousness (*ālayavijñāna*); Sthiramati (P Mi 195b4–5).

[38] Reading *yatiṁ* as Lévi suggests (LII, p. 109 n. 18.1), following the Tibetan *sdom brtson*.

[39] Lévi queries the second *na* in *nāsau na bhāvaṁ* (LI, p. 60.4), and the Tibetan *de ni yod pa ma yin no /* omits it.

nonexistence of the (real) elephant and so on, and the nonexistence of the (real) elephant, and so on, is just the existence of such an (illusory) form.

> 21. Likewise, the appearance of duality is there, but its reality is not found. And therefore existence and nonexistence are ascribed to forms and so on.

Thus there is the appearance of duality in unreal construction but there is not the reality of duality.[40] Therefore, existence and nonexistence are attributed to forms and so on which in reality are the (relative processes of) unreal construction.

> 22. Therein, existence is not exactly nonexistence and nonexistence is not exactly existence; the nondistinction between existence and nonexistence is attributed to material things and so on.

Here, existence is not nonexistence, inasmuch as there is an appearance of duality. Here, nonexistence is not existence, inasmuch as there is no reality to duality. It is a nondistinction of existence and nonexistence which is attributed to material things and so on, for it is exactly the existence of an appearance of duality which is in fact the nonexistence of duality.

> 23. This is asserted in order to refute the (two) extremes of reification and repudiation, and in order to reject progress (toward a dualistic Nirvāṇa) made by means of the individual vehicle.

Why then is this total unity and nondistinction of existence and nonexistence asserted? To reject the two extremes of reification and repudiation[41] respectively, and to reject (the value of) progress achieved by means of the individual vehicle. In fact, when one knows that the nonexistent is nonexistent, one does not engage in reifications. When one knows that the existent is existent, one does not engage in repudiations. When one finally knows the nondistinction of the two, ex-

---

[40] Compare *MAV* I.2ab: *abhūtaparikalpo 'sti dvayaṁ tatra na vidyate.*

[41] *Samāropāpavāda* (LI, p. 60.17). *Samāropa* or reification is the erroneous affirmation of a quality not actually present, while *apavāda* or repudiation is the denial of that which actually is. See *Kośa* V, p. 18.

istence does not disgust one any longer, and so one does not (try to) transcend (the world) by means of the individual vehicle.

> 24.[42] The cause of error and error itself are considered to be the idea of matter and the idea of nonmateriality (respectively);[43] in the absence of one, the other would not exist.

The idea which causes the error of matter is the idea "matter," which we call "matter." But the error of matter itself is considered to be the idea of nonmateriality. If the idea of matter did not exist, the other, the idea of nonmateriality, would not exist, because it would lack a cause.

> 25. Because of the error of perceiving the matter of an illusory elephant, duality is mentioned; there is no duality there as it seems, but there is just the perception of duality.

> 26. Because of the error of perceiving the image of a skeleton, duality is mentioned; there is no duality there as it seems, yet there is just the perception of duality.

Because of an error of perceiving the material form of an illusory elephant, (subject-object) duality is mentioned. There is (in reality) neither subject nor object of cognition, but there is nevertheless the perception of duality. And one who contemplates the image of a skeleton,[44] because of the error of cognizing such a thing, speaks of duality and so forth as above.

---

[42] This verse is also found in the second chapter of the *MS*.

[43] dBal Mang here (81b3 *ff.*) clarifies: "Here there is the general demonstration of the establishment of the subject as illusory, and the detailed explanation. First, verbally speaking, there are two types of ideas: 1) the idea of forms, the cause of error, the objective five sense-objects and the five sense-faculties; and 2) the idea of the formless, the fruitional, the subjective sixfold system of consciousnesses. Hence… (the first part of the verse). These two are not substantially dichotomous, because the cause of error, the objective, is not subtantially different (from consciousness), and so the other, the subjective consciousness, is not substantially different; hence 'one not existing, the other becomes nonexistent.'"

[44] This is an allusion to the death-ground contemplation in the yogi's *aśubhabhāvanā* (meditation upon the ugly). For references see *La Somme* p. 18. dBal Mang clarifies this (82a3) as being the kind of hallucination commonly experienced by the novice yogi who meditates on ugliness in the burning ground.

27. Naturally erroneous things both exist and do not exist, just like illusions; because they exist as (relative), because they do not exist as (imaginatively constructed), and because of the (ultimate) undifferentiability of their existence and their nonexistence.

Things identifiable as error, having the nature of the resistances, both exist and do not exist, just like illusions. Why? They exist because they exist as such, as the (relative process of) unreal construction. They do not exist because they do not exist as such, as (the imagined reality of) subject and object.

They both exist and do not exist, because of the indistinguishability of their existence and nonexistence. And since the nature of illusion is also like that, they are said to be "like illusion."

28.[45] Practices which serve as remedies are taught to lack intrinsic identity and to be illusory; because they do not exist as such, do[46] exist as such, and do not exist as such.

The practices which were taught by the Buddha as remedies, the foundations of mindfulness and so forth, are shown to lack any identity, to be illusions. Why? "Because they do not exist as such," as they are apprehended by the naïve. "Because they do exist as such," as taught (to be illusorily there).[47] "Because they do not exist as such," as manifested by the Buddha – (in the form of his deeds, such as) conception, birth, renunciation, unexcelled perfect enlightenment, and so forth. Without

---

[45] The first two *pāda*s as printed by Lévi (LI, p. 61.16): *tathā 'bhāvāt tathā 'bhāvāt* / are confirmed by Sthiramati (P Mi 200a1–6). In the Chinese (T.31.612b28) the first *abhāvāt* is *bhāvāt* and the relevant portion of the commentary reads: "because such as these exist (*ti*) as they are apprehended by the naïve." In the *MSA kārikā*s and the Tibetan translation the second *abhāvāt* should be *bhāvāt* and the relevant portion of the commentary reads: "because they exist (*yod pa*) as taught."

[46] The Sanskrit (LI, p. 61.16) reads here *'bhāvāt*, which accords with Sthiramati's gloss below, that the Dharmas in the sense of "teachings" do not exist in the way they are expressed. However, the Tibetan (D Phi 169b7) clearly reads *yod*, and it makes better sense this way, according with the commentary below emended to read *tathā bhāvādyathā deśitāṁ* following the Tibetan *ji ltar bshad pa de ltar yod pa'i phyir*.

[47] The Buddha's scriptures do not (ultimately) exist in the mode (*tshul*) in which they were taught, that is, as words, names, and letters; see Sthiramati (P Mi 200a4–5). This reading seems inferior to that rendered by the Tibetan. See previous note.

having identity, without being really discoverable, they appear; and therefore they are like illusions.

> 29. It is like an illusory king being conquered by an illusory king –
> the victor-children are without pride[48] concerning all practices.

The practices which are remedies are like an illusory king, because of their power of purification in the process of the elimination of addictions. And addictive actions also are like a king, because of their power of producing (more) addictions. Thus the conquest of addictions by the remedial practices should be seen as like the defeat of an (illusory) king by an (illusory) king. And because they know this, the bodhisattvas are without pride regarding the two tendencies.

A verse on the meaning of the similes:[49]

> 30. The supremely enlightened buddhas proclaimed again and again that created things are like illusions, dreams, mirages, mirror-images, shadows, echoes, water-moons, and magical incarnations;[50] (referring respectively to the) six (senses), (their) six (objects), both (mind and functions), again the pair of six (internal media and) six (external media), and the (last) three each to one (buddha speech, mind, and body).

The Lord said that things are like illusions and so forth, up to magical incarnations.[51] The things like illusions are the six internal media; in the absence of any real self or soul, they appear (to exist as ego-centering foci). Things like dreams are the six external media, because truly the sense objects do not exist (externally). Two things are like mirages: the mind and the mental functions, because they produce error. Furthermore, six things are like mirror-images: the six internal media, because

---

[48] The Sanskrit (LI, p. 61.23) reads *nirmāra* for *nirmāṇa*.

[49] The Tibetan lacks this phrase (D Phi 170a5).

[50] These eight similes form the body of stock similes illustrating *dharmanairātmya*; see *VKN* pp. 132–133 and n. 23; also p. 176. For references see *La Somme* pp. 21–22. Two other similes are usually found together with these eight, *ākāśa*, or space, and *gandharvanagara*, the city of the Gandharvas.

[51] For example, the *Pañcaviṁśati-* and *Śatasāhasrika-prajñāpāramitāsūtras*; see *Le Traité* pp. 357–387.

they are the reflections of previous evolutionary acts. Six are like shadows – these are the external media, because they are the shadows of the internal media, produced under their control. These two sets of six make up a pair. Like echoes are the phenomena of teaching.[52] Like the water-moon-images are the phenomena based upon concentration; concentration resembles water in its clarity. Like magical incarnations (are the buddhas') emanations of deliberate birth, which lend themselves to all actions without being affected by addictions.

A verse on the investigation of the object:

> 31. The entire objective reality is experienced as unreal imaginative construction, as neither real nor unreal, as nonconceptual, and as neither conceptual nor nonconceptual.

"Unreal imaginative construction" is mental construction which does not conform to transcendental intuition. "Neither real nor unreal" is that (conceptual construction) which does conform to (such intuition), such as the aids to penetrative insight. "The nonconceptual" is suchness and its transcendental intuition. "Neither conceptual nor nonconceptual" is the mundane intuition attained in the aftermath of transcendental intuition. And that is the entire objective reality.

Two verses investigating defilement and purification:

> 32. Discriminative constructions evolve from their own realm with a dualistic appearance, functioning with addictions and misknowledge; (yet in reality) they are devoid of any substantial duality.

"From their own realm" refers to their seed[53] which is the fundamental consciousness. The appearance of duality is the appearance of subject and object. These (constructions) function together with misknowledge and addictions. They are free of any substantial duality, (without any) substantial subject or any substantial object. Addiction should be investigated in this way.

---

52 *Deśanādharmāḥ* (LI, p. 62.16). Sthiramati (P Mi 201b3–4): "Although an echo does not exist as a natural(ly produced) sound (*sgra'i rang bzhin du med mod kyi*), it is audible; similarly no teachings exist in the way (they seem when) taught (*chos thams cad ji ltar bshad pa bzhin du yod pa ma yin yang*), yet they are audible, like an echo."

53 Following Lévi's suggestion (based on the Tibetan *rang gi sa bon*) to read *svabījād* in place of Ms. *bhāvāṅgād* (LI, p. 63.5), which is obviously corrupt.

> 33.[54] (Those discriminative thoughts) enter the reality where non-duality appears, attaining the special (Dharma-)objective,[55] through cultivation of stability in their own (true) realm; it is like the hide and the arrow.

"Attaining the special objective" is to encounter the Dharma-objective discussed above.[56] "Through cultivation of stability in their own realm" refers to the suchness of discriminative thoughts, which is their own realm; they stand therein when the mind is focused on name(-only). "Cultivation" is self-conditioning by the path of meditation. These discriminative thoughts function without any appearance of duality in that person who has achieved the foundational transmutation. "Like the hide and the arrow," hide loses its hardness and becomes supple, and an arrow is heated in the fire to become straight. In the same way, when one who has achieved the foundational transmutation arrives at the liberation of intellect and wisdom by the meditation of serenity and insight, his discriminative thoughts no longer function with an appearance of duality. Thus purification should be investigated.

Two verses on the quest of information-only:[57]

> 34.[58] It is mind which is asserted as appearance of duality, and likewise appearance of lust and so on, and appearance of faith and so on; there is no afflicted or pure thing other than it.

Only mind is asserted to be the appearance of duality, the appearance of subject, and the appearance of object. Thus it is that also which is claimed to be the appearance of the addictions such as lust and the appearance of the virtuous phenomena such as faith. And there is nothing other than such appearance, neither anything afflicted such as lust or virtuous such as faith; nor is there any dualistic thing other than the appearance of duality.

---

[54] In the Chinese (T.31.613a23) *pāda*s a and b are: "Having perceived those three objects one should stand in one's own element."

[55] The Tibetan *thob pa yi* reads *āptem̐* for *āptim̐* (LI, p. 63.8).

[56] See XI.6–7.

[57] *Vijñaptimātratā* (LI, p. 63.16). The doctrine of mind-only (*cittamātra*); see *Siddhi* pp. 416–432.

[58] The Chinese omits (T.31.613b3).

> 35. Thus mind functions as various appearances and as having various aspects. And because just such appearance exists and does not exist, there is no (such reality-status) of things.[59]

It is mind alone which unfolds under various appearances, sometimes under the appearance of lust or of hate, or else of other phenomena, and also simultaneously under various aspects such as faith. Appearances are existent and nonexistent in a mind which is in a state of addiction or virtue. But phenomena themselves have no (existence or nonexistence) either afflicted or virtuous, because they have no nature apart from appearance.

Eight verses on the quest of nature. The first verse is a summary, the rest the explanation:

> 36. The perfect buddhas, to benefit living beings, taught analytically the identified, its identity, and (the process of) identification.[60]

This is the summary.

> 37.[61] Mind has its views, its states, and its changelessness: this summarizes the identified; when analytically differentiated, it is immeasurable.

---

[59] The text of this verse is problematical. As originally printed by Lévi (LI, p. 63.22) it read: *yathā dvayapratibhāsādanyo na dvayalakṣaṇaḥ / iti cittaṁ citrābhāsaṁ citrākāraṁ pravartate.* However, in his translation, following the Tibetan and the Chinese, what he has printed as the first two *pāda*s is replaced with the commentary to the previous verse, and what he has printed as the beginning of the commentary to our verse, i.e., *tathābhāso bhāvābhāvo na tu dharmāṇāṁ mataḥ*, is now *pāda*s c and d with *tathā* and *mataḥ* replaced by *tatra* and *vataḥ*. Although the last *pāda* is unmetrical it is in harmony with the sense. Ui would correct this *pāda* to *na tu dharmābhāsaṁ tataṁ* though he cites no grounds for such an emendation. Sthiramati (P Mi 204b2–7) confirms Lévi's corrections. See LII, vs. 35 n. 1, 2; and Ui, p. 615.

[60] *Lakṣya, lakṣaṇa, lakṣaṇā* (LI, p. 64.5). In Sanskrit grammar *lakṣya* is that which is to be indirectly expressed, *lakṣaṇa* that which makes the *lakṣya* known, and *lakṣaṇā*, that which places the two terms into relation. Lévi (LII, p. 116, n. 1) cites the classical example: *Gaṅgāyāṁ ghoṣaṁ* "a tumult on the Ganga (river)." The *lakṣaṇa* is the expression "on the Ganga" – an actual physical impossiblilty which the intellect remedies by supplying the idea of "shore" – for example, "on the shore of the Ganga." The idea of "shore" is the *lakṣya*. The association of ideas which introduced the notion of "shore" is *lakṣaṇā*.

"Mind" here is consciousness and matter. "Views" then are mental functions. "States" are the anomalous phenomena detached from mind (and matter). "Changelessness" is the uncreated, such as space, since it permanently functions according to its informative concept.[62] Such are in summary the five categories of the identified; however, in detail, its categories are beyond measure.

> 38. The cause of the concept of objective referents corresponding to verbalization, its instincts, and thence also objective perceptions – such is the nature of the imaginatively constructed (identity).

"Identity" is, in brief, threefold: the imagined identity and so on. The imagined identity is threefold: the cause of the concept of the objective referent corresponding to verbalization; the instinct for verbal expression; and the referent which is perceived due to such an instinct even without – among those not skilled in linguistic conventions – the concept of referent corresponding to verbalization.[63] The concept of the referent corresponding to intentional expression is a mental function, (the same as) the concept of (objective) referents corresponding to verbalization. Its object is its cause. Thus, that to be imaginatively constructed, and that cause (of imagination), instinct – both are simply the imaginatively constructed identity.

> 39. The projection of (disparate) name and referent corresponding to name and referent – the process of unreal mental construction – such is the imaginatively constructed identity.

---

[61] The Chinese (T.31.613c4) has: "Common (*gong*- commentary explains as form), mental, view, structure (*wei*), and the changeless. In brief there are five things which are 'identified;' if one were to explain them extensively they would be limitless."

[62] *Tadvijñapternityaṁ tathāpravṛttem* (LI, p. 64.11). Sthiramati (P Mi 205b4–6) explains that when the uncreated noumena of space, the two cessations (*nirodha*) or the ultimate reality appear before the mind, they appear to lack the characteristics of production or destruction (*skye ba dang 'jig pa*). Compare *AS* p. 63: *kiṁ upādāya sa nirodhaṁ punar asaṁskṛtaṁ ity ucyate / lakṣaṇatrayavirahitaṁ upādāya / /* "Why is 'cessation' called uncreated? Because it lacks the three characteristics (of birth, duration, and disappearance)."

[63] Compare Dharmottara's commentary on *Nyāyabindu* I.5; see Stcherbatsky, *Buddhist Logic*, vol. II.

Another formulation: "Corresponding to name and referent" means according to name and referent. "Projection of name and referent" means perception of name and referent. When the object is perceived according to the name, or the name perceived according to the object, that is the object of unreal mental construction, which is the imaginatively constructed identity. Everything imaginatively constructed is indeed either name or referent.

> 40. Having a threefold threefold appearance, with the nature of subject and object, (the very process of) unreal mental construction (itself) is the relative identity.

Here, (unreal mental construction) is "having a threefold threefold appearance," since within it there are two kinds of threefold appearance. The (first) threefold appearance is the appearance of word, meaning, and objective referent.[64] The second threefold appearance is the appearance of mentality, subjectivity, and conceptual construction. "Mentality" is that (mind) which is always addicted. "Subjectivity" is the fivefold group of sense-consciousnesses. "Conceptual construction" is mental consciousness. The first threefold appearance has the nature of the object; the second has the nature of the subject. Thus this (process of) unreal mental construction (itself) is none other than the relative identity.

> 41. Nonexistence, existence, existence and nonexistence in equality, peaceless peace, and freedom from discriminative construction – this is the perfect identity.

The perfect reality is suchness. It is indeed the nonexistence of all imagined things, and it is existence (of the relative), since it exists through the nonexistence (of the imagined). It is the equality of existence and nonexistence, because such existence and nonexistence are indivisible. It is peaceless, because of the incidental minor addictions,[65] and it is peace since it is naturally purified. It is without dis-

---

64 *Pada, artha, deha* (LI, p. 65.2). Usually *artha* can mean either "sense" or "referent" in the Fregean sense. This is an unusual distinction between *artha* as linguistic meaning, and *deha* as "body" or "objective referent." This is a fascinating resonance with Frege.

65 *Upakleśa* (LI, p. 65.10). The minor (*upa*) addictions (*kleśa*). There are twenty minor addictions: 1) anger (*krodha*), 2) vindictiveness (*upanāha* or *upanāhana*), 3) hypocrisy (*mrakṣa*), 4) envy (*īrṣyā*), 5) spite (*pradāśa*), 6) stinginess (*mātsarya*), 7) dissimulation (*śāṭhya*), 8) duplicity (*māyā*), 9) violence (*vihiṁsā*), 10) conceit (*mada*), 11) lack of conscience

(cont'd)

criminative construction since it is beyond the range of discrimination, given that it is free of fabrications. Thus the threefold identity of suchness has been elucidated; its intrinsic identity, its identity with respect to addiction and purification, and its identity of freedom from discriminative construction. Thus also the threefold identity has been expressed.

> 42. Perceiving the spontaneous teaching, holding the appropriate conscientious attitude, fixing the mind on the element, and viewing objects as (both) existent and nonexistent: (such is the fivefold yogic process of identification).

The stage of yoga, again, has a fivefold process of identification: the ground, the product, the mirror, illumination, and the foundational. The ground is the spontaneous Dharma, realized by the Buddha and taught by him as the spontaneous result of his realization. The product is the appropriate conscientious attitude. The mirror is the fixing of the mind on the element, also called meditative concentration, which was defined above as fixing it upon name.[66] Illumination is the transcendent wisdom that sees objects as existent and nonexistent; it sees precisely the existence of the real and the nonexistence of the unreal. "The foundational" refers to the foundational transmutation (in the deepest consciousness).

> 43. One arrives here at equality, since the spiritual gene of noble beings is immaculate, equal, distinguished, without excess or deficiency; this is accepted as the process of identification.

This is the arrival at equality with the other noble ones in the uncontaminated realm, which is the spiritual gene of the noble ones and the immaculate, noble gene of the buddhas. It is equal due to its equality in liberation with the disciples and hermit sages. It is distinguished by five distinctions: distinction of thorough purification, since the addictions along with the instincts are thoroughly

---

(*āhrīkya*), 12) shamelessness (*atrapa* or *anapatrāpya*), 13) inertia (*styāna*), 14) excitement (*auddhatya* or *uddhata*), 15) disbelief (*aśraddha* or *aśrāddhya*), 16) indolence (*kausīdya*), 17) heedlessness (*pramāda*), 18) forgetfulness (*muṣitasmṛtitā*), 19) distraction (*vikṣepa*), 20) inattention (*asaṁprajanya*). All these functions are clearly described in the *Vijñāptimātratāsiddhi*, Sthiramati's commentary on Vasubandhu's *Triṁśika*. See the version by R.S. Tripathi and S. Dorje (Leh, Ladakh: Central Institute of Buddhist Studies, 1984).

66 See XI.6, 33.

purified; distinction of universal purification, since the field is universally purified; distinction of body, since it is the body of truth; distinction of beatitude, because uninterrupted spiritual beatitude fills the society; and distinction of evolutionary activity, since the aims of living beings are persistently accomplished by means of emanational (buddha-)deeds such as the (bodhisattva's) life in the Tuṣita heaven. It has no deficiency upon the cessation of the tendency to addiction. It has no excess in the production of the tendency to purification. Such is the process of identification, also called the five stages of yoga.

So thereby the identity (of reality), the identified (reality bearing that identity), and identification (the process of coming to realize that identity) occurs.

Six verses on the inquiry into liberation:

> 44. From the total transmutation of the seed, there is the transmutation of the appearance of places, objects, and bodies; this is the uncontaminated realm, and it has a universal basis.

The "transmutation of the seed" is the transmutation of the fundamental consciousness. (It produces) transmutations of consciousnesses which appear as places, objects, and bodies. This is the uncontaminated realm that is liberation. It has a universal basis – it holds sway for the disciples, the hermit buddhas, and the buddhas.[67]

> 45. Through the mutation of mentality, perceptivity, and discriminative construction, there is a fourfold mastery over the nonconceptual, the land, intuition, and action.

The word "mutation" (*āvṛtti*) is used in the verse for "transmutation" (*parāvṛtti*). The four masteries are exercised over the nonconceptual, the land, intuition, and action respectively.

> 46. The four masteries exist on the three stages, the immovable, and so on; two in one stage, one in each other respectively.

---

[67] It is generally held in both the disciple and bodhisattva vehicles that the liberations (*vimukti*) of disciples, hermit sages, and buddhas are identical; see *MSABh* XI.53 and *VKN* p. 422.

This fourfold mastery exists in the three stages from the immovable and so on. In one stage, the immovable, it is twofold: there being mastery[68] over the non-conceptual due to the freedom from conceptuality in non-intentionality, and (mastery) over the land due to the perfect purification of the buddha-land. In each of the two next stages, there is one mastery respectively: mastery over intuition in the stage of good genius due to the attainment of the distinguished intellectual knowledges, and mastery over action in the stage of cloud of Dharma due to the unobstructedness of actions guided by the superknowledges.

> 47. The genius (bodhisattva), having found here the two kinds of selflessness which pervade all existence, and having recognized equality, enters into reality, through subjectivity. Then, by fixing her mentality there, even that (subjectivity) no longer appears here; and that non-appearance is liberation, the supreme freedom from perception.

Another instruction on liberation. Having recognized the two kinds of selflessness which are found in the three worlds, and having known this twofold selflessness as being equal, by virtue of the nonexistence of the constructed person and the constructed thing, but not by virtue of total nonexistence, the bodhisattva enters into reality, which is sheer information, "through subjectivity," which means "this is sheer subjectivity." Then, her mentality having arrived at (the realm of) sheer information, that reality no longer appears, (even) as sheer information. When it does not appear any longer, then that is supreme liberation, which is the freedom from perception, through the nonperception of persons and things.

> 48. When from (the gathering of) the stores, there are both base and product, one sees name-only. In seeing name-only, there is seeing, and afterwards no more seeing (even of that name-only).

Another instruction. "The base" here means learning. "From gathering the stores" means that one who is well-endowed with the stores has gathered them previously. "Product" means appropriate conscientious attitude. "Seeing name-only" refers to (perception of) simple verbal expression devoid of sense. One truly sees name-only, that is, information-only, since one says to oneself: "'Name' is the four

---

68 The Tibetan reads *vaśitā* (*dbang ngo*) again in this sentence in the commentary.

systems apart from form." Having seen it, afterwards he does not see it anymore, that is, the object not existing, he does not see its information. This absence of perception is liberation.

> 49. That mind functions with its negative conditioning, ensnared by the vision of self; nevertheless, it is asserted that there is cessation by fixing that (mind) within.

Another mode of instruction. This mind accompanied with negative conditioning functions in the lifetimes. The words "ensnared by the vision of the self" show the cause of negative conditioning. It is tied up by the two types of visions of a self,[69] and consequently is susceptible to negative conditioning. But this is stopped by fixing the mind within, that is, by fixing the mind in mind itself, since there is no longer any perception of objects.

Two verses on the investigation of freedom from intrinsic reality:

> 50.[70] Realitylessness is advocated because (things) do not exist as selves or with their intrinsic natures, do not endure in intrinsic objectivity, and do not exist as they are perceived.

Because they do not exist by themselves, things lack intrinsic reality, but depend on conditions. Since they do not exist by their intrinsic natures, they lack intrinsic reality, for once they have been terminated, they do not reproduce themselves out of their intrinsic natures.[71] Since they do not stand in their own intrinsic reality, they lack intrinsic reality, since they are momentary. Such should be understood as the three kinds of intrinsic realitylessness which accompany the three characteristics of created things. They lack intrinsic reality, since they do not exist as they are perceived. "Do not exist" (in the compound *tadabhāvāt*) means "do not intrinsically exist" (*tad* = *sva*). It is like naïve persons' perceptions of intrinsic reality, as permanence, happiness, purity, self, or else as some otherwise imaginatively constructed nature; there is no such intrinsic reality, and therefore the intrinsic realitylessness of things is accepted.

---

[69] The self of persons (*pudgala*) and of phenomena (*dharma*).

[70] This verse and the following are also found in the second chapter of the *MS*.

[71] Lévi's Sanskrit reads *punastenātmana* (LI, p. 67.19), supported by the Tibetan *yang de'i bdag nyid du*.

51. Realitylessness establishes nonproduction, noncessation, primordial peace, and natural liberation, since each is the basis of the succeeding one.[72]

As things lack intrinsic reality, they are established as without production and so on. In fact, the absence of intrinsic reality is nonproduction. What is not produced is unceased. What is unceased is in a state of primordial peace. What is in primordial peace is in a state of natural liberation. Thus, by these realitylessnesses, each serving as basis of the succeeding, (there are) intrinsic realitylessness, nonproduction, and so on.[73]

A verse in the *ārya* meter on the investigation of the tolerance of the nonproduction of things:[74]

52. The tolerance of the nonproduction of things is recommended, in the light of their beginning, sameness, otherness, intrinsic identity, self, transmutation, addiction, and distinction.

Tolerance of the nonproduction of things is a tolerance in terms of the eight nonproductions. In terms of the origin of cyclic life, it is without original production. In terms of sameness or otherness in prior and later things, in cyclic life things previously produced are not produced (again) as the same, since once produced they do not reproduce themselves from their intrinsic realities; nor is there production of (intrinsically) other things, as things are not produced in unprecedented forms. In terms of intrinsic identity, the imaginatively constructed reality is never produced. In terms of self-production, the relative reality (is unproduced). In terms

---

72 Compare with *SN* VII.1 (as restored by Lamotte): *niḥsvabhāvāṁ sarvadharmā anutpannāṁ sarvadharmā aniruddhā adiśantāṁ prakṛtiparinirvṛtāṁ*, and the following passage from the *Ratnameghasūtra* cited in *Prasannapadā* p. 98: *adiśantā hyanutpannāṁ prakṛtyaiva, ca nirvṛtāṁ / dharmās te vivṛtā nātha dharmacakrapravartate*. On the doctrine of the three *niḥsvabhāvatas* see *La Somme* p. 23; *Siddhi* pp. 556–561; and Thurman, *Tsong Khapa's Speech of Gold*, pp. 209–252.

73 Compare the commentary here with *SN*, (Lamotte ed.) VII.8.

74 *Anutpattidharmakṣānti* (LI, p. 68.4). As explained in *MSABh* XIV.23–26 the state of tolerance (*kṣānti*) is realization that the "external world" does not exist apart from the mind. This results in the overcoming of the distraction of objectivity (*grāhyavikṣepa*) but the distraction of subjectivity (*grāhakavikṣepa*) remains. This "tolerance" is achieved on the third of the four degrees of the path of application (*prayogamārga*), and is considered "mundane" (*laukika*). See LII, vs. 52 n. 1, *VKN* pp. 411–413, *HTV* pp. 164–165.

of transmutation, there is never any production of the perfect reality. In terms of abandonment of addictive processes, (there is no production) because those who have attained the knowledge of termination of contamination do not see any production of addictions. In terms of distinction (there is no production), since any distinctions between the truth bodies of the buddhas are not produced. This explains the tolerance of the nonproduction of things in terms of these (eight) things.

Seven verses investigating the unique vehicle:[75]

> 53.[76] There is uniqueness of vehicle because of the sameness of reality, selflessness, and liberations; because of the differences of spiritual genes; because of the attainment of two aspirations; because of emanated incarnations; and because of culmination.

"Sameness of reality" means that there is one vehicle, since the disciples and so on do not have different ultimate realms; because "vehicle" (*yāna*) means "destination" (*yātavyam*). "Sameness of selflessness" means there is one vehicle, since the disciples and so on hold in common that the self does not exist; because "vehicle" (*yāna*) means "goer" (*yātā*). "Sameness of liberation" means there is one vehicle, since "vehicle" means "going" (*yāti*).

"Difference of spiritual genes" means there is one vehicle, since those undetermined in their disciples' spiritual gene become transcendent by means of the universal vehicle; because "vehicle" means "they go by it" (*yānti tena*).

"Attainment of the two aspirations" means that there is one vehicle, since the buddhas discover their own aspiration in all beings, and because even disciples are determinate in spiritual gene, who have in previous lives gathered the stores of enlightenment, attain the buddha-aspiration by the power of the Buddha, through gaining the faith that their lives are not alienated (from the buddhas'), through their gaining their portion of the excellence of the grace of the Transcendent Lord. Thus there is uniqueness of vehicle for the Buddha and disciples because of their sameness in attainment of aspirations.[77]

---

[75] *Ekayāna* (LI, p. 68.14).

[76] This verse and the following are found in the tenth chapter of the *MS*.

[77] This passage is quite difficult to understand. With the help of Sthiramati (D Mi 197b–198a), the two aspirations achieved seem to refer to the buddha's achievement of his aspiration in realizing the sameness of himself and other beings, and the achievement of the disciples who have attained the disciples' Nirvāṇa through their own vehicle, yet who re-

(cont'd)

"Emanation" means that there is one vehicle. As it was said: "On hundreds of occasions I attained final Nirvāṇa by means of the disciples' vehicle" in order to manifest an emanation for the sake of the disciples.

Finally, "culmination" means that there is one vehicle, since vehicle means "whence there is no higher destination."[78]

Buddhahood has only the one vehicle; and it is thus that one should understand the statements in such and such discourses that there is one (vehicle) as having such and such intended implications. But it is not the case that there are not three vehicles.

For what purpose have the buddhas sometimes taught with a certain intention the uniqueness of vehicle?

> 54.[79] The buddhas have taught the one vehicle for the sake of those who are not determined, to attract some and to hold the others.

"To attract some" refers to those of the disciple gene, who are not determined, and "to hold others" refers to those of the bodhisattva gene who are still not determined.

> 55. There are two kinds of disciples who are not determined: those who have and those who have not realized the goal of the vehicle. Those who have realized the goal are dispassionate or are not dispassionate; these two (kinds of disciples) being inferior.

There are two kinds of disciples who are not determined: those who have realized the goal of the vehicle have seen the truth and have transcended by way of

---

member that they once in former lives practiced the bodhisattva deeds and so will eventually attain buddhahood, eventually entering the buddha vehicle. They have only a partial sameness with the Buddha's intention, so they are said to enjoy only a portion of the Lord's grace. This is how Vasubandhu interprets the one vehicle doctrine without giving up the three vehicle idea.

78 *Yānam* is here glossed as *yataḥ pareṇa yātavyaṁ nāsti* (LI, p. 68.26–27).

79 This verse is quoted in *AAA* p. 331.

the universal vehicle,[80] and those who have not realized the goal of the vehicle, who have seen the truth yet have not transcended by way of the universal vehicle. Those who have realized the goal are dispassionate or are not dispassionate, depending on (the intensity of) their lust. These two mentioned are inferior (to the undetermined bodhisattva), and progress very slowly. Those who have realized the goal are said to be of two types.[81]

> 56. Those two, through the dedication to (continued) existences of one who has attained the noble path, become endowed with a life of inconceivable dedication.

Those who have realized the goal should be understood as becoming endowed with an inconceivably dedicated life. By dedication to the noble path acquired, they reincarnate in the worlds with an inconceivable dedication; that is why inconceivable dedication (is mentioned).

> 57. One type advances through life by the power of his vows; and the other becomes involved (in the world) through emanations created by his application of his non-returner status.

Of the two, the one who is not dispassionate undertakes lives voluntarily by the power of his vows.[82] The other, by the power of his non-returner's stage, takes (reincarnation) by emanation (of mind-made bodies).[83]

> 58. Both are considered very slow to progress, because they delight in Nirvāṇa, and because their habitual (disciple's) mind is again and again given to self-indulgence.

---

[80] dBal Mang (80b) is critical of Vasubandhu's commentary and (presumably) Sthiramati's elucidation when they mention that these disciples "transcend by way of the universal vehicle."

[81] This phrase is absent in the Tibetan (D Phi 175b2).

[82] See XVIII.74–76.

[83] *Anāgāmi* (LI, p. 69.21). The third of the four degrees of discipleship in the individual vehicle. Those who attain it are never again born in the desire realm (*kāmadhātu*), according to traditional doctrine. Yet, as Sthiramati explains (D Mi 200b–201a), they can take rebirth voluntarily by the power of their *samādhi*, creating mind-made (*manoja*) emanation bodies with which to accomplish the aims of beings.

Because they delight in Nirvāṇa, they both are considered slow to progress, since their perfect enlightenment is long delayed. Too frequently they indulge their habitual disciple's attitude, (always) associated with revulsion (for life).

> 59. Not having accomplished her purpose, and born in a time without a buddha, she strives to achieve the contemplations, longing to become an emanation (buddha). Relying upon that, she attains supreme enlightenment.

The non-dispassionate one who has seen the truth has not accomplished her purpose, having more to learn. Being born in a time when there is no buddha, she strives for the sake of contemplation, longing to become an emanation (buddha). Relying upon such an emanation, she gradually attains supreme enlightenment. Hinting at these three stages, the Lord said in the *Śrīmālā Sūtra*: "Having been a disciple, he becomes a hermit buddha, and finally a buddha; as in the example of fire."[84] When she is first in the state of seeing truth, in a time deprived of a buddha, she strives for contemplation for herself. She renounces her natural body and acquires a magical emanation body, and finally attains supreme enlightenment.

A verse investigating the sciences:

> 60. If he has not applied himself to the five sciences, even the supreme saint will never arrive at omniscience. Therefore, he makes effort in those (sciences), in order to criticize and care for others as well as for the sake of his own knowledge.

There are the five sciences: inner science, and the sciences of logic, linguistics, medicine, and artistic technologies. This verse shows that the bodhisattva should pursue all in general in order to attain omniscience. In specific, he should investigate logic and linguistics in order to criticize those who have no faith in that (universal vehicle). (He should investigate) the science of medicine and the artistic sciences in order to care for others who have need of them. He should investigate the inner science for his own omniscience.[85]

---

[84] This passage is not to be found in any extant version of that work; see Alex Wayman, *The Lion's Roar of Queen Śrīmālā* (New York: Columbia University Press, 1974), p. 26.

[85] On the five sciences (*pañcavidyāsthāna*) see also *BBh* p. 68.

Thirteen verses investigating the nourishing of the element. These verses indicate certain attitudes associated with the transcendences for the purpose of fulfilling the transcendences and completely nourishing the element.

> 61. (The conscientious attitudes that nourish the element of the transcendences are) satisfaction in obtaining their cause, remembrance of their basis, desire for the common good, and faith that accords with enlightenment.

The list of conscientious attitudes goes from satisfaction in obtaining the cause to affirming the supreme self.

The conscientious attitude of satisfaction in obtaining the cause, which is the first, is that of the bodhisattva who has the spiritual gene, who sees in herself the gene of the transcendences and nourishes the element of the transcendences by her satisfaction in having obtained the cause. Immediately then there follows the conscientious attitude of remembrance of their basis, as, having that spiritual gene, she conceives the spirit of unexcelled perfect enlightenment. Indeed, the bodhisattva, seeing in herself the spirit of enlightenment as the basis of the transcendences, adopts this attitude: "Certainly these transcendences will be perfected, since I have thus discovered the spirit of enlightenment."

Once the spirit of enlightenment has been produced, there is the attitude of desire for the common good, applied to the welfare of self and others through the transcendences, considering: "May the benefit of these transcendences be shared with others! And may it not be otherwise!" In applying herself to the welfare of self and others, she fully realizes the meaning of reality, which is the unaddicted liberative art, and immediately there follows the conscientious attitude of faith that accords with enlightenment, becoming motivated as follows: "Just as the lord buddhas have been, are, and will be perfectly enlightened in the transcendences, so I believe (I also will become)." Thus should be understood all the stages (of these conscientious attitudes).[86]

> 62. (Further conscientious attitudes are) joy from the four powers, inexhaustible determination, and the fourfold practice concerning resistance and remedy.

---

[86] Following the Tibetan (D Phi 176b6), reading the Sanskrit *evaṁ sarvatrānukramo veditavyaḥ* (LI, p. 71.15) at the end of the paragraph where it more logically fits.

The conscientious attitude of joy from the powers is the joy of the experience of the four powers. The four powers are those of the abandonment of the resistances, the full ripening of the gathered stores, the care of self and others, and the giving of the evolutionary and homogeneous results in the future.

The conscientious attitude of the inexhaustible determination, at the beginning of the development of enlightened qualities in oneself and other living beings, arises when one determines not to be exhausted, either by the perverse activities of living beings or by all the sufferings which fall upon one.

For the sake of obtaining supreme enlightenment, there arises the conscientious attitude of the fourfold practice directed toward the resistances and their remedies: the confession of stinginess and so on which are the resistances to generosity and so on; the congratulatory approval of the remedies, generosity and so on;[87] the request to the Buddha to teach the Dharma that possesses these remedies; and the total dedication of everything to enlightenment.

> 63. (Further) conscientious attitudes (that nourish the transcendences are) faith, receptivity, eagerness to share, armor, devotion, delight, and (artful) effort.[88]

There is the conscientious attitude of faith in the teaching and import that concern the transcendences, which begins from intensifying the power of faith. Beginning from the investigation of the teaching, there is the conscientious attitude of receptivity, which embraces the teaching and applies it without any condescension. Beginning from (receiving) instruction, there is the conscientious attitude of eagerness to share, which has the purpose of elucidating for others the teaching and its import.

Beginning from practice, there is the conscientious attitude of armoring, as one dons one's armor in order fully to perfect one's generosity and so on. There is the conscientious attitude of prayerful devotion, which undertakes to seek occasions for the full perfection of those (transcendences). There is the conscientious attitude of delight coming from rejoicing: "Ah! I must surely realize total success in the

---

[87] For the resistances to the transcendences see *MSABh* XVI.8–13.

[88] The Sanskrit *manaskriyā* (LI, p. 72.4), and the Tibetan *bya ba'i yid*, at first seems an alternative form of *manasikāra*, but its indicating a further attitude is made clear by the commentary, which glosses *kriyā* by *upāyopasaṁhitakarma* (*thabs dang ldan pa'i las*).

practice of generosity and so on!" These (latter) three conscientious attitudes in particular must be applied to precepts and instructions.

There is the conscientious attitude of artful effort, which keeps all calculating thought intent upon every kind of generosity and so on (with the other transcendences).

> 64. (A further conscientious attitude is) the persistent, high enthusiasm for the sixfold generosity and so on, (fourfold) in gaining power, developing (living beings), worshipping, and serving (teachers); (and another is) sensitivity.

The conscientious attitude of enthusiasm is fourfold. (It aims) to gain power in giving gifts and so on, (these transcendences themselves being) sixfold, from generous generosity up to wise generosity, likewise in the case of the sixfold morality and the rest. (It aims) to develop living beings by using the (four) social practices, (here constituted) only by transcendent acts. (It aims) to worship, which means worship by the giving of goods and honor and worship by practicing the other transcendences. (Fourth,) one should recognize the conscientious attitude of enthusiasm in the service of a spiritual teacher for the sake of (receiving) unerring instruction in the transcendences.

The conscientious attitude of sensitivity consists of the four immeasurables: love, which brings about the practice of generosity and so on; compassion for living beings entrenched in stinginess and so on; joy for living beings who are generous and so on; and equanimity through wishing them to be free of addiction.

> 65. (Further conscientious attitudes are) shame at the undone or badly done, guilt, delight in one's objectives, the consideration of fatigue as an enemy, and the intention to compose and to publish.

The conscientious attitude of shame comes from the working of conscience in the cases of giving and so forth which one failed to do, or did incompletely or incorrectly. Seized by shame, one soon feels guilty, (which moves one) to take action or to desist from action. The conscientious attitude of delight in one's objectives such as giving and so on comes from joy,[89] as it holds the mind without wavering.

---

[89] The Sanskrit reads *dhṛtim* (LI, p. 72.25–26), but the Tibetan reads *mgu ba*, translating an original *tuṣṭiṁ*, which seems preferable in this context, though the other is surely possible.

The conscientious attitude of indefatigability proceeds from considering exhaustion an enemy when one is engaged in giving and so on. The conscientious attitude of inspiration to compose proceeds from the ambition to compose treatises concerning the transcendences. The conscientious attitude of publication begins from knowledge of society, proceeding from the ambition to publish these same treatises in the world adapted to the audience.

> 66. In (the aim of) perfect enlightenment, there is (the conscientious attitude of) self-reliance upon such (virtues of one's own as) generosity, and not upon such (deities) as God (*īśvara*). (Another conscientious attitude is) the intellectual insight into the faults and excellences of both (resistances and remedies).

In the process of attaining enlightenment, there is the conscientious attitude of self-reliance, as one relies upon (one's own) generosity and so on, and not upon God and so on. The conscientious attitude of intellectual insight proceeds from insight into the faults and excellences of the resistances (to the transcendences), stinginess and so on, and their remedies, generosity and so on.

> 67. (Further conscientious attitudes are) joy in remembrance of accumulation, awareness of great purposefulness, and the willingness for practice, for nondiscrimination, for steadfastness, and for rising to occasions.

The conscientious attitude of joy in the remembrance of accumulation works in the accumulating of (deeds of) giving and so on, from seeing (them as) the accumulation of the stores of merit and knowledge. The conscientious attitude of awareness of great purposefulness comes from seeing that generosity and so on, being (virtues) corresponding to the accessories of enlightenment,[90] have the purpose of achievement of the great enlightenment.

The conscientious attitude of willingness is fourfold. There is the conscientious attitude of willingness for practice, coming from the will to meditation on serenity and transcendent insight. There is the conscientious attitude of willingness

---

90 The Tibetan reads *byang chub kyi phyogs dang mthun pa'i dngos po'i don gyis*, which emends Lévi's Sanskrit (LI, p. 73.11) from *bodhipakṣe bhāvārthena* to *bodhipakṣānukūla-bhavārthena*.

for nondiscrimination, coming from the will to skill in liberative art for the sake of succeeding in the transcendences. There is the conscientious attitude of willingness in steadfastness, coming from the will to uphold teaching and meaning concerning the transcendences. There is the conscientious attitude of willingness to rise to occasions, coming from the motivation derived from sincere vows.

> 68. (Further conscientious attitudes are) the awareness of ability to rise above the seven kinds of false habits; four kinds of surprising ideas; and four kinds of unsurprising ideas.

There is the conscientious attitude of awareness of (one's) ability to rise above the seven kinds of false habits. The seven kinds of false habits are: taking that which is not for that which is; taking the faulty for the excellent; taking the excellent for the deficient; misperceiving permanence and happiness in all creations; misperceiving self in all things; and misconceiving Nirvāṇa as lacking peace. The remedies taught for these (false habits) are the three concentrations on voidness[91] and so on, and the four epitomes of the Dharma.[92]

There is the conscientious attitude with four surprising ideas: the ideas, concerning the transcendences, of magnificence, long persistence, disregard of reward, and disregard of evolutionary benefit. There is also the conscientious attitude with four unsurprising ideas. These four unsurprising ideas are: that the transcendences, magnificent and time-consuming, culminate in the fruit of buddhahood; and also that (the bodhisattva, aware) that both (magnificence and persistence) are involved,

---

[91] The concentrations on voidness (*śūnyatā*), signlessness (*animittā*), and wishlessness (*apraṇihitā*) are the "three doors of liberation"; see *MSABh* XIII.1. Sthiramati (P Mi 214b1 *ff.*) explains that concentration on voidness cures taking the nonexistent (constructed) reality as really existent, concentration on wishlessness cures taking the faulty for the excellent, and concentration on signlessness cures taking the excellent as the deficient. He then relates the concentration on voidness to the empty and selfless aspects of the holy truth of suffering; he relates the concentration on wishlessness to the impermanent and suffering aspects of the holy truth of suffering, and to the four aspects of the holy truth of origin, as well as to the four aspects of the holy truth of the path; and he relates the concentration on signlessness to the four aspects of the holy truth of cessation. Thus, he makes it understandable how these two latter concentrations enable one to abandon the false habits of taking the faulty (world of suffering, origin, and path) for the excellent and taking the excellent (realm of Nirvāṇa) as the deficient.

[92] Sthiramati gives his version of the four epitomes (P Mi 2147 *ff.*): all created things are impermanent; all contaminated things are suffering; all things are selfless; peace is Nirvāṇa.

achieves equanimity of mind toward self and others; that though such (bodhisattvas practicing the transcendences) have won the worship of the excellent Indra and the other gods, they do not worry about rewards; and that, though they have obtained a body and a fortune which excel those of the whole world, (the bodhisattva) does not worry about (gaining any) evolutionary benefit.

> 69. (Other conscientious attitudes are) equanimity towards all beings, awareness of greatness, expecting a reward for others (due to their) excellences, the threefold hope, and the unremitting (attitudes).

The conscientious attitude of equanimity results from the ambition to treat all beings equally in terms of generosity and so on. The conscientious attitude of awareness of greatness[93] comes from understanding the transcendences as conferring benefit upon all beings. The conscientious attitude seeking reward (for others) results from (enjoying seeing) others engaged in the excellences of generosity and so forth. The conscientious attitude of hope comes from hoping for three states of (success of) the transcendences (to obtain) among living beings: the culmination of the bodhisattva stages, the culmination of the buddha stage, and the accomplishment of the aims of beings. The unremitting conscientious attitude comes from the ambition not to waste any opportunity for generosity and so forth.

> 70. (Other conscientious attitudes are) the determination not to fall short in putting into practice the Buddha's teaching, disappointment with beings who fail in it, and joy for (those who) progress (in it).

The conscientious attitude of true application comes from intending not to fall short in correctly putting it into practice. The conscientious attitude of disappointment is directed towards beings who are deficient in generosity and so forth. The conscientious attitude of joy is directed toward beings who progress in generosity and so forth.

---

[93] In his reconstruction of this lacuna in the Sanskrit Ms., Lévi reads *mahātmadṛṣṭi* (LII, p. 132, n. 68), for the Tibetan *bdag nyid chen po mthong ba*. We prefer to read this *mahātmyādṛṣṭi*, or even better *mahātmyādarśana*, emending also the second part of the first line of the verse as *saṁdarśanaśca mahātmyām*. For the use of *mahātmyā* by Maitreya and Asaṅga, see XIV.37.

> 71. (Further) conscientious attitudes are disrespect for counterfeit practice, respect for the genuine, disassociation (from resistances), and longing for the prophecy and the determined destiny.

The conscientious attitude of disrespect is directed at the counterfeit practice of the transcendences. The conscientious attitude of respect is directed at genuine practice. The conscientious attitude of disassociation comes from the motivation to control the resistances such as stinginess and so on with generosity and so on.[94] The conscientious attitude of longing is twofold: the attitude of longing to obtain the prophecy of one's perfection of the transcendences, and the attitude of longing to obtain the condition of the stage of certain destiny of (perfecting) the transcendences.

> 72. (Further conscientious attitudes are) the will to engagement through foresight, observation of equality, and affirmation of one's own excellence from engagement in the best practices.

The attitude of the will to engagement (in the transcendences) through foresight is motivated by the thought: "A bodhisattva must necessarily practice generosity and so forth wherever she goes." The attitude of observation of equality in generosity and so on is the wish always to accomplish the transcendences together with other bodhisattvas. The attitude of affirmation of oneself as excellent comes from awareness of one's own excellence due to one's engagement in the superior practices of the transcendences.

> 73. These virtuous conscientious attitudes follow the ten transcendences.[95] They always increase the element of the bodhisattvas.

This is a concluding verse. The meaning is self-evident.

Two verses on the types of investigation of the teaching:

---

[94] "with generosity and so on" is from the Tibetan (D Phi 179a4: *sbyin pa la sogs pas*), though it is lacking in Lévi's Sanskrit edition (LI, p. 74.16).

[95] The six transcendences, generosity, morality, etc., plus skill in liberative art (*upāya-kauśalya*), vow (*praṇidhāna*), power (*bala*), and intuition (*jñāna*).

> 74–75. For the brave (bodhisattva), investigation is considered in terms of growth, universal responsibility, and greatness; through their abandonment, non-abandonment, and mastery. The bodhisattvas' investigations[96] are proclaimed to (take place at the levels of) being unincorporated, incorporated,[97] lightly incorporated, and fully incorporated (in the truth body); with much pride, with slight pride, and without pride.

There are thirteen types of investigation of the teaching: in terms of growth, increasing faith in (the teaching) which has been heard; in terms of universal responsibility, through the stream of the door of truth; in terms of greatness, when one has obtained the masteries. (Here,) "abandonment" (refers again to) the first, "non-abandonment" to the second, and "mastery" to the third.

The "unincorporated" (level) is created from hearing and reflection, and still lacks the body of truth. The "incorporated" level is created from meditation, in the stage of action out of faith. The "lightly incorporated" refers to (the first) seven stages. The "fully incorporated" refers to the other (three) stages. "With much pride" refers to the stage of action out of faith. "With slight pride" refers to the first seven stages. "With no pride" refers to the last three stages.

A verse on the investigation of the causality[98] of the teaching:

> 76. For the brave (bodhisattvas), the teaching is the cause of (their) marks in the form (realm), of their health in the formless (realm), of their power through the superknowledges, and of their inexhaustibility.

In the form (realms), the Dharma is the cause of the (bodhisattvas') auspicious marks. In the formless (realms), it is the cause of health, because it cures the sicknesses of the addictions. It is the cause of their power by means of the super-

---

96 The Tibetan reads *byang chub sems dpa' rnams kyi tshol ba* which reflects an original of the last line of the second verse *bahusūkṣmamānā nirmāṇā ca bodhisattvaiṣṭi matā* instead of *bahumānasūkṣmamānā nirmāṇā caiṣaṇābhimatā* (LI, p. 75.9) (keeping the line at seventeen syllables).

97 *Asakāyā*, (LI, p. 75.12) revealed by the commentary below to be a contraction of *akāyā* and *sakāyā*.

98 The Tibetan, erroneously, *gnyis* for *nyid*.

knowledges. It is also the cause of inexhaustibility, since it is not interrupted even in the remainderless Nirvāṇa.

Therefore it is said in the *Dialogue with Brahma Sūtra*:

> Endowed with four ideas, the bodhisattvas investigate the teaching: the idea of (the teaching as) a jewel, as it is difficult to obtain; the idea of (it as) medicine, as it cures the sicknesses of the addictions; the idea of (it as) wealth, as it is not wasted; the idea of (the teaching as) Nirvāṇa, as it cures all suffering.[99]

The (auspicious) marks are like jewels because they beautify; from such causality comes the idea of the teaching as like a jewel. There is the idea of it as medicine, since it is the cause of health. There is the idea of it as wealth, since it is the cause for the (bodhisattvas') power through the superknowledges. There is the idea of it as Nirvāṇa, because it is the cause of (the bodhisattvas') inexhaustibility.

A verse on the investigation of discriminative constructions:

> 77. The victor-children should absolutely avoid discriminative constructions of nonexistence, existence, reification, repudiation, unity, diversity, intrinsic identity, qualification, habitual naïve realism, and nominalistic substantialism.

There are ten kinds of discriminative constructions that the bodhisattva should completely abandon.[100]

To remedy the discrimination of nonexistence, it is said in the *Transcendent Wisdom Scripture*:[101] "Here, the bodhisattva exists as merely a bodhisattva." To remedy the discrimination of existence, it is said: "He does not see any bodhisattva at all." To remedy the discrimination of reification, it is said: "Śāriputra – form is empty with respect to intrinsic reality." To remedy the discrimination of repudiation, it is said: "It is not by voidness (that matter is void)...."

---

99 This passage is found in the *Āryabrahmaviśeṣacintaparipṛcchāsūtra* (mdo, Phu, 31a6–8). See also LI, pp. 75–76, n. 4.

100 On the ten discriminations see also Dignāga's *Prajñāpāramitāpiṇḍārtha* vs. 19–58; *La Somme* pp. 115–118; etc.

101 On the sources of the subsequent quotations from the *Prajñāpāramitā* see *VKN*, p. 47, n. 19. See also Conze, *The Large Sūtra on Perfect Wisdom*, Part One, p. 53 n. 3.

To remedy the discrimination of unity, it is said: "Voidness of matter is not matter." To remedy the discrimination of diversity, it is said: "Apart from voidness there is no matter; matter is voidness, voidness is matter."

To remedy the discrimination of intrinsic identity, it is said: "Matter is merely a name." To remedy the discrimination of qualification, it is said: "Matter has neither production nor destruction, neither addiction nor purification."

To remedy the discrimination of addiction to naïve realism, it is said: "Language is an artificial thing." To remedy the addiction to naïve substantialism, it is said: "The bodhisattva does not see any names at all; not seeing them at all, she is not addicted to attaching them to referents."

> 78. Thus the beautiful genius with tremendous effort embodies the investigation of his own thatness through the two realities.[102] He always serves as refuge for living beings, being as full of excellences as the ocean.

This concluding verse shows the three kinds of greatness of investigation: greatness of liberative art, because with a tremendous effort he lives the quest of thatness by means of conventional and ultimate realities[103] – "thatness" here means "truth"; greatness of altruism, because he becomes a refuge for living beings; greatness of individualism, because he is full of excellences like the ocean.

---

[102] See *Prasannapadā* on *Mūlamadhyamakaśāstra* XXIV.8.

[103] *Satya* (LI, p. 76.23). Omitted in the Tibetan.

CHAPTER XII

Teaching the Dharma

One verse rejecting stinginess in teaching the Dharma:[1]

> 1. In many extravagant acts of charity, the brave (bodhisattvas) are always joyously giving to suffering beings (their own) lives and fortunes, (so) hard won (and yet) insubstantial. So is there any need to mention (their constant giving of) the magnificent Dharma which always helps beings in every way, which is not hard won, and which is inexhaustible when freely given, even increasing more?

Out of compassion for suffering beings, the bodhisattvas constantly give with a magnificent abandon (even their) lives and fortunes which, although hard to obtain, are insubstantial because perishable. So what need to mention (their giving) the Dharma which is neither hard to get nor perishable when freely given, even increasing all the more.

Two verses on the uselessness and usefulness of the Dharma:

> 2. The Lord Buddha did not, in fact, teach the (ultimate) Dharma, since it is individually realized within. Still, the compassionate ones, like huge boa-constrictors, (first) attract people toward their own reality with their reasonable teachings, (which work) like the boa's paralyzing saliva, and (then) make them fall into the gaping mouth of their own peace, which is perfectly pure, universal, and inexhaustible.

The buddhas are compared to boa-constrictors. "The gaping mouth of their own peace" is the body of truth. (It is) "perfectly pure" because it is purified of the

---

[1] dBal Mang (97b7) introduces this chapter: "Once one has discovered the Dharma, one must practice it oneself and teach it to others...."

objective and addictive obscurations and their instincts. It is "universal" to all buddhas, and "inexhaustible" because of its eternality.

> 3. Thus the meditative practice of yogis is not useless, and thus the teaching of the bliss-lords is not useless. If the import were understood through study alone, meditation would be useless; and if one were to engage in meditative practice without study, teaching would be useless.

Therefore the meditative practice of yogis is not useless because through its power the Dharma to be realized individually is comprehended. And teaching is not useless because it attracts people toward their own reality by means of reasonable teachings. The second half of the verse shows the way in which both meditative practice and teachings are useful. The rest is easy to understand.

A verse on the analysis of teaching:

> 4. The teaching of superior beings comes from scripture, realization, and mastery. It issues forth from the mouth, from all forms, and from space.

"From mastery" refers to the teaching of those who have entered the great stages. "From all forms" refers to teachings issuing forth even from trees, musical instruments, and so on. The rest is self-evident.

Two verses on the perfection of teaching:

> 5. The bodhisattvas' perfect teaching should be recognized as extensive, doubt-dispelling, acceptable, and twofold in its demonstration of reality.

This verse explains (perfect teaching as constituted) by four elements. The *Dialogue with Brahma Sūtra* states:

> The bodhisattvas, great spiritual heroes, share the great gift of the Dharma, themselves in possession of four qualifications: full comprehension of the holy Dharma, cultivation of their own wisdom, success in the deeds of noble persons, and (the ability to) demonstrate (both) addictional and liberational (realities).

First their teaching becomes extensive through great learning. Second, doubts are dispelled from their great wisdom, since it resolves others' doubts. Third, it is fit for acceptance since their deeds are irreproachable. And fourth, they can teach thatness in a twofold way, (using) both realities (to teach) both the reality characterized as addictional and the reality characterized as liberational.

> 6. The teaching of these best heroes is gentle, modest, tireless, clear, varied, reasonable, intelligible, non-exploitive, and universal.

In this second verse, (the bodhisattvas' teachings are said to be) "gentle" because they do not speak rudely even when insulted by others; "modest" because they feel no pride in praise or success; "tireless" because they are inexhaustible; "clear" because they teach completely, free of the reticence of bad teachers; "varied" because they are never redundant; "reasonable" because they do not contradict validating reason; "intelligible" because their words and syllables are easily comprehensible; "non-exploitive" because they are not aiming for special favors from the faith (of their students); and "universal" because they range over all three vehicles.

A verse on the perfection of speech:

> 7. The speech of the victor-children is powerful, gentle, eloquent, sensible, appropriate, non-exploitive, measured, and expansive.[2]

"Powerful" means public, because it reaches the whole audience. "Gentle" means attractive. "Eloquent" means distinct, because the syllables are well-articulated. "Sensible" means understandable, because it is sensibly expressed. "Appropriate" means worthy of hearing, because it is attuned to the disciples. It is "non-exploitive," because it is not aiming toward wealth, honor, or fame. "Measured" means not disagreeable, because measured speech never becomes boring. "Expansive" means unconstricted.

Two verses on the perfection of syllables:

> 8. (The bodhisattvas' syllables are perfect because they) teach, explain, are adapted to the vehicles, soothe, make sense, are appropriate, liberate, and favor.

---

[2] Following Lévi's reconstruction from Tibetan of this "*vers mutilé*" (LII, p. 141 n. 7.1): *adīnā mādhurā sūktā pratītā vāgjinātmaje / nirāmiṣā yathārhā ca pramitā viśadā tathā / /*

(The bodhisattvas' syllables are perfect) because reasoned words and letters teach in summary without contradiction by validating cognition. They explain in detail by means of compositions that do not contradict the summary teachings. They adapt to the vehicles by interpretations uncontradicted by (any of) the three vehicles. They soothe by apt words free of harshness. They make sense by artfully employing well-known ideas to make their points. They are appropriate by being suitably adapted to the disciples. They liberate through their reverence, as they always aim for Nirvāṇa. And they favor, containing the eight elements of cultured intellects,[3] as they conform to the holy eightfold path of learners.

> 9. These in sum are recognized as the perfection of the syllables of these best heroes; but the speech of the bliss-lords is infinite and inconceivable with its sixty elements.[4]

"Inconceivable with its sixty elements" refers to the sixty aspects of a buddha's speech explained in the *Teaching of the Lord of Secrets Sūtra*:[5]

> Furthermore Śāntamati, the speech of the transcendent lords issues forth endowed with sixty aspects. It is kindly, gentle, beautiful, appealing, pure, and so forth at length. It is "kindly" because it encourages the roots of virtue of the beings. It is "gentle" because its encounter brings immediate happiness. It is "beautiful" because of its excellent content. It is "appealing" because of its excellent expression. It is "pure" because it conveys the aftermath (intuition) of unexcelled transcendence. It is "stainless" because it is dissociated from all addictions, bad habits, and instincts. It is "luminous" because the words and phrases are lucid. It is "attractive" because it has the excellence of the power to dissolve the convictions of evil-minded fanatics. It is "worth hearing" because it leads to transcendence through practice. It is "unassailable" because it is not over-

---

[3] The Sanskrit *nipaka* (LI, p. 79.12), translated by the Tibetan *'grus skyong*, and glossed by Sthiramati as *mkhas pa sbyor pa* (P Mi 231a–b), refers to the cultured minds of the seven types of persons on the learners' path, from "stream-winner" up to just before "saint."

[4] Following the Tibetan *de mdor*, which indicates a reading of *samāsataṁ jñeyā* for *vijñeyā sarvathā* in the middle of the first line (LI, p. 79.13).

[5] *Guhyakādhipatinirdeśa* (LI, p. 79.15). The list also occurs in *MVy*.

whelmed by any opposing critics. It is "melodious" because it delights. It is "disciplined" because it is the remedy for passion and so on. It is "without harshness" because it has the art of pleasantly announcing the precepts. It is "without severity" because it shows the means of deliverance from transgressing those (precepts). It is "well-disciplined" because it gives instruction in the three vehicles. It is "pleasant to the ear" because it is the remedy for distraction. It is "physically satisfying" because it generates meditative concentration. It is "mentally satisfying" because it effectively generates intense joy by means of transcendent insight. It is "gladdening to the heart" because it resolves all doubts. It is "creative of joy and bliss" because it releases from false certainties. It is "not disturbing" because there is no regret about its practice. It is "eminently understandable" because it supports the perfect learned wisdom. It is "to be realized" because it supports the perfect reflective wisdom. It is "transparent" because it reveals the teaching without the (bad) teacher's closed fist. It is "lovable" because it is loved by those who through it attain their goal. It is "delightful" because it is instills enthusiasm in those who have not yet attained their goal. It is "authoritative" because it truly reveals the inconceivable Dharma. It is "informative" because it truly teaches the inconceivable Dharma. It is "reasonable" because it is not contrary to validating cognition. It is "appropriate" because it teaches appropriately for the disciples. It is "without redundancy" because it is never pointless. It is "energetic as the lion's roar" because it terrifies all religious fanatics. It is "sounding like an elephant's trumpeting" because of its magnificence. It is "sounding like the crash of thunder" because of its profundity. It is "like the voice of the dragon-king" because it is agreeable. It is "like the kinnaras' song" because of its sweetness. It is "like the kalaviṅka's song" because it is penetrating and always changing. It is "like Brahma's cry" because it spreads afar. It is "like the pheasant's call" because it presages all success and good fortune. It is "sweet as the voice of (Indra), the king of the gods," because it is unsurpassable. It is "like the sound of the drum" because it heralds victory over all demons and rivals. It is "not haughty" because it is unaffected by praise. It is "not lowly" because it is unaffected by blame. It is "immersed in language" because it completely integrates the characteristics of all aspects of

> linguistics. It is "grammatically impeccable" because it never errs due to any lapse of memory. It is "never fragmented" because it attends to the needs of the disciple at all times. It is "undaunted" because it is unconcerned with wealth and honor. It is "irrepressible" because it is beyond all reproach. It is "joyful" because it is indefatigable. It is "comprehensive" because it exhibits skill in all the sciences. It is "holistic"[6] because it brings about the simultaneous accomplishment of all the aims of beings. It is "continuous" because its flow is not cut off. It is "playful" because it employs many kinds of expressions to bring out a point. It is "fulfilling all words" because it enables one expression to convey multiple verbal ideas. It is "satisfying to the faculties of all beings" because it causes one meaning to convey multiple meanings. It is "irreproachable" because it keeps its promises. It is "unchangeable" because it can be applied at a future time. It is "unwavering" because it is presented without haste. It "resounds through all audiences" because it is heard equally in audiences far and near. It is "endowed with the best of all forms" because it transforms all worldly matters into illustrations (of the Truth).

Four verses on the greatness of teaching:

> 10. (Teaching proceeds) with frequent repetition for those who understand through concise statements and those who understand through detailed explanations, using speech and reasonable words which expound, analyze, and resolve doubts.

(Teaching) is given expression through speech. It makes the subject known with reasonable words. With exposition, analysis, and resolution of doubts respectively, it sets the subject forth, analyses it, and explains it. Teaching uses frequent repetition and opens up the subject, setting it forth distinctly in order to develop a strong certainty. It is taught in summary to those who understand through concise statements, and it is fully elucidated for those who understand through detailed explanations.

---

[6] *Akhilā* (LI, p. 80.26). Tibetan *tha ba dang bcas pa'i ched.*

11. The teaching of the buddhas is beneficial, being pure of the three sectors (of an action). Furthermore, it should be recognized as exempt from the eight faults.

"Pure of the three sectors" refers to (freedom from division into the following three): the means of teaching, (namely) speech and words; the actuality of teaching, via the modes of summary statements and so forth; and the persons taught, those who understand through concise statements and those who understand through detailed expositions. These teachings should be known as exempt from eight faults, respectively:

12. Six of the faults are laziness, lack of understanding, importunity, non-definitiveness, indecisiveness, and inconclusiveness.

These are (six of) the eight faults: laziness and lack of understanding, (teaching at) an inappropriate occasion, non-definitiveness of meaning, non-resolution of doubts, and non-termination of doubting. (The two final faults are):

13. (The last two faults are) weariness and stinginess. These (eight) are considered the (main) defects of communication. Since the buddhas' teaching is free of them, it is unexcelled.

"Weariness" is what would make one unable to teach often. "Stinginess" is what would make one not give a full explanation.

Two verses on the perfection of content:

14. This teaching is virtue, because it causes devotion,[7] joy, and intelligence; it has a twofold meaning, is easy to understand, and expounds the religious life which has four excellences.

15. It is unique in its application which has nothing in common with others, and it accomplishes the termination of the addictions of all three realms. It is pure by nature and pure from (accidental) taints; such is considered the spiritual life with its four excellences.

---

[7] *Bhakti* (LI, p. 81.22).

The teaching which correctly expounds the spiritual life with its four excellences is virtuous in its beginning, middle, and end, since it is the cause of devotion, joy, and intelligence, through study, reflection and meditative concentration, respectively. "Devotion" is faith and trust. "Joy" is the great delight of realizing one's potential for attainment through definite understanding by means of reason. "Intelligence" is the intuition of reality by means of the concentrated mind. "Twofold meaning" is its excellent meaning concerned with both conventional and ultimate realities. "Easy to understand" refers to its verbal expression, which is good because its words and phrases are sensible. The religious life has four excellences: it is unique, having nothing in common with others; it is fulfilling, because it fulfills the abandonment of the addictions of the three realms; it is completely pure because of its natural purity, free from contamination; and it is completely purified, having completely purified all taints, since the processes of those who have terminated contaminations are completely pure.

Two verses on the analysis of intentional implications:[8]

> 16–17. There are four types of ulterior implications: introductory implications concerned with the disciples; natural implications concerning the three realities; therapeutic implications for the control of faults; and transformational implications concerning the profundity of expressions.

In the buddha's teaching method, (statements having) ulterior implication are fourfold: such implicative (statements) are introductory, natural, therapeutic, and transformative.

The introductory ulterior implicative considers the disciples; in order to introduce them to the teaching and not to frighten them (by the idealistic teaching), the (external) existence of form and so on is taught.

The natural implicative considers the three realities, the imaginatively constructed and so on, teaching that all things are devoid of intrinsic reality and are unproduced, (implying their imaginative non-reality, relative non-self-production, and perfect non-ultimacy).

---

[8] An analysis of the next two difficult verses that assisted greatly our understanding was given by Michael Broido in his "Abhiprāya and Implication in Tibetan Linguistics," in *Journal of Indian Philosophy* 1–2 (1984): 1–33.

The therapeutic implicative refers to the control of faults, as will be explained below in the two verses which explain and recommend the supreme vehicle as having the remedies for the eight obscurations.

The transformative implicative refers to the profundity of expressions, for example: "Substantial-minded in the insubstantial, well-established in the reverse, well-afflicted by addictions, they acquire supreme enlightenment." Here, there are the following ulterior implicatives: "Substantial-minded in the 'insubstantial'" refers to those free of distraction as "substantial-minded," meaning "mindful of the substantial thing," because distraction is a diffusion[9] of the mind. "Well-established in the reverse" refers to being established in the opposite of permanence, happiness, purity, and self; that is, in impermanence and so forth; "well-established" meaning "not ruined." "Well afflicted by addictions" means greatly afflicted by the stress and strain of austerities over a long time.

One verse on the analysis of intentional hints:

> 18. The intentional hint should be understood as fourfold, intending equality, another meaning, another time, and personal disposition.

There are four types of intentional hint. There is the hint of equality, such as that in "It was I myself who was at that time the perfect Buddha, Vipaśyin," hinting that the Dharma-body is undifferentiated. There is the hint of another meaning, such as that in "All things are unreal and unproduced and so on," as this hints at another non-literal meaning. There is the hint of another time, such as that in "Those who aspire to Sukhāvatī will be born there," hinting at another time. And there is the hint of personal disposition, as, for example, when the same root of virtue is praised in some and yet disparaged in others, in the (case where the former are beginners and the latter more advanced and yet) complacent with merely minimal (virtue).

These two verses condense the extensive scriptures of the universal vehicle and have the benefits (of the scriptures of the universal vehicle). They are:

---

[9] Here there is a pun on the word *sāraṁ*, translated "substance" (sometimes "essence"), in that the word *visāraṁ*, meaning "diffusion," from *visṛj-* "to release," contains the same phonemes. The pun is missed in the Tibetan which translates both *vikṣepaṁ* and *visāraṁ* as *rnam gyeng*. The whole passage is difficult, in any case.

> 19–20. Living beings are obstructed by contempt for the Buddha and the Dharma, laziness, complacency with slight achievement, passionate and proud behavior, guilt, and the deviance of the uncommitted. (The Buddha) explained the supreme vehicle as the remedy of those, causing the abandonment of all obstructive faults.

> 21–23. The genius, the best hero, who applies herself to understand two verses, either in letter or spirit, obtains a tenfold benefit; total increase of element, supreme joy at the time of death, voluntary reincarnation, memory of all former lives, encounters with the buddhas, learning the supreme vehicle from them, faith endowed with intelligence, the two doorways, and the swift enlightenment.

These are five verses (beginning) with "contempt for the Buddha and the Dharma." "Deviance of the uncommitted" refers to those uncommitted bodhisattvas who deviate from the universal vehicle. "Explanation of the supreme vehicle" refers to the teaching of the universal vehicle. An expression which remedies the obscuration which is contempt for the Buddha is such as: "It was I myself who was at that time the perfect Buddha, Vipaśyin." A statement that remedies that obscuration which is contempt for the Dharma is such as: "Having served buddhas equal in number to the sands of the Ganges, understanding of the universal vehicle arises." A statement which remedies that obscuration which is laziness is such as: "Those who will aspire to Sukhāvatī (buddhaverse) will be born there," and "By merely recollecting with faith the name of the Transcendent Lord Vimalacandraprabha one will certainly attain unexcelled perfect enlightenment."

A statement which remedies the complacency obscuration is such as when the Lord disparages a gift and so on, which he praised at another time. A statement which remedies the passionate behavior obscuration is such as when the Lord praises the magnificence of the buddhaverses. A statement which remedies the proud behavior obscuration is such as when the Lord praised the surpassing excellence of some buddha. A statement which remedies the guilt obscuration is such as when it is said: "Even those who injure the buddhas and bodhisattvas will all go to heaven." A statement which remedies the obscuration which is the deviance of the uncommitted is such as the prophecies that the great disciples will become buddhas, or such as the teaching of the universal vehicle.

"Total increase of the element" means increase of all elements which have the universal vehicle as their basis, because through freedom from its obscurations, faith in the whole universal vehicle is obtained. "The two doorways" are the doorway of meditative concentration and the doorway of mnemonic spells. Two types of these benefits apply to the present life, and eight types to future lives; it should be understood that one gradually attains to higher and higher excellence.

One verse on the benefit of teaching:

> 24. Thus, the bodhisattva who has a good intellect, is untiring, loving, of good repute, and well-endowed with knowledge of good methods, becomes an excellent philosopher; when he teaches, he shines brilliantly among the people just like the sun.

Excellence of a philosopher has five causes, and its benefit is sun-like brilliance, as such a person is greatly admired for his inspiring of the world. The five causes of the excellence of a philosopher are that he teaches without confusion, repeatedly, without exploitive motivation, with acceptable expressions, and in attunement to the disciples.

CHAPTER XIII

Practice

Six verses on the analysis of practice:[1]

> 1. With the twofold intuition[2] of the selflessness of persons and things, the genius should abandon falseness and authenticity with regard to duality by means of three (concentrations).

This (and the next five verses) explain the following scriptural passage: "Understanding the import and understanding the teaching, he practices the Dharma and cultivates the corresponding realizations; practicing the harmonious, he lives by the corresponding realizations."[3]

Intuitive knowledge of the selflessness of persons and things is twofold because neither exists as either subject or object. Concerning the falseness and authenticity in the duality (of being and nothingness), there are three abandonments: the concentration on voidness, focused on the nonexistence of the constructed reality,

---

[1] dBal Mang (82b5) introduces his comment on this chapter by saying: "In order for one's teaching to others of the Dharma one has investigated to become beneficial, it is necessary for one to practice that Dharma oneself...." Sthiramati remarks perhaps more cogently that, having investigated the Dharma, one helps others by teaching it to them (subject of the previous chapter), whereas one helps oneself by practicing it oneself. He gives the vivid example of a man holding a lamp, by whose light others see and he can see himself. If the man were blind, then only others can see, and he, ironically, cannot see himself. The implication is that one who does not practice what he preaches is blind to his own benefit. dBal Mang's idea is also true, of course, in that a person who does not practice himself is likely not to teach others very beneficially.

[2] *Dvedhā* (LI, p. 84.15). Sthiramati remarks that this twofoldness (he uses the more usual *dvidhā*) of intuition here applies to both types of selflessness. That is, the person is realized as selfless, as object as well as subject, and things are realized as selfless, as subject as well as object.

[3] Canonical cliché, found widely in Pāli sources as well as in Mahāyāna texts; see LII, pp. 152–3, vs. 1, n. 2, 3. Sthiramati commments that the first verse elucidates the first phrase, "understanding the import."

and the wishless and signless (concentrations), focused on the existence of the relative and perfect realities. These three mundane concentrations are not false, in that they lead to transcendent intuition, and they are not authentic because they are not transcendent.

> 2. The knower of import (*arthajño*) knows that all teachings are like boats;[4] as he abandons complacency with (mere) learning, he thereby comes to be called a "knower of Dharma."

Thus a knower of import knows that all the teachings, the discourses and so forth, are like boats. This causes him to abandon complacency with mere erudition, and therefore he becomes a knower of the Dharma.

> 3. Having thus penetrated the two (selflessnesses) with the alienated individual's intuition, he cultivates the corresponding realizations in order to perfect that intuitive wisdom.

Having penetrated the two selflessnesses, as previously explained,[5] with the alienated individual's twofold intuition of meaning and teaching, (the bodhisattva) practices in order to perfect his intuitive knowledge. Thus he practices the corresponding realizations.[6]

---

[4] *Kola* (LI, p. 85.3). Tibetan *gzings*. Chinese *fa* (raft). The simile appears in *MN* I.135 and *Vajracchedikāprajñāpāramitāsūtra* (in *Mahāyānasūtrasaṁgraha* pp. 772–73). dBal Mang states that this verse concerns the bodhisattva who practices on the application path, and Sthiramati remarks that this verse comments on the phrase "knows the teaching" in the quote from sūtra given in comment to the first verse. The idea is that, knowing the teachings as like boats, the bodhisattva uses it in the accumulation path to gain learning and wisdom born of learning (crossing the river with the boat), but then moves on to apply this learning in thought and meditation (leaving the literal teaching like the boat on the shore).

[5] Reading *yathoktaṁ*, following Lévi's emendation of *yathākramaṁ* (LI, p. 85.10), as supported by the Tibetan *ji skad bshad pa'i*.

[6] *Anudharma* (LI, p. 85.10). See Edgerton p. 27 s.v. idem; LII, p. 153 n. 2. According to Sthiramati (P Mi 277b7–8; D Mi 249b7) the *anudharma* here are the four aids to penetration, heat and so on (see XIV 23–26), which complete the stage of action in faith (*adhimukticaryābhūmi*), as they are the stages of meditation leading immediately into the insight path, the first of the holy (*ārya*) paths. dBal Mang (103ab) explains this verse and the following verse as describing the transition from common, alienated person to holy person, from application path to insight path, from mundane intuition to transcendent intuitive wisdom.

4. Then she attains transcendent, unexcelled intuition, and becomes the equal of all bodhisattvas on the first stage who have such a nature.

"Then she attains transcendent, unexcelled intuition," because there is no vehicle more excellent. (She is) "equal to all bodhisattvas on the first stage," the stage of the joyous, "who have such a nature," being on that stage. Thus she practices harmoniously, because she is equal to the bodhisattvas of that stage.

5. Having accomplished the total termination of the insight-abandoned addictions, he applies himself to meditation in order to abandon the objective obscurations.[7]

The meaning of the verse is self-evident.

6. By coordinating the situational and nonconceptual intuitive wisdoms, (the bodhisattva) cultivates the harmonious realizations on the remaining stages.

This last (verse) shows the cultivation of harmonious realizations. "By means of the situational and nonconceptual" (refers to the aftermath) intuition in the situation of the stages, and to the nonconceptual intuition. "Coordinating" means integrating their functions, since they are mutually inseparable. "Cultivation of harmonious realizations" has been shown in these two verses.[8]

Four verses concerning the scope of vigilance in practice:

---

[7] Reading *heyānāṁ* and *hānāya* for *jñeyānāṁ* and *jñānāya* is clearly indicated by all Tibetan versions.

dBal Mang (103b) remarks that this verse concerns the bodhisattva entering the meditation path, quoting Sthiramati as saying that the bodhisattva here proceeds from the second through the tenth stage, since Sthiramati follows the system of having nine rounds of abandonments for both afflictive and cognitive obscurations.

[8] This sentence is omitted in the Tibetan translation.

> 7. The place where the genius practices has the virtues of being convenient for livelihood, a good neighborhood, a salutary location, an excellent community, and suitable for yoga.[9]

The scope of vigilance is demonstrated as encompassing the four spheres,[10] a favorable place and so forth. This verse describes residence in a favorable place. It should have "easy livelihood," so that the necessities of life such as robes and alms-food are obtained with little difficulty. It should be in a "good neighborhood," so that evil people such as thieves do not dwell there. It should be a "salutary location," so that it is a place free from disease. It should have a "supportive community," so there are friends who share a common morality and philosophy. It should be "conducive to yoga practice," so that in the daytime there is little commotion and senseless chatter, and at night there is little noise and so forth.

> 8. (The practitioner who needs a teacher) should recognize (as) the eminent holy person that bodhisattva who has vast learning, who has seen the truth, who is a wise philosopher, who is loving and indefatigable.[11]

This second (verse) shows (the spiritual teacher to be a truly reliable) holy person when he has the good qualities of doctrinal learning, realization, eloquence, non-exploitativeness, and non-indolence.

> 9. The authentic devotedness of (the bodhisattva) herself is shown in her good orientation, good equipment, good meditation, good transcendental determination, and good application.

This third (verse) shows that (the bodhisattva's) personal authentic devotedness is incorporated in her proper conscientious attitude when (she) takes the holy Dharma as her goal, when she succeeds in gathering the stores, when she systematically practices the meditation of serenity and transcendent insight, when she is not

---

[9] See LII, vs. 7 n. 1, for references on the "agreeable place" from the *Maṅgalasutta*, and its commentary by Buddhaghoṣa, as mentioned by Childers, *Journal of the Royal Asiatic Society*, n.s. IV, 328.

[10] *Cakra* (LI, p. 86.5), lit. "wheel."

[11] The commentators inform us that this is the second sphere within the scope of vigilance.

complacent with slight attainments, and when she applies herself constantly and reverently.

> 10. (The bodhisattva can be aware that) his merit gathered in former lives is the cause of his happiness, opportune birth,[12] health, concentrative power, and intellectual discernment.

The fourth (verse) shows how merit previously gathered has a fivefold causal impact. It is the cause of happiness in that (the bodhisattva) is happy in a pleasant place. It is the cause of opportune birth in that he wins an embodiment in which he can rely on a holy person. And because (such merit also) is the cause of his health, concentrative power, and wisdom, his own authentic devotedness may become fulfilled.

Three verses on the transcendence of addictions by means of the addictions themselves:[13]

> 11. Since no thing is found outside of the ultimate realm, the buddhas consider that passions and so on constitute their own transcendence.[14]

The Lord said: "I say that apart from passion there is no transcendence of passion. The same is true for hate and delusion."[15] This verse shows the intended

---

[12] *Kṣaṇopapatti* (LI, p. 86.20). Not to be born in any of the eight inopportune conditions (*aṣṭāvakṣaṇāṁ*). According to *MVy* 2299–2306 they are: 1) hell beings (*narakāṁ*), 2) animals (*tiryañcaṁ*), 3) hungry ghosts (*pretāṁ*), 4) long lived gods (*dīrghāyuṣo devāṁ*), 5) the borderlands (*pratyanta janapadaṁ*), 6) handicapped (*indriya vaikalyaṁ*), 7) wrong views (*mithyā darśanaṁ*), 8) a time when a Tathāgata does not appear (*tathāgatānāṁ anutpādaṁ*).

[13] The idea that one is liberated from the addictions by the addictions is more common to universal vehicle texts than is usually thought. The *Vimalakīrti* is most explicit about it, especially in the chapter "Family of the Tathāgatas" (see Thurman, *HTV*, VIII). It is more widely recognized as a theme of Buddhist tantrism; see Dasgupta, *An Introduction to Tantric Buddhism*, pp. 123–124.

[14] The Chinese (T.31.622b6 *ff.*) translates: "There is no element of passion apart from the ultimate realm; thus do the buddhas say that passion drives out passion, and so on with the others." *Pāda*s a & b are quoted in *AAA*, p. 381.

[15] Sthiramati (P Mi 281b6) cites a passage from the *Śatasāhasrikāprajñāpāramitāsūtra*: *'dod chags kyis 'dod chags 'byin pa gzhan par nga mi smra* / "I do not say otherwise than that passion drives out passion."

implication here. Since no thing is found apart from the ultimate realm, that is, there is no thing apart from reality, the reality of passion and so on is therefore called "passion," and also "transcendence of passion." This should be understood as the intended implication (of such scriptural statements).

> 12. Since no thing is found outside of the ultimate realm, the geniuses consider just that as the intended implication of the teaching of the addictive reality.[16]

It is said: "Misknowledge and enlightenment are the same,"[17] and such is the indication in the instructions concerning the addictive reality. Misknowledge is (called) the reality of enlightenment through metaphoric designation.

> 13. Thus, one properly engages with the passions and so forth, and thereby becomes liberated from them; such is their transcendence.[18]

It is in properly engaging with passions and so on that one is liberated from them. Thus once their (reality) has been fully realized (as both frustrating and empty), they are transcended. This is the intended implication here.[19]

Two verses on the abandonment of the attitudes of the disciples and hermit sages:

> 14. Even when dwelling in the hells for the sake of beings, the most terrible suffering is not harmful in the least to the victor-children;

---

[16] In the Chinese (T.31.622b12) *pāda*s c and d are: "thus, as it is said, addiction is enlightenment."

[17] Sthiramati (P Mi 282b4) cites a passage from the *Śatasāhasrikāprajñāpāramitāsūtra*: *ma rig pa dang byang chub gcig ste / gang ma rig pa de byang chub / byang chub de ma rig pa ste / de gnyis su med cing gnyis su byar med pa /* "Misknowledge and enlightenment are one. Misknowledge is enlightenment and enlightenment, misknowledge, nondual and indivisible."

[18] According to the *Prajñopāyaviniścayasiddhi* (cited in Dasgupta, op. cit., p. 122) sympathy (*kṛpā*) is called lust (*rāga*) because it gladdens (*rañjati*) or saves (*rakṣati*).

[19] Sthiramati (D Mi 254a–b) comments on the proper engagement with the addictions as twofold, realizing their harmful relative nature and so determining to gain freedom from them, and realizing their ultimate voidness and so seeing the possibility of freedom from them.

but even those geniuses are harmed by the various virtuous discriminations prevalent in the individual vehicle, such as that between the excellence of peace and the evil of existence.

15. Not even a continuous residence in hell interferes with the impeccable and magnificent enlightenment of the (bodhisattva) geniuses; but the other vehicle's false notion of a self-benefiting supreme coolness[20] causes interference, even though (they might enjoy) a state of highest bliss.

Of these two verses, the second proves the first. Their meaning is self-evident.

Four verses to refute the fear of unreality and natural purity:

16. Things do not exist, yet they are perceived. There is no addiction, yet there is purification. It is like a magical illusion or the sky.[21]

17. Though a technically accurate painting lacks height and depth, they appear there. Likewise, there is never any duality in unreal construction, yet it appears.

18. When water is muddy and then clears, its clarity is not produced by that (muddiness) but is just the removal of the taint. The principle is just the same in the purification of one's own mind.

19. It is accepted that the mind which is always naturally luminous[22] is flawed by accidental faults; and it is decreed that there is no other mind apart from the mind of reality which is naturally luminous.

---

[20] *Paramaśīta* (LI, p. 87.24). The selfish Nirvāṇa of the individual vehicle; see Sthiramati (P Mi 284bl).

[21] Compare VI.1. This verse also appears in the second chapter of the *MS* (*La Somme* p. 119).

[22] *Cittaṁ prakṛtiprabhāsvaraṁ* (LI, p. 88.9). Also *Bhāṣya* on XVIII 43–44. On the natural luminosity of mind see *VKN* pp. 53–54.

That things do not exist yet are perceived frightens the immature.[23] That there is naturally no addiction in the ultimate realm yet there is a subsequent purification frightens the immature. Such fears are removed by establishing that these things are like illusion, or like the sky, respectively. In the same way, fear is removed by the examples of the lack of height or depth in a picture, and water which has been stirred up and allowed to become calm, respectively.

The fourth (verse) shows the mind to be like water. Just as water is naturally pure but polluted by accidental pollutants, mind is accepted as naturally luminous but flawed by accidental faults. It is decreed that apart from the reality-mind there is no other mind of a relative nature which has natural luminosity. Therefore, "mind" is to be understood here as the "suchness of mind."

Four verses to reject (the suspicion that the bodhisattva will commit) offenses driven by his passions:

> 20. The bodhisattva has in her very marrow as great a love for beings as towards an only child. She is therefore accepted as always beneficial.
>
> 21. Because she works for the benefit of beings she does not offend from passion; and any hatred for all beings is utterly precluded.
>
> 22. For a pigeon who greatly cherishes her young and stays and gathers them to herself, anger is precluded; it is just the same for a compassionate one concerning beings who are her children.
>
> 23. Where there is love, the thought of anger ceases. Where there is peace, malice ceases. Where there is benefit, deceit ceases. And where there is comforting, there is no more intimidation.

The love of the bodhisattva for beings is here implied to be passionate, but any offenses (born of passion) are impossible for them, because (their love) causes them to work for the benefit of beings. The example of the pigeon is (cited) due to (its) great passion, its extremely intense love for its young. For a compassionate bodhisattva, it is impossible (for her) to be angry at corporeal beings. Bodhisattvas, as they are loving, work for the welfare of beings through being loving towards

---

[23] Following the Tibetan (D Phi 188b4 *ff.*).

them, pacifying their malice, bringing about their benefit, and producing their happiness. Thus, love and so on prevent anger and its successors, malice and so on.

Five verses on the types of practice:

> 24. Like a sick man with (foul but)[24] good medicine, (the bodhisattva) engages in the life-cycle, and like a doctor with the sick he engages in practice[25] with living beings.
>
> 25. He practices with himself as with an untrained servant,[26] and he engages his own desires in practice, like a merchant with his wares.[27]
>
> 26. He engages in action like a clothes dyer (dyes his) clothes;[28] like a father with his infant son, he practices nonviolence with beings.[29]

---

[24] The Chinese (T.31.623b2) renders *pāda*s a and b: "He well engages in cyclic life like a sick person taking bitter medicine." That some text might have had such a reading is supported by Sthiramati's use of the same idea in his commentary (D Mi 259a4).

[25] The identical Sanskrit *pratipadyate* (LI, p. 89.9–10) is translated both *'jug par byed* and *sgrub par byed*, the former leaning towards "engaging," or "putting into practice," and the latter toward "practicing."

[26] Sthiramati (P Mi 289a1–3) comments: Just as one energetically corrects an untrained servant with blows, etc., so does the bodhisattva tame his passions. He alludes to the example of the skilled horsetrainer in the *Kāśyapaparivarta* (*Ratnakūṭa*), sec. 108: "Kaśyapa, it is like a son who is skilled in training horses; whenever a horse stumbles, rears, or acts viciously he curbs it and so tames it that it never again becomes wild. Just so, Kaśyapa, is the monk who practices yoga; whenever he perceives mental instability he takes measures to curb it, and he so curbs the mind that it never again becomes wild." See Edgerton p. 121 s.v. *utkhumbati*, p. 202 s.v. *khaṭuka*.

[27] Sthiramati (P Mi 289a5): "As a merchant hopes to make a lot of money for his family by selling a small amount of merchandise, so the bodhisattva, through the practice of transcendent generosity, amasses the five desirable objects (the objects of the senses) and a great deal of wealth, and gives it all to living beings."

[28] Sthiramati (P Mi 289a 5–7): "As a clothes dyer dyes and washes, etc. a cloth clean of stains, so the bodhisattva purifies his body, speech, and mind and practices the ten virtuous actions. This exemplifies transcendent morality."

[29] An example of transcendent tolerance.

27. His practice is as continual as the rubbing of fire sticks together by one wishing fire;[30] like a trustworthy person he engages in practice to fulfill his universal responsibility.[31]

28. He practices with wisdom about the facts as a magician (knows the true nature of his illusions). In whatever way, and wherever there is practice, it is all accepted as the bodhisattva's.

This verse elucidates how and where there is practice. How? Like a sick person and so on with good medicine and so on. Where? In the life-cycle and so on, because he frequents the life-cycle having understood it by means of analytical (wisdom). Through compassion he does not abandon beings who are afflicted with the passions because he has thoroughly made up his mind with his own vows, has gradually increased his wealth through the transcendence of generosity and so forth, has purified the acts of body and so forth, does not become enraged by harm done by beings, strives incessantly in the cultivation of virtue, does not relish the savor of meditative concentration, and is not in error regarding the facts.[32]

One verse on the purification of the three spheres of engaging in practice:

29. He always exerts himself with magnificent heroic effort, striving to purify the development of both (self and other). Gradually, with supreme, impeccable, and nonconceptual intelligence, he attains the unexcelled accomplishment.

The purification of the three spheres should be understood as the nondiscernment of practitioner, to-be-practiced, and actual practice through the nonconceptual intuition of the selflessness of things. "He strives to purify the development of both" refers to (both other) beings and himself.

---

30 An example of transcendent energy.

31 The Chinese (T.31.623b9) translates *pāda*s c and d: "He well practices meditative concentration like a trustworthy person is responsible for his wealth."

32 From Sthiramati's commentary (D Mi 260b6 *ff.*) we learn that the merchant example illustrates generosity, the dyer morality, the father tolerance, the fire-sticks effort, the trustworthy person contemplation, and the magician wisdom.

Chapter XIV

Precept and Instruction

Fifty-one verses on the analysis of precept and instruction:[1]

> 1. (The bodhisattva) emerges (into the stage of action in faith) in one incalculable eon; and increasing (her) faith, she is as full of virtuous qualities as the ocean is full of water.

"Increasing (her) faith (in the universal vehicle)," it reaches a state beyond measure. The rest is self-evident.

> 2. Thus provided with the stores (of merit and wisdom), the victors' spiritual child, primordially pure, with fine intellect and good will, applies himself to the meditative practice (of the path of application).

(He is) "primordially pure" because (his) bodhisattva vow is pure and because (his) universal vehicle view of reality is precise through his unerring grasp of

---

[1] Sthiramati (D Mi 261b *ff.*) explains the relevance of this chapter in this place: "Here, we are in the context of explaining the education (of the bodhisattva); the specifics of the aspects of such education are those of motivation, (application), self-benefit, other-benefit, culmination and so on. In the chapter on manifold faith in the Dharma, the specifics of motivation were taught. 'Investigation of the Dharma' taught application. 'Engagement in Practice' taught self-benefit. 'Teaching the Dharma' taught other-benefit. Now, the specifics of culmination are to be taught. The bodhisattva who has engagement, in order to culminate and purify the paths of insight and meditation, should seek precepts and instructions. Also other(s) must be placed in precepts and instructions."

dBal Mang more briefly (107b) says that "in order to put engagement into practice, one must hear precepts and instructions, so one must learn precepts and instructions, which are the methods of intensifying that (engagement). In this we have the person who learns, how to find word and meaning, the sequence of the conscientious attitudes which are the meaning of precepts, the greatness of precepts, the actuality of precepts, and the fruit of precepts."

its import. He has a "fine intellect" due to long study (of the scriptures). He has "good will" because (his mind is) free of impediments.

> 3. Then she obtains from the buddhas extensive instruction in the "Dharma-stream" (concentration) in order to attain extensive serenity and intuition.[2]

This verse is self-evident.

> 4. Then first that ascetic should focus his mind upon the teaching of the discourses and so forth which reveals the import of nonduality, (starting with) the name of the Sūtra and so on.
>
> 5. Then he should progressively examine the details of the text and analyze its import inwardly and accurately.
>
> 6. Having ascertained its meanings, he should concentrate them in (his memory of) the teaching. Then he should form a powerful will to realize their import.

The teachings consist of (the categories of) discourse, hymn, and so on. "The name of the Sūtra and so on" refers, for example, to the *Discourse on the Ten Stages* and so on. He should first focus his mind upon it.

These three verses indicate six (kinds of) thought: basic thought, discursive thought, analytic thought, ascertaining thought, synthetic thought, and finally willful thought.

Basic thought has for its object the name of the teachings of the sūtras and so on, having heard instruction (given by another) or arrived at by oneself; as for example impermanent, painful, empty, selfless, strictly nonexistent, and so on.

Discursive thought is that with which one follows the details of the text (chapter divisions, number of verses, number of letters, etc.) of those teachings, sūtras and so on, which have been taken as objects by (their) names.

Analytic thought is that with which one analyzes phonemes and meanings. One analyzes meaning in four ways: by calculation, comparison, examination, and

---

[2] According to dBal Mang, this verse begins to describe the process of seeking words and meaning of precepts and instructions.

discernment. Calculation means "grouping," as for example, "matter constitutes ten media and a portion of another";[3] or, "sensation is the group of six sensations." Comparison is perceiving the even[4] measure of the characteristics of the things enumerated without exaggerating or underestimating (their number). Examination is investigation through the validating cognitions. Discernment is the observation of what has been calculated, compared, and examined. One analyzes phonemes in two ways: in combination where they have meaning, and in isolation where they do not.

Ascertaining thought is that by which one ascertains the signs of an object according to its examination or analysis.

Synthetic thought is, for example, concentrating the meaning analyzed into the basic thought (and so on), to (create) a total synthesis.

Willful thought is the will-power associated in function with whatever object one apprehends, be it the object of meditative concentration, of its fulfillment, of the fruition of asceticism, of entrance to the stages, or of distinctive attainments (such as the superknowledges).

Indeed it is the mind itself which appears as the object and there is no object apart from mind. Whether one knows (the reality of) only mind or not, just mind itself is the object, no other. Thus the six (kinds of) thought are established as objects.

> 7. She should investigate (the sūtras) and thoroughly examine them with a continuous mental inquiry. Further, she should experience (them) by means of conscientious attitudes which are nonverbal and experientially uniform.
>
> 8. She should know the path of serenity to be the synthesis of the words of the teaching and so on, and she should know the path of transcendent insight to be the analysis of their meanings.
>
> 9. She should know that the integrated path is the combination (of both serenity and insight); she should prevent depression and pacify excitement.

---

[3] Non-informative matter (*avijñaptirūpa*) belongs to the mental object medium (*dharma-āyatana*).

[4] Reading Sanskrit *sama* for *śama*, following the Tibetan (D Phi 190b3): *mtshan nyid la … 'tsham par 'dzin pa'o* /. Bagchi concurs (p. 162, n. 6.3).

> 10. Then, when she gains balance in that orientation, she should cultivate equality; applying herself perseveringly and devotedly.

Eleven (types of) conscientious attitudes are shown by these four verses. (There are the first contemplation attitude) with consideration and analysis, (the second contemplation attitude) without consideration and with only analysis, (and the third and fourth contemplation attitudes) free of considerative and analytic processes.

(Differentiated cognitively, they are) the attitude of serenity, the attitude of transcendental insight, and the attitude of integration.

(Differentiated functionally, they are) the attitude whose function is preventive, the attitude whose function is pacifying, and the attitude whose function is equalizing.

(Differentiated by orientation, they are) the attitude of perseverance and the attitude of devotion.[5]

> 11. When he has focused the mind on the objective, he should not let its continuity waver. Being quick to recognize its wavering he should again draw it back there.

> 12. The intelligent should repeatedly draw the mind within away from external objects. Then he should tame it, seeing the virtue in concentration.

> 13. Seeing the fault of distraction he should cease any distaste for concentration, and in the same way quell avarice, anxiety, and so forth, when they arise.

> 14. The ascetic should then obtain free-flowing (concentration) in his mind, (first) with volitional effort and then, from its repeated practice, without volitional effort.

---

[5] These eleven types of conscientious attitude are elucidated by Sthiramati in great detail (D Phi 265b *ff.*), and more concisely by dBal Mang (109b *ff.*).

These four verses show the means of stabilization through the nine states of mind. One stops the mind, stabilizes it, fixes it, focuses it, tames it, calms it, utterly quiets it, streamlines it, and perfectly concentrates it.[6]

> 15. Thereafter, once she has acquired a great[7] physical and mental fluency she should be recognized as having acquired (a suitable) conscientious attitude. Then increasing it
>
> 16. through a prolonged development, she should acquire fundamental stabilization. In purifying it in order (to obtain) the superknowledges, she attains the best competence
>
> 17. in contemplation. Through the attainment of the superknowledges, she travels to the (various) universes in order to worship and listen to buddhas beyond measure.
>
> 18. Having worshipped innumerable buddhas for innumerable aeons, her mind thereby gains the supreme competence.

One should construe "best competence" with "in contemplation." "For innumerable aeons" means (aeons) whose number is beyond measure. The remaining verses are self-evident.

> 19. Then he obtains the five benefits, the precursors of purity. Then he becomes the vessel of purity and goes on to the unexcelled.

---

[6] This analysis of the process of the stabilization of mind into nine successive states of mind became extremely famous in Indian and Tibetan Buddhism. It is taught in great detail in the *YBh*, in the works of Kamalaśīla, and eventually in the Tibetan writings, such as Tsong Khapa's *Great Stages of the Path*. See Alex Wayman, *Calming the Mind and Discerning the Real* (New York: Columbia University Press, 1978), introduction; Thurman, *Tsong Khapa's Speech of Gold*, introduction; Hopkins, *Meditation on Emptiness*, Ch. I.8.

[7] *Tanukāṁ* (LI, p. 92.14). The Tibetan (D Phi 191b1) has *che*, meaning "great degree," but Sthiramati supports the Sanskrit with *chung ngu* (D Mi 268a1), though the verses (D Phi 19a7) agree with the *Bhāṣya*. dBal Mang has *chen po* as well, and under analysis that reading is preferable. Passing beyond the ninth state of mind, the kind of fluency attained should be quite powerful by all accounts.

> 20. The entire mass of negative conditioning is dissolved every moment, and body and mind are totally filled with fluency.
>
> 21. He fully recognizes the unannihilated appearances of things; he discerns the nonconstructed signs of total purity.
>
> 22. In this way, the genius always and everywhere accomplishes the embrace of the cause for the fulfillment and purification of the body of truth.

Then he obtains the five benefits which are the precursors of purity. "Purity" is the stage of the pure universal responsibility. Having obtained them he becomes the vessel of purity. "Unexcelled" refers to the unexcelled vehicle. In "for the fulfillment and purification of the body of truth," "fulfillment" is the tenth bodhisattva stage, "purification" the buddha stage. Of the five benefits, three belong to serenity and two to transcendent insight. These are the mundane attainments.

> 23. Having become such, the bodhisattva in meditative concentration does not perceive any objects separate from her mental discourse.
>
> 24. In order to increase her illumination about things she exerts a strong effort; by the intensification of such illumination, she remains in mind-only.
>
> 25. Then she perceives that all objects are reflections in the mind, and then she abandons the distraction of objectivity.
>
> 26. Then only the distraction of subjectivity remains, and she soon experiences unobstructed meditative concentration.

After this come the aids to penetration (of the application path). When the bodhisattva's mind is in such a concentration she does not perceive any thing apart from her inner mental discourse. Perceiving the mental discourse itself appearing as general and specific characteristics is the condition of (the aid to penetration called) "heat."

The (subsequent) illumination is mentioned in the *Kṣāranadī Sūtra*: "Illumination is a designation of (the aid to penetration called) 'tolerance' in the investigation of things."

In order to increase this investigation of things, she maintains a firm, strong effort through persevering energy. This is the "peak" (aid to penetration).

Through the increase of illumination about things, she remains in mind-only because she realizes: "this is nothing but mind." Then she perceives the mere reflectedness of all objects in the mind and no objects other than the mind. Then she abandons the distraction of objectivity and only the subjectivity distraction remains. This is her condition of (the aid to penetration called) "tolerance."

Then she will quickly experience unobstructed meditative concentration. This is the condition of (the aid to penetration called) "world-triumph."

Why is it called "unobstructed"?

> 27. (It is unobstructed) because the distraction of subjectivity is abandoned immediately afterwards; and so the states of heat and so on should be recognized in their due order.

"The states of heat and so on" are the aids to penetration.

> 28. Further, he attains the unexcelled, transcendent intuition, free from perceptions of duality, nonconceptual, and free of taints.

From here on is the condition of the path of insight. "Free from the perception of duality" means that it is free from the perception of subject and object. "Unexcelled" means that there is no higher intuition. "Nonconceptual" means that it is free from the conceptualizations of subject and object. "Taintless" means that the insight-abandoned addictions are eliminated. It is said that this intuition is free from dust and stain.

> 29. This, her foundational transmutation, is accepted as the first (bodhisattva) stage. Only after innumerable aeons does she proceed to perfect purity.

The meaning of the verse is self-evident.

30. Then, when he fully realizes the equality of the realm of truth, he attains the constant awareness of the sameness of himself and all beings.

31. His awareness of his sameness with beings (is attained) in (their common) selflessness, suffering, duty, and non-expectation of reward, and also in his sameness with the other victor-offspring.

Having realized the equality of reality through the objective selflessness, he obtains the constant awareness of the sameness of himself and all beings, by means of five samenesses. (These are the) sameness in selflessness and sameness in suffering, since there is no difference between the selflessness and suffering of the processes of self and others; the sameness of duties, since he and others have the same need to eliminate suffering; the sameness of not expecting rewards, since he has no more eagerness for rewards from others than (he would for rewards received) from himself; and the sameness with other bodhisattvas, since his realizations are like their realizations.

32. She sees the creations of the three realms as unreal imaginative constructions, with her well-purified nondualistic intuition.

She sees the creations of the three realms as merely unreal imaginative constructions, through her completely purified transcendental intuition. "Nondualistic" means that it is not divided into subject and object.

33. When she has attained the state beyond (duality) and the freedom from insight-abandoned (addictions), then her path of insight is proclaimed.

By seeing the realm of truth as a state beyond subject and object, she realizes freedom from those addictions abandoned (by insight).

34. Having understood the voidness of nonexistence, the voidness of existence, and also the voidness of intrinsic identity, he is pronounced "a knower of voidness."

The bodhisattva is called a "knower of voidness" because he knows three types of voidness. The "voidness of nonexistence" is the imaginatively constructed reality, because it does not exist through its intrinsic identity. Also, the "voidness of existence" is the relative reality, which does not exist in the way it is imagined, but does exist through its intrinsic identity. And "natural voidness" is the perfect reality, because its voidness is its intrinsic reality.

> 35. The ground of signlessness should be recognized as the utter termination of conceptualization, and the ground of wishlessness as unreal mental construction (itself).

The ground of signlessness should be recognized as the complete termination of conceptualization. The ground, that is objective, of wishlessness is unreal mental construction (i.e., the relative reality) as objective.[8]

> 36. It is accepted that the victor-offspring always obtain all the various accessories of enlightenment simultaneously with the path of insight.

It should be understood that simultaneously with the path of insight, all the various accessory qualities of enlightenment of the bodhisattva, such as the foci of mindfulness, are obtained.

> 37. Having realized intellectually that beings are mere creations, selfless, and a mere expanse of suffering, and having abandoned the view of the useless self, (the bodhisattva) discovers the view of the great self which has the great goal.

> 38. She has here a view of self without a view of self, intense suffering without any suffering, and she accomplishes the goals of all, expecting no reward, just as one accomplishes one's own benefit (without asking) oneself (for reward).

> 39. Her mind is free with supreme freedom, yet she is bound with long and heavy chains; not seeing any end of suffering, she just applies herself and sets to work.

---

[8] Following the Tibetan (D Phi 193a7–b1) in slight variance from the Sanskrit.

> 40. The mundane person is unable to bear even his own suffering in this life, what need to mention the combined suffering of others until the end of the world – it is unthinkable! But the bodhisattva is just the opposite.
>
> 41. The love and tenderness for beings, the energy and indefatigability of the victor's spiritual offspring, these are the supreme wonder of all worlds! Yet they are not that (wondrous), because of (the bodhisattvas' awareness of the) sameness of themselves and beings.

These five verses express the greatness of the bodhisattva who has attained the path of insight.

"The view of the useless self" refers to the addicted materialistic view. "The view of the great self which has the great goal" is the view of the self which has attained the awareness of the sameness of self and beings. It has a great goal because it causes the accomplishment of the goals of all beings. "Without a view of self" means being without the useless (view of self). The view of self with the great goal is attained by one who is without suffering produced in his own continuum, yet who suffers intensely because of its production in the continua of all beings.

"Free in mind" means free from the (addictions) abandoned by insight. "With supreme freedom" means thanks to the supreme vehicle. "Bound by long and heavy chains" means chains which come from the continua of all beings. "Although she does not see the end of suffering," because the realms of beings are infinite, like space, "she applies herself" to make an end to the sufferings of beings. "And she sets to work" for the welfare of limitless beings.

"The bodhisattva is the opposite" means that she is able to bear the combined sufferings of all living beings, for as long as the world lasts.

The love and tenderness to benefit and gladden beings – which the bodhisattva possesses by his efforts on their behalf – and his tirelessness: (these) are the greatest wonders in the world. Yet they are not wondrous at all, because (bodhisattvas feel that) beings are the same as themselves.

> 42. Then on the remaining stages here on the path of meditation he applies himself to the cultivation of the two sorts of intuition.

43. Nonconceptual intuition perfects the buddha-qualities. The other (aftermath intuition) causes the development of beings in accordance with their situations.

44. This meditative cultivation reaches transcendence after two incalculable aeons; attaining the final meditation, the bodhisattva receives anointment.[9]

45. He arrives at the diamond-like meditative concentration, unbroken by conceptualization, and obtains the final foundational transmutation, untainted by any obscurations.

46. And he obtains universal omniscience, which is the unexcelled exaltation from which he accomplishes the welfare of all beings.

These verses show the path of meditation. The two types of intuition are the nonconceptual, by which one's buddha-qualities are purified, and the situationally attuned mundane intuition, the aftermath of transcendent intuition, by means of which one causes the development of beings.

Having achieved the final meditation after two incalculable aeons, the anointed bodhisattva obtains the diamond-like meditative concentration. It is diamond-like because it cannot be destroyed by conceptualizing thought and by instinctual propensities. Then he obtains the final foundational transmutation which is untainted by the addictive and objective obscurations. And he obtains omniscience, the unexcelled state from which he accomplishes the welfare of beings by displaying perfect enlightenment and perfect liberation for as long as the cycle of suffering endures.

47. Thus, (the bodhisattva who achieves the Dharma-stream *samādhi*) always sees the rarely visible (Buddha Śākya)muni (as if before her), and feels intensely satisfied in mind by the force of faith derived from the matchless learning (gained from him); how could she fail to give it the greatest value?

---

[9] Sthiramati (P Mi 325.3.7, folio 313a7) says: "after culmination of the meditative path, the bodhisattva is anointed by the radiance of the transcendent lords of the ten directions."

48. Ever urged by the always present transcendent lords to stand in the doorway of the Dharma, dragged from the abyss of faults as if pulled by the hair, (the bodhisattva) is forcefully established in enlightenment.

49. Having entirely overcome the whole world everywhere by completely purified insight and nonconceptual understanding, and having dispersed the great darkness, she illuminates the world far and wide, like a great sun.[10]

These three verses show the greatness of precepts. Whoever receives precepts (drawn from) the stream of doors of the Dharma will constantly see the buddhas and hear the matchless Dharma from them. He will have great faith, his mind satisfied by the intensity of pure faith. Thus the constant vision of the buddhas has a great value. The rest is self-evident.

50. The buddhas always justly praise realistic dedication to one's individual concerns, while condemning false obsession (with them).[11] Here, for the superior beings who are intent on stability and discernment, the victors systematically teach all kinds of teachings about what assists and hinders (such serenity and insight), which they must implement and avoid (respectively) in order to

---

[10] The Tibetan locates this verse next to the last one, and places the Sanskrit verse 50 right after verse 48, running the two paragraphs of commentary together. The *MSA Kārikās* also follow that order (D Phi 20b). Because this verse is considered self-evident by the commentator, there is no evidence from him as to which location is preferable.

dBal Mang considers the verses 47 and 48 to describe the greatness of precepts, the Tibetan verse 49 (Skt. 50) to encapsulate the actuality (*ngo bo*) of precepts and instructions, and the Tibetan verse 50 (Skt. 49) along with 51 to describe the fruition of precepts and instructions. His explanation is plausible considering the content, as the solar bodhisattva fits nicely in the concluding depiction of the fruition of the path.

Nevertheless, we have left this verse here anyway, to honor the Sanskrit, as there seems to be no serious improvement of the flow of meaning by following the Tibetan.

[11] Reading *nindāmithyāprayukte* for Lévi's *nindāmīrṣyāprayukte* (LI, p. 97.6), following the Tibetan (D Phi 194b5) *log par sbyor la smod mdzad.* This concern with authentic self-concern, the quest of wisdom and the body of truth, as opposed to false self-concern, the egoistic pursuit of saṁsāric goals, makes much better sense than a cryptic singling out of envy among the numerous mental afflictions.

> achieve the expansiveness of the yoga of the teaching of the blissful buddhas.

This verse shows the fourfold instruction. Concerning supreme morality, (the buddhas) praise bodhisattvas realistically dedicated to their individual concerns and criticize those falsely obsessed (with them).[12] Concerning supreme mind and supreme wisdom, (they) teach to those intent on stability and discernment all sorts of teachings which assist and hinder, which are respectively to be implemented and avoided. "Yoga" here refers to the meditation of serenity and insight.

> 51. Thus, ever full of the store of beauty, the foremost heroes who always obtain the personal precepts from the ascetic buddhas attain the very expansive meditative concentration of mind and proceed to the far shore of the ocean of excellence.

The meaning of this concluding verse is self-evident.

---

[12] This last phrase, reinforcing the Tibetan reading of the verse (see note above), is missing in the Sanskrit.

Chapter XV

Action Endowed with Liberative Art[1]

A summary (of the preceding "how to learn" section):

1. (The process of learning (chapters 10–14) what is to be learned (chapters 1–9) consists of the chapters on) abundance of faith, investigation of the Dharma, teaching, corresponding practice, and authentic precept and instruction.[2]

Four verses analyzing action endowed with liberative art:

2.[3]As the earth is considered the universal support of forests, beings, mountains, and rivers, so the wise proclaim that the three types of actions are the universal (support) of the virtues of generosity, and so forth.

---

[1] dBal Mang (117a5) comments that one should not be complacent about just having received the precepts, but one should practice all that has been explained, which practice must be combined with skill in liberative art. This is taught in summary and in detail. This chapter is the summary, identifying the ground of artful skill, the way of becoming artful, and the best attainment of artful skill.

[2] This summary verse is placed by the Tibetan *Bhāṣya* (D Phi 195a) and explained by Sthiramati (D Mi 283a) as if it should occur at the end of the Precept chapter, as it logically summarizes the unit of chapters 10–14. It could just as well go there, but we prefer to follow the arrangement of Lévi's Sanskrit, which places it at the beginning of the 15th. The *Kārikā* version (D Phi 21a1) places it at the beginning of the 15th as well. If we consider that this chapter begins the third section, the practice itself, as the faith chapter begins the section on the method for the practice, it is useful for each section to begin with a summary recapitulating the preceding section.

[3] Our numbering of the verses in this chapter varies from Lévi's, since we moved the summary to the end of the previous chapter, following the Tibetan.

This verse shows liberative art as originative, because all kinds of virtue such as transcendent generosity and the accessories of enlightenment originate from the three (types of artful) action. "The wise" refers to the bodhisattvas. Forests and so on are mentioned in order to indicate food, foragers,[4] habitat, and inhabitants.

> 3. Here in this world, great ordeals of various kinds over many aeons do not overcome the physical, verbal, and mental actions of the enterprising spiritual children of the victor.

> 4. Just as in self-protection one should keep one's body away from poison, weapons, lightning-bolts, and enemies, just so the victor-offspring should keep their three actions away from both individual vehicles.

These two verses teach liberative art as recuperation from weariness in the universal vehicle or from descent into other vehicles, respectively. "Overcoming" indicates weariness. Action associated with the individual vehicles is compared to poison and so on because it leads to the development of the inferior dedication of that vehicle, severs virtuous roots on the universal vehicle, fails to produce future virtuous roots, destroys the crop of virtuous roots already produced, and hinders the attainment of the perfection of buddhahood.

> 5. The threefold discrimination between agent, objective, and action is never apprehended; thus, from such an incorporation of liberative art, the actions of (the bodhisattva) become perfectly pure, infinite, and transcendent.[5]

This fourth verse shows the purificative liberative art, purifying action by purifying the three spheres, as neither agent, object, nor action is apprehended. "Infinite" means inexhaustible.

---

[4] Following the Tibetan *nye bar spyod pa po*. Sthiramati (D Tsi 2a *ff.*) explains that the four things that depend on and spring from the earth – habitat, inhabitant, immobile, and mobile things – are represented by forest, being, mountain, and river. These also apparently represent things included in the realm of evolution, although no strict correspondence is presented.

[5] The Tibetan *las rnams dag pa mtha' yas de yi pha rol 'gro* (D Phi 195b6) takes the *anantaṁ* (LI, p. 98.14) with *viśuddhi* and *pāragaṁ* as a separate adjective, or else all three as separately qualifying *karma*, rather than taking *viśuddhipāragaṁ* as one compound.

Chapter XVI

The Transcendences

A summary verse as a table of contents of the transcendence (chapter):

> 1. One should understand their number, nature, order, and etymologies; the excellence of their practice, their analysis, summary, resistances, excellences, and mutual determination.

Six verses on the analysis of the number (of the transcendences):

> 2. (Four give) the exalted estate of perfection of wealth, body, society, and effort. (The last two give) freedom from the power of addictions and constant unerringness in duties.

This is the first (verse). There are four types of exalted estate from the (first) four transcendences: perfect wealth from generosity; perfect body from morality; perfect society from tolerance, since in future lives one will be loved by many people from having served them; and perfect effort from energy, since one succeeds in all terminal actions. The fifth (transcendence) gives freedom from the power of the addictions, since contemplation conquers addictions. The sixth (transcendence) gives unerringness in duties, through thorough knowledge of the reality of all undertakings.

Thus, the transcendences are six in terms of (the first three types of) exalted estate, effort, non-addiction, and unerringness in duties.

> 3. A person dedicated to the needs of beings acts with detachment, non-aggression, and tolerance; and he always fulfills his own aims with the basic (energy), stability, and liberation.

This is the second (verse). The bodhisattva who is truly dedicated to the aims of living beings accomplishes them with detachment, non-aggression, and tolerance of aggression, through, respectively, the transcendences of generosity, morality, and tolerance. He accomplishes his own aims in all ways through three (transcendences), with the basic (energy), with mental stability, and with liberation. For, relying on effort, with contemplation and wisdom respectively, he stabilizes the unstable mind and then liberates the stabilized mind. Therefore, the transcendences are six (also) from the point of view of individualistic and altruistic aims.

> 4. Others' aims become (the bodhisattva's) own aims on account of (his) nondepletion, nonviolence, tolerance of violence, indefatigability in action, charisma, and eloquence.

This is the third (verse). Through giving and so on, all the bodhisattva's (aims) become exclusively altruistic aims, since, (in terms of the transcendences) respectively, he is not depleted by (giving) his possessions to others, is nonviolent, is tolerant of others' violence, is tireless in his works of friendliness (to beings), is charismatic through his (contemplative) powers of magic and so on, and is eloquent in teaching, as (his wisdom) cuts through (beings') doubts. Therefore, altruistic aims[1] become the bodhisattva's own aims, because (he considers) others' duties[2] as his own duties, and thus attains great enlightenment. Thus, the transcendences are six (also) in terms of the exclusive altruism of (the bodhisattva's) aims.

> 5. The whole supreme vehicle is epitomized in the (bodhisattva's) disinterest in possessions, intense reverence, indefatigability in both (tolerance and effort), and nonconceptuality in yoga.

This is the fourth (verse). The bodhisattva takes no delight in pleasures, having no regard for them in his giving. Through his sincere adoption of morality, he shows his intense reverence for the bodhisattva precepts. Through tolerance and effort he is unwearying in (bearing the) suffering caused by beings and by nature and in his intense dedication to virtue. Through contemplation and wisdom his yoga is free of conceptuality, being comprised of serenity and insight. This epitomizes the entire universal vehicle. Thus the transcendences are six with respect to their epitomizing the universal vehicle.

---

[1] The Tibetan reads as *parārthāḥ* in nominative, not in ablative as Ms. *parārthāt* (LI, p. 99.18) awkwardly reads.

[2] The Tibetan translates both *artha* and *kārya* by *don.*

> 6. One is a path to non-attachment to objects, another (a path) to the control of distractions of that attainment, another the non-forsaking of beings, another an increase, and the others for the purification of obscurations.

This is the fifth (verse). Generosity is a path of non-attachment to objects, because the repeated practice of generosity frees one from such attachments. Morality is a path of[3] the control of distractions from attaining one's aim; (for example), one who takes the monk's vow in order to attain his goal (of liberation) thereby prevents all distractions arising from evolutionary works. Tolerance is a path of not forsaking beings, because one is not revulsed by any suffering or any sort of harm (received while helping beings).[4] Effort is a path of the increase of virtue, because virtue increases[5] for one who initiates effort. Contemplation and wisdom constitute a path of the purification of obscurations, because those two clear up the addictive and objective blocks.

"Path" here means "liberative art." Thus the transcendences are six with respect to the path in all its forms.

> 7. The victors expound the six transcendences considering the three educations: the first (education) includes three (transcendences), the other two (educations comprise) the last two (transcendences), and the one (remaining transcendence accompanies) all three (educations).

This is the sixth (verse). The first education, supreme morality, includes three transcendences along with their stores and correlates: through (the transcendence of) giving, (the bodhisattva) disregards her property; (then she can) undertake (the transcendence of) morality; and then she can preserve that undertaking through (transcendent) tolerance, by not responding aggressively to aggression, and so on.

---

[3] The word path (*mārga*) is missing in the Skt. in these sentences, but *lam* is present in the Tibetan version (D Phi 197a1).

[4] Lévi reads this "*…des douleurs à subir pour rendre service à autrui*" (LII, p. 178), presumably reading *sarvopakāraduḥkha* (LI, p. 100.7), even though he enters the alternative *sarvāpakāraduḥkha*, which fits the Tibetan *gnod byed thams cad kyi sdug bsngal*.

[5] Lévi reads *tadvṛddhigamanāt* (LI, p. 100.8), instead of Bagchi's *tadbuddhigamanāt* (98.12).

"The other two (educations)" are (those of) supreme mind and supreme wisdom. They are comprised by the last two (transcendences, those of) contemplation and wisdom, respectively. "The one" transcendence of effort is included in all three educations, because effort accompanies all of them.

Six verses on the analysis of (their) characteristics:

> 8. Generosity weakens its resistance, goes with nonconceptual intuitive wisdom, fulfills all wishes, and develops beings in three ways.

The bodhisattvas' generosity has four characteristics. It weakens its resistance, because it abandons avarice. It goes with nonconceptual intuition because it applies to the realization of the selflessness of things. It fulfills all wishes because it gives anyone whatever he wishes. It develops beings in three ways, since, attracting beings through generosity, the (bodhisattva) involves them in (whichever of) the three vehicles according to their destinies.

> 9. Morality weakens its resistance, goes with nonconceptual intuition, fulfills all wishes, and develops beings in three ways.
>
> 10. Tolerance weakens its resistance, goes with nonconceptual intuition, fulfills all wishes, and develops beings in three ways.
>
> 11. Effort weakens its resistance, goes with nonconceptual intuition, fulfills all wishes, and develops beings in three ways.
>
> 12. Contemplation weakens its resistance, goes with nonconceptual intuition, fulfills all wishes, and develops beings in three ways.
>
> 13. Wisdom weakens its resistance, goes with nonconceptual intuition, fulfills all wishes, and develops beings in three ways.

The characteristics of (transcendent) morality and so on are understood as fourfold, like those of generosity. Their resistances are, respectively, immorality, anger, laziness, distraction, and false wisdom. (Transcendent) morality and so on fulfill all wishes in (dealings with) others, by (respectively) restraining body and speech, tolerating injury, helping, gladdening, and resolving doubts. (The transcendences of) morality and so forth develop beings by attracting them and developing them in (whichever of) the three vehicles.

One verse on the analysis of their order:

> 14. They are taught in their order because the latter arises dependent on the former, they have progressively superior status, and they grow progressively subtle.

Generosity and so on are taught in that (usual) order for three reasons.

Each arises dependent on its precedent. One who disregards property is concerned with morality, the moral person becomes tolerant, the tolerant person exerts his effort, an energetic person produces meditative concentration, and a concentrated person intuitively understands the real.

They progress from inferior to superior. Generosity is inferior and morality superior, and so on up to contemplation is inferior and wisdom superior.

They grow progressively subtle. Generosity is coarse, easy to enter and easy to practice, while morality is more subtle, harder to enter and practice; and so on up to coarser contemplation and subtler wisdom.

One verse on the analysis of their etymologies:[6]

> 15. (The six transcendences are named for connoting, respectively, that) poverty is removed, coolness is obtained, anger is destroyed, there is dedication to excellence, the mind is held firm, and there is intuitive knowledge of the ultimate.

As it takes away poverty, it is called "generosity."[7] As it confers coolness, it is called "morality," since one who has it is not burned by the addictions of involvement with objects. As it is the destruction of anger, it is called "tolerance," as it terminates anger. As it is exertion for excellence, it is called "creative effort," as it is

---

[6] *Nirvacana* (LI, p. 101.20) for the more usual *nirukti* (Tibetan *nges pa'i tshig*).

[7] These etymologies are fanciful, but must have had some currency in the Buddhist world. The connotation of each term is put into a short phrase, where each word contains a syllable of the name of the transcendence. As in the following table (LI, p. 101.24–102.2):

dāridryamapanayati = dāna	*vareṇa yojayati = vīrya*
śaityaṁ lambhayati = śīla	*dhārayati adhyātmaṁ mana = dhyāna*
kṣayaḥ kruddher = kṣānti	*paramārtha jānātyanayā = prajñā*

dedication to virtuous practices. As it holds the mind within, it is called "contemplation." And as it realizes ultimate reality, it is called "wisdom."

A verse on the analysis of their realization:[8]

> 16. For all of the (transcendences), realization is said to be based on condition, conscientious attitude, aspiration, liberative art, and mastery.

The realization of the transcendences is fivefold, from being based on conditions up to being based on mastery.

When based on conditions, there are four types of realization. Based on the cause, realization is the repeated practice of the transcendences on the strength of the spiritual gene. Based on development, it (is the repeated practice of the transcendences) on the strength of a perfect body. Based on prayerful vow, it (is the repeated practice of the transcendences) on the strength of a previous vow. Based on the strength of analytical discernment, it is the repeated practice of the transcendences on the strength of wisdom.

There are four types of realization of the transcendences based on conscientious attitudes. (The realization of the transcendences through) the attitude of faith is faith in the scriptures which treat all the transcendences. (The realization of the transcendences through) the attitude of appreciation is appreciation of the transcendences already achieved by viewing them as virtues. (The realization of the transcendences through) the attitude of congratulation is the rejoicing in the generosity and so on of all beings in all universes. (The realization of the transcendences through) the attitude of delight is taking pleasure in the excellence of the future transcendences of oneself and all beings.

The realization of the transcendences based on aspiration is sixfold: (as based on) insatiable aspiration, expansive aspiration, joyous aspiration, helpful aspiration, unsullied aspiration, and virtuous aspiration.

The bodhisattva has an insatiable aspiration for generosity. She would bestow on even one being in only one instant universes as numerous as the sands of the Ganges filled with the seven jewels, lives as numerous as the sands of the Ganges, and likewise also eons as numerous as the sands of the Ganges in every instant. Just as she gives to the one single being, so she should give by the same amount to

---

[8] *Bhāvanā* (LI, p. 102.3) translated "realization" to preserve the double sense of "mental focus in awareness" and "actually bring into being/make real."

all the many realms full of beings who are to be fully matured for unexcelled, truly perfect enlightenment. Such is the bodhisattva's insatiable aspiration for generosity.

The bodhisattva does not neglect that process of giving even for a single moment; he does not discontinue it until he sits on the seat of enlightenment. Such an aspiration is the bodhisattva's expansive aspiration for generosity.

The bodhisattva who cares for beings with her giving becomes more happy, not (thinking) that the beings so cared for by her generosity (should be happy). Such an aspiration is the bodhisattva's joyous aspiration for generosity.

When the bodhisattva thus gives to those beings, he truly regards those he helps as being more helpful to him than he himself (is to them); because (he thinks) "they serve as the very foundation (for my attainment) of unexcelled perfect enlightenment." Such an aspiration is the bodhisattva's helpful aspiration for generosity.

A bodhisattva who has amassed such vast merit from generosity has no desire for reward or for evolutionary development. Such an aspiration is the bodhisattva's unsullied aspiration for the realization of the transcendence of generosity.

The bodhisattva rejoices in the evolutionary development resulting from such a vast mass of giving (as coming) to beings and not to herself. Taking all beings as (sharing a) common (destiny), she develops them towards unexcelled perfect enlightenment. Such an aspiration is the bodhisattva's virtuous aspiration for realization of the transcendence of generosity.

The bodhisattva's insatiable aspiration for (realizations) from the realization of the transcendence of morality up to the realization of the transcendence of wisdom is as follows: in bodies as numerous as the sands of the Ganges, in lives as long as eons as numerous as the sands of the Ganges, the bodhisattva, even though always deprived of possessions, should manifest the four behaviors in the great billion world universe filled with fire. And he should realize (eons of transcendent moral actions in) a single moment of the transcendence of morality up to (eons of transcendent wisdom in) a single moment of the transcendence of wisdom. By the same means he should realize (the development from) a mass of morality up to a mass of wisdom, through which unexcelled perfect enlightenment is realized; because the bodhisattva's aspiration for (realizations from) the realization of the transcendence of morality up to the realization of the transcendence of wisdom is insatiable. Such an aspiration is the bodhisattva's insatiable aspiration for the realization of the transcendence of morality (and so on) up to the insatiable aspiration for the realization of the transcendence of wisdom.

So long as the bodhisattva does not sit on the seat of enlightenment she does not relax the process of the realization of the transcendence of morality up to the process of the realization of the transcendence of wisdom; she does not discontinue it. Such an aspiration is the bodhisattva's expansive aspiration for the realization of the transcendence of morality up to the realization of the transcendence of wisdom.

The bodhisattva, in helping (beings) through the realization of transcendent morality up to the realization of the transcendence of wisdom, becomes happier than those beings he helps. Such an aspiration is the bodhisattva's joyous aspiration for the realization of the transcendence of morality up to the realization of the transcendence of wisdom.

The bodhisattva regards beings as more helpful than herself, for she thinks "they are helpful in such realization of the transcendence of morality up to the realization of the transcendence of wisdom, and I am not; because they are the very foundation (for my attainment) of unexcelled perfect enlightenment." Such an aspiration is the bodhisattva's helpful aspiration for the realization of the transcendence of morality up to the realization of the transcendence of wisdom.

A bodhisattva who has amassed vast merit from the realization of the transcendence of morality up to the realization of the transcendence of wisdom has no desire for reward or evolutionary progress. Such an aspiration is the bodhisattva's unsullied aspiration toward the realization of the transcendence of morality up to the realization of the transcendence of wisdom.

The bodhisattva rejoices in the evolutionary progress of beings – and not of himself – from the mass of merit coming from the realization of transcendent morality up to the realization of the transcendence of wisdom. Regarding all beings in common, he develops them towards unexcelled perfect enlightenment. Such an aspiration is the bodhisattva's virtuous aspiration for the realization of the transcendence of morality up to the realization of the transcendence of wisdom.

The realization based on liberative art has three types. By nonconceptual intuition she discerns the purification of the three spheres (of action; that is, the giver, the giving, and the recipient). Such is the liberative art for perfecting all conscientious attitudes.

The realization based on mastery has three modes: mastery over body, mastery over conduct, and mastery over teaching. Mastery over the body should be recognized in the two bodies of a transcendent lord, the intrinsic reality (body) and the beatific (body). Mastery over conduct is to be recognized in the emanation body by which he shows conduct that corresponds in all its aspects to all beings. Mastery over teaching is the irresistibility in the teaching of the six transcendences in all their forms.

There are twelve verses summarizing the analysis. Generosity and the rest are each analyzed under six headings. The six headings are reality, cause, result, activity, endowment and function.

Two verses on the analysis of generosity:

> 17–18. The wise person should truly practice generosity, having understood it as motivating the presenting of gifts (to beings), as based fundamentally in the will, as leading to perfection of wealth and body, as caring for both (self and society), as completing (the stores), as being endowed with freedom from avarice, and as the giving[9] of the teaching, of goods, and of security.

The presentation of gifts to those who receive them is the reality of generosity. It is caused by the volition that naturally emerges from freedom from greed and so on. It results in perfection of wealth and (of future life) embodiment which includes length of life, as (explained) in the *Scripture on the Five Points.*[10] Its activity is assistance to self and other and completion of the stores of (merit and wisdom that become) great enlightenment. Its endowment with freedom from avarice is present among those who are not avaricious. Its function is analyzed into the giving of the teaching, of material goods, and of security.

Two verses on the analysis of morality:

> 19–20. The wise person should practice morality, having understood it thus: as having six elements, as aimed at the realization of serenity, as granting good lives and stability, as (serving as) basis, peace, and fearlessness, as endowed with the store of merit, and as attained conventionally or naturally on the part of those ordained in vows.

---

[9] *Dṛṣṭa* (LI, p. 104.8) seems to have no function here, and is not translated in the Tibetan. *Sṛṣṭa* "releasing" would correspond to the Tibetan *gtong*, and would add something useful.

[10] *Pañcasthānasūtra* (LI, p. 104.11). See LII, p. 184, n. 17–18.1. He cites the *Pañcaka-nipāta* of the *Aṅguttaranikāya* (XXXVIII (III, 42)), where the five things gained as evolutionary reward of giving food are said to be life-span, good social position (color), happiness, strength, and eloquence: *Bhojanam bhikkhave dadamāno dāyako paṭiggāhakānaṁ pañca ṭhānāni deti / katamāni pañca / ayuṁ deti vaṇṇaṁ deti sukhaṁ deti balaṁ deti paṭibhānaṁ deti / /*

Its reality is that it has six elements. The six elements are (those traditionally mentioned,) from "living morally (she is ordained in an individual liberation vow)" up to "she disciplines herself in her commitments to the precepts."[11]

"Aimed at the realization of serenity" indicates its cause, because one takes it up with the ambition for Nirvāṇa.

"Granting good lives and stability" indicates its result, because by morality one goes to good migrations and because the mind becomes stabilized through freedom from discontent and so on, respectively.

"Basis, peace, and fearlessness" indicates its activity. Morality is the basis of all virtue, is peace, pacifying the burning of the addictions, and is fearlessness, because fear, sin, and enmity based on killing and so forth are not produced.

Its endowment is the store of merit, because one always preserves the activities of body, speech, and mind.

"Attained conventionally or naturally on the part of those ordained in vows" describes its function. "Attained conventionally" (refers to morality) cultivated through vows of individual liberation, and "attained naturally" (refers to morality) cultivated through vows of the contemplative and the uncontaminated (realms); this analyzes its three types of functions. And "on the part of those ordained in vows" indicates its ground of function.

Two verses on the analysis of tolerance:

> 21–22. The wise person should practice tolerance, having understood it thus: as patience, endurance, and knowledge;[12] (as arising) from compassion and the support of the teaching; as taught to have five benefits; as accomplishing the aims of both (self and society); as universally supreme asceticism; and as considered threefold on the part of those (who are tolerant).

---

[11] Sthiramati (D Tsi 19a3–4) explains that the six factors are that "the moral person 1) is ordained with the vows of individual liberation; 2) is perfect in ritual regulation (*cho ga*); 3 & 4) is perfect in behavior and its range; 5) sees the danger in even the slightest shortcoming; 6) disciplines himself in his commitments." This seems to correspond well to the Pāli passage quoted by Lévi (LII, p. 185, n. 2), from *Āgama*, III, 135: *idha bhikkave bhikkhū sīlavā hoti, pātimokkhasaṁvarasaṁvuto viharati, ācāragocarasampanno, anumattesu vajjesu bhayadassāvī samādāya sikkhati sikkhāpadesu.*

[12] *Marṣādhivāsanajñānaṁ* (LI, p. 105.6) does not seem well matched by the Tibetan / *mi mjed ji mi snyam shes dang* /

"Patience, endurance, and knowledge" is the reality of the threefold tolerance: the tolerance which is patient with harm – here "patience" (*marṣa*) means "being patient" (*marṣaṇā*); the tolerance which endures suffering; and the tolerance which embodies the teaching, respectively.

"From compassion and the support of the teaching" indicate its causes, "support of the teaching" showing how it is undertaken through morality and incorporated from learning.

"Taught to have five benefits" indicates its result, as it is stated in scripture: "There are five benefits of tolerance; not much enmity, not much divisiveness, abundance of happiness and joy, ability to face death without regret, and rebirth in exalted heavens after the loss of the body."[13]

"Accomplishing the aims of both (self and society)" indicates its activity of patience and endurance. As it is stated: "He who accomplishes the aims of both self and others is the one who, while aware of others' anger, immediately controls his own."[14]

"Universally supreme asceticism" indicates its endowment, as it is said: "Tolerance is the supreme austerity."

"On the part of those" indicates the ground of its function, since it functions among the tolerant. "Considered threefold" indicates the analysis of its function, as already stated in the threefold analysis of (the reality of) tolerance.

Two verses on the analysis of effort:

> 23–24. The wise person should practice effort, having understood it thus: as true enthusiasm for virtue; as based on faith and will; as increaser of excellences such as mindfulness; as remedy of addictive tendencies; as endowed with virtues such as nongreed; and as sevenfold among those (who are enterprising).

---

[13] There is an odd lacuna in Sthiramati here (D Tsi 20a), so he does not comment on this scriptural passage. Lévi (LII, p. 186, n. 1) cites a helpful Pāli passage (*Aṅguttara*, III, 254): *pañc'ime bhikkhave ānisaṁsā khantiyā. bahuno janassa piyo hoti manāpo, na verabahulo hoti, na vajjabahulo, asaṁmūḷho kālaṁ karoti, kāyassa bhedā paraṁmaraṇā sugatiṁ saggaṁ lokaṁ upapajjati.*

[14] Lévi (LII, p. 186, n. 2) again helpfully quotes an exact Pāli match (*SN* I, 162–3): *ubhinnam atthaṁ carati attano ca parassa ca / paraṁ saṅkupitaṁ ñatvā yo sato upasammati / /*

"True enthusiasm for virtue" indicates its reality; "for virtue" excludes enthusiasm for other activities, and "true" excludes the religious fundamentalists' enthusiasm for liberation and so on.

"Based on faith and will" indicates its cause, for a confident and purposeful person engages her effort. "Increaser of excellences such as mindfulness" shows its result, since excellences such as mindfulness and meditative concentration are produced in one whose effort is engaged.

"As remedy for addictive tendencies" shows its activity, as it is said: "The enterprising person dwells in happiness unperturbed by sinful, nonvirtuous habits."

"Endowed with virtues such as nongreed" shows its endowment.

"Among them" means "among the energetically enterprising," indicating the ground of its function, and "sevenfold" indicates the analysis of its function, which is mental and physical effort constantly and carefully exerted in the three educations, supreme morality and so forth.

Two verses on the analysis of contemplation:

> 25–26. The wise person should practice contemplation, having understood it thus: as the inner stability of mind; as established in mindfulness and effort; as source of happiness; as mastery of superknowledges and stations; as the foremost practice; as threefold, found among those (contemplatives).

"Inner stability of mind" indicates its reality.

"Established in mindfulness and effort" indicates its cause, as trance is achieved when the objective is not forgotten and effort is exerted.

"Source of happiness" shows its result, since the result of contemplation is the development of immunity from harm.

"Mastery of superknowledges and stations" shows its activity, since contemplation gives mastery over the superknowledges and over the holy, divine, and sublime stations.

"The foremost practice" indicates its preeminence, as it is said: "Concentration is the foremost of all practices."

"Among those" shows that the ground of its function is among contemplatives, and "threefold" shows the analysis of its function, as it functions with both consideration and analysis, without consideration and with analysis alone, and without either consideration or analysis. Alternatively, (it is threefold as) accompanied with pleasure, accompanied with delight, or accompanied with equanimity.

Two verses on the analysis of wisdom:

> 27–28. The wise person should practice wisdom, having understood it thus: as true discernment of objects; as based on meditative concentration; as good liberator from addiction; as (enabling) the life of wisdom and excellence in teaching; as supreme among practices; and as threefold, found among those (who are wise).

"True discernment of objects" indicates its reality; "true" means objects which are "not false," and excludes authentic discernment of mundane duties.

"Based on meditative concentration" shows its cause, as the concentrated mind intuitively understands reality.

"Liberator from addiction" shows its result, since there is liberation from addictions through discernment, mundane, slightly transcendent, and greatly transcendent.

"Life of wisdom and excellence in teaching" shows its activity, since it enables one to live as unexcelled among those who live for wisdom and to teach the authentic teaching.

"Supreme among things" shows endowment with supremacy, as it is said: "Wisdom is the supreme of all things."

"Threefold as found among those" indicates its function, as it functions among the wise with a three-fold differentiation into mundane, slightly transcendental, and greatly transcendental.

So are stated the analyses of generosity and so on, each with a sixfold analysis.

One verse in analysis of inclusion:

> 29. All good practices should be known as distracted,[15] concentrated, and both, each of which include two transcendences.[16]

"All good practices" are the practices of generosity and so on. "Distracted" includes the first two transcendences, because both generosity and resolutely engaged morality are not meditatively concentrated. "Concentrated" includes the last two because of the stability of contemplation and the wisdom that accords with reality. "Both" includes tolerance and effort, because both have both concentrated and non-concentrated (forms).

---

[15] *Vikṣipta* (LI, p. 107.3).

[16] Literally, "these are fully included by two, by two, by two transcendences."

Six verses on the analysis of the resistances:

> 30. The generosity of the bodhisattvas is not attached, not attached, not attached, not attached, not attached, not attached, and not attached.

The resistant tendency to generosity consists of seven types of attachment: attachment to wealth, attachment to relaxation, attachment to easy complacency,[17] attachment to reward, attachment to evolutionary progress, attachment to resistance due to the failure to overcome the instinctual habit attached to the resistance, and attachment to distraction. Attachment to distraction is of two kinds: attitudinal distraction from interest in the individual vehicle, and discriminative distraction from discriminating between giver, recipient, and gift. Thus, since it is free from the sevenfold attachment, the non-attachment of generosity has been repeated seven times.

> 31. The morality of the bodhisattva is not attached, not attached, not attached, not attached, not attached, not attached and not attached.

> 32. The tolerance of the bodhisattva is not attached, not attached, not attached, not attached, not attached, not attached, and not attached.

> 33. The effort of the bodhisattva is not attached, not attached, not attached, not attached, not attached, not attached, and not attached.

> 34. The contemplation of the bodhisattva is not attached, not attached, not attached, not attached, not attached, not attached, and not attached.

---

[17] Here Lévi's Sanskrit reads *pakṣapātasaktiḥ* (LI, p. 107.12) which the Tibetan omits, and which seems out of place in this context.

> 35. The wisdom of the bodhisattva is not attached, not attached, not attached, not attached, not attached, not attached, and not attached.

As generosity has been described as "not attached," the same should be understood in the other cases, from morality up to wisdom. In the place of non-attachment to excellent wealth (in the case of generosity), non-attachment to immorality and so on (the opposites of the other transcendences) should be understood. Attachment to resistances results from not overcoming their instinctual propensities. Discriminative distraction results from discriminatively discerning the three spheres (of actions) in various situations appropriate (to the other transcendences).

Twenty-three verses on the analysis of excellences:

> 36. Out of compassion, the buddha-offspring, when they meet a suppliant, always give up even their own lives, without desiring any reward from others and without interest in any desired result. Such generosity exalts all beings in the three enlightenments; and generosity fully integrated with intuitive wisdom remains inexhaustible in the world.

The meaning is self-evident.

> 37. The buddha-offspring always take up the triple morality consisting of restraint and exertion. They do not desire heaven, and even when they reach it they generate no attachment to it. Such morality exalts all beings in the three enlightenments; and morality fully integrated with intuitive wisdom remains inexhaustible in the world.

Morality is threefold: restrictive morality, morality embracing virtuous practices, and morality which works for the benefit of beings. The nature of the first is restraint, and the nature of the other two is exertion.

> 38. The buddha-offspring undergo great austerities and all the injuries inflicted by people; not for the sake of heaven, not from inability, not from fear, and not from desire for benefit. Unexcelled tolerance exalts all beings in the three enlightenments; and toler-

> ance fully integrated with intuitive wisdom remains inexhaustible in the world.

"Unexcelled tolerance" refers to the tolerance of voluntary endurance of suffering and the tolerance of patience with injuries inflicted by others, in their order of development.

> 39. The buddha-offspring exert incomparable effort, by nature defensive and progressive, in order to slaughter the army of the addictions of themselves and others and to attain the holy enlightenment. Such effort exalts all beings in the three enlightenments; and effort fully integrated with intuitive wisdom remains inexhaustible in the world.

This refers to defensive effort and progressive effort.

> 40. The buddha-offspring totally perfect contemplation endowed with many meditative concentrations. Sustaining themselves with the finest bliss of contemplation, they remain in lowly lives through their compassion. Such contemplation exalts all beings in the three enlightenments; and contemplation fully integrated with intuitive wisdom remains inexhaustible in the world.

It (is) "endowed with many meditative concentrations" because it incorporates the limitless concentrations of the bodhisattvas.

> 41. The buddha-offspring totally know everything to be known, along with its thatness. Their intellect does not generate attachment even to cessation (in Nirvāṇa), how much less to involvement (in the life-cycle)?[18] Thus, intuitive wisdom exalts all beings in the three enlightenments; and wisdom fully integrated with (the needs of) beings remains inexhaustible in the world.

---

[18] The Tibetan reads *nirvṛtau* (LI, p. 109.8) as *nirvāṇau* and *saṁvṛtau* as *saṁsārau*, which makes the verse more explicit, and may have been the reading of the Sanskrit text the Tibetan translators used. To retain the Sanskrit word-play however, we have used both versions, bracketing the Tibetan.

"Along with its thatness" refers to the general nature (of things), including their ultimate reality, and the selflessness of subjects and objects. "Everything to be known" refers to the knowable divided into infinite categories (of things), by nature particular and conventional and so on.

Generosity and so on, fully integrated with nonconceptual intuitive wisdom, are inexhaustible, since they are not exhausted even in the Nirvāṇa without remainder. "Wisdom fully integrated with (the needs of) beings" means that due to compassion, one does not forsake beings.

The summarized meaning of these six verses is taught by a seventh verse:

> 42. In sum, magnificence, non-exploitiveness, greatness of aim, and inexhaustibility should be understood as the four excellences of generosity and so forth.

The magnificence of generosity and so on is made clear by the first quarter; by the second, their freedom from exploitiveness; by the third, their greatness of aim, since they bring about the great aim of beings; and by the fourth, their inexhaustibility. Thus, by these verses, one should understand the four excellences (of the transcendences).

> 43. The petitioner is pleased with encounters (of the donor) and fulfillment (of desires), is unhappy (without these), and is (generally full of) hopes. The compassionate (bodhisattva) donor outdoes him (in each respect) due to his extravagant dedication.

A person who is a petitioner gains pleasure from encounter with a donor and from fulfillment of wishes when getting whatever he wants, is unhappy when he does not encounter (the donor) and does not have his wishes fulfilled, and is (generally) hopeful for such encounters and fulfillments.

But that (person's happiness, unhappiness, and hopefulness) is always outdone by the bodhisattva (donor), who is even more happy to encounter the petitioner and to fulfill his wishes, and is even more unhappy not to encounter him and not to fulfill his wishes. Therefore, the compassionate donor outdoes (the petitioner) always by his extravagant dedication (to giving).[19]

---

[19] We had to rearrange the syntax of the Sanskrit here to avoid the awkwardness of passive construction.

44. With his compassion, he always freely gives away his lives, wealth, and wives to beings; and he is overjoyed. How then would he not maintain his refusal of these (things from others)?

"Refusal of these" is refusal of life, wealth, and wife belonging to others. This shows the excellence of his morality, opposed to the three evil physical actions.

45. Moved by compassion, she has no concern (for herself), is even-minded, fearless, and totally generous. How could such a holy person speak falsely in order to harm another?

This shows the excellence of the (bodhisattva's) refusal to utter falsehoods. Lies are spoken out of self-concern, concerned for one's body and life. Or else (they are spoken) for the sake of others, out of love for a dear person or out of fear, such as fear of a king. Otherwise, (lies are spoken) for the sake of some wealth, in order to gain profit.

(But) "the bodhisattva has no concern" for her own body and life. She is "even-minded" with regard to all beings because she has the attitude that they are the same as herself. "She is fearless," because she has transcended the five fears. "She is totally generous" to petitioners, because she has renounced all ownership. For what reason (then,) would she utter a falsehood?

46. He desires to help (all) equally, is kindly, terrified of making others suffer, and is devoted to educating beings; (thus he is) very far from the three faults of speech.

The bodhisattva desires to help all beings equally; how could he engage in slander for the purpose of creating dissensions between friends? He is kind, as his motive is to dispel others' suffering, and he is terrified of making others suffer; how could he indulge in harsh speech for the purpose of making others suffer? He is truly dedicated to educating beings; how could he engage in idle chatter? Therefore he is very far from the three faulty types of speech, slander, abusive speech, and idle chatter.

47. All-giving, compassionate, and expert in the arising of things in relativity; how could she endure any form of mental addiction?

Greed, aggression, and false convictions, respectively (are the three evil mental actions).

This (above description)[20] should be recognized as (elucidating) the excellence of the bodhisattvas' purity of morality, through its association with the special qualities which remedy (the ten types of) immorality.

> 48. The compassionate (bodhisattva) always considers it a help when he is harmed and always finds pleasure in suffering that helps others; so what is there to tolerate for such a person?

When an injury must be tolerated, the bodhisattva will be able to consider it a help, since it causes his development of tolerance. When suffering must be endured, the bodhisattva will be able to find pleasure even in that suffering, as it serves as cause of helping others. For such a person, in whom the notions "injury" and "suffering" do not arise, what is there to tolerate?

> 49. Since she has transcended the perception of others as "others," and since she always cherishes others very much more than herself, the compassionate person engaged in austerities finds effort both not difficult and very difficult.[21]

The compassionate person is the bodhisattva. Whatever difficult tasks (are undertaken) for the sake of others, her effort is both not difficult and very difficult. How is it not difficult? (It is) because (her efforts are) free from considering others as "other," and because she loves others more than herself at all times. How is it very difficult? (Very difficult) effort (is required) to become free from the perception of "other" and to love others more than oneself.

> 50. For three (types of persons), contemplation is considered (to give only) slight happiness or selfish happiness, to be suppressed, (either) perishable (or) exhausting, and quite delusive. (But) for the bodhisattvas it is the reverse.

---

[20] Vs. 44–47.

[21] Lévi's emendation following the Tibetan is here preferable (LI, p. 111, n. 1).

The contemplation of mundane persons gives slight happiness, and that of disciples and hermit buddhas selfish happiness. For mundane persons contemplation becomes suppressed by the materialistic (views), and for disciples and hermit buddhas it becomes suppressed by (their dualistically conceived) Nirvāṇa. It is easily perishable for mundane persons, and exhausting for disciples and hermit buddhas, because they are exhausted in the Nirvāṇa without remainder. It is quite delusive for all of them, their delusions being addicted and unaddicted, respectively.

For the bodhisattva (it is the reverse). His contemplation gives great happiness, such happiness being both self-gratifying and altruistic. It is irrepressible, not perishable, not exhausting, and free from delusion.

> 51. The three knowledges are like groping about in the darkness, or like a lamp under cover.[22] But the knowledge of the compassionate (bodhisattvas) is unrivalled, just like the rays of the sun.

Groping about with the hand in the dark (gives) knowledge whose object is small in scope, not immediate, and unclear; such is the knowledge of alienated individuals. A lamp in a cave[23] (gives) knowledge which is limited, immediate, and yet not very impeccable; such is the knowledge of the disciples and hermit buddhas. The rays of the sun (give) knowledge which is totally immediate and extremely impeccable; such is the knowledge of the bodhisattvas. Thus it is without rival.

> 52. (Transcendent) generosity is considered supreme from the point of view of embodiment, substance, process, dedication, cause, intuition, field, and reliance.[24]

The (supreme) embodiment is the bodhisattva.

As for the substance, in material giving, personal[25] substance is supreme. In giving security, (the supreme substance) is the freedom from fear for those terrified

---

[22] Lévi's emendation *dīpaiśchanne* (LII, p. 195, n. 51.1) for *dīpairnunnaṁ* follows the Tibetan.

[23] Following Lévi's emendation *yathā gahvarake* for *yathāvacarake* (LII, p. 195, n. 51.2) according to the Tibetan *phug tu*.

[24] Sthiramati's quoted version (D Tsi 36b4–5) of this verse is quite different from this version, and that of the translation of the *Kārikās*.

by the hellish states and the life-cycle. In giving the teaching, (the supreme substance is) the universal vehicle.

The (supreme) process is compassion.

The (supreme) dedication is the ambition for the fruition of great enlightenment through such (giving).

The (supreme) cause consists of the instincts developed by repeated practice of transcendent generosity in former lives.

The (supreme) intuition is the nonconceptual intuition with which one gives gifts in complete purity of the three sectors (of the act), free of discrimination of giver, gift, and recipient.

Its (supreme) field is fivefold, consisting of the petitioner, the sufferer, the protectorless, the evildoer, and the virtuous. Among the (first) four, each subsequent field is superior to its precedent, and in their absence the fifth is the best.

Its (supreme) reliance, relying on which gifts are given, is threefold, consisting of conviction, conscientious attitude, and meditative concentration. "Conviction" is the attitude of faith as described in the context of the analysis of meditative realization.[26] "Conscientious attitude" consists of attitudes of appreciation, congratulation, and delight as taught in the same place. "Meditative concentration," for example (the meditations of) "sky-treasury" and so forth, is like the mastery taught in the same place.

Thus it is that generosity is supreme, because of the supremacy of embodiment and so forth. This should be understood as the (eightfold) instruction here; who gives, what he gives, whereby, for what purpose, from what (cause), integrated with what, to whom, and in how many ways.

> 53. Morality is supreme from the point of view of embodiment, substance, process, dedication, cause, intuition, field, and reliance.

> 54.[27] Tolerance is supreme from the point of view of embodiment, substance, process, dedication, cause, intuition, field, and reliance.

---

[25] Literally, "inner" (*adhyātmikaṁ*, LI, p. 111.23). Sthiramati explains (D Tsi 37a1) that "inner" here means pertaining to the giver's own body, as in the bodhisattvas' giving their eyes, limbs, head, and so on.

[26] See above, verse 16.

[27] Lévi's Ms. is missing this verse on tolerance. He restores it from the Tibetan, according to the invariant pattern of the other five verses, but, out of reverence for the Sanskrit, he pre-

(cont'd)

55. Effort is supreme from the point of view of embodiment, substance, process, dedication, cause, intuition, field, and reliance.

56. Meditation is supreme from the point of view of embodiment, substance, process, dedication, cause, intuition, field, and reliance.

57. Wisdom is supreme from the point of view of embodiment, substance, process, dedication, cause, intuition, field, and reliance.

The supreme substance of morality is the bodhisattva's vow. (The supreme substance) of tolerance is the deprivation of (one's own) life by inferior or weak persons. (The supreme substance) of effort is the realization of the transcendences and the conquering of their resistances. (The supreme substance) of contemplation is the bodhisattvas' meditative concentrations. (The supreme substance) of wisdom is suchness. The field of all the rest such as morality is the universal vehicle. The rest should be understood as above (in the elucidation of generosity).

58. Though he himself were hurt for many eons, the bodhisattva would love generosity if it made even one being happy; what need to mention the opposite case!

If the generosity of the bodhisattva were to give happiness to only one being, although he himself were harmed for many eons, he would yet love it because of his distinctive compassion. How much more (would be his joy) if many beings are made happy and he himself is benefited for many eons!

59. Because embodied beings desire wealth, the intelligent bodhisattvas give them that very thing. (In fact,) it is because of the body that beings desire wealth, and the intelligent give up that very thing to them hundreds of times.

Here, the first half is explained in the second half.

---

serves the numbering of the verses according to the lacuna, calling this restored verse "53 bis." We see no purpose in this excessive adulation of the Sanskrit, so from here to the end of this chapter our numbering will be one higher than that of Lévi's.

60. If his mind does not suffer even when giving up the body itself, what can one say concerning things of small value? Such is his transcendent (generosity). And when he is even gladdened by (suffering), it is even more transcendent.

"If his mind does not suffer even when giving up the body itself" shows his transcendent (generosity). But when he is made happy by that suffering "it is even more transcendent" – it is transcendent of transcendent (generosity).

61. A petitioner is not happy even when he receives absolutely all that he desires, but the genius is still happier by giving all she has in this world for the happiness of the petitioner.

"Receives absolutely all that he desires" means receives in proportion to his desire. "By giving all she has" means up to giving her own life.

62. Even when laden with wealth, a petitioner does not consider himself wealthy; but the genius, impoverished by having given away all his wealth, believes himself all the more wealthy.

63. A petitioner who has received money in abundance does not consider that he has received a service from the giver who has obliged him; but the genius, when she has properly satisfied the petitioner with beautiful gifts, thinks of him as a great benefactor.

(It is the effect) of (her) distinctive compassion. The meaning of the two verses is self-evident.

64. Corporeal beings are free from sorrow and well at ease, having taken all his fortune from him, as on the road one picks a tree rich in edible fruits. Yet none other than the bodhisattva is rich with the delight in giving.

"Rich with the delight of giving," he who enjoys the wealth of delight in giving is to be known as none other than the bodhisattva. The meaning of the rest is self-evident.

> 65. It is taught that effort should be understood through analysis into principal, its cause, activity, types, support, and remedy for the four obstructions.

Effort should be understood in terms of six categories: principal, its cause, activity, types, support, and remedy for the four obstructions. This is the concise statement; the following verses explain it:

> 66. Effort is the best among the host of virtues, for later attainment relies upon it. With effort (one at once attains) a very happy situation, as well as mundane and transcendent accomplishments.

"Effort is the best among the host of virtues" teaches that it is the principal of all virtuous practices. "For later attainment relies upon it" teaches that it is the principal cause, since relying upon effort all virtuous qualities are attained.

"Though effort one attains at once a very happy situation as well as mundane and transcendent accomplishments" teaches its activity. Through effort, in fact, one achieves a supremely happy situation in the present life, and one becomes assured of mundane and transcendent accomplishments.

> 67. With effort one attains the wanted pleasures of life; with effort one becomes endowed with powerful purity; with effort one passes beyond the materialistic (views) and becomes liberated; and with effort one awakens to supreme enlightenment.

This formulation teaches the activity of effort by an analysis of mundane and transcendent accomplishments. "Powerful" refers to the mundane accomplishment (of purity) which does not endure forever.

> 68–69. Effort has decrease and increase; rules over liberation; is the remedy for its resistance; enters into reality; transforms people; and has a great aim. Under other names the buddhas proclaim all kinds of effort. Armor-effort is the first, and then follows exertion-effort systematically employed, intrepid-, unshakeable-, and insatiable-(effort).

This is the analysis of its types. In the context of the authentic abandonments, effort has decrease and increase, in the decrease of unvirtuous phenomena in two (abandonments), and in the increase of virtuous phenomena in two (abandonments). In the context of the spiritual faculties, effort rules over liberation, because the spiritual faculties have the sense of ruling over liberation. In the context of the powers, it is the remedy for the resistance, because the powers have the sense of not being overwhelmed by resistances. In the context of the branches of enlightenment, effort enters into reality, because they are classed in the path of insight. In the context of the branches of the path, it is transforming, because it is the ground for foundational transmutation in the path of meditative realization.

Effort has a great aim; its nature is transcendent since it is concerned with the aims of self and others. It is "armoring effort" because it is a donning of armor for engagement in practice. It is "engaged effort" when it has been engaged in such application. It is "intrepid effort" because it is free of discouragement even about the magnificent objective. It is "unshakeable effort" because it is undisturbed by sufferings such as heat and cold. It is "insatiable effort" because it is not contented with realizing just a little.

It is of these, "armor-effort" and so forth, that scripture states: "Powerful, energetic, mighty, overpowering, it does not shirk the responsibility of virtuous practice," respectively.

> 70. Again, effort is inferior, mediocre, and outstanding with respect to its embodiment, which is the person engaged in the three vehicles. Effort is considered as having a small aim or a great aim, according to whether motivation and intellect are feeble or extremely magnificent.

This teaches types of effort through an analysis of its embodiment. This embodiment is the person engaged in the three vehicles, and for those persons, effort is to be understood as inferior, mediocre, and outstanding, respectively. Why? On the basis of whether motivation and intellect are feeble or extremely magnificent. Motivation and intellect are feeble for those engaged in the two individual vehicles, because they are governed solely by their own aims. They are extremely magnificent for those engaged in the great vehicle, because they are governed by the aims of others. Therefore effort has, respectively, a small aim, or a great aim, depending on whether it is governed by the individual's aims or by all others' aims.

> 71. The enterprising person is not overcome by wealth. The enterprising person is not overcome by addictions. The enterprising

> person is not overcome by weariness. The enterprising person is not overcome by success.

This analyzes (effort) as the remedies of the four obstructions. The obstructions to generosity and so forth are fourfold, preventing one from engaging in generosity and so forth. They are attachment to wealth, from being completely taken over by it; attachment to addictions, from becoming obsessed with their full enjoyment; weariness, because of total exhaustion from repeatedly engaging in giving and so forth; and success, from becoming complacently satisfied with even a small achievement of generosity and so forth. Effort is to be known as fourfold according to such analysis of its resistances.

One verse on the analysis of mutual determination:

> 72. The ascertainment of the six transcendences is to be understood in all ways by means of mutual inclusion, differentiation, teaching, and process.

Ascertainment (of the nature of the transcendences results) from mutual inclusion. The giving of fearlessness includes morality and tolerance, for it is by means of those two that (the bodhisattva) gives fearlessness. The giving of the teaching includes meditation and wisdom, for it is by means of those two that one gives the teaching. Both (types of giving) include effort, and thus (through effort) one gives both. The virtue-accomplishing morality includes all the other (transcendences) such as giving. Thus the mutual inclusion of tolerance and so forth are also to be worked out appropriately.

Their ascertainment by means of differentiation (is as follows): generosity is sixfold, generosity-generosity, morality-generosity, and so on up to wisdom-generosity, because of the adherence of morality and so on in the processes of others.[28]

Their ascertainment by means of the teaching should be understood as the mutual inclusion of whatever scriptures are seen to relate to the topics of generosity and so forth and whatever references to generosity and so forth appear in the scriptures.

Their ascertainment by means of causal process is as follows: generosity is the causal process for morality and so forth because one progresses in morality when

---

[28] dBal Mang and Sthiramati do not comment on this way of subdividing each transcendence by analyzing each one in connection with to all the others.

one is indifferent to wealth. Also morality is the causal process for giving and so forth, because those ordained in the vow of a monk renounce all they own, and because when they stand in morality they develop tolerance and so forth.

The practice of the morality which includes virtuous practices is the causal process of all (transcendences) such as generosity. In a parallel way, one should work out how each of the other transcendences such as tolerance mutually serve as each other's causal processes.

Seven verses on the social practices. There are four social practices: giving, pleasant speech, accomplishment of aims, and consistency of behavior. Concerning them:

> 73. Generosity is considered the same as above. Pleasant speech, accomplishment of aims, and consistency of behavior are considered as teaching those (transcendences) to people, inspiring them to practice, and setting an example accordingly.

"Generosity" is accepted as the same as the transcendence. "Pleasant speech" teaches the transcendences. "Accomplishment of the aims" inspires people. The word "those"[29] refers to the transcendences. Therefore one teaches the transcendences and inspires people to practice the transcendences. "Consistency of behavior" refers to practicing oneself what one has recommended to others. Why are these considered the four social practices? For others they are:

> 74. A beneficial art, a means of holding, an impeller, and likewise an example; these are to be known as the four social practices.

Generosity is a "beneficial art" because by giving beings worldly goods physical benefit arises. Pleasant speech is a "means of holding" because it enables the uneducated to understand a perplexing notion. Fulfilling aims is an "impeller" because it impels (people) towards virtue. Consistency in practice is an "example," because when they see that the one involved practices as she teaches they are motivated to engage in virtue and conform to (that example).

---

[29] *Tad* (LI, p. 116.7) in the singular root form as in compound.

75. Through the first, one becomes receptive, through the second devoted, through the third one practices, and through the fourth there is purification.

Through giving worldly goods one becomes receptive, because one becomes well disposed to the teaching. Through pleasant words one comes to have faith in the teaching because one's doubts are resolved and the meaning made clear. Through fulfilling beings' aims one practices according to the teaching. Through consistency of behavior one perfects one's practice through perseverance over a long time. This is the activity of the social practices.

76. The four social practices are considered to be included in two groups, (pertaining to) worldly goods and to the teaching. (The last three) pertain to the teaching, consisting of objective, (practical, and purificative teachings).

The Lord has also taught two social practices, bringing people together by means of worldly goods and bringing them together by means of the teaching. These two social practices include the four. Bringing together by means of worldly goods includes the first, and bringing together by means of the teaching includes the rest.

Furthermore, the teaching has three types: teaching objectives, practices, and purifications, (corresponding to the last three social practices) respectively.

77. Analyzing its types, the social practice is understood as inferior, mediocre, and superior; generally useless, generally useful, and totally successful.

This analyzes the types of social practice. The bodhisattvas' association is to be understood as inferior, mediocre, and superior among those who are engaged in the three vehicles, respectively. It is generally useless in (bodhisattvas on) the level of action from faith. It is generally useful for those who have entered the (bodhisattva) stages. And it is totally successful on the eighth stage and above, because (such an advanced bodhisattva) necessarily fulfills the aims of beings.

78. All those engaged in gathering a retinue rely on that method (of the social practices); for the achievement of all the aims of everyone it is praised as an art of happiness.

All engaged in gathering a retinue rely on that liberative art consisting of the four social practices. It serves to fulfill all aims of all, and the buddhas have praised it thus as an art of happiness.

> 79. All beings either have been gathered together, will be gathered together, or are gathered together now. Thus, that (art) is the path of evolutionary progress for beings.

This shows that for the evolutionary progress of beings in the three realms, the four social practices are the path of the one vehicle, for there is no other path.

> 80. Thus the (bodhisattva's) mind is always unattached to wealth. Her soul at rest, she has gone beyond serenity, restraint, and effort. She no longer discerns existence, objects, or causal processes, and she embraces the company of beings.

This shows how the bodhisattva, when she stands in the six transcendences as they have been taught, employs the social practices; for she achieves her individual and altruistic aims, respectively, through the transcendences and the social practices.

Chapter XVII

Worship, Service, and the Immeasurables[1]

Seven verses on the analysis of the worship of buddhas:

> 1. With a mind of profound faith,[2] (the bodhisattva performs) physical and imaginary worship of the buddhas with (offerings) such as robes, in order to perfect the two stores (of merit and wisdom).
>
> 2. Yet the perfect worship of the buddhas is the non-apprehension of the three (sectors of action) by those good people who have vowed that the buddhas' incarnation be not in vain.

---

[1] dBal Mang (130b1) contextualizes this chapter as follows: "As (the bodhisattva) must wish to fulfill his own aim with the six transcendences and must not weary in the social practices in order to fulfill the aims of others, (fourth) there are the methods of making those two (sets of practices) powerful; there is the worship of the Three Jewels as the remedy of miserliness, the reliance on the spiritual teacher as the remedy of false morality, and the contemplation of the immeasurables as the remedy of the disciples' false practices."

Sthiramati (D Tsi 47a1 *ff.*) adds that worship of the buddhas and reliance on the teacher remedies the attachment to one's own success that is a danger as the transcendences lead to the consummation of own's own aim, as the offering of material things counteracts the attachment to possessions, and the reliance on the spiritual teacher remedies one's attachment to the pleasures of body and life. In the process of fulfilling others' aims with the social practices, the bodhisattva without the immeasuarables will weary, lose his impartiality, and will not tame beings. So the immeasurables remedy this tendency and cause the bodhisattva never to abandon beings.

[2] The Tibetan has *rab dang* not *zab dang*, and Sthiramati has *shin tu dang ba'i sems kyis*, reading *gāḍha* as "extremely" rather than "deep."

> 3. Another (type of worship) is by means of the development of immeasurable living beings; and still others are with material or mental (resources), from faith and sincere resolve.
>
> 4. Other (types of worship) are (performed) with sympathy, tolerance, realistic practice, the facing of the facts, realization, liberation, and with suchness.

With these four verses it should be understood that:

> 5. Worship is elucidated in terms of object, materials, causal process, dedication, cause, intuition, field, and resources.

The object (of worship) is the buddhas, both present and absent. The materials (which are offered in worship) are robes, (alms, bowls, incense,) and so on. The causal process is the mind endowed with profound clarity. The dedication is to the completion of the stores of merit and intuition.

The cause is the previous vow "May I not allow the birth of the buddha to be in vain!" The intuitive wisdom is nonconceptual as there is no apprehension of worshipper, worshipped, and worship.

The field is immeasurable beings; "by the development of beings" refers to the process of planting (the seed of buddhahood) in them by the performance of that (worship). The resources are material and mental. In this context, worship which depends upon material objects is (worship by offering) robes and so on, and (worship) which depends upon the mind consists of the attitudes of appreciation, congratulation, delight, and faith as previously explained. For example, faith in the universal vehicle teaching is the reason for the conception of the spirit of enlightenment. Here (in verse three), for reasons of meter, "sincere resolve" (*nidhāna*) is used for "vow" (*praṇidhāna*).

"Sympathy" is for living beings. "Tolerance" is for the sufferings involved in the performance of austerities. "Realistic practice" is the practice of the transcendences. "Facing facts" is the proper attitude towards things, which does not distort reality. "Realization" of things is the realization of reality on the path of insight when the realistic view is produced. "Liberation" is that of the disciples when they are freed from the addictions. And "suchness" is that whereby great enlightenment is attained.[3] These are the different types of worship.

> 6. And (worship) is twofold; from being cause or effect, being personal or through others, and with (offering) wealth and devotion or with (offering) practice.

> 7. And worship is considered inferior (when devotional and material) or superior (when practical), prideful or without pride (when accompanied by wisdom). Worship with practice (is near or far), according to migration and vow.

Another classification of the types (of worship) is according to differences in time and so on. In this context past (worship) is a cause, and present (worship) an effect. Present (worship) is a cause, future (worship) an effect. Thus one should understand past, present, and future (worship) in terms of cause and effect.

"Personal" is (either personal worship such as offering one's body or) internal (worship such as listening and thinking about the Dharma). "By others" is (either causing others to worship or) external (worship with goods, robes, etc.).[4]

(Worship with) "wealth and devotion" is gross, with "practice," subtle. (Worship in) the individual (vehicle) is inferior, in the universal (vehicle) superior. Again, (worship) accompanied by pride is inferior, without pride, superior, because of the latter's nondiscrimination of the three sectors.

(Worship through practice) to be performed at another time is distant, in the present, near. When (worship) is interrupted for (a number of) lives (in different migrations) it is distant, (when it continues) uninterrupted (in this life), it is near. Again, the worship which is vowed in the future is distant, that which one vows to perform (in this life) is near.

If one asks: "What is the supreme worship of the buddhas?" –

---

[3] Thus under mental offerings of worship, all the *Mahāyāna* practices on different levels become a sort of worship, following a pattern typical of *Mahāyāna* scriptures. This passage is reminiscent of the *Vimalakīrti*, where Vimalakīrti teaches the layman Sudatta the meaning of *Dharmayājña*, or where the Buddha Bhaiṣajyarāja teaches the prince Candracchattra about the "Dharma-worship." (See Thurman, *HTV*, pp. 39–41, 98–99.)

[4] Sthiramati (D Tsi 50a2–3) explains these in this way.

> 8. The supreme worship of the buddhas comes from one's own mind; that is, from faith in the teaching, from aspiration, from mastery, from full incorporation of arts born of nonconceptual intuition, and from joining with all (bodhisattvas) in unity of purpose.

The worship of the buddhas from one's own mind is to be understood as supreme. It has five modes: faith in the teaching of the universal vehicle combined with worship; aspiration which is of nine kinds – appreciative, congratulatory, rejoicing, insatiable, expansive, joyful, helpful, unsullied, and virtuous, which have been explained in the context of the realization of the transcendences; mastery in the meditative concentrations such as the "sky-treasury"; full incorporation of liberative art developed through nonconceptual intuition; and joining with all the great bodhisattvas in unity of purpose, through mingling and combining of duties.

Seven[5] verses on the analysis of service of the spiritual teacher. With the first five and a half verses:

> 9. Service is shown in terms of ground, material, process, dedication, cause, intuition, field, and resource.

> 10. One should serve a (spiritual) friend who is disciplined, tranquil, serene, outstanding in good qualities, energetic, rich in (knowledge of) scripture, awakened to reality, skilled in speech, compassionate, and indefatigable.

A friend with these qualities is the ground of service. "Disciplined" means that the senses are restrained due to moral discipline. "Tranquil" means that the mind is internally quieted by discipline in meditative concentration. "Serene" means the instinctual addictions are eradicated by the discipline of wisdom. "Outstanding in good qualities" means that he is unequalled and non-deficient. "Energetic" means that he is not indifferent to the welfare of others. "Rich in scripture" means that his learning is not inferior. "Awakened to reality" means that he understands reality. "Skilled in speech" means that he is skilled in the techniques of

---

[5] We count eight verses, from vs. 9–16. First there is a goup of five and a half verses (9–14ab), then a group of one and a half verses (14cd–15). That would total seven verses up to there, but then note below that the next verse, vs. 16, is introduced as "the seventh verse."

speaking. "Compassionate" means that his mind is free from the desire for material possessions. "Indefatigable" means that he teaches the Dharma continuously and reverently.

> 11ab. One should serve the spiritual teacher with devotion, wealth, attendance, and practice.

These are the materials of service.

> 11cd. The genius with an aspiration to realize the Dharma truly should humbly approach the spiritual teacher at the proper time.

This is the threefold process (of service): the desire to know, knowledge of the proper time, and freedom from pride.

> 12ab. The (spiritual teacher) who has no greed for devotion and wealth should cause (his disciple to) dedicate himself to practice.

In service, dedication is towards practice, and not towards (providing) devotion and wealth.

> 12cd. The brave[6] (bodhisattva) who practices as taught should please the mind of such (a spiritual teacher).

The cause of service is practice in accordance with what has been taught, because that is what pleases the mind of such (a spiritual teacher).

> 13ab. Having attained intellectual skill in the three vehicles, one should strive in the accomplishment of one's own vehicle,

Intuitive wisdom comes from skill in the three vehicles.

---

[6] The Tibetan (D Phi 212b2–3) does not translate *dhīraḥ* (LI, p. 120.9), or, more probably, contains the typographical error *bstan pa* for *brtan pa*; the *Kārikās* do translate with *brtan pa* (D Phi 25b4), and Sthiramati (D Tsi 52a6–7) with *blo can*, reading *dhīmān*.

> 13cd. in order to develop immeasurable beings and to create a pure land.

The field of service is twofold: immeasurable beings and a thoroughly pure buddhaverse; since, having learned the Dharma, one instills it in those (beings) and one stands in that (land).

> 14ab. One should serve the spiritual teacher in order to inherit his teachings and not to inherit his worldly goods.

These are the resources of service. One should serve the spiritual teacher for the inheritance of the Dharma, not for the inheritance of worldly goods.

One should understand the different varieties of service through the following verse-and-a-half:

> 14cd–15ab. The genius should serve the spiritual teacher externally through cause and effect (services) and (internally) by proceeding through the door of the Dharma; by listening to the lessons, by application in the mind, and by perseverance with and without pride.

"Through cause and effect," as above (in verse six), differentiates (services) into past and so forth.

"By proceeding through the door of the Dharma" and "the genius should externally serve the teacher" differentiates between internal and external (services). "Proceeding through the door of the Dharma" refers to the (internal) stream of the door of the Dharma. "Externally" is used for "outside."

"Listening to lessons and application in mind" refer to gross and subtle (services). Learning is gross, whereas reflection and meditation, applications in mind, are subtle.

"Perseverance with and without pride" differentiates between inferior and superior (services).

> 15cd. The genius should serve the spiritual teacher through practice, according to migration and vow.

This differentiates far and near and should be understood as (in verse seven of this chapter) above.[7]

Again, if one asks: "What is supreme service?" The seventh verse[8] (answers):

> 16. Supreme service of the good teacher comes from one's own mind; that is, from faith in the Dharma, from aspiration, from mastery, from full incorporation of the arts born from nonconceptual intuition, and from joining (all bodhisattvas) in unity of purpose.

(The meaning of this is) as above (in verse 8).

Twelve verses on the analysis of the immeasurables:

> 17. In the brave (bodhisattvas), the sublime stations eliminate resistances, possess nonconceptual intuition, operate with three objects, and develop the maturity of beings.

The sublime stations are the four immeasurables: (the immeasurables of) love, compassion, joy, and equanimity. In the bodhisattva they have four characteristics. They eliminate resistances (– malice, violence, displeasure, and attachment, respectively). They possess the distinctive remedy (– nonconceptual intuition). They have a distinctive function concerning their three objects: beings, things, and the objectless. And they have a distinctive activity because they cause beings to mature.

They have beings and things as their objects, but in relation to what kinds of beings or things do they operate? And what kind of object is the objectless?

> 18. For the brave they function in relation to those who seek happiness, are tormented by suffering, are happy, and are addicted; in

---

[7] In the context of vs. 7 above, Sthiramati indicates that the two kinds of worship, according to migration and vow, are types of worship *by practice*. Here, we assume the same intent, though the wording weakens that interpretation, as it lists "practice" as second in the list in *gatiprayogapraṇidhāna* (LI, p. 121.5), whereas *prayogād* (LI, p. 119.2) was first in the list in vs. 7.

[8] As mentioned above in the note before verse 9, this would appear to be an eighth verse in this series.

> relation to the things in which such (beings) are indicated; and in relation to their suchness.

When their object is beings they function for those who "seek happiness" and so on up to for those beings who "are addicted." "Love" has the mode (of desiring) that beings be happy; "compassion" has the mode (of desiring) that (beings) be free from suffering; joy has the mode (of desiring) that (beings) not be separated from happiness; and equanimity has the mode of causing beings to become free from addictions in the midst of (pleasant and unpleasant) experiences.

When their object is things, it is the things in which they are indicated, that is, where the (beings and) states are indicated.[9]

When their object is objectless they function concerning their suchness (that is, in relation to the suchness of beings and things). They are objectless because (on the eighth stage, when the bodhisattva attains tolerance of noncreation), the (sublime stations) are nonconceptual, as if objectless.

Furthermore:

> 19. Love is objectless because its object is suchness, it is purified by the attainment of tolerance, it has two activities, and it destroys the addictions.

---

[9] There seems to be some confusion between the *dharma* that means "teaching" and the *dharma* that means "thing" or "process." In this traditional formulation of the three types of compassion and so on, that which is *dharmālambana* is always considered to be that which is felt by the bodhisattva on the stages, or by the enlightened disciple or hermit buddha, who has seen through the illusion of self and personality and sees beings as mere impersonal processes, or things, yet still feels love for them.

Sthiramati (D Tsi 54b7 *ff.*) quotes the *YBh* as defining *dharmālambanamaitrī* as the love of the disciple and the hermit sage, since they see "these phenomena (of beings) as just the processes (*dharma*) of the five systems such as form, without personality or being...." He goes on to quote the *AMN*, which defines it as being the love of the bodhisattva engaged in deeds (on the stages before the eighth), "where they see beings as the purity of the ultimate realm (*dharmadhātu*)." Here Sthiramati has quoted sources using *dharma* as referring to things and to reality, and not to teachings; yet he leaves the matter there.

In the context of his commentary above, it almost seems as if Vasubandhu is thinking of *dharma* as "teaching, in which the stations are taught" – the most natural way to translate *taddeśite dharme / yatra te vihārā deśitā* (LI, p. 121.23). We would expect dBal Mang to elucidate this problem, but he appears not to notice.

Love is objectless for four reasons: because its object is suchness; because it is purified by attaining the tolerance of the noncreation of things on the eighth stage and by the growth of its element; because of its two activities, since love is accompanied by physical and verbal activity which are (its) homogeneous results; and because of its destruction of addictions.

Addictions have been said to be an object; as it has been said: "When mind-made knots are unraveled, the object is terminated."

> 20ab. They are mutable, immutable, over-appreciated by the sentimental, and not (so over-appreciated by those more developed in mind).

The sublime stations are fourfold. "They are mutable" or susceptible to loss, when they are liable to destruction. "They are immutable" or capable of duration and intensification, when they are not subject to destruction. "They are over-appreciated," that is, addicted, and "not over-appreciated," or unaddicted. "By the sentimental" refers to those whose minds are not expansive, who long for the pleasure (of the meditation of the sublime stations). This is an analysis of the types of sublime states with regard to their liability to loss and so on.

> 20cd. The bodhisattvas take their stand in those (forms of the stations which are) immutable and free of attachments.

Not in those which are mutable or over-appreciated.

> 21. If their nature is not concentrated, if they are feeble or mediocre, if they are of an inferior stage, if they are of an inferior aspiration or accompanied by pride, they are inferior; otherwise they are superior.

This is a division (of the sublime states) into weak and strong. The weak are of six kinds: those naturally not concentrated; those which although concentrated are weak or mediocre; those which are of a stage inferior to the higher bodhisattva stages; those imbued with inferior aspiration and accompanied by pride, (as they are) among the disciples; and those which lack the tolerance of the uncreatedness of things.[10] All of these are inferior, that is weak. "Otherwise they are superior"; those opposite to the above are strong.

> 22. When a genius has dwelt in the sublime stations and is born in the desire realm, she then completes the stores and matures living beings.

> 23. She is never deprived of the sublime stations and is always free from their resistances; despite violent circumstances, or even carelessness, she does not degenerate.

(The sublime stations are) classified as to cause, effect, and sign. "When she has dwelt in the sublime stations" refers to the cause. "She is born in the desire realm," among its beings, refers to the evolutionary effect. "She completes the stores" refers to the determined effect. "She develops living beings" refers to the heroic effect. "She is never deprived of the sublime stations" refers to the homogeneous effect. "She is free from their resistances" refers to the disjunctive effect. "Despite violent circumstances she does not degenerate" refers to the sign. "Despite carelessness" refers to situations when the remedy is not immediately present.

Four other verses classify virtues and faults:

> 24. The bodhisattva who is malicious, violent, unhappy, and addicted to malice and lust, undergoes many kinds of troubles.

These are faults. In the absence of the sublime stations one becomes prey to their opposing resistances. Malice and so on are respectively the resistances to love and so on. Addiction to malice and lust is the resistance to impartiality.

How does he undergo many kinds of troubles?

> 25. These addictions destroy (the bodhisattva) himself, destroy other beings, and totally destroy morality. Damaged, impoverished, defenseless,

---

[10] This sixth type of inferior station is not mentioned in the verse.

26. rebuked by the teacher, he loses good repute. In the next life he is born in the inopportune states, is deprived of that which he had or had not acquired, and he undergoes great suffering in his mind.

The first three phrases show the troubles which he suffers of injury to himself, injury to others, and injury to both.

The six phrases, "damaged" and so on, show the increase of the disagreeable in the present life. How does it increase? He is reproached by himself, by others, and the gods as well. The teacher, other wise people, and his fellow students criticize him in the name of the Dharma. Word of his evil reputation spreads in all the directions. This is shown by the verses from "damaged" to "loss of good repute" respectively.

The three remaining phrases show respectively the increase of the disagreeable in the immediate future and in the future life, and that he experiences mental suffering generated by that, and despair. These are the misfortunes indicated.

27. One well established in love and so on has none of these faults; without being addicted he does not abandon the life-cycle, (staying) for the sake of beings.

This shows the two[11] virtues which apply to (one well established on) the sublime stations: absence of the faults described, and, although lacking the addictions, non-abandonment of the life-cycle for the sake of beings.

28. No one has a feeling of love even towards (loved ones) such as an outstanding only child, anything like that (love) the victor-offspring feel for beings.

This shows the intensity of the love and so forth of the bodhisattvas.

Within the analysis of compassion, there are two verses concerning its various objects:

---

[11] Lévi's Sanskrit has *trividhaṁ guṇaṁ* (LI, p. 123.24), but the Tibetan has *yon tan rnam pa gnyis* (D Phi 214b6), which makes better sense. Although Lévi did not catch this in LII (p. 212), Bagchi (120.7) does suggest emending *trividhaṁ* to *dvividhaṁ* in agreement with the Tibetan. This has the effect of making the *akliṣṭasya* in the following phrase a quality of the implied subject ("one well established in love") rather than a third virtue possessed by such a subject.

> 29. Enflamed, under the power of enemies, oppressed by suffering, enveloped in darkness, traveling a difficult road, bound with great chains,
>
> 30. greatly fond of food mixed with poison, strayed from the path, remaining on the wrong path, of little strength – the (bodhisattva) takes compassion upon such beings.

(Living beings are) "enflamed" by attachment to pleasure, devoted to sense-pleasure. (They are) "under the power of enemies," impeded by the deeds of devils, even when engaged in virtue. They are "oppressed by suffering," overcome by pain in the hells, and so on. They are "enveloped in darkness," when, as butchers and the like, they are wholly given over to evil conduct due to ignorance of the evolutionary consequences of their actions.

"Traveling a difficult road" refers to those who miss the principle of final liberation because they do not radically sever the continuum of the cyclic life. "Bound with great chains" refers to those heterodox fundamentalists fixed on liberation, because they are bound with the tight chains of various wrong views. "Greatly fond of food mixed with poison" refers to those who are addicted to the pleasure of meditative absorption – for them the pleasure of meditative absorption is addicted, like delicious food mixed with poison, and should be shunned accordingly.

"Strayed from the path" refers to those arrogant persons who have wandered from the path of liberation. "Remaining on the wrong path" refers to those of uncertain (disciple or bodhisattva) genealogy who set out on the individual vehicle. "Of little strength" refers to those bodhisattvas whose stores are incomplete.

These ten types of living beings are the objects of the bodhisattva's compassion.

One verse showing the five results of compassion:

> 31. Enlightenment is not far away at all from the victors' spiritual heir who relies upon the Dharma which prevents violence, is the seed of superior enlightenment, brings happiness (to oneself) and delivers (other beings), causes the desirable, and naturally imparts itself.

"Prevents violence" refers to the disjunctive result (of compassion), because its resistance, violence, is destroyed. (The Dharma) "is the seed of superior enlightenment" refers to the determinant result. To others and oneself respectively, it "brings happiness" and "delivers (other beings)," which are heroic results. "Causes the desirable" refers to the evolutionary result. "Naturally imparts itself" refers to the homogeneous result, because it gives the result of distinctive compassion in the future. When one relies upon such fivefold compassion, buddhahood should be understood as not far off at all.

One verse on not being located either in the life-cycle or in liberation:

> 32. The compassionate best genius understands that everything included in the life-cycle is naturally both suffering and also selfless, and so neither becomes disgusted nor damaged by any faults.

Having thoroughly understood all of the life-cycle as it is in reality, the bodhisattva, due to compassion, does not become disgusted, and, due to extreme intelligence, is not damaged by any faults. Thus he does not dwell either in Nirvāṇa nor in the life-cycle, respectively.

One verse on the thorough knowledge of the life-cycle:

> 33. When she observes the natural suffering of the world, the loving (bodhisattva) suffers; yet she knows just what it is as well as the means to avoid it, and so she does not become exhausted.

"She suffers" means that she feels compassion. "She knows what it is" means that she knows suffering just as it is, and the "means to avoid suffering" means that she knows that by which it is destroyed. Thus, knowing the suffering of the cyclic life just as it is and (also knowing) the means of renouncing it, the bodhisattva does not become exhausted thanks to her distinctive compassion.

Two verses on the varieties of compassion:

> 34. The compassionate have four types of mercy: natural, analytic, from former cultivation, and from the purity attained by overcoming its resistance.

This (fourfold mercy) should be understood as proceeding respectively from the excellence of the (bodhisattva's) spiritual gene, from an analysis of virtues and faults, from its cultivation in former lives, and from the attainment of detachment. When its resistant tendency, violence, is abandoned, "purity is attained," that is, detachment is attained.

> 35. That is not mercy which is not equal or constant, not from universal responsibility nor from practice, and not from detachment nor from nonperception; likewise, one without mercy is not a bodhisattva.

(Compassion is) "equal" towards (beings whether) happy (or sad) and so on, being aware that whatever is experienced in this life is misery. (It is) "constant" because it is not exhausted in the remainderless Nirvāṇa. It is from "universal responsibility" for those who enter the (bodhisattva) stages and attain the resolve to (realize) the equality of self and others. It is "from practice," because it functions to deliver from suffering. It is from "detachment," when its resistance, violence, is abandoned. It is from "nonperception," when the tolerance of things' nonproduction is attained.

Five verses on the comparison of compassion to a tree:

> 36. Compassion, tolerance, ambition, resolution, life, and the full evolution of living beings; this is the great tree of compassion beginning with the root and ending with the superior fruit.[12]

The tree of compassion should be known in its root, trunk, branches, leaves, flowers, and fruits. Its root is compassion, tolerance its trunk, ambition for the sake of beings its branches, resolutions for beautiful lives its leaves, beautiful life its flower, and the evolutionary fulfillment of beings its fruit.

> 37. If compassion were not the root, there would be no endurance of difficult deeds. If the genius could not bear up under suffering, she would have no ambition for the sake of beings.

> 38. (Even) a genius without such ambition would not make the resolution for perfect lives. If she did not manifest beautiful lives, then she would not develop beings.

---

[12] Lévi (LI: 125.22 and note 1) emended Skt. and translated a list of "flowers, leaves, and fruits." We follow Tib. and original Skt. Ms. " from roots to superior fruits."

These two verses establish that compassion and so on are of the nature of root and so on, due to the analogy of how each (member of each set) gives rise to the next.

> 39. One should recognize that love is the watering (for the tree) of compassion; its broad growth comes from joyous willingness to undergo suffering; and the vast spread of its branches comes from fitting conscientious attitudes.
>
> 40. The growth and fall of leaves comes from the unbroken series of resolutions. Fertile flower and fruit come from success in the two objectives, personal and social.

These two verses display the tree of compassion using the analogy of watering the root of a tree and so forth.

Compassion has been called the root. Love is the water sprinkled upon it because it causes it to grow. In fact, one who has the thought of love suffers from the sufferings of others. Then from the suffering produced in the bodhisattva compassionately devoted to the aims of beings, happiness arises which causes the broad growth, that is, the growth of tolerance, which is called the trunk, and the trunk is broad.

From fit conscientious attitudes comes an abundant spread of branches in the universal vehicle. Ambition has been called the branches. The growth and fall of leaves is analogous to resolutions because the series of vows is unbroken: when one ceases another begins.

From success in the personal objective, that is, the development of one's own continuum, life is like a fertile flower. From success in the social objective, that is, the development of others' continua, there is the fertile fruit, the evolutionary fulfillment of living beings.

One verse on the benefit of compassion:

> 41. Who would not be compassionate toward beings who are the source of the virtue of universal mercy? There is a matchless happiness even in that suffering which mercy for them generates.

The second half of the verse shows the virtue of great compassion. The rest is self-evident.

One verse on the non-attachment of compassion:

42. The mentality of those compassionate (bodhisattvas) permeated with mercy does not rest even in quietude; how then could they become fond of worldly happiness or even of their own lives?

All people are fond of worldly happiness and of their own lives, and the mentality of disciples and hermit buddhas, who are not attached (to either), still rests in Nirvāṇa, where all suffering is quieted. But the mentality of bodhisattvas does not resort even to Nirvāṇa, because they are permeated with compassion. How much less, then, will they be fond of both (worldly happiness and living).

Three verses on the distinctive affection of compassion:

43. (Ordinary) love which is irreproachable and not mundane is never found; but merciful love in the genius (bodhisattvas) is blameless and transcendent.

The love of such as father and mother is made of craving and so is liable to reproach. (The love of) those who dwell in mundane compassion, though irreproachable, is still mundane. But the love of bodhisattvas is made of compassion and is both irreproachable and transcendent.

How is it irreproachable?

44. The world stands upon the great flood of suffering, in the great darkness of ignorance;[13] how could the art of saving it, indeed, fail to be irreproachable?

One should construe the great flood with suffering and the great darkness with ignorance. The rest is self-evident.

How is it transcendent?

45. Not to mention others, not even perfect saints nor privately enlightened sages have such a love for the world; how could it fail to be transcendent?

---

[13] Emending the Sanskrit *duḥkhājñānamahaughe mahāndhakāre ca* (LI, p. 127.8) to *duḥkhājñānamahaughamahāndhakāre ca*, following the Tibetan (D Phi 217a6) *sdug bsngal dba' rgal che dang mi shes pa'i / mun pa che la...* and the commentary which specifices the distribution of the two similes.

"Privately enlightened sages" means "buddhas who are enlightened by themselves." The rest is self-evident.

One verse on the significance of terror and delight:

> 46. When they have no (personal) suffering, suffering brought to the bodhisattvas by mercy terrifies them at first, but once it is experienced, causes them extreme delight.

"When they have no suffering" refers to an absence of suffering. The suffering of bodhisattvas which is brought them by their mercy for beings terrifies them at first, on the stage of action through faith, because they do not have experience of what suffering is like in the equality of self and others. But when it is experienced on the stage of pure universal responsibility, it causes delight. This is the meaning.

One verse on the surpassing of happiness by compassionate suffering:

> 47. Merciful suffering surpasses every mundane happiness, and is missed even by one who has accomplished his own aim; what could be more supremely wondrous!

There is nothing more wondrous than this: that the bodhisattva's suffering born from compassion becomes happiness, and surpasses all mundane happiness. Even the saints who have accomplished their own aims lack that happiness, not to speak of others.

One verse on the benefit of mercy-driven generosity:

> 48. Generosity accompanied by compassion generates the happiness of generosity in the brave. Happiness from enjoying things of the three realms does not touch the slightest portion of it.

The happiness from enjoyments in the three realms does not approach that happiness, does not touch a portion of that happiness. This is the meaning of the second half (of the verse). The rest is self-evident.

One verse on the acceptance of suffering through mercy:

> 49. Through mercy, for the sake of beings he does not (even) forsake the life-cycle made of suffering; what suffering will the compassionate bodhisattvas not embrace in order to accomplish the benefit of others?

All suffering, in fact, is included in the suffering of the life-cycle. In accepting that he accepts all suffering.

One verse on the growth of its fruits:

> 50. Compassion, generosity, and fortune always increase for the merciful (bodhisattva); and therefrom come the happinesses born of love, helpfulness, and powerful ability.

Three things increase for bodhisattvas in all lives from the practice of compassion: compassion from its repeated practice, generosity from the force of compassion, and fortune from the force of generosity. And from these three, three happinesses come forth as results: happiness born of love due to compassion, happiness born of helpfulness due to generosity, and happiness born of the ability to act to assist beings with that fortune.

One verse on encouraging generosity:

> 51. "I increase, I cause increase, I fully develop (beings), I gladden, I attract, and I lead" – it is as if compassion encourages those weak in generosity.

It is necessary to connect "in generosity" and "those who are weak." It is as if compassion uses six virtues to encourage bodhisattvas weak in generosity. It increases naturally; it increases by fortune it brings; it brings beings to evolutionary maturity with generosity; it produces happiness in the giver; it attracts the stores of great enlightenment; and it leads one close to great enlightenment.

One verse on the experience of happiness due to the happiness of others:

> 52. How could one who from mercy suffers in the presence of suffering become happy without making (others) happy? Thus the merciful (bodhisattva) makes himself happy by making others happy.

Due to compassion the bodhisattva suffers with the sufferings of others. How could he become happy if he does not create happiness in (other) beings? Thus it should be known that the bodhisattva makes himself happy by giving happiness to others.

Six verses on mercy's instructions to generosity:

53. The compassionate one, uninterested in her own happiness, instructs, as it were, her own generosity: "Make others happy with gifts of wealth; otherwise I also will have no happiness, as (mine and others' happiness are) indistinguishable (for me)."[14]

The compassionate one, in fact, is not happy apart from the happiness of others. Because there is no distinguishing her happiness (from that of others), the bodhisattva, without that (happiness of others), does not desire that happiness which is her own[15] fruit of generosity.

54. "To beings I have given gifts, as well as the fruits (of that giving), since their happiness is my happiness. If you owe me any duty, you must reward them (even more) abundantly."

"In giving gifts, I have given the fruit of generosity with the gift to beings, because their happiness is my happiness. Hence you should reward them as much as possible." "Reward" is in the imperative mood. (Thus) the bodhisattva instructs generosity with compassion.

55. "The giver, though he hates wealth, keeps getting wealth even more abundant and beautiful; but I do not think of that as happiness because for me there is just more continuity in giving."

It is just in the nature of things that the fortune of a giver who turns away from wealth becomes more abundant and more beautiful, due to the magnificence of his mind. "But I, (continues compassion,) do not consider such persistence of wealth to be happiness, because I am continuous in giving. I desire uninterrupted generosity, not happiness."

---

[14] The Tibetan (D Phi 218b2) / *yang na tha dad min bde bdag la'ang min* / reads a Sanskrit original that included a negative and the personal pronoun in the locative or dative; e.g., *vā nātmano 'pyayutasaukhyaṁ* /, which would restore that last *pāda* to a more proper length for the meter.

[15] Following the Tibetan and Lévi's suggested emendation.

> 56. "You always observe me compassionately letting go of all that I have; so can't you recognize that, 'She has no interest in my fruits'?"

"Since I perpetually relinquish, out of compassion, all the fruits of generosity, do you not understand that I have no interest in the fruits of my generosity?" In this way the bodhisattva instructs generosity.

> 57ab. "I will not delight in generosity if I do not relinquish any fruit I get."

For:

> 57cd. "To remain even an instant without generosity is not to delight in generosity."

The meaning of the verse is self-evident.

> 58ab. "You do not give fruits to one who does not (give) because you expect reward; you are not my equal."

"You, (continues compassion's lesson to generosity,) give fruits to whomsoever practices you; thus you are not my equal regarding rewards because I..."

> 58cd. "do not expect reward. I give your fruits to others voluntarily."

This is self-evident.

Two verses on compassionate generosity:

> 59. For the spiritual offspring of the victors, compassionate generosity is irreproachable, pure in basis, beneficial, protective, unsolicited, and unsullied.

It is irreproachable because generosity does no harm to others. It is pure in its basis, giving appropriate objects excluding poison, weapons, and intoxicants. It is beneficial, since what is gathered through generosity is applied to virtue. It protects, giving to others without depriving one's associates. It is unsolicited, since, even without being requested, one gives of one's own accord once one has understood (the recipients are) needy or deprived, and since the honorable (recipients) do not solicit (one's donations). It is unsullied, free of desire for reward or evolutionary development.

In another way:

> 60. For the spiritual offspring of the victors compassionate generosity is total, vast, excellent, continual, joyous, non-exploitive, and pure, inclined towards enlightenment and virtue.

It is total because it gives (both) internal and external objects. It is vast, giving things in abundance. It is excellent, giving the best things. It is continual, giving continually. It is joyous, giving cheerfully without deliberation. It is non-exploitive, as it is unsullied (as explained in the previous verse). It is inclined towards enlightenment because it tends towards great enlightenment. It is inclined towards virtue as it is conducive to benefit (as explained in the previous verse).

> 61. A voluptuary does not obtain any satisfaction in enjoyments like the satisfaction which comes to a compassionate one from renunciation, her mind satiated with the three pleasures (of giving, helping, and gathering the stores).

The three pleasures are the pleasure of generosity, the pleasure of helping others, and the pleasure of gathering the stores. The rest is self-evident.

A verse on compassion as accomplishing the transcendences:

> 62. (The transcendences are motivated by) compassion for the pitiable, compassion for the violent, compassion for the disturbed, compassion for the reckless, compassion for those dependent on sense-objects, compassion for those addicted to falsehood.

The "pitiable" are the stingy. The "violent" are the immoral who do harm to others. The "disturbed" are the angry. The "reckless" are the lazy. Those "dependent on sense-objects" are those whose minds are distracted by sense objects. Those who are "addicted to falsehood" are those with false wisdom, such as the fanatics, and so forth. "Compassion for the pitiable and so forth" is compassion for those in the conditions that are opposed to the transcendences. It causes the accomplishment of the transcendences, since it eliminates their opposing resistances. Thus, it is called the "compassion accomplishing the transcendences."

A verse to show the conditions for compassion:

> 63. The compassion of the bodhisattvas comes from happiness, from suffering, and from the (anaesthesia) which is linked with them. The compassion of bodhisattvas comes from a cause, from the (spiritual) mentor, and from its intrinsic reality.

The first half shows the objective condition of compassion. Compassion is born from three kinds of suffering in taking the three types of sensation as objects. The (anaesthetic) sensation without happiness or suffering is linked to happiness and suffering because it leads to them once again.

The second half shows the causal, controlling, and antecedent conditions of compassion which are respectively the cause, the spiritual mentor, and intrinsic reality.

A verse on the greatness of compassion:

> 64. The compassion of bodhisattvas should be understood as equal by virtue of its aspiration, practice, detachment, nonperception, and purification.

It is equal, because whichever of the three kinds of sensations he experiences he knows that all sensation is suffering. (It is thus equal) because of its aspiration, as it is produced through will; because of its practice, as it saves; because of its detachment, as it abandons the violence which is its resistant tendency; because of its nonperception, not perceiving any compassion for self and others; and because of its purification, since on the eighth stage one attains the tolerance of the noncreation of things.

> 65. The superior meditative practice of love and so forth comes from one's own mind, from faith in the teaching, from resolve, from mastery, from nonconceptualization, and from oneness.

One should understand the meaning according to the explanation given above.[16]

> 66. Thus, producing great faith in the Lord Buddha, intensely worshipping him with great material things and constant reverence, and constantly serving the beneficial mentor who has many virtues, she who has compassion for people attains complete success.

This shows succinctly and in order the qualities of worship, service, and the immeasurables as they have been explained. The compound, "great-materials-constant-reverence-worship"[17] is analyzed as follows: she worships greatly with great material things and with constant reverence. "Reverence" connotes right practice. Thus she worships with wealth, reverence, and practice. The "beneficial mentor who has many virtues" refers to virtues other than those. He is called "beneficial" because he is compassionate. She attains complete success, attaining success in her own aims as well as in others' aims.

---

[16] See XVII.8.

[17] *Mahadupadhidhruvasatkriyābhipūjī* (LI, p. 131.24).

Chapter XVIII

The Accessories of Enlightenment

Sixteen verses on the analysis of conscience:[1]

> 1. The conscience of the brave (bodhisattva) is free from (its own) resistant tendency, is associated with nonconceptual intuition, holds (even) blameless objectives to be inferior, and brings evolutionary maturity to beings.

This shows the four characteristics of the bodhisattva's conscience, through the perfection of (its) nature, association, objective, and activity. Its objective is both blameless and inferior; that is, the bodhisattva's conscience (considers) that even though the vehicle[2] of the disciples and hermit buddhas is blameless, it is inferior by comparison with the universal vehicle.[3] How does conscience bring maturity to beings? It installs[4] others in that same kind of conscientiousness.

---

[1] dBal Mang (142a4 *ff.*) describes the continuity at this point in the text in a useful way: "As it is necessary to perfect the six transcendences from the persepctive of fourteen faculties such as the sense of shame, secondly there is the way of being skilled in liberative art from the point of view of the accessories of enlightenment. In this there are four sections, the way of establishing the ground through morality, the way to cease reifications through learning and reflecting, the way to put into practice the accessories of enlightenment, and the art of developing their power. In the first, there are the sense of shame in the restraining morality, the bravery in the morality accomplishing beings' aims, and the indefatigability in the morality that gathers virtue."

[2] *Yānaṁ* is absent in Lévi (LI, p. 132.9); its insertion here is a suggested emendation by Bagchi (p. 128.6). *Theg pa* is present in the Tibetan (D Phi 220b3).

[3] This definition of conscientiousness is puzzling, as to why it should be definitionally connected with the bodhisattva's sense of the difference between the two vehicles. Neither dBal Mang nor Sthiramati clarify this satisfactorily. Perhaps the vehicle difference – individual versus universal orientation – comes into play, since the bodhisattva's conscience will not let him or her rest from practicing the altruistic transcendences. The individual vehicle orienta-

(cont'd)

2. When resistances to the six transcendences increase and their remedies decrease, the bodhisattvas' guilty conscience becomes intolerable.

This is the bodhisattvas' guilty conscience derived from increase and decrease. An increase of the transcendences' resistances[5] and a decrease of their remedies provoke an intensive feeling of guilt.

3. The brave (bodhisattvas) feel a guilty conscience when they are lazy in the practice of the six transcendences and (yet) energetic in actions attuned with the addictions.

This is the guilt (arising) from non-engagement and engagement. Non-engagement in the practice of the transcendences and engagement in activities which are attuned with addictions, such as not guarding the doors of the senses, generate a guilty conscience (in bodhisattvas).

4. Conscience is inferior when its nature is unconcentrated, when it is feeble or mediocre, when it is on a lower stage, when it has inferior aspiration, and when it is filled with pride. When it is otherwise, it is superior.

This (shows) conscience as weak and strong. The sense of the verse is to be understood according to the explanation above.[6]

---

tion toward individual liberation, while the same as the orientation of the last two transcendences, contemplation and wisdom (which also aim to satisfy individualistic desires for freedom, and are therefore also blameless), would be inferior if pursued without simultaneously pursuing the altruistic transcendences of generosity, morality, and tolerance.

[4] As Lévi points out (LII, p. 225, n. 2), two lines are missing in the Sanskrit here. Thus, in the next few lines we have followed the Tibetan (D Phi 220b3–4) and Lévi's reconstituted Sanskrit (LII, p. 225, n. 2; compare Bagchi, p. 128.7–11). As Sthiramati (D Tsi 82b) comments as if this verse were integral to the text, and as dBal Mang (142b) fits it into the flow of meanings in relation to the causal analysis of conscience, we see no reason to call it *1 bis* as does Lévi, rather than alter the numbering of the verses he gives in his Sanskrit edition. Thus, our numbering is one greater than his for the remainder of this chapter.

[5] See XVI.8–13.

[6] See XVII.21.

With the following four verses and three verses respectively, he shows the resistance to conscience and the analysis of its faults and virtues:

> 5. (Even a bodhisattva) genius devoid of conscience persists in passions due to inappropriateness; (for) anger, callousness, and pride destroy both beings and morality.

This shows how one can harm oneself, harm others, and harm both self and others.[7] "Due to inappropriateness" (means) because of inappropriate attitudes. How does callousness destroy beings? By neglecting beings' aims.

> 6.[8] He is (both) disturbed by remorse (and) suffers the loss of the respect (of others). And therefore the angelic host that believed in him[9] and the teacher as well, lose their concern for him.

> 7ab.[10] His religious associates, spiritual offspring of victors, reproach him, and he becomes publically notorious in that very life.

This shows the unpleasantness which (the bodhisattva) creates (for himself) in the present life. He is despised by himself, by others, by the gods and the teachers, respectively. He is reproached by his intelligent fellow students in the name of the Dharma and his wicked reputation spreads throughout the world.

> 7cd.[11] And in other (lives), he is born in unfavorable conditions.

This shows the unpleasantness which he creates (for himself) in future lives, since he will be reborn in unfavorable conditions.

---

[7] Canonical formula; see LII, p. 226, vs. n. 4.1, quoting *SN* IV, 339: *attavyābādhā ya pi ceteti paravyābādhāya pi ceteti ubhayavyābādhāya pi ceteti.*

[8] The Chinese omits this verse.

[9] Sthiramati explains (supporting Lévi's reading, LII, p. 226, n. 5.1: *śrāddhāmānuṣasaṁghāt*) that a bodhisattva has an angelic host that follows his or her career from life to life and believes in him and assists in his endeavors, and that that host ceases this activity when the bodhisattva becomes too lazy and dissipated. See Sthiramati (D Tsi 84b1 *ff.*).

[10] The Chinese omits.

[11] Prose in the Chinese (T.31.640b25 *ff.*).

> 8ab.[12] Thus, concerning virtuous qualities, she destroys both those already obtained and those not yet obtained.

This shows the unpleasantness she creates for herself in both the present life and future lives by losing both the virtuous qualities which she has obtained and those she has not yet obtained.

> 8cd. She lives in suffering, and hence her mind also loses all well-being.

This shows that she experiences (both) suffering derived from that (heedless behavior) and the associated mental functions such as anxiety.

> 9ab. None of these faults adhere to the buddha-offspring who have conscience.[13]

Beginning from here the virtues of conscience are to be understood. Because the faults (above) do not arise:

> 9cd. Such an enlightened person is always born among gods and humans.

This is its evolutionary effect.

> 10ab.[14] Because of conscience, the (bodhisattva) genius quickly perfects the stores (necessary) for enlightenment.

---

[12] The Chinese omits all of vs. 8 (Ms. vs. 7).

[13] *Hrī* ("conscience") (LI, p. 133.18). It is defined in *BBh* p. 171 as guilt (*lajja*) for negative behavior (*avadyasamudācāra*) through recognizing its unsuitability in oneself, as opposed to *vyapatrāpya* which is shame for bad behavior born of fear and respect for others. See also *AS* p. 6, and *Kośa* II pp. 170–173.

In Abhidharmic Tibetan, *lajja* is translated as *ngo tsha* (rendered "guilt"), *hrī* as *ngo tsha shes pa* ("conscience"), and *vyapatrāpya* as *khrel yod pa* ("shame," or "sense of shame"). In this translation however, *ngo tsha* and *khrel* are used interchangeably for *hrī* and *lajja*.

[14] Vs. 10 (Ms. vs. 9) is prose in the Chinese translation (T.31.640c).

This is its determining effect.

> 10cd. The victor-offspring is not wearied by (his working for the) evolutionary development of living beings.

This is the heroic[15] effect.

> 11ab.[16] She always lives free of resistances and endowed with remedies.

These are disjunctive and homogeneous effects, that is, freedom from resistances and endowment with the remedies, respectively.

> 11cd. In this way the victor-heir with a conscience obtains such benefits.

This shows that she does not possess the faults and obtains the benefits already described.

> 12. The fool, since devoid of conscience, is tainted by faults, no matter if he is disguised with fine clothes. But the victor-child who is clothed with conscience is free of any taint of fault, no matter if he is quite naked.

This (shows) conscience as the most excellent garment. Even one who is clothed in other garments is tainted with faults if he lacks conscience; and even one who is naked is impeccable if he has conscience.

> 13ab. Conscientious victor-children, like space, are not defiled by concerns.

"By concerns" (means) by mundane concerns.

---

[15] *Puruṣakāra* (LI, p. 134.1). Tibetan *skyes bu byed pa*.

[16] Vs. 11 (Ms. vs. 10) is prose in the Chinese translation.

> 13cd. One adorned with conscience shines in the company of victor-children.

This verse shows that conscience is like the sky and like an ornament.

> 14ab. The bodhisattvas' conscientiousness towards disciples is like the tenderness of a mother.

(This is) because (they feel) ashamed to abandon living beings who need saving.

> 14cd. Conscience is a defense against all the faults of the life-cycle.

It serves (the bodhisattva) like an army of elephants, horses, and so on. The similes of clothing and so on show conscience to be a remedy against passions while at rest, a remedy against mundane concerns while in motion, conducive to association with spiritual friends, conducive to the evolutionary development of living beings, and conducive to unaddicted migration through the life-cycle.

> 15. She rejects all (faults), she approves all (virtues), she never engages (in evil), and she always engages (in virtues): these are the signs of conscience in the conscientious person.

This shows the four signs left by the conscience of a conscientious person. That is, she rejects all faults and does not engage (in faulty actions), she approves all virtues and engages (in virtuous acts).

> 16. The main meditative realization of conscience comes from one's own mind: from devotion to the teaching, from aspiration, from mastery, from nonconceptual (wisdom), and from unity.

The explanation of this (verse) is as above.[17]

Seven verses on the analysis of courage:[18]

---

[17] Explained in the context of worship, as in XVII.8.

[18] *Dhṛti* (LI, p. 135.5). *BBh* p. 171.21 explains the nature (*svabhāva*) of the bodhisattva's production of the power of courage (*dhṛtibalādhānatā*) as the firm taming of addicted states

(cont'd)

> 17. The courage of bodhisattvas excels all others by its nature, varieties, and firmness.

> 18. Courage is considered to consist of effort, concentration, wisdom, heroism, and endurance. Thereby the bodhisattva proceeds fearlessly, (undisturbed) by the three (hindrances).

This shows the nature of courage, its synonyms, and the means to achieve it. "Effort" and so on is its nature, "heroism" and so on its synonyms. The last (phrase describes) the means to achieve it. (Undisturbed) by which three (hindrances) does the bodhisattva proceed fearlessly?

> 19. In the course of actions, fear arises from discouragement, distraction, and delusion. Therefore "courage" is recognized as comprising a triple spontaneity.

During all activities, fear arises from a depressed attitude, due to a lack of enthusiasm; from wavering, due to mental instability; or from delusion, due to not knowing the appropriate liberative art. The remedies are effort and so on, respectively. Therefore the word "courage" is to be known as comprising three spontaneous qualities, effort and so on. "Spontaneous" means that they are performed without deliberation.

> 20–22. The courage of the brave (bodhisattva) is born naturally, in vows, in abandon, in practice for living beings, in learning the profound and the magnificent, in the difficulty of taming disciples, in the inconceivability of the victors' bodies, in various ordeals, in the non-renunciation of the cycle of life, and in the totally non-ad-

---

of mind (*kliṣṭacittasanniyacchanatā*), avoidance of the power of addictions (*kleśavaśānanuyāyitā*), discipline of the acceptance of suffering (*duḥkhādhivāsanaśīlatā*), and unswerving practice in the face of fear and terror (*bhayabhairavairāmukhaiḥ samyak prayogāvikampanatā*).

Sthiramati (D Tsi 88a4) explains the relevance of these verses on courage, saying that "conscience is the most important quality conducive to the meditation of the thirty seven factors of enlightenment, and when the conscientious bodhisattva engages in meditative practice, he must have courage and heroic vigor in three practices – effort, concentration, and wisdom – in order not to be afflicted by laziness, distraction, and false wisdom. And since courage is derived and achieved through conscience, it is taught after teaching conscience."

dicted. It is unequalled by others, and so (the bodhisattva) is considered champion of the brave.

These three verses show the types of courage according to spiritual gene, spiritual conception, self-interest, other-interest, the import of reality,[19] power, the development of living beings, and supreme enlightenment. "Abandon" is to be understood as disregard of body and life on the part of one intent upon his own interests. There are also types (of courage) based on ordeals, deliberate incarnation in the life-cycle, and the totally non-addicted.[20]

23. The heroine is not shaken by wicked friends, sufferings, or the hearing of the profound, just as Mt. Sumeru (is not shaken) by butterflies, the wind of wings, or the ocean('s depths).

This shows the firmness of the bodhisattva's courage. The three similes are to be understood as corresponding to the threefold unshakability (that is, by discouragement, distraction, or delusion).

Two verses on the analysis of indefatigability:[21]

24. The indefatigability of the bodhisattvas is peerless in three things: thirst for learning, great effort, and (tolerance of) suffering; and it is grounded in conscience and courage.

25. The indefatigability of the genius is considered to be his intense zeal for universal enlightenment. It is not perfected, perfected, and totally perfected, on the (various) stages.

---

[19] Following Lévi's emendation according to the Tibetan. See LII, p. 230, n. 19–21.1.

[20] *Asaṁkleśataḥ* (LI, p. 136.2). Sthiramati (P Tsi 106b8–107a1; D Tsi 90a3–4) explains that when the bodhisattva is born into the life-cycle for the sake of beings he is uncorrupted by the addictions.

[21] *Akheda* (LI, p. 136.6). *BBh* p. 172.6 gives five reasons for the bodhisattva's mental indefatigability (*aparikhinnamānasatā*): 1) she is naturally powerful (*prakṛtyā balavān*); 2) her practice of mental indefatigability is constant (*punaṁ punarabhyastā*); 3) her energy is art-directed (*upāyaparigṛhītena vīryārambheṇa prayukta*); 4) she has sharp analytical power due to her wisdom (*tīvreṇa ca prajñāpratisaṁkhyānabalena samanvāgata*); 5) and she is supported by compassion and sympathy (*kāruṇyacittamanukampācittaṁ... pratyupasthitaṁ*).

These two (verses) show indefatigability through its manifestations, ground, nature, and types. The three manifestations are insatiability in learning, heroic striving over a long period of time, and (tolerance of) suffering in the life-cycle. Relying both upon conscience and courage, he feels guilt when weariness arises, and so he does not let it arise. Indefatigability's intrinsic nature is intense zeal for universal enlightenment. When this zeal abates, fatigue arises. It is not perfected on the stage of action in faith, perfected on the next seven stages, and well-perfected on the rest. These are its types.

Two verses on the knowledge of sciences:

> 26–27.[22] The brave bodhisattvas' knowledge of sciences is distinctive by subject matter, concern, activity, nature, inexhaustibility, and successful fruition. It is contained in the doors of concentration and retention. It causes the evolutionary development of beings and the upholding of the holy Dharma.

The subject matter of the knowledge of sciences consists of the five sciences: inner science, logical science, linguistic science, medical science, and artistic technological science.[23] Its concern is to accomplish the aims of self and others.

Its function, in the first (science), is one's own practice and its communication to others. In the second (science), it is to understand faults (in practice and communication) and refute the arguments of others. In the third (science), it is for oneself to express the eloquent (teaching), and to make it understood by others. In the fourth (science), it is the alleviation of the sicknesses of others. And in the fifth (science), it is to share (one's own welfare) with others.

The nature of the knowledge of sciences consists of these five subjects which have been studied, retained, verbally mastered, critically examined, and insightfully penetrated. Having heard them, they are successfully retained, rehearsed, their meaning is examined with a clear mind, their faults and virtues are understood in due order, and good and bad elucidations are ascertained.[24]

---

22 The Chinese summarizes vs. 26–27 (Ms. 25–26) in a single verse (T.31.641c5–6).

23 See XI.60.

24 Compare *BBh* p. 172.

It is "inexhaustible" because it is not terminated in any remainderless Nirvāṇa. "Successful fruition" is ontological and phenomenological omniscience.[25]

The bodhisattvas' knowledge of sciences is contained in the doors of concentration and retention. It causes the evolutionary development of beings, since he accomplishes their aims through concentration. And it causes the upholding of the holy Dharma, because he retains it in memory by the spells of retention.

Four verses on knowledge of the world:[26]

> 28. (As expressed) by body, speech, and knowledge of realities,[27] the peerless worldly knowledge of the brave (bodhisattvas) stands out from all others.

How (is it expressed) by body?[28]

> 29a. The brave ones always smile.

How by speech?

> 29b. They are always polite.

What is its purpose?

> 29c. To make beings receptive.

To make (beings) receptive for what purpose?

---

[25] *Sarvadharmasarvākārajñatā* (LI, p. 137.1).

[26] *Lokajñatā* (LI, p. 137.3–4). Compare *BBh* pp. 172–175.

[27] *Satya* (LI, p. 137.5) here refers to the "noble truths," as they are usually called. The following passages show that "fact" or "reality" is a much better translation than "truth," as what is intended is an objective thing, a *jñeya*, and not some sort of proposition or religious revelation.

[28] The four quarters of this next verse are clear in Lévi's Sanskrit (LI, p. 137.7–14), the Tibetan (D Phi 223b2–4), and in the *Kārikās*, (D Phi 29b1–2), as well as in Lévi's translation (LII, p. 232). For some reason Bagchi (p. 132.13–16) mixes up verse and commentary in his formatting, making the first two questions and *pāda*s a and b seem to be prose commentary, and the next two questions and *pāda*s c and d seem to be the verse.

29d. For practice of the holy Dharma.

How from the point of view of knowledge of realities?

30.[29] The continuous creation of the worlds proceeds from two realities; and their cessation (also proceeds) from two. Thus she who knows them is said to know the world.

The creation of the world, the repetitious cycle of life, proceeds from two facts which correspond to what is created (the fact of suffering) and the means by which (it is created, the fact of origin). Its cessation (also) proceeds from two (facts), the fact of cessation and the fact of path, corresponding to what ceases and the means by which (it ceases). Therefore one who knows them is said to know the world, because she is endowed with the knowledge of the creation and cessation of the world.

31. For the sake of the extinction and the attainment of those (realities), the genius applies himself to the (noble) facts; for it is by knowledge of the facts that an intelligent (bodhisattva) is pronounced "a knower of the world."

This indicates the function of knowledge of the world. It is for the extinction of the realities of suffering and origin and for the attainment of the realities of cessation and path.

Three verses on the analysis of the reliances:[30]

---

[29] Vs. 30 (Ms. vs. 29) and *pāda*s a and b of vs. 31 (Ms. vs. 30) form a single verse in the Chinese (T.31.641c28). The remaining two *pāda*s of 31 (Ms. vs. 30) form part of the commentary.

[30] *Pratisaraṇa* (LI, p. 138.2). On the reliances see *VKN* p. 380, n. 23, and *Kośa* IX 246–248. *MVy* 1546–1549 enumerates them in a different order: reliance upon the meaning (*artha*) rather than on the letter (*vyañjana*); reliance upon the teaching (*dharma*) rather than on the teacher (*pudgala*); reliance on intuition (*jñāna*) rather than dualistic consciousness (*vijñāna*); reliance on definitive meaning (*nītārtha*) rather than upon interpretable meaning (*neyārtha*). In *BBh* pp. 174–175 the third and fourth items of our list are also reversed.

> 32. (The four reliances are on) the holy Dharma that is (literally) taught, its intended meaning, its authoritative definitive meaning, and its inarticulable attainment.

This is the nature of the reliances. "Authoritative meaning" is that meaning which is declared and elucidated by (a buddha,) a personification of reason, or by a teacher authorized by such (an enlightened one). "Inarticulable attainment" is the transmundane intuition of realization, because it is inexpressible. The rest is self-evident.

> 33. Here (in these four reliances) is taught the refutation of any critic, of the literal expression, of its false understanding, and of its verbalized attainment.

The first reliance refutes any person who rejects the sacred Dharma. The second refutes the literal sense but not the intended sense. The third refutes a false understanding, wrongly determined. The fourth refutes a verbalized intuition, which is not inwardly experienced.

> 34. (Using the reliances,) the (bodhisattva) geniuses do not suffer any ruinous loss through their faith, investigation, hearing properly from another, and through their nonverbal intuitive wisdom.

These are the benefits of the reliances. Through the first reliance one does not lose his faith in the sacred Dharma. Through the second, one investigates the intentional sense himself. Through the third, one hears the pattern of unerring meaning from another. Through the fourth, one achieves transmundane intuitive wisdom.

Four verses on the analysis of spiritual intellectual knowledge:[31]

> 35. The bodhisattvas' four spiritual intellectual knowledges are considered peerless, due to their knowledge of formulation, nature, language, and knowledge (itself).

---

[31] *Pratisaṁvid* (LI, p. 138.17). Also see XX–XXI 47; *AS* pp. 99–100; and Dayal pp. 259–267. *MVy* 197–200 lists them: *dharmapratisaṁvid, artha-, nirukti-, pratibhāna-*. For a bibliography see *La Somme* 54.

First, the knowledge of formulation is of as many nominal formulations as there are of any single thing. The second, (knowledge) of nature, is that of knowing the name corresponding to the referent. The third, (knowledge) of language, is that of knowing the language spoken in each of the countries. The fourth, (the knowledge) of knowledge, is one's own inspired eloquence.[32] This is the definition of the spiritual intellectual knowledges.

> 36. (The four spiritual intellectual knowledges are needed, since) one who is engaged in teaching (must know) of what the teaching consists and by what (means it is taught); and the teaching of both the Dharma and (its) meaning happens only through speech and knowledge.

> 37. Spiritual intellectual knowledge is fourfold, the presentation and explanation of the Dharma, the complete revelation of both (in language), and the overwhelming of all objections.

This states the reasons why there are four. It is necessary for one who is engaged in the teaching (of Dharma to know) of what the teaching (consists) and by what (means it is taught). Of what does the teaching consist? Teaching and meaning. By what (means is it taught)? By speech and by knowledge.

The teaching of the Dharma and its meaning refers to the presentation and explanation of the Dharma. The teaching by speech is the complete making available of both. Teaching by knowledge is for the refutation of objections. Therefore intellectual knowledges are four in number on the basis of knowing what is taught and by what means.

---

[32] The explanation of the four intellectual knowledges (*pratisaṁvids*) here differs somewhat from that in *BBh* p. 176.7: "*Dharmapratisaṁvid* is the meditative knowledge (*jñāna*) of all things in all their formulations (*paryāya*) with respect to their existence as they are and as they appear (*yāvadbhāvikatayā yathāvadbhāvikatayā*)." In the case of *artha-pratisaṁvid* both *MSABh* and *BBh* employ the term *lakṣaṇa* which our text links to the name (*nāma*) corresponding to the referent (*artha*), and the *BBh* takes it as the characteristics of things with respect to their existence as in *dharma-pratisaṁvid*. As for *nirukti-pratisaṁvid*, *MSABh* employs the term *vākya* in the sense of a regional language (see *MN* III, 234), whereas *BBh* p. 176.11 has *nirvacana* which is explained as the knowledge of the etymological explanations of things. As for *pratibhāna-pratisaṁvid*, the meaning is unclear. In *MSABh* vs. 36–37 (Ms. vs. 35–36) it is related to skill in public speaking, but in *BBh* it is the meditative knowledge of the varieties (*prabheda*) of things. See also *Kośa* VII, p. 89 *ff.*

> 38. It is called "spiritually intellectual knowledge" (*pratisaṁvid*), because it is the experiential realization (*pravedanā*) that follows arrival at spiritual (*pratyātmaṁ*) equanimity (*samatām*), and (its function is) to destroy all doubts (of others).

This shows the etymology and function of spiritual knowledge. Through transmundane intuition one arrives within the inner mind at the equality of all things in their suchness; and later on, one's experiential realization through aftermath intuition is called "spiritual intellectual knowledge." This is the etymology of spiritual intellectual knowledge.[33] Its function is the destruction of all the doubts of others.

Four verses on the analysis of the stores:[34]

> 39. The bodhisattvas' store, consisting of merit and wisdom, is unequalled, one (part) leading to ascendance in the cycle of life, the other to unaddicted living.

This shows the substance and purpose of the store. The store is twofold. The store of merit leads to ascendance in the cycle of life. The store of wisdom leads to unaddicted living.

> 40. Generosity and morality constitute the store of merit, wisdom (the store of) wisdom, three others, (tolerance, effort, and contemplation, constitute) both (stores), and (the first) five (transcendences also) constitute the store of wisdom.[35]

---

[33] The etymology of *pratisaṁvid*: *prati*- (*pratyātmaṁ*), *saṁ*- (*samatām*), *vid*- (*pravedanā*). See LI, p. 139.12).

[34] *Saṁbhāra* (LI, p. 139.16). See also VI.6, XVI.19–20, *ŚBh* p. 337, *BBh* pp. 22–23. For a bibliography see *La Somme* 29.

[35] Sthiramati (D Tsi 101b–102a) has some interesting remarks in this connection, which are worth paraphrase. The first two transcendences are the store of merit, as generosity produces wealth and morality produces human and divine lives. Wisdom is the wisdom store, in its realization of universal voidness and its incorruptibility by afflictions. Tolerance belongs to both, non-retaliatory and voluntary suffering tolerances being merit, and reality-assuring tolerance being wisdom. Effort helping beings is merit and practicing the teaching of voidness is wisdom. Contemplations of the world, formless, and form realms is merit, and con-

(cont'd)

This shows that the two stores encompass the transcendences. Both stores are formed through the power of tolerance, effort, and concentration. Therefore three are of both stores. Moreover, all (the first) five transcendences pertain to the store of wisdom, because they are conducive to the development of intuition.

> 41. Virtue is achieved (*āhārah*) repeatedly from continuous (*saṁtatyā*) dedication to realization (*bhāvanām*); such is the store (*saṁ+bhā+rah*) which enables the brave (bodhisattva) to accomplish all goals.

This shows an etymology and the function of the "stores" (*saṁbhāraḥ*). "*Saṁ*" means "continuous," "*bhā*," "being dedicated to practice," and "*raḥ*," "repeated achievement."[36] Its function is shown by "to accomplish all goals," because it makes possible the achievement of individualistic and altruistic goals.

> 42. The brave (bodhisattvas) gather the stores for the sake of entry (into the stages), for the sake of (attaining the) signless (at the seventh stage), for the sake of effortlessness (on the eighth and ninth stages), for the sake of the consecrated anointment (on the tenth stage), and for the sake of the culmination (of buddhahood).

These are the types of stores. On the stage of practice in faith, the stores lead to entry upon the stages. On the first six stages, they lead to the seventh stage, the "signless," where signs no longer operate. On the seventh stage, they lead to the "effortless" which includes the next two stages. On those two, the stores lead to the consecration (of anointment with buddha-wisdom) which constitutes the tenth stage. And on that stage, the stores lead to the culmination which is the buddha stage.

Three verses in analysis of the foci of mindfulness:[37]

---

templation leading to realization of selflessness is wisdom. And the first five transcendences are also wisdom, when practiced with the nonperception of the three action-sectors.

36 This is a folk-etymology of *saṁbhāra*: *saṁ-* (*saṁtatyā*), *bhā-* (*bhāvanāmāgamya*), *raḥ-* (*bhūyo bhūya āhārah*).

37 This begins the treatment of thirty-seven accessories of enlightenment (*bodhipakṣika* or *bodhipakṣyadharmāḥ*). They are: four foci of mindfulness (*smṛtyupasthāna*), vs. 43–45; four perfect abandonments/exertions (*samyakprahāṇa*), vs. 46–50; four bases of magic (*ṛddhipāda*), vs. 51–55; five spiritual faculties (*indriya*), vs. 56; five strengths (*bala*), vs. 57; seven

(cont'd)

> 43.[38] The (bodhisattva) geniuses' meditation of the foci of mindfulness distinctively excels all others' (mindfulness), because it is unequalled in fourteen aspects.

What are the fourteen?

> 44–45. It is distinctively outstanding with respect to ground, remedy, entry, objective, conscientious attitude, and attainment; with respect to conformity, cooperation, thorough knowledge, life, degree, triumph, meditative practice, and success.

The bodhisattvas' meditative practice of the foci of mindfulness is distinctively outstanding in these fourteen respects.

(Its) ground (is distinctive), because it is founded on the wisdom born from learning, reflection, and meditation on the universal vehicle.

---

factors of enlightenment (*bodhyaṅga*), vs. 58–64; eight branches of the path (*aṣṭāṅgamārga*), vs. 65–66 (Ms. vs. numbers all one less). For a bibliography see *ŚBh* p. 288, n. 1; *Le Traité* pp. 1119–1137.

The *Vijñānavādin* view of the thirty seven factors is given in *BBh* pp. 176–177: "How does the bodhisattva practice (*yogaṁ karoti*) the thirty seven factors of enlightenment? The bodhisattva, relying on his four spiritual knowledges, knows the thirty seven factors of enlightenment as they are through art-integrated-knowledge (*upāyaparigṛhītena jñānena*) but not directly (*na sākṣātkaroti*). He knows them as they are according to the system of two vehicles; the system (*naya*) of the disciple's vehicle and the system of the universal vehicle. He knows them as they are in the system of the disciple's vehicle according to their exposition in the *ŚBh* (*ŚBh* p. 288 *ff.*). And how does the bodhisattva know the thirty seven factors of enlightenment as they are according to the universal vehicle? The bodhisattva stands, considering the body in the body but without conceiving the body existing as the body (*naiva kāyaṁ kāyabhāvato vikalpayati*) (the point of view of the disciples); or as totally nonexistent (*nāpi sarveṇa sarvamabhāvataṁ*) (the point of view of the *Mādhyamika* Centrists); but he knows the inexpressible nature of the reality of the body (*kāyanirabhilāpyasvabhāvadharmatā*). This is his focus of mindfulness examining the body in the body in an ultimate sense (*pāramārthikī*). On the superficial level, the bodhisattva's focus of mindfulness examining the body in the body should be understood according to the knowledge of the system of innumerable categorizations (*apramāṇavyavasthānanayajñānānugataṁ*). The remaining foci of mindfulness and the rest of the factors of enlightenment should be understood in the same way."

[38] Compare the Chinese version (T.31.643a5).

(Its) remedial power (is distinctive) because it enters into the objective selflessness of such things as the body, by using the concepts of impurity, suffering, impermanence, and selflessness as remedies against the four mistaken notions.[39]

(Its) entry (is distinctive) because the four foci of mindfulness cause self and others to enter into the facts of suffering, origin, cessation, and path respectively, as taught in the *Analysis of Center and Extremes*.[40]

(Its) objective (is distinctive) because it takes the bodies and so on of all beings as its objects.[41]

(Its) conscientious attitude (is distinctive) because the body and so on is not perceived.

(Its) attainment (is distinctive) because it leads neither to severance nor nonseverance from the body, and so on.[42]

(Its) conformity (is distinctive) because it conforms to the transcendences which remedy its resistances.

(Its) cooperation (is distinctive) because it cooperates with mundane persons, disciples, and hermit buddhas; since (bodhisattvas) practice the foci of mindfulness in order to teach them.

(Its) thorough knowledge (is distinctive), since through its thorough knowledge that the body is like an illusion its unreal nature becomes manifest. Through

---

39 The four are: to take the impure for the pure, the painful for the pleasurable, the impermanent for the permanent, the not-self for the self; see *Kośa* V p. 21.

40 See the *MAVBh*.1 (Pandey p. 125). As found in Sthiramati (P Tsi 123b6–124a2; D Tsi 104b2 *ff.*) the passage reads: "Bad conditioning (*gnas ngan len*) corrupts (*yongs su bsgos pa*) the body; when examined one enters into the fact of suffering. As bad conditioning is the nature (*mtshan nyid*) of the conditioned (*'du byed*), therefore whatever has bad conditioning (*gnas ngan len rnams*) is contaminated (*zag pa dang bcas pa*) with the suffering of conditioned existence (*'du byed kyi sdug bsngal*) and is entirely suffering. Sensation (*tshor ba*) is the cause of craving (*sred pa*) (in the twelve part chain of dependent origination) and when examined one enters into the fact of origin. The mind is the basis of the investment in a self (*bdag tu mngon par chags pa'i dngos po*); when examined one enters into the fact of cessation, because one is no longer fearful of self annihilation (*bdag chad pa*). By examining mental objects one enters into the fact of the path because there is entirely no delusion (*kun tu gti mug med pas*) over the mental objects of addiction and purification."

41 Compare *AMN* 16115–6: *ji ltar na byang chub sems dpa' lus la lus kyi rjes su lta zhing gnas she na / de rang gi lus dang gzhan gyi lus la lus kyi rjes su lta zhing gnas te /* "How does the bodhisattva persist in examining the body in the body? He persists in examining his own body and the bodies of others in their bodies."

42 See *AMN* 161a6–161b3.

its thorough knowledge that sensation is like a dream, it is experienced as false. Through its thorough knowledge of the natural luminosity of the mind, (it is realized) as like open space. And through its thorough knowledge of the coincidentality of things, (they are realized as coincidental), just as minor blemishes such as dust, smoke, clouds and mist are coincidental in the sky.

(Its) life (is distinctive) because in voluntary rebirth in the world as a universal monarch and so on, (the bodhisattvas') body, experience, and the rest are especially excellent because they are totally free of addictions.

(Its) degree (is distinctive) as even if it is feeble, it is far superior to others' mindfulness-practice because the faculties are naturally sharp.

(Its) triumph (is distinctive) as when they perfect their (mindfulness on the eighth stage), their practice is effortlessly resonating and harmonizing.[43]

(Its) practice (is distinctive) as such perfect practice does not come to an end even in the remainderless Nirvāṇa.

And (its) culmination (is distinctive) because it succeeds on the ten stages and (finally) in buddhahood.

Five verses on the analysis of realistic exertion:[44]

> 46.[45] The brave (bodhisattvas') realistic exertion is unmatched by any beings; it is practiced as the remedy of the faults of the foci of mindfulness.[46]

---

[43] Sthiramati (D Tsi 107a1 *ff.*) explains that "resonating and harmonizing" practice refers to eighth stage bodhisattvas, where mindfulness is perfected. On that stage, when one bodhisattva meditates mindfulness, others automatically are drawn into the state (hence "combined,") and when others meditate on them, oneself effortlessly enters mindfulness ("harmonically"). Alternatively, he continues, mindfulness in the first instant on the eighth stage is called "resonating," and from then on until the entry into the ninth stage is called "harmonizing."

[44] *Samyakprahāṇa* (LI, p. 141.13). On the linguistic history of this term see Dayal pp. 101–102, and Edgerton p. 389 s.v. *prahāṇa*. That *prahāṇa* is an incorrect form for *pradhāna* is indicated in the *MSABh* to Ms. vs. 49 (LI, p. 142.9–10; see the commentary to our vs. 50 below) in which the correct verb *pradadhāti* ("intensifies") is used indicating the author's knowledge that the term is derived from the root *dhā* rather than the root *han* ("abandon"). This latter meaning is recognized only by the Tibetan translators (*yang dag par spong ba*). Compare the following passage from *Kośa* VI p. 285: "Why is *vīrya*, energy, called right effort (*samyakpradhāna*)? Because body, speech, and mind are, by means of energy, put into action (*pradhīyate*)." See also *AS* p. 82 where the correct verb is used in the explication of the four *samyakprahāṇas*. The four are enumerated in *MVy* 956–958.

This is the general[47] definition of "realistic exertion": "realistic exertion (functions) to remedy the resistances that flaw the above-mentioned practice of the foci of mindfulness." Further, it has particular types:

> 47–49. The ingenious bodhisattvas practice the remedies of the resistances in order to enjoy the life-cycle, abandon the hindrances, relinquish (misleading) attitudes, enter the stages, stand in the signless, obtain the prophecy, develop beings, receive consecrating anointment, purify the (buddha-)land, and proceed to perfection.

These are the types of the practice of realistic exertion; undefiled full enjoyment of the successes of the cycle of life; abandonment of the five hindrances;[48] abandonment of the attitudes of disciples and hermit buddhas; entry into the stages; stability in the signless on the seventh stage; the obtainment of the prophecy (of future buddhahood) on the eighth; the evolutionary development of beings on the ninth; the consecrating anointment on the tenth; the purification of the buddha-land on (these last) three; and perfection on the buddha stage.

One should understand that the practice of realistic exertion is the remedy of the tendencies resistant to these (achievements). These are the types of this practice:

> 50. Such a yoga-practice, with associated processes, based on the will, is called "remedial tendency" in the realistic exertions.

---

[45] Compare the Chinese translation (T.31.643b5).

[46] As mentioned in the note just above, *prahāṇa* (LI, p. 141.15) is considered a distorted Sanskritization of Pāli *padhāna*, which unambiguously means "exertion." The Tibetan, following the Sanskrit, took it as "abandonment" (*spong ba*). In terms of meaning, two of the four are efforts of restraint or prevention, which might cogently be called "abandonments," but two are positive exertions to increase and achieve new virtues, which are clearly exertions and not abandonments. So we have departed from Tibetan usage here to restore what seems to be the original thrust of the term.

[47] The Tibetan reads *sāmānyaṁ* (*spyi*) for Lévi's *samastaṁ* (LI, p. 141.18).

[48] The five hindrances (*nivāraṇa*) according to *AS* p. 48 are: zeal for pleasure (*kāmacchanda-nivāraṇa*), hostility (*vyāpāda-*), indolence-languor (*styānamiddha-*), excitement-anxiety (*auddhatyakaukṛtya-*), doubt (*vicikitsā*).

This statement reveals the meaning of these verses. "Thereby one generates will, strives, exerts efforts, controls the mind, and truly intensifies it."[49] "Strives" indicates the practice of the yoga called "will-based serenity and insight." "With associated processes" indicates meditation accompanied by the processes of serenity, control, and equanimity. How does one meditate? One "exerts efforts" to remedy depression and excitement which afflict serenity and control. How does one "exert efforts"? One "controls the mind" and "truly intensifies it." Here "control" is by means of critical wisdom, and "true intensification" is by means of serenity.[50] Attaining equality, one concentrates in equanimity. This yoga practice is called "the remedial tendency" in all the types of realistic exertion explained above.

Five verses on the analysis of the magic powers:

> 51.[51] The brave (bodhisattvas) have four magic powers which are naturally superior, generated for the accomplishment of all goals, both of self and others.

"The accomplishment of all goals" is to be understood as applying to mundane and transcendent (goals). The rest is self evident.

> 52.[52] The general arrangement of the geniuses' magic powers is presented in terms of basis, type, liberative art, and manifest realization.

This is the presentation, the rest is explanation.

---

49 *Chandaṁ janayati / vyāyacchate vīryamārabhate / cittaṁ pragṛhṇāti / samyak pradadhāti /* (LI, p. 142.5–6).

50 This reading accepts Lévi's editing following the Tibetan; see LII, p. 239, n. 49.2.

51 The *ṛddhipāda* are literally the "feet of magic," which bodhisattvas and saints develop as a by-product of their meditative achievements. We will depart from the many complex translations that have been advanced with this translation of "magic powers." See Dayal, pp. 104–106.

For a bibliography of the *ṛddhipāda*s see *Le Traité* pp. 1124–1125. See also *AS* p. 73 and *Kośa* VI p. 285. As energy (*vīrya*) is regarded as the nature of the four perfect exertions, so is *samādhi* the nature of the four *ṛdhipāda*s which are: will (*chanda*), thought (*citta*), energy (*vīrya*), and investigation (*mīmāṁsā*).

52 Compare the Chinese version (T.31.643b28).

> 53. It is stated that based upon the transcendence of contemplation, its type and its art are fourfold, its realization sixfold.

The transcendence of contemplation is its basis. Its four types correspond to the analysis of concentration into will, effort, motivation, and investigation. It has four arts and six realizations. What are its four arts?

> 54. The first has the nature of energy,[53] the second the nature of assistance, the third the nature of determination, and the fourth the nature of remedial tendency.

Among the eight meditative applications in (the context of) the exertions, will, striving, and faith are energy arts, since one who has faith and ambition strives. Adeptness constitutes an assistance (art). Mindfulness and alertness are determination (arts), because by the former the mind does not diffuse itself among objects and by the latter the diffusion is easily recognized. Motivation and equanimity are remedial arts because they are remedies of the affects of depression and excitement and of the addictions (in general). What are the six manifest realizations?

> 55. The manifest realizations are vision, instruction, sporting living, prayerful vow, mastery, and attainment of good qualities.

"Vision" is the fivefold eye; physical eye, divine eye, the holy wisdom eye, the Dharma eye, and the buddha eye.[54] "Instruction" is the six superknowledges, because their employment gives knowledge respectively of speech, thought, whence one comes, and where one goes, which (knowledge) is powerfully instructive of renunciation.[55]

"Sporting living" indicates that the bodhisattvas, through their creative concentrations, play (in the dramas of the worlds) by means of various emanations. "Prayerful vow" indicates that the prayer-empowered bodhisattvas, through the dis-

---

[53] *Vyāvasāyika* (LI, p. 142.23) is translated both here and in the commentary below by the Tibetan *'bad par byed pa*, lit. "causing striving." Although its more usual Sanskrit meaning is "determination, decision" and that is how Lévi translates, Monier Williams (p. 1033) gives "strenuous effort" as the primary meaning of the masculine noun, supporting the Tibetan.

[54] See I.

[55] See VII.

tinctiveness of their vows, sport by means of their vow-born intuitive wisdom. "It is not easy to reckon (the bodhisattva's) body, light, and voice," as it says at length in the *Discourse on the Ten Stages*.[56]

"Mastery" indicates the ten masteries described in that same text.[57] "Attainment of qualities" indicates the attainment of the powers, fearlessnesses, and qualities exclusive to a buddha. These are the six manifest realizations, such as vision.

One verse on the analysis of the five spiritual faculties:[58]

> 56. Enlightenment, practice, excellent learning, serenity, and insight should be understood as the bases of faith and the other (spiritual faculties) in the context of their function of achieving goals.

Enlightenment is the basis, that is the objective source, of the spiritual faculty of faith. Bodhisattva practice is the basis of the faculty of effort. Learning about the universal vehicle is the basis of the faculty of mindfulness. Serenity is the basis of the faculty of concentration. Transcendent insight is the basis of the faculty of wisdom. Because of their purposive orientations, faith and the rest are called "spiritual faculties" in the sense of their control (over objectives to be achieved).

One verse on the analysis of the (five) spiritual powers:[59]

> 57. Although faith and the rest are considered to be addicted when entering the stages, they are (still) called "powers" because of the lack of power of their resistant tendencies.

The meaning of the verse is self-evident.

Seven verses analyzing the factors of enlightenment:[60]

---

[56] See *DBhS* p. 9.30–11.2.

[57] See VII.

[58] *Indriya* (LI, p. 143.16). See also *AS* p. 74; *Kośa* II pp. 11–112, VI p. 286; *AMN* 168b2–169a4. For a bibiography see *Le Traité* pp. 1125–1127. The five are faith (*śraddhā*), effort (*vīrya*), heedfulness (*smṛti*), concentration (*samādhi*), and wisdom (*prajñā*).

[59] *Bala* (LI, p. 143.22). The difference between the faculties and the powers is one of intensity; see *AS* p. 74.

[60] *Bodhyaṅga* (LI, p. 144.1). See *Le Traité* p. 1128, *AS* p. 74, *Kośa* pp. 281–284. The seven factors are: mindfulness (*smṛti*), analysis (*pravicaya*), effort (*vīrya*), joy (*prīti*), adeptness (*praśrabdhi*), concentration (*samādhi*), and equanimity (*upekṣā*).

> 58. The scheme of the factors of enlightenment is set forth for one who has entered the stages, based upon her understanding of the equality of all things and beings.

This shows that the factors of enlightenment are arranged in the order in which one achieves realization. In the condition of being on the stages, one understands the equality of all things and of all beings through (the facts of) objective selflessness and the equality of self and others, respectively.

In the following, (the author) compares the factors of enlightenment to the seven jewels (of the monarch), such as the wheel:[61]

> 59ab.[62] Mindfulness ranges everywhere in order to conquer knowable facts as yet unconquered.

"In order to conquer knowable facts as yet unconquered" (likens mindfulness) to the precious wheel of the universal monarch, (which she needs) for her conquest of lands as yet unconquered.

> 59cd. (The bodhisattva's) analysis causes the defeat of all signs of conceptual thought.

Just as the precious elephant causes the defeat of foes.

> 60ab. His effort swiftly progresses toward total enlightenment.

He rapidly produces the superknowledges, just as the precious horse swiftly travels across the great earth surrounded by oceans.

> 60cd. He will always be fulfilled by his increasing joy in the illumination of the Dharma.

---

[61] In the canonical literature the *bodhyaṅga*s are referred to as jewels or gems (*ratna*); see Dayal p. 154 for references.

[62] Compare the Chinese translation (T.31.644a29 *ff.*).

The light of the Dharma increases for the bodhisattva who makes effort; therefore his joy delights him in all his lives as the precious wish-granting-jewel delights the universal monarch with its special radiance.

> 61ab.[63] Liberated from all obscurations, she becomes blissful through adeptness.

She overcomes all bad conditioning (with adeptness), just as the universal monarch experiences happiness with the precious queen.

> 61cd. Success in her desired aim is generated through concentration.

Just as the wealth of the universal monarch (is generated) from the precious householder.

> 62. Through equanimity he lives in all situations just as he likes, always living in exaltation because of his aftermath and nonconceptual wisdoms.

"Equanimity" is nonconceptual intuitive wisdom, whereby the bodhisattva dwells anywhere, just as he likes; and it is followed by his living in its aftermath intuition, the two (intuitions) successively alternating. He builds himself a dwelling of nonactivity there, by living in nonconceptual intuition. In similar fashion, the precious general of a universal monarch leads the advance of the fourfold army when necessary, leads them away when they must retreat, and prepares a camp where the fourfold army may rest without fatigue.

> 63.[64] The bodhisattva endowed with such virtues is like the universal monarch, always surrounded by the factors of enlightenment, which are like the seven precious jewels.

---

[63] Compare the Chinese version (T.31.644b4 *ff.*).

[64] In the Chinese translation (T.31644b8) this verse appears in prose immediately after Lévi vs. 61.

This concludes the comparison of the factors of enlightenment with the seven jewels.

> 64. (The seven may be designated as) a basic factor, a natural factor, third, a transcendence factor, fourth, a benefit factor, and a threefold factor of non-addiction.

This shows the factors of enlightenment and in what way they are factors. Mindfulness is the basic factor because everything functions in dependence upon it. The analysis of things is the natural factor, because it is the nature of enlightenment. Effort is the transcendence factor, because its continuity is unbroken as long as enlightenment is not attained. Joy is the benefit factor, because it is the happiness of mind. Adeptness, concentration, and equanimity constitute the factors of non-addiction. The addictionless factor is known as threefold, analyzed into cause, effect, and actuality.

Two verses on the analysis of the branches of the path:[65]

> 65–66.[66] Beyond that (achievement of the factors of enlightenment),[67] (the bodhisattva) experiences (a new) attunement to (such) realistic understanding, a (new) interpretation according his realistic understanding, and a (new) engagement based on that interpretation. (He also experiences) the purification of the three actions and the contemplative cultivation of remedies for the objective obscurations, the path (-obscurations), and the (obscurations of achieving the) distinctive qualities.

---

[65] The bibliography on the eightfold path is quite extensive. For a summary of canonical sources see *Le Traité* pp. 1129–1132. The eight branches are: realistic view (*samyagdṛṣṭi*), realistic consideration (*samyaksaṁkalpa*), realistic speech (*samyagvāc*), realistic behavior (*samyakkarmānta*), realistic livelihood (*samyagājīva*), realistic exertion (*samyagvyāyāma*), realistic mindfulness (*samyaksmṛti*), and realistic concentration (*samyaksamādhi*).

[66] Vs. 65–66 (Ms. vs. 64–65) are a single verse in the Chinese (T.31.644c2).

[67] Sthiramati (D Tsi 122a1 *ff.*) explains that the bodhisattva practices the seven factors of enlightenment on the insight path, during the first bodhisattva stage, abandoning the affective and cognitive obscurations on that level. "Beyond that," then, refers to the practice from the second to the tenth bodhisattva stages, during which the eight branches of the holy path are mobilized.

Beyond the factors of enlightenment, the realistic view is attunement to the realistic understanding (of selflessness). The discernment of such an understanding is realistic consideration, which is also the engagement with such an interpretation, as contained in the discourses of the Lord, through which its import is understood.

"Purification of the three actions" constitutes realistic speech, realistic action, and realistic livelihood, since (all three) include both verbal and physical actions.

Realistic effort, (mindfulness, and concentration) constitute "the cultivation of remedies" for objective obscurations, path-obscurations, and obscurations of the distinctive qualities, respectively. Realistic effort tirelessly cultivates for a long time the remedies for objective obscurations. Realistic mindfulness cultivates the remedy for the obscurations of dedication to the path, by the exclusion of depression and excitement from the processes of serenity, control, and equanimity. Realistic concentration cultivates the remedy for obscurations of the accomplishment of special qualities.

Such is the arrangement of the path in its eight branches.

Three verses on the analysis of serenity and transcendent insight:[68]

> 67. Serenity and transcendent insight (arise) from the mind staying in the mind and from the critical discernment of things grounded on that perfect stability.

Depending upon realistic concentration, the mind stays focused in the mind, and there ensues the critical discernment of things; these are to be understood as mental serenity and transcendent insight, respectively, for which concentration is indispensible. This is the definition of serenity and insight.

> 68ab. Universal, partial, and not partial; they are accepted as causal.

Mental serenity and transcendent insight are universal because one must cultivate them in order to obtain whatever excellence one may desire. According to the discourse: "The monk having said 'O may I be free from desire,'" and so on at length, "that monk must practice just these two teachings, mental serenity and transcendent insight." Serenity and insight are partial when one cultivates either se-

---

[68] For a bibliography see *La Somme* 33. See also XI.8–12. *BBh* p. 177 states the *Vijñānavādin* view of *śamatha* and *vipaśyanā*: The bodhisattva's nonconception (*avikalpa*) of any thing whatsoever is his serenity, and the knowledge of things' ultimate reality – i.e., the knowledge of the system of innumerable categorizations of things – is insight.

renity or insight (alone). They have both parts when one cultivates them both in integration. Serenity and insight are accepted as causal for bodhisattvas on the stage of faithful action.

> 68cd–69. For the brave (bodhisattva), serenity and insight constitute the all-accomplishing yoga, functioning on all stages, in penetration, in renunciation, in signlessness, in the uncreated, and in purification and purity.

"They are accepted as causal" and so on shows the types and functions of serenity and insight. "Yoga" is to be understood as liberative art. "Penetration" is the entrance to the first stage. "Renunciation" applies as far as the sixth stage, because by those (concentrations on those stages), (the bodhisattva) renounces involvement with the signful. "Signlessness" is the seventh stage. The "uncreated" consists of the three other stages because they arise without volition. "Volitional creation" operates in "the created" and its nonexistence (on those stages) is termed "uncreated." In these three stages, the buddha-land is totally purified and buddhahood is attained; which are, respectively, "purification" and "purity."

Two verses on the analysis of skill in liberative art:[69]

---

[69] *BBh* pp. 178–179 distinguishes two types of skill in liberative art: 1) for one self, leading to the acquisition of buddha qualities (*buddhadharmasamudāgama*); and 2) for others, for the development of beings (*sattvaparipāka*). Each is sixfold.

The first set of six is: 1) compassionate regard for all beings (*sarvasattveṣu karuṇāsahagatā apekṣā*); 2) thorough knowledge of all creations as they are in reality (*sarvasaṁskāreṣu yathābhūtasarvaparijñānaṁ*); 3) desire for the intuition of unexcelled, perfect enlightenment (*anuttarasamyaksaṁbodhijñāne spṛhā*); 4) non-renunciation of cyclic life (*saṁsārāparityāgaṁ*); 5) unaddicted journeying through cyclic life (*asaṁkliṣṭa...saṁsārasaṁsṛtī*); and 6) burning effort (*uttaptavīrya*).

Upāyakauśalya for others is comprised of the four social practices (*saṁgrahavastu*). By employing them the bodhisattva: 1) assures an immense fruition of the meager roots of virtue of beings (*sattvānāṁ parīttāni kuśalamūlāni a p ramāṇaphalatāyāmupanayati*); 2) brings about immense roots of virtue with little effort (*alpakṛcchrena...pramāṇāni kuśalamūlāni saṁjanayati*); 3) removes the obstacles obstructing beings' acceptance of the Buddha's teaching (*buddhaśāsanapratihatānāṁ sattvānāṁ pratighātamapanayati*); 4) brings over those staying in the middle (of the path) (*madhyasthānavatārayati*); 5) develops those who have been brought over (*avatīrnān paripācayati*); and 6) liberates those who have been developed (*paripakvān vimocayati*).

> 70–71.[70] The skill in liberative art of the bodhisattvas is unequalled on all stages, in fulfillment of the Buddha's teachings, in developing beings, in swiftness of attainment, in purity of deeds, and in not terminating their careers; relying on such skill, they succeed in all their aims.

This shows the types and functions of skill in liberative art. The liberative art that fulfills the buddhas' teachings is nonconceptual intuition. (The liberative art) that evolutionarily develops beings consists of the four social practices.

(The liberative art) of swiftness in attainment of perfect enlightenment consists of repentance, congratulatory joy, earnest resolution, and dedication, as in (the repentance) "I repent all my sins!" up to (the resolution) "May my wisdom become perfect enlightenment!" (The liberative art) in purity of deeds consists of the doors of concentrations and retentions, because through them one accomplishes the aims of all beings. (The liberative art) of not terminating the career consists of the unlocated Nirvāṇa.

In these five liberative arts on the five stages, the bodhisattvas have a skill unequalled by others.

Such is the analysis (of liberative art). Its function is the accomplishment of all goals of self and others.

Three verses on the analysis of retentions:[71]

> 72–74. Retentions are small or great, arising from evolutionary maturity, cultivated learning, or concentration. When great, further, they are of three types. They are weak in those geniuses who have

---

[70] Quoted in *AAA* p. 294.

[71] *Dhāraṇī* (LI, p. 147.9). *BBh* pp. 185–186 treats four types of *dhāraṇī*: 1) *dharmadhāraṇī* or the acquisition of such powers of memory and understanding (*smṛtiprajñābalādhānatā*) that one is able to retain (*dhārayati*) upon mere hearing innumerable texts as composed and arranged including names, words, and phonemes with which he is neither familiar, nor which he has recited (*śrutamātrakeṇaivānāmnātān vacasā 'paricitān nāmapadavyañjanakāyasaṁgṛhītānanupūrvacaritānanupūrvasamāyuktān*); 2) *arthadhāraṇī*, the same as above except one retains the meaning (*artha*); 3) *mantradhāraṇī*, the acquisition of such powers of concentration (*samādhivaśitā*) that mantra-formulae (*mantrapadāni*) confer blessings upon beings (*sattvānāmadhitiṣṭhanti*) to allay many kinds of sicknesses (*anekavidhānām…saṁśamanāya*); and 4) *kṣāntilābhāyadhāraṇī*, the bodhisattva considers, weighs, and examines (*cintayati tulayatyupaparīkṣate*) mantras such as *iṭ miṭi kiṭibhiṁ kṣāntipadāni svāhā* spoken by the Tathāgata for obtaining a bodhisattva's tolerance.

> not entered the stages, mediocre in those on the impure stages, and great in those on the pure stages. Bodhisattvas, repeatedly relying on such retentions, illuminate the holy Dharma and uphold it always.

This shows the types and functions of retentions.

They are of three types: either the evolutionary effects of actions in previous lives, derivatives from the cultivation of learning when one has studied much in the present life because of a special capacity for understanding and retention, or (the fruition of) reliance upon concentration.

When (retentions are developed) from maturity and exercise of learning, they should be understood as small; and when from concentration, great.

The great (retentions are) also threefold: for those who have not entered the first seven stages, they are small; for those on the stages yet not purified, they are mediocre; but for those on the remaining stages, completely purified, they are great. This is the typology of retention. Its function is the elucidation and upholding of the holy Dharma.

Three verses on the analysis of the solemn vow:[72]

> 75–77.[73] The solemn vow is mind, associated with will and impelled by intuition; and, in the brave (bodhisattvas), it is unequalled in all stages. It should be understood as an effective cause, as its fruition comes from the mind alone; though arisen from thought alone, it is effective, as it will bring forth accomplishment in the future. It is various, great, and pure on the ever-transcending stages. In bodhisattvas, it accomplishes goals of self and others, until the perfect enlightenment.

---

[72] *Praṇidhāna* (LI, p. 147.22). *BBh* pp. 186–187 distinguish five types of vows: 1) *cittotpāda-praṇidhāna*, the vow to generate the spirit of enlightenment; 2) *upapatti-*, the vow to be born in circumstances conducive to the welfare of beings; 3) *gocara-*, the vow to attain the true discernment of things (*samyagdharmapravicaya*), and to attain the realm of the cultivation of virtuous practices such as the immeasurables (*apramāṇādikuśaladharmabhāvanāviṣaya*); 4) *samyak-*, the vow to perform meritorious deeds and acquire the bodhisattva excellences (*guṇa*); and 5) *mahā-*, the great vow, worship of the Tathāgatas, preservation of their teachings, reincarnation in the Tuṣita heaven, and so forth.

[73] Vs. 75–77 (Ms. vs. 74–76) are summarized in the Chinese (T.31.645c1).

Here, the solemn vow is elucidated as to its intrinsic nature, ground, stage, types, and functions. "Mind associated with will" is its intrinsic nature. Intuition is its ground. (It operates) on all stages.

It serves as a cause because it has an immediate result from the will, and in the future also accomplishes the desired aim. That is has an immediate result from will is to be understood from the achievement of the desired aim from the will alone. As it is said: "Of the vows with which the powerful bodhisattvas sport, it is not easy to reckon their amount!" and so on at great length.

It is "various" on the stage of faithful practice, where it is said: "May I be such and such!" (It is) "great" in the ten great vows of the bodhisattva who has entered the stages. It is "purified" in the ever-transcending stages, since purity is always of a higher and higher quality until enlightenment.

These are its types. Its function is the accomplishment of the aims of self and other.

Three verses on the analysis of the three concentrations:[74]

> 78. The twofold selflessness, the basis of the self-habits, and their permanent eradication should be understood as the sphere of the three concentrations.

The sphere of the three concentrations should be understood as threefold. The selflessness of persons and things constitutes the sphere of the concentration upon voidness. The basis of the habitual notions of both (persons and things) as selves, which is the five appropriative systems, is the sphere of the concentration upon wishlessness. The total eradication of its basis is the sphere of the concentration upon signlessness. Furthermore:

> 79ab. Concentration should be understood as threefold, according to object, subjectivity, and actuality.

The concentrations which are the subjectivities of the threefold objective sphere are the concentrations on voidness and the rest. Therefore, according to object, subjectivity, and actuality, concentration should be understood as threefold. They are, respectively:

---

[74] These are the three doors of liberation (*vimokṣamukha*); see *ŚBh* p. 267, n. 3, *VKN* p. 48, n. 16. Compare *BBh* pp. 187–188.

> 79cd. Nonconceptual, aversive, and always pleasurable.

The concentration upon voidness is nonconceptual because there is no conceiving of persons or things as selves. (Concentration on) wishlessness is eliminates the basis of self-habits. (Concentration on) signlessness is at all times associated with pleasure in the eradicating of such a basis (of self-habits).

> 80. It is well known that the concentrations upon voidness and so forth have three aims: thorough knowledge, abandonment, and realization.

(Concentration on) voidness is for the thorough knowledge of the selflessness of persons and things. (Concentration on) wishlessness is for the abandonment of the basis of those self-habits. (Concentration on) signlessness is for the purpose of realizing the cessation of such (self-habits).

Two verses analyzing the epitomes of the teaching:[75]

> 81. From the desire to benefit beings, four epitomes of the teaching have been taught to bodhisattvas as the causal basis of the concentrations.

"All creations are impermanent, all creations are suffering." This has been taught as the causal basis of the concentration upon wishlessness. "All things are selfless" (is the causal basis of concentration on) voidness. "Nirvāṇa is peace" (is the causal basis of concentration) on signlessness. What is meant by "impermanent" up to "peace"?

> 82. For the (bodhisattva) geniuses, those four (respectively) have thus the meanings of unreality, un(real) discrimination, imaginative construction, and the eradication of discriminative construction.

---

[75] *Dharmoddāna* (LI, p. 148.23). See *VKN* p. 165, n. 51. Sthiramati (D Tsi 131b1 *ff.*) discusses the relevance of analyzing the four epitomes at this point, saying that they are the content of the three concentrations, and therefore are appropriately discussed here. The long discussions following of momentariness and of selflessness fit into the same category, presumably, though Sthiramati does not comment on them in the same way.

For bodhisattvas the meaning of "impermanent" is "unreal." Whatever is not permanent is impermanent, and for them that is the imaginatively constructed identity.

The meaning of "suffering" is "discriminative construction of the unreal," and such is the relative identity.

The meaning of "selfless" is "imagination-only." The word "thus" in the verse is for emphasis. The constructed self does not exist, it is construction-only. Thus the meaning of "selflessness" is the nonexistence of the constructed identity.

The meaning of "peace" is "eradication of discrimination"; it is the absolutely perfect identity, which is Nirvāṇa.

Also, the meaning of "impermanent" is to be understood as "momentary annihilation," which refers to the relative identity. In order to establish that, (there are) ten verses analyzing momentariness:[76]

> 83. (All creations are momentary:)[77] because (otherwise, their function) would be unreasonable; because production is from a cause; because of contradiction (between creation and cessation); because (a non-momentary production) could not endure on its own; because (another cause of destruction) does not exist; because its (impermanent) nature must be uniform; because of conformity; because of cessation;
>
> 84. because of the perception of change; because of the nature of causes and effects; because of influence; because of mastery; and because of conformity to what is pure and to beings.

The thesis (under discussion, namely,) "all created entities are momentary," will be stated later on.[78] How is it proven?

---

[76] *Kṣanikatva* (LI, p. 149.12). On the doctrine of momentariness consult Stcherbatsky's *Buddhist Logic*, and Mukherjee's *Buddhist Philosophy of Universal Flux*. See also *Kośa* IV pp. 4–8, *ŚBh* pp. 473–486, *BBh* pp. 188–190, *Hetubindu* 341b5–345b2, *Pramāṇavārttika* I 192 *ff.*

[77] As the commentary explains below, this thesis (*kṣaṇikaṁ sarvasaṁskṛtaṁ*), for which the rest of this and the following verses are reasons, is only stated below in verse 89 (Ms. vs. 88). We have moved it here in brackets as a reminder.

[78] See XVIII.89 (Ms. vs. 88) below.

It is because without momentariness the function of creations would be unreasonable. "Function" means continuous activity, which is unreasonable without origination and annihilation every moment. However, if continuous activity[79] is taken to mean a prior cessation and a subsequent production with an interval of duration, there could be no function immediately after (cessation), because of discontinuity, as it is not reasonable that what has arisen should exist for an interval without continuity. Why? It is because production is caused; in fact, all created entities originate, that is, come into existence through a cause. If what has already come into existence were to exist at a later time, it must indubitably exist through a cause, because without a cause it would not have come into existence to begin with. It is, however, impossible for it to continue to exist through that cause (which brought it into existence), because the causal efficacy (of the original cause) has already been employed in bringing it into existence, and no other cause is found. Therefore, one should realize without any doubt that at every moment another entity comes into existence having a prior cause. Thus, without continuity (of momentary causations), it is illogical for what has arisen to exist at an intermediate period.

Again, one might accept that what has arisen does not originate again – for the sake of which a cause would be required – but that what has arisen becomes extinct, not merely upon its arising, but at some other time later on. Through what (we ask) does it become extinct later on? If it is through the cause of its origination, it becomes unreasonable. Why? It is because origination and cessation are contraries, and contraries are not seen to have the same cause, as for example light and shade, or heat and cold. There is also contradiction of cessation (occurring) at another time. From what? From the discourses, for the Lord has said: "O monks, creations are like illusions, they arise and pass away; they are temporary, their existence is fleeting."[80] (There is also contradiction) from the attitudes of meditators. When they consider the arising and passing away of creations they see their cessation moment by moment, otherwise they would not have the revulsion, freedom from attachment, or liberation as others do who see (such) cessation at the time of death, and so on.

---

79 This argument for momentariness turns on the definition of "continuous function" (*prabandhena vṛttiṁ = pravṛttiṁ*), which Vasubandhu insists means continuous momentary reproduction, against the Vaibhāṣika notion of a production, a bit of duration, and a cessation. dBal Mang (156b) and Sthiramati (D Tsi 134a7 *ff.*) comment on the argument, without identifying the players.

80 Compare *MN* I.137.

If a creation which has arisen were to subsist for an interval it would either subsist on its own, having the capacity to subsist on its own, or (it would exist) through some cause of subsistence. Its self-subsistence is unreasonable. Why? Because it does not subsist on its own later on. Why is it not able to subsist forever? Because (to do so) through a cause of subsistence is unreasonable as such a cause does not exist, that is, no such thing is found.

Again, one might object saying that things subsist even without a cause of subsistence because there is no cause of destruction, but that when the cause of destruction obtains, they are subsequently destroyed as darkness is by fire. That is unreasonable, since it does not exist, that is, no subsequent cause of destruction exists whatsoever. To say that darkness is destroyed by fire (is to say what is) unproven; but its capacity to generate a dissimilar entity is proven. In relation to it, the continuum of darkness is apprehended as dissimilar, but a total absence of efficient operation is not. The water which is boiled through contact with fire gradually diminishes until it becomes so much reduced that finally it is apprehended as never having originated at all, but it does not instantly cease to exist upon contact with fire.

It is contrary to reason for anything which has arisen to subsist, because its nature is uniform. The Lord has taught that the impermanence of a created entity is its nature, its uniform (nature). If it were not destroyed as soon as it arose it would not be impermanent at any other time, and it would follow that its nature of impermanence would not be uniform.

Again, one might object saying that as production is new every moment, there could be no recognition (in the form) "This is just that." That comes about (we say) due to the conformity of similarity, like a magician's props with which he creates illusions. The cognition comes about through resemblance, not from (a thing's continued) existence.

How do we know that? Through cessation; for whatever remains exactly the same will never cease forever, since it would never differ from its first moment; and that is why one cannot assert "this is exactly that."

(We) also (know that) because of a perception of change at the conclusion. Change means becoming different, and if it did not commence at the very outset then one would never perceive a change at the conclusion in either internal or external things. Therefore difference begins at the very beginning, gradually increases, and finally manifests obviously, like milk in the state of cream. So long as the difference is subtle it is not perceived, and so long as there is the conformity of similarity it is cognized as "This is exactly that" – thus it is proven. Therefore, because there is a difference at every moment, momentariness is proven.

How is it proven? By the nature of causes and effects, that is, because causes are momentary and effects are momentary. Mind is proven to be momentary. Its cause consists of other creations, the eye and so forth. Therefore it has been proven that they also are momentary. However, it is impossible for what is momentary to come into existence from what is not momentary, as in the case of the impermanent from the permanent.

Further, all creations are the effects of mind. How is this known? (It is known) because of influence, mastery, and conformity to what is pure and to living beings. All creations, the eye and so forth, together with their bases are influenced by mind and develop along with it because they conform to its auxiliaries. Therefore they are the effects of mind.

Mind is the master of creations; as the Lord said: "The world is led by mind, drawn by mind, it is at the mercy of each thought as it is born."[81] In the same way it is said: "Name and form are conditioned by consciousness";[82] they are therefore the effect of mind.

(It is known) because they conform to the pure mind of yogins. As it is said: "The monk absorbed in contemplation, endowed with magic powers, attains mastery over the mind; and if he believes that the forest of wood is gold, it will be so for him."[83] Therefore created entities are the effect of the mind.

And also because of conformity to beings. For beings who are sinful, external objects are dreary, and for those who are virtuous, they are excellent. Therefore, because of their conformity to mind, it is proven that creations are the effect of mind as well as (that they are) momentary. It is unreasonable that the momentary should have an effect which is not momentary since (effect) conforms to (cause).

Thus it has been demonstrated in two verses that creations are, without exception, momentary. The next five verses are understood to establish (the momentariness of) internal creations:

> 85.[84] There are fourteen kinds of the life[85] (of internal creations.
> They are all momentary,) as they are utterly initial, developed,

---

[81] This corresponds to *SN* I, 39. *AN* II, 177 gives the same in prose.

[82] In the twelvefold chain of dependent origination; e.g., *SN* II, 6.

[83] This is found in *SN* I 116.

[84] Summarized in the Chinese (T.31.647a11).

growing, embodied, changeable, evolutionarily developed, inferior, superior,

86. luminous, non-luminous, relocatable, seminal, non-seminal, and arisen like reflections –

87. (which they are) because of their distinctive cause and size, because their expansion would be impossible and unreasonable, because embodiment would be impossible,

88. because duration would be impossible, because there would be no ultimate change without initial destruction in the inferior and superior, and also in the luminous and non-luminous,

89. because there is no progress, because duration would be implausible, because conclusion would be implausible, and because of their conformity to mind; (again,) all mental creations are momentary.

How is momentariness proven by the verses: "All creations are initial, developed," down to "all creations are momentary"?

The life of internal creations is of fourteen kinds. "Initial (life)" is the first manifestation of self-existence. "Sustained (life)" is subsequent to the first moment of birth. "Growing (life)" comes about through the nourishment of food, sleep, continence, and absorption. "Embodied (life)" refers to the birth of visual consciousness and so on through the support of the eyes and so on. "Changeable (life)" refers to the changes in complexion and so forth brought about by desire and so forth. "Evolutionarily developed (life)" refers to the conditions of embryo, childhood, youth, middle age, and old age. "Inferior and superior (lives)" are lives in the wretched and happy migrations, respectively. "Luminous (life)" refers to lives in (the two highest heavens of the desire realm, that is the heavens of) "fantastic pleasure" and "vicarious fantastic pleasure,"[86] and in the form realm and formless realm (heavens), because such births depend only on mind. "Non-luminous (life)"

---

[85] Skt. *utpāda*. As will be seen from the commentary below, *utpāda* here is being used in the context of describing the psycho-biological process of the development of beings.

[86] *Nirmitakāma, paranirmitakāma* (LI, p. 152.1–2); see LII, p. 254, n. 2.

refers to lives elsewhere. "Relocated (life)" refers to death in one place and birth in another. "Seminal (life)" refers to (all life) except the final body of the saint. "Non-seminal (life)" refers to that final body. "Reflection-like (life)" refers to the life of mental creations called "reflections" through the power of concentration in the contemplations of the eight liberations.

Regarding these fourteen kinds of life of internal creations, they are understood as momentary on the basis of the reasons "because of their distinctive cause and size" and so on.

To begin with, "because of a distinctive cause" applies to initial life. If that life did not have a distinctive cause one would not subsequently apprehend greater and greater differences in the function of future creations, because its cause would not be distinctive; and when it is distinctive, momentariness is proven because it becomes different from those that follow.

"Distinctive size" applies to developed life. "Size" means "dimension." Without change moment by moment there could be no difference in size.

"Because growth is impossible" applies to growing life. Growth is the basis. Without momentariness it would be impossible because it would remain as it is. And "because growth would be unreasonable" means that growth would be contrary to reason without the generation of greater nourishment every moment.

"Because it would not be embodied" refers to embodied life. If the embodiment stood still, it would be unreasonable for the embodied not to stand still, just as it would be unreasonable for the rider of a stopped chariot not to also stay stopped; otherwise embodiment would be impossible.

"Because duration would be impossible" and "because there would be no ultimate change without initial destruction" apply to changeable life and evolutionary (life), for if something were to remain as it is, it would be impossible for it to change through desire and so on, and there could be no evolution into other states; because where there is no initial destruction there will be no ultimate change.

Momentariness should be understood to apply to the inferior and superior lives in the same manner as changeable life and evolutionary life. If creations remained as they are, instincts for action could not develop for lives in the wretched or happy migrations. However, gradual development is possible because there are various changes in the continuum.

Momentariness obtains in the case of luminous and non-luminous lives in the same way. First, in the case of the luminous, if it remained the same, its dependence upon mind would be impossible; and in the case of the non-luminous, without initial destruction ultimate change would be impossible.

"Because there is no progress" refers to relocatable lives. "Progress among creations," action characterized by transmigratory relocation, would be implausible. The creation progressing to another place must be identified as created or uncreated. If it is created, then as there would be no development in its progress, it would just be still, and progress would be implausible. If it is uncreated, there is no progress and "progression" would be implausible. If one imagines that such action applies to a creation stationary in that migration, it is implausible, because a stationary thing does not go to another place. Or if one imagines that such (action) applies to a creation standing in another migration, it is also implausible, as (the creation) would not have gotten there without action (already having served its function). An action is not perceived separate from the creation in one place or another. Therefore, there is no progress in creations other than lives in continuity in different migrations. And because such is absent, momentariness is established.

The progress characterized as unhindered life in other places is recognized as due to various causes. It comes about by the power of mind as in the occasion of walking about and so on. It comes about by the impetus of former actions, as in the between state. It comes about by the force of projection, just as an arrow is shot. It comes about by the force of connection, like the progress of riders of chariots or ferry boats. It comes about by flexibility, like grasses moved by the wind. It comes about naturally, as wind progresses straight ahead, fire upwards, and water downwards. It comes about by magic power, as some things are moved by the power of spells and drugs, iron by the power of a magnet, other things by the power of a magician.

In the case of seminal and non-seminal lives, momentariness is to be understood by the "implausibility of duration" and that "of conclusion," for without a causal entity at every moment, it is impossible for what remains as it is to become a seed at another time, and it will not cease to be a seed at the last moment; just as it is implausible for it to be a seed at a prior moment and not a seed at the final moment. What does not exist, cannot have a final end. Thus a conclusion is implausible.

Momentariness due to conformity with mind should be understood in the case of reflection-like life, both because of conformity to mind and because at every moment it is born from the power of mind.

Thus it has been established that all internal creations are momentary.

Now, three verses establish the momentariness of the external:

> 90–92.[87] The (four) elements and the six objects are declared to be momentary: (water) because of evaporation and increase; (wind) because of natural motion, increase, and decrease; (earth) because of its origin from those (other elements) and its four transmutations, the same (reasons) applying to colors, odors, tastes, and textures; (fire) because of its dependence on fuel; (sound) because of the perception of variation; (mental-medium-objects) because of their conformity to mind; and because of inquiry. Thus external (creations) also are momentary.

What is external? The four primary elements; and the six objects, namely, forms, odors, tastes, textures, sounds, and mental-medium-forms. Thus the primary elements and the six objects are declared to be momentary. Why is this declared?

Water (is momentary) because of its evaporation and increase. The water of springs, lakes, ponds, and so on is perceived gradually to evaporate and increase, neither of which would be possible without change in every moment, because a cause for a subsequent difference would not exit.

Wind (is momentary) because it moves by nature and increases and decreases. What is at rest cannot move by nature, due to lack of motion; this has already been established. And it cannot increase or diminish because it remains as it is.

Earth (is momentary) because of origin from them and because of four transmutations. The word "them" indicates water and wind. In the period of cosmic evolution, earth is formed by water and wind together; therefore, because it is an effect, it should be understood as momentary. And four transmutations of earth are perceived: wrought by the various actions of beings; wrought from injuries, such as earthquakes; wrought by the elements, fire and so on; and wrought by time, brought about over a long duration. Such transmutations are impossible without momentariness because a cause of destruction does not exist. As for the momentariness of color, odor, taste, and tangibility, it is to understood by similar reasons as in the case of earth, and so on.

Fire is momentary because it arises in dependence upon fuel. When fire is produced the fuel produced along with it does not remain as it is and that fire cannot remain which has burnt up the fuel. One cannot say at the end that without

[87] Vs. 90–92 (Ms. vs. 89–91) are summarized in the Chinese (T.31.648a6 *ff.*).

fuel it remains as it was. It is to conform to the composition of the verses that color and so on are mentioned first and fire afterwards.

As for the sound of bells and so on, for example, its momentariness is known by the perception of variation because without momentariness its variation from moment to moment could not be perceived.

Mental-medium-form is momentary, as proven by its conformity to mind according to the previous explanation.[88]

Therefore it is established that the external is momentary.

"Why prove the momentariness of all creations?"

One should inquire of the opponent of momentariness: "Why do you accept the impermanence but not the momentariness of all creations?"

If he answers: "Because change is not apprehended every moment," this must be said to him: "Why do you not accept the momentariness of things which are well known to be momentary such as lamps, flames, and so on, inasmuch as things are never perceived in a state of non-motion?"

If he were to reply: "Because they are not perceived later as before," one should say to him: "Why do you not accept the same for creations?"

If he were to say: "Because it is not the same for creations other than lamp-flames, and so on," this should be said to him: "Difference is of two kinds: difference in nature and difference in function. If it is a natural difference of which you speak, the example is unsuitable because the nature of a thing cannot be employed as an example of it, like fire of fire and cow of cow. But if it is a difference in function, the example of a lamp-flame is suitable because it is well known that it follows as a consequence of momentariness."

Then one should further inquire: "Do you accept that when a chariot is standing at rest a man mounted in the chariot is in motion?"

If he says "no," then this should be said to him: "For the eye and so on to stand at rest, and the consciousness it supports to be continually in motion, that is impossible."

If he were to say: "But in the case of a lamp-flame which depends on a wick, is not the wick seen to remain at rest when the lamp-flame is in continual motion?" – this should be said to him: "It is not seen, because a change is continually being produced in the wick at every moment."

If he were to say: "If there is momentariness, then why is the momentariness of creations not established (obviously) as in the case of the lamp-flame?" – this

---

[88] See XVIII.89 (Ms. vs. 88).

should be said to him: "Because of a fundamental mistake, their momentariness is not known because their function persists in a coordinated series. Since each instance exists one after the other, one mistakenly thinks that it is one and the same. Otherwise, there would be no erroneous idea that the impermanent is permanent. When that (erroneous idea) does not exist there will be no addiction; not to speak of purification."

This inquiry, resulting from the refutation of objections, established the momentariness of all creations.

Twelve verses analyzing selflessness, to establish the selflessness of persons:[89]

> 93. The person is identifiable as conventionally existent and not substantial; since it is not perceived, is a distortion, is addictive, and is from an addicted cause.
>
> 94. It cannot be pronounced either same or different from those (systems), because of two faults: it would be absurdly consequent either that the systems would be the self, or that the self would be substantial.
>
> 95. If it were substantially existent, its inexpressible necessity would have to be expressed. An unnecessary (self), inexpressible as either the same as or different from (the systems), is quite implausible.
>
> 96. By definition, by worldly consensus, and according to scientific treatises, it is unreasonable to (maintain) the inexpressibility of fire and fuel; since they are, indeed, perceived dualistically.
>
> 97. Since consciousness arises in the case of (subject-object) duality, (the person) is not its condition, because it is not necessary. Therefore (the person) is not properly posited as (the agent, variously designated as from) "beholder" to "liberator."
>
> 98. If it (had) lordship, it would not engage in impermanent (pleasure-consciousness) and disagreeable (pain-consciousness). (If

---

[89] Compare the Chinese translation (T.31.648b26).

it were substantial,) its functional character would remain to be proved; and it would prevent the threefold perfect enlightenment.

99. The person's function is not self-originated in seeing and so forth, for three reasons. (Nor) is there any conditionality in its function. (Nor) is there any non-functional seeing and so forth.

100. The self-origination of its function in seeing and so forth is implausible, because of its non-agency, its impermanence, and its (need for) continuous, simultaneous function.

101. Its conditionality is not logical, because of the prior absence of an enduring entity, because of the impermanence of a destroyed entity, and because there is no third alternative.

102. All things are selfless, they are voidness in an ultimate sense; and therefore the perception of self was taught to be merely a mistake.

103. In the contexts of addiction and purification, the notion of "person" indicates a degree of resolution, a degree of engagement, and a degree of continuity.

104. If there was a (real) "person," it would be unnecessary to (indicate it in order to) generate a conviction of self; and from their habituation (to self) from beginningless time, either all beings would be effortlessly liberated, or there could be no liberation.

Should one say "the person exists" or "the person does not exist"? To explain, (it is stated:) "The person should be said to exist designatively and not substantially." Thus, one would say it has "designative existence" and "substantial nonexistence." Thus, adopting a non-simplistic position, one does not incur the faults of absolutism or nihilism.

How is it known that "It does not exist as a substance"? It is known by its nonperception. It is not perceived as a substance like matter and so on.

Here, one objects that "perception" means mental cognition and it is not the case that the person-advocates do not mentally cognize a person. Even the Lord said: "As merely an immediate experience, one apprehends a self, and cognizes it!" So, how can one say that it is not perceived?

In perceiving thus, it is not perceived as a substance. Why? Because it is a mistaken notion. The Lord said that "To think that the selfless is a self is mistaken." Therefore, to take it as a person is mistaken.

How is this understood? By means of its addictedness, which is the addictedness whose nature is the addiction of the materialistic views of "I" and "mine"; it being impossible for the unmistaken to be addictive. How is it to be known that it is addicted? Because it serves as an addicted cause. Passion and the other addictions are generated with it as cause.

As for the fact called "matter," with respect to which "person" is designated, should it be said that the person is the same or different? To explain, it is said that "Therefore it should not be said to be either the same or different." Why? Because of two faults. From which two faults? "Because it would be absurdly consequent that the body-mind-systems be the self, or that the self be substantial." If they were the same, the consequence is that the systems would be the self, and the person would be substantial. And if they were different, the consequence is the substantial existence of the person. Therefore it is right not to speak of the person, except for its existing as a convention, as a consequence of which it is established that (its sameness or difference from the systems) is an impredicable matter.

To those who overstep the teaching of the Teacher and accept the existence of a substantial person, it should be said: "If it were substantial, its inexpressible necessity would have to be expressed." Why? "An unnecessary (self), inexpressible as either the same as or different from (the systems), is quite implausible."

Here they may object that "it is just by this example that we ought to accept the inexpressibility (yet reality) of the person, as for example fire cannot be said to be either the same as or different from fuel." One should answer them thus: "By definition, by common consensus, and according to the sciences, it is unreasonable to insist upon (the example of) the inexpressibility of fire and fuel, since they are perceived dualistically."

With regard to sameness and difference, fire is the fire element, and fuel consists of the remaining elements. Their natures are different, and thus fire is different from fuel (by definition). In worldly (consensus) they are established as different, since wood and so forth, the fuel, is seen without fire and fire without fuel. It is not right to say that in the sciences the Lord did not say anywhere that nothing could be said of fire and fuel. How is it known that fire exists without fuel? Because it is perceived, carried by the wind it can be seen blazing from a great distance. If one were to say that in this case the wind is the fuel – it is by that very reason that the difference of fire and fuel is established. Why? "Because there is perception of both." That proves it. Two things are perceived there, the fire, and the wind as fuel.

If they say: "There is only the person, which is the beholder..." up to "the conscious one, the agent, enjoyer, knower, and liberator"; we answer "It is impossible as the beholder..." up to "it is impossible as the liberator." If they then rejoin that it should be the agent of those consciousnesses called "beholding" and so on, either by its causal nature or by its ownership, we then answer: "Since consciousness arises in the case of duality, (the person) is not its condition." Why? Because it is unnecessary. No capacity is perceived of it in that situation. "If it had ownership, it would not engage in the impermanent, and the disagreeable." If it is the owner, then it would not engage in the impermanent pleasure consciousness and the disagreeable pain consciousness. Therefore because of that twofold implausibility, it is impossible that it be the "beholder" up to the "liberator."

Moreover, if the self existed as a substance, "its functional character would remain to be proven." If it existed as a substance then its activity would be apprehended, just like, for example, the character of vision and pure form and so forth, as regards the eye. And that is not the case for the person. Therefore it does not exist as a substance.

If its existence as a substance were accepted, then the Lord Buddha's "threefold perfect enlightenment would be prevented" – the profound perfect enlightenment, the distinctive perfect enlightenment, and the transcendent perfect enlightenment. By the clear understanding of a person, there would be no profound perfect enlightenment whatsoever; it would not be distinctive from that of the heterodox, and it would not transcend the world. Thus, if buddhahood were to be held (as the enlightenment of a real person), it would be understood by all the world, accepted by the religious fanatics, and would remain for a long time in the life-cycle.

If the "person" is the "beholder" up to the "knower," then in beholding and so on it must either have a function or not have a function. If it has a function, that function is either self-originated, or brought about by chance, or by its cause. "The person's function in seeing is not self-originated because of three faults." "By three faults" is to be explained by "(Nor) is there any conditionality in its function." The negation is to be supplied. If it has no function, then it becomes established that "(Nor) has it beholding and so on without function." With respect to beholding and so on, how can the person be the beholder when there is no function (of beholder) up to knower?

Three faults have been mentioned; which three faults? "It is impossible that the person's function in beholding and so forth is self-originated because of its non-agency, its impermanence, and its continuous, simultaneous function." If, with respect to beholding and so forth, there is accidental function, from which there is beholding and so forth, then the person is their agent. How can it be the beholder up to the knower, because if it comes about accidentally there is no relation, the function will never exist, and it would not be impermanent? If the function is permanent the fault will arise that the functioning of beholding and so forth will be simultaneous and eternal. Therefore, with respect to vision and so forth, it is impossible that the function be self-originated.

"Its conditionality is implausible, because of the prior absence of the enduring, because of the impermanence of the destroyed, and because of the lack of a third alternative." If one suggests that function has the person as its cause, it is impossible that that which remains as it is be a cause, because of prior absence. If it be in the condition of a cause, the person will never be without existence. Why? Because the function will not have prior existence at the time when it will not have arisen, and it is impossible that what has been destroyed should be a cause as it would follow that the person is impermanent. Nor is there a third alternative, for that does not exist which neither endures nor is destroyed. It is thus implausible that the person is the cause of function.

Therefore, depending on this partial chain of arguments, the person is not perceived to be substantial. "All things lack self, they are ultimately voidness; and therefore the perception of a self has been taught as simply a mistake."

Among the epitomes of the Dharma, the Lord taught that "all things are selfless." And according to the *Ultimate Voidness* (*Discourse*):[90]

"There is action and its evolutionary effect, but an agent who forsakes this (set of) systems and takes up other systems is not perceived apart from its symbolic designation."

According to the *Pañcaka* (*Discourse*),[91] there are five disadvantages of the perception of a self:

"One comes to a conviction of self, one comes to a conviction of soul. One becomes no different from the religious fanatics. One enters a wrong path. And one's mind does not incline to voidness, does not believe in voidness, and does not remain in voidness. One does not have faith, and one's saintly qualities are not cultivated."

Thus also according to scripture (the self) is implausible.

---

[90] Sthiramati (P Tsi 204a) refers to this as a *śrāvakasūtra*, but we have been unable to identify it. See *ŚBh* p. 382, n. 2 for parallels.

[91] See LII, p. 264, n. 7.

The Lord has indicated "a person" in various places, setting up the person as the understander (*parijñātāvin*), the bearer of the burden (*bhārahāraḥ*), the pursuer of faith, and so on. If it is asked: "If it does not exist substantially, why was it indicated?" (One answers:) "With respect to addiction and purification, the notion of 'person' indicates a degree of resolution, a degree of engagement, and a degree of continuity." In the context of addiction and purification, without the designation "person" it would be impossible to indicate the degrees of prevention, engagement, and continuity. According to the *Parijñā Scripture*: "The addicted are the things to be understood. Understanding is purification." According to the *Bhārahāra Scripture*:[92] "The burden and the bearer of the burden are the addicted. Casting off the burden is purification." Without the designation "person" who understands, or is the bearer of the burden, it would be impossible to teach the degrees of engagement, and of their continuity.

The accessories of enlightenment are of many types, when divided according to the paths of application, vision, meditation, and culmination. And without the designation of a "person" who pursues faith, it will be impossible to indicate the degrees of their engagement and continuity. This rule is to be thus maintained against one who asks: "If the person does not exist substantially, why was it indicated?"

Otherwise the indication of "a person" will be useless. One cannot say that it was done to generate the conviction of self because: "The conviction of self is not to be generated," since it has been already produced primordially. Neither is it for its habituation, because if the habituation to the view of a self were conducive to liberation, then "all would be liberated without effort," inasmuch as the view of a self is present in all who have not seen the (holy) truths. Yet they are in fact not liberated.

If previously the self has not been perceived as selfless, then, at the time of the realization of the truth, one will take (that too) as self. It is just as if one previously has not taken suffering for suffering, he will not apprehend it (as suffering) later on. One remains afterward as before, and so there will be no subsequent liberation. If a person were to exist (substantially) there would be no avoiding the (habits of) "I" and "mine," the craving for self, and the addictions which have them for their cause. Therefore "there could be no liberation."

The "person" cannot be accepted as (substantially) existing. If it existed, those faults will become imperatively consequent.

---

[92] The *Parijñā* and *Bhārahārasūtras* are found in the *Saṁyuktāgama* (Tok., XIII, 2, 15b) as well as in the Pāli *Saṁyutta*; see LII, p. 264, n. 9.

> 105. Thus, bodhisattvas, always endowed with such virtues, both
> do not neglect their own aims and do accomplish the aims of others.

This is the brief exposition of the function of the virtues such as conscience and courage.

Chapter XIX

Excellences

Three verses on the analysis of wonders:[1]

> 1–2. This (transcendent conduct) of the genius (bodhisattvas) is considered wondrous: the total sacrifice of the body, the (sacrifice) of perfections[2] for a vow, the tolerance for the weak, the energetic initiative without regard to body and life, the refusal to savor the pleasures in contemplations, and the nonconceptuality in intuitive wisdom.

> 3. And these are considered most greatly wondrous: the taking birth in the clan of the transcendent lords, the winning of the prophecy (of future enlightenment), the anointment of consecration (in the buddha wisdom), and enlightenment (itself).[3]

In the (first) two verses the wonders of practice are explained from the point of view of the six transcendences. The sacrifice of one's own body is the wonder of generosity. The renunciation of extensive perfections is the mark of the vow of morality. The rest is self-evident.

---

[1] *Āścarya* (LI, p. 160.12). *BBh* p. 193.7 counts five wonders: 1) disinterested love (*niṣkāraṇavatsalatā*); 2) tolerance of infinite suffering (*aprameyaduḥkhasahiṣṇutā*); 3) knowledge of the means to tame (*vinayopāyajñatā*) living beings; 4) penetration of the difficult to understand import of supreme reality (*paramadurvijñānatattvārthānupraveśa*); and 5) inconceivable power (*acintyaprabhāvatā*).

Sthiramati (D Tsi 178b3 *ff.*) explains that the bodhisattva path has been completely taught in the accessories of enlightenment chapter, so now it is relevant to explain the excellences achieved by the bodhisattva through the practice of that path.

[2] The sacrifice of perfections (*saṁpatti*) here indicates the bodhisattva's giving up of any righteous sense of moral perfection.

[3] The Sanskrit (LI, p. 160.18) has a singular here and at the end of the above verse, and lacks the "great" (Tibetan *che*). Our emendation is to avoid awkward brackets.

The third verse explains the wonders of fruition from the point of view of the four fruits of the bodhisattva: on the first and eighth and tenth stages there are the three learner's fruits, and on the buddha stage there is the superior[4] fourth fruit of the master.[5]

A verse analyzing the non-wondrous:[6]

> 4. (The bodhisattvas') dedication to these (transcendences) is not wondrous, having reached detachment, compassion, highest meditative practice, and equanimity (about self and other).

"To these" is to the transcendences. Having achieved detachment, dedication to generosity is not a wonder, nor, having achieved compassion, is (dedication to) morality and tolerance wondrous. Having achieved supreme meditative realization and so become free of discrimination and calculated activity on the eighth (bodhisattva) stage, dedication to energetic effort is no wonder. Nor is dedication to all the transcendences any wonder, once one has attained equality of concern for self and others and so has become just as unwearying in concerns of others as in concerns of self.

Three verses on equality of concern:[7]

> 5. Beings' love for themselves, for mates, children, friends, and relations is not equal to the genius (bodhisattvas' love) for (all) beings.

> 6. Impartial to suppliants, unbroken in firmness of morality, tolerant in all cases, great in effort to achieve all aims of beings,

---

[4] Reading *agra* with the Tibetan *mchog* against the Sanskrit *atra* (LI, p. 160.22).

[5] In the Chinese (T.31.650b3) the commentary relates the four fruits to the four stages of the disciple: stream-winner, once returner, non-returner, and saint.

[6] *Anāścarya* (LI, p. 160.23). *BBh* p. 193.13 counts five non-wonders: 1) undergoing suffering for the sake of helping others (*parahitahetukaṁ duḥkhamabhyupagacchati*); 2) the voluntary acceptance of cyclic life in order to purify living beings (*sattvapariśuddhimevādhipatiṁ kṛtvā saṁsāram abhyupagacchati*); 3) zeal for teaching the Dharma (*dharmadeśanāyai prayujyate*); 4) willing release (*āśayataṁ samutsṛjati*) of roots of virtue to others; and 5) regarding all the purposeful actions of others as one's own (*parakārysvakārya iva sarvaparakāryārthakriyāsu saṁdṛśyate*).

[7] *Samacittatā* (LI, p. 161.4). Compare *BBh* p. 194.

> 7. always skilled in contemplation, and discrimination-free in wisdom: so should be recognized the bodhisattvas' equanimity of concern.

One verse is on equality of concern for beings, and two on the transcendences.

Beings' love for themselves and so on is neither even-minded nor constant;[8] therefore, they sometimes even kill themselves. But the bodhisattvas' (love) for all beings is both equal-minded and constant.

In terms of the transcendences, (they have) equality of regard in generosity and so on, since they are impartial toward suppliants. (They are equal minded) in morality, since (they do) not ever violate it even in the slightest way. "Tolerant in all cases" means (that they are tolerant) without distinctions of country or era or beings. (They are) "great in effort to achieve all aims of beings," since they are equal in their dedication to the aims of self and others and to the aim of all that is virtuous. The rest is self-evident.

Sixteen verses on the analysis of helpfulness:[9]

> 8–9. The genius (bodhisattvas') helpfulness for beings is deemed to consist in (their) establishing them as vessels, furthering them in morality, bearing their offences, going to work to accomplish their aims, engaging them with the teaching, and resolving their doubts.

These two verses describe the manner of the bodhisattvas' helpfulness through the six transcendences. By generosity, they establish beings as vessels of virtuous activities. By meditation, they engage them (in the teaching)[10] by means of their (own) endowment with distinctive power. The rest is self-evident.

The remaining verses show (the bodhisattvas') helpfulness by comparing them to mothers, and so on:

---

[8] Reading with the Tibetan *mnyam pa nyid dang ldan pa yang ma yin la gtan du yang ma yin te /.*

[9] *Upakāritva* (LI, p. 161.17). Compare *BBh* p. 194.

[10] Reading the Tibetan (D Tsi 241a1) *'dzud par byed de / / mthu'i khyad par...* for *...byed do / / mtha'i....*

> 10–11. The spiritual offspring of the victors are like mothers to beings through five activities: they always sustain beings with an equal attitude; they give them birth in a holy place; they cause them to grow with virtues;[11] they protect them against harm; and they educate them in what must be learned.

"Like mothers to beings" means like beings' mothers. A mother renders five types of assistance to her children: she bears them in her womb; gives them birth; nurses them, (that is) nourishes them and raises them; protects them from harm; and teaches them to speak. The five activities of the bodhisattva are to be known through this example. "Holy place" is to be understood as (a land) blessed with the holy Dharma.

> 12–13. The spiritual offspring of the victors are like fathers to beings through five activities: they always cause faith to grow in all beings; they engage them in their educations in supreme morality and so on; (they engage them) in liberation; they petition the buddhas (for them); and they purge their obscurations.

A father renders five types of assistance to his children: he plants their seed; he teaches them crafts; he matches them with suitable mates; he entrusts them to spiritual mentors; and he renders them free from debt so they do not have to pay any inherited debts.

The five activities of the bodhisattva are known through this example. Faith is the seed for living beings' attaining the holy embodiment. The educations are crafts. Liberation is the mate, because they experience the bliss of the joy of liberation. The buddhas are the spiritual mentors, and the obscurations are the debts.

> 14–15. The spiritual offspring of the victors are like relatives to beings through five activities: they conceal the teaching from unworthy beings; they reprove (beings') lapses from the disciplines; they praise their excellences; they give useful advice; and they alert them to (dangers from) any devils.

---

[11] The Tibetan *dge ba* should read *dge bas* following the Sanskrit *kuśalair* (LI, p. 162.4).

Relatives provide five types of assistance: they keep secrets; they reprove bad conduct; they praise good conduct; they render assistance when need be; and they turn them away from dangerous situations.

The five activities of the bodhisattvas may be understood through this example: they keep the teaching of the profound truth secret from the unworthy; they deprecate (beings') lapses from the disciplines; they praise their excellences;[12] they give useful advice for realization; and they alert (beings to) the actions of devils.

> 16–17. The spiritual offspring of the victors are like friends to beings through five activities: their own minds are not confused[13] about addiction and purification; they totally give mundane and transcendent perfections; they are tireless; they never disassociate (themselves from beings); and they always seek (beings') happiness and benefit.

That one is a friend who is never opposed to the health and happiness of their friend; who (tirelessly) secures their benefit and happiness; never falls out with them; and who always desires their wealth and happiness. Likewise, bodhisattvas are to be known as a friend to beings through five activities. "Mundane perfection" is happiness, because one experiences happiness through it. "Transcendent" (perfection) is (true) health, because it is the remedy to the illness of the addictions.

> 18–19. The spiritual offspring of the victors are like servants to beings through five activities: they always strive to develop beings; they speak of authentic renunciation; they are tolerant of those who act perversely; they give the two perfections; and they are skillful in liberative arts.

A servant behaves properly for his master[14] through five activities: his diligence is excellent; he is not deceitful about his duties; he is tolerant of reproaches, blows, and so on; he is clever in carrying out all tasks; and he is skillful and knowledgeable of arts.

---

[12] *Yathākramaṁ*, "respectively" (LI, p. 163.1) is untranslated here since our translation already sorted out the verbs and nouns.

[13] Read *abhrānta* with the Tibetan *ma 'khrul ba* against the Sanskrit *aśrānta* (LI, p. 163.3).

[14] The Sanskrit omits (LI, p. 163.15); the Tibetan (D Phi 242a2) reads *jo bo la*.

The five activities of the bodhisattva may be understood through this example. The "two perfections" are to be known as mundane and transcendent (perfections).

> 20–21. The spiritual offspring of the victors are like teachers to beings: they have attained the tolerance of the uncreatedness of things; they teach all the vehicles; they promote success in yoga; they have a pleasing countenance; and they do not look for reward and evolutionary development (for themselves).

Teachers assist their pupils in five ways: they are themselves well-instructed; they cause them to learn everything; they make them learn quickly; they have a pleasing countenance like those who are compassionate; and they have no concern for material wealth.

The five activities of the bodhisattva should be understood through this example.

> 22–23. The spiritual offspring of the victors are like preceptors for beings: they exert themselves to accomplish the aims of beings; they cause them to complete their stores (of merit and wisdom); they cause those with stores already completed to be liberated quickly; they cause them to abandon their resistant tendencies; and they provide them with various mundane and transcendent perfections.

A preceptor assists those who live together (under her teaching) through five activities: she gives them their novitiate vows of renunciation; she gives them their full ordination; she instructs them how to abandon faults completely; she supports them with material needs; and (she supports them) with the teaching.

The five activities of the bodhisattva should be understood through this example.

Two verses on the analysis of requital:[15]

> 24–25. Beings who appropriately requite the kindness of the bodhisattvas are those who engage in the six transcendences, being

---

[15] *Pratikāra* (LI, p. 164.5), *lan du phan 'dogs pa*. Compare *BBh* p. 194.

> unattached to possessions, not remiss in moral discipline, endowed with grateful recognition, and dedicated to practice.

"Appropriately" means in accordance with the assistance rendered to them by the bodhisattvas. Because they are unattached to wealth, they stand in generosity. Because they do not break their moral discipline, (they stand) in morality. Because they are endowed with gratitude, (they stand) in tolerance. In fact, out of gratitude for the bodhisattvas' assistance they become lovers of tolerance. "Dedicated to practice" means that they practice effort, contemplation, and wisdom, referring to the means and the place of their practice.

One verse on the analysis of expectation:[16]

> 26. They always expect increase, decrease, evolution of beings, (their) special progress on the stages, and unexcelled enlightenment.

Bodhisattvas always expect five conditions: the increase of the transcendences; the decrease of their resistant tendencies; the evolution of living beings; (their) special progress on the stages; and (their) unexcelled perfect enlightenment.

One verse on the analysis of effective practice:[17]

> 27. The victors' spiritual offspring are always effective in eliminating fear, in authentic spiritual conception, in the resolution of doubts, and in giving instruction on practice.

The bodhisattvas' practice should be recognized as effective in accomplishing the aims of beings in four ways: in not indulging in fear of the profound and magnificent teaching; in the authentic conception of the spirit of enlightenment; in the resolution of doubts concerning the spirit of enlightenment already conceived; and in giving instructions on the practice of the transcendences.

---

[16] *Āśāsti* (LI, p. 164.14). The five things wished for according to *BBh* p. 194.22 are a bit different: 1) the advent of a buddha (*buddhotpāda*); 2) hearing the *Bodhisattvapiṭaka* from him; 3) the power to develop living beings (*sattvaparipācanapratibalatā*); 4) the attainment of perfect enlightenment (*samyaksaṁbodhiprāptiṁ*); and 5) attainment of the like by the host of disciples (*abhisaṁbuddhā bodhiśca śrāvakasāmagrī*).

[17] *Abandhyaprayoga* (LI, p. 164.18). See also *BBh* p. 195.

Two verses on the analysis of authentic application:[18]

> 28–29.[19] The brave (bodhisattvas) show their authentic application in giving without expectation, in being moral without desire for good rebirth, in tolerance in all situations, in endeavor in the production of all virtue, in contemplation without (addiction to) formlessness,[20] and in wisdom integrated with liberative art.

As it is stated extensively in the *Jewel Heap Scripture*: "By giving without expectation of evolutionary benefit" and so on.[21]

Two verses on the analysis of the qualities conducive to downfalls and excellences:[22]

> 30. The causes of the brave (bodhisattvas') downfall are attachment to possessions, laxity,[23] pridefulness, a liking for pleasures, indulgence (in transic experiences), and superstitious notions.

> 31. On the contrary, the bodhisattvas firm in tendencies remedial to those (downfalls) are endowed with the qualities conducive to excellence.

The resistances to the six transcendences are the pitfalls, and their remedies are recognized as the excellences.

Two verses on the analysis of counterfeit and genuine virtues,[24] the first verse having six quarters:

---

[18] *Samyakprayoga* (LI, p. 165.2). See also *BBh* p. 195.

[19] These two verses are quoted in *AAA* p. 378.

[20] The Tibetan (D Phi 243a2) has misprinted *yin* for *min*, which is the word in the *MSA* itself (D Phi 33b6), and in Sthiramati (D Tsi 193b1 *ff.*), who explains that the bodhisattva contemplates without desiring entry into formless realms, since therein he will not evolve toward buddhahood, nor will he be able to benefit others in their development.

[21] This corresponds to *Kāśyapaparivarta* #24: *vipākapratikāṁkṣiṇa tyāgaṁ*; see also #25 of the same work.

[22] *Parihāṇiviśeṣabhāgīyadharma* (LI, p. 165.7). Compare *BBh* p. 194–195.

[23] *Sacchidratvaṁ* (LI, p. 165.9), (Tibetan: *nyams bcas*, Sthiramati: *ral bcas*) meaning having "gaps" or "tears" or "holes" in one's moral armor.

32–33. Boasting,[25] pretending,[26] faking a loving expression, acting with a temporary show of diligence, (artificially) calming body and speech, and being well skilled in eloquent speech while devoid of real practice (of these virtues): these are taught as counterfeit for bodhisattvas, while the opposite are taught as genuine for those really engaged in practice.

With reference to the six transcendences, boasting and so on are understood as counterfeit bodhisattva qualities. The meaning of the rest is self-evident.

One verse on the analysis of discipline:[27]

34. By their practices of generosity and so on, on all stages, the geniuses discipline the six kinds of resistant tendencies of beings.

There are six types of tendencies resistant to the six transcendences: stinginess, corrupt morality, hatred, laziness, distraction, and confused knowledge, respectively. The rest is self-evident.

Three verses on the analysis of prophecy:[28]

35–36. The genius (bodhisattvas) receive prophecies of two kinds, varying according to time and person, and also in relation to enlightenment and prophecy itself. Another (prophecy) is called "great," because by attaining the tolerance of the noncreation of things pride and willful struggle come to an end, and they become one with all the buddhas and bodhisattvas.

37. (Such) prophecy consists of field, name, time, name of eon, retinue, and duration of the holy teaching.

---

[24] *Pratirūpakabhūtaguṇa* (LI, p. 165.14). Compare *BBh* p. 197.

[25] *Pravāraṇā* (LI, p. 165.15), but *pratāraṇā* according to LII, p. 272, n. 32.1. The Tibetan translation has *sprul pa*, and Sthiramati *stobs pa*, as the first counterfeit practice (corresponding to false generosity).

[26] *Kuhanā* (LI, p. 165.15). Tibetan *tshul 'chos pa*.

[27] *Vinaya* (LI, p. 165.21). Compare *BBh* p. 197 on the ten types of ethical disciplines (*vinaya*).

[28] *Vyākaraṇa* (LI, p. 166.2). See *VKN* pp 189–194, and compare *BBh* p. 196.

Prophecy varies according to person, because prophecy relates to a person with respect to genealogy, spiritual conception, presence, or absence. It varies according to time, because prophecy relates to a limited or unlimited time. Also, prophecy occurs in relation to enlightenment and also in relation to prophecy (itself). As it is said: "A transcendent lord of such-and-such name, or such-and-such time, will prophecy thus."

There is another, the great prophecy, which occurs on the eighth stage when one has attained tolerance of the noncreation of things, having overcome the pride which says "I will become a buddha" as well as all reifying strivings, having become one with all buddhas and bodhisattvas, by no longer experiencing any difference between their processes and one's own.

Again, prophecy specifies the land and so on, as it is said: "In such a buddha-land of such a name in such a time there will appear such a buddha, in an eon of such a name, and his assembly will be of such a kind, and the duration of his holy Dharma will last for such a time."

One verse of six quarters on the analysis of attaining predetermination:[29]

> 38. Becoming predetermined (for enlightenment) for the geniuses consists of success, life, indefatigability, perpetual realization, unremitting meditation and successful activity, and obtaining effortless tolerance in all situations.

Becoming predetermined is shown to be sixfold based upon the six transcendences. One becomes predetermined in terms of success, because (through generosity) one always gains the success of extensive wealth. One becomes predetermined in terms of life, because one always embraces life according to one's desire. One becomes predetermined in terms of indefatigability, because one is never wearied by the suffering of the life-cycle. One becomes predetermined in terms of perpetual realization, because (the process of) meditative realization never ceases. One becomes predetermined in terms of unremitting meditation and accomplishment of duties, because one never abandons meditation and one always accomplishes the duties of beings. One becomes predetermined in terms of attaining the spontaneous

---

[29] *Niyatipāta* (LI, p. 166.17). *BBh* p. 197 gives three conditions which insure the attainment of enlightenment: 1) gene (*gotra*); 2) conception of the spirit of enlightenment (*bodhicittotpāda*); and 3) power (*vaśitāprāpta*).

tolerance of things' nonproduction, because one always stands spontaneously in nonconceptual wisdom.

One verse of six quarters on the analysis of involuntary duty:[30]

> 39. Involuntary duty for the geniuses on all stages includes offering worship, undertaking of the educations, compassion, cultivation of virtue, vigilance in (preserving) solitude, and also non-complacency (in one's understanding of) the meaning of what one learns.

The six involuntary duties are based upon the six transcendences. The verse is self-explanatory.

Two verses on the analysis of constant duty:[31]

> 40–41. Constant duty for the geniuses on all stages is to know the drawbacks of desire, to be aware of aberrations, to accept suffering, to cultivate virtue, not to over-indulge in pleasure, and not to conceptually reify signs.

Six things must always be done in order to accomplish the six transcendences. The verse is self-explanatory.

One verse of six quarters on the analysis of the principal matter:[32]

---

[30] *Avaśyakaraṇīya* (LI, p. 167.2). Compare *BBh* p. 197 on the five indispensible conditions for the attainment of enlightenment: 1) initial conception of the spirit of enlightenment (*prathamaścittotpāda*); 2) sympathy for living beings (*sattveṣvanukampā*); 3) intense endeavor (*uttaptavīrya*); 4) competence in all the branchs of knowledge (*sarvavidyāsthāneṣu yogyatā*); and 5) indefatigability (*akheda*).

[31] *Sātatyakaraṇīya* (LI, p. 167.7). *BBh* p. 197 counts five duties which should be constantly performed: 1) diligence (*apramāda*); 2) protection (*sanāthakriyā*) of the miserable and protectorless; 3) worship of the Tathāgata (*tathāgatapūjā*); 4) knowledge of negligence (*skhalitaparijñānam*); and 5) keeping the spirit of enlightenment in the forefront (*bodhicittapūrvāṅgama*) of all activity.

[32] *Pradhānavastu* (LI, p. 167.13). *BBh* pp. 197–198 distinguishes ten qualities for which the bodhisattva is considered the greatest of people: 1) bodhisattva gene (*bodhisattvagotraṁ*); 2) initial conception of the spirit of enlightenment (*prathamaścittotpāda*); 3) endeavor and wisdom (*vīryaṁ, prajñā*); 4) agreeable speech (*priyavāditā*); 5) transcendent realization (*tathāgata*); 6) compassion (*karuṇā*); 7) the fourth contemplation (*caturthaṁ dhyānaṁ*); 8) voidness concentration (*śūnyatāsamādhiṁ*); 9) cessation absorption (*nirodhasamāpattiṁ*); and 10) skill in liberative art (*upāyakauśalya*).

42. The principal matters of the transcendences for the geniuses are considered to be the giving of the teaching, the purity of morality, the tolerance of the uncreated, the exerting of effort in the universal vehicle, the standing with compassion to the end, and wisdom.

The six types of principal matter relate to the six transcendences. In this context "purity of morality" refers to the morality cherished by the holy ones. "Standing with compassion to the end" is the fourth meditation joined with measureless compassion. The rest is self-explanatory.

Four verses on the analysis of nominal classification:[33]

43. For the genius (bodhisattvas) on all stages the classification of teachings should be understood as a classification of sciences distinguished by the various forms such as discourse.

44. The classification of truths is sevenfold, based on suchness. The classifications of reasons and vehicles are fourfold and threefold.

45. Appropriate conscientious attitude, authentic conviction endowed with a result, analysis by means of validating cognition, and the inconceivable should be understood to be the four(fold classification of) reasons.

46. Vehicles are accepted as threefold on the basis of differences in aspiration, teaching, application, preparation, and achievement.

Nominal classification is fourfold through differences in nominal classification of teaching, truth, reason, and vehicle. The classification of teachings is understood as the classification of the five sciences in the various forms such as discourse and verse. Other sciences, being included within them, are taught to the bodhisattvas on the great vehicle.

The classification of truths is sevenfold, based on suchness: suchness of function, suchness of mark, suchness of construction, suchness of habits, suchness of wrong practice,[34] suchness of purity, and suchness of right practice.

---

[33] *Prajñaptivyavasthāna* (LI, p. 167.18). The four "nominal classifications" *dharma-*, *satya-*, *yukti-*, and *yāna-* are treated extensively in *BBh* pp. 198–199.

The nominal classification of reasons is fourfold: relational reason, functional reason, logically established reason, and reality reason.[35]

The classification of vehicles is threefold: disciple vehicle, hermit buddha vehicle, and universal vehicle.[36] "Relational reason" is the proper conscientious attitude toward the three vehicles; because in relation to that, by that condition, the transcendent realistic view arises. "The functional reason" is the realistic view together with its cause and effect. "The logical reason" is investigation by validating cognitions, such as direct perception. "Reality reason" is the state of the inconceivable – the reality being already established, it is not conceived (by a reasoning process, such as) "Why? Because realistic view arises from proper attitude!" or "Because the result will be the termination of addictions."

The classification of the three vehicles is to be understood through five aspects: aspiration, teaching, practice, preparation, and achievement. Here, the inferior aspiration, teaching, application, preparation of stores, and authentic achievement are those of the disciple vehicle, and the superior are those of the universal vehicle. The teaching of the Dharma is superior according to aspiration and according to desire. As it is taught, so it is practiced; as it is practiced, (so is there) preparation of the stores; as there are stores, so there is the achievement of enlightenment.

One verse on the analysis of investigation:[37]

> 47.[38] (The four investigations are) the investigation of name and referent as mutually incidental, and the investigation of both (ascriptive and descriptive) designations as mere (designations).

---

[34] Compare *MAV* pp. 101–103 which discusses the seven *tathatā* (LI, p. 168.3) of our text under the designation *tattva*. See *Siddhi* pp. 534–535. The equation *tathatā* = *satya* goes back to Pāli *tatha* which is the equivalent to *sacca*, so e.g., *cattāri tathāni* = *cattāri saccāni*; see Edgerton p. 248 s.v. *tathatā*, and PTSD p. 295 s.v. *tatha*. In *BBh* p. 198 the truths are enumerated from a single truth up to a tenfold truth, but the *BBh* is silent on the sevenfold truth of our text.

[35] The four reasonings (*yukti*) are taught in *Saṁdhinir* X.7 and briefly treated in *AS* p. 81.

[36] Compare *BBh* p. 199 on the three vehicles discussed in the context of seven topics.

[37] *Paryeṣaṇā* (LI, p. 168.16). The four investigations and the four thorough knowledges of reality (*yathābhūtaparijñāna*, see vs. 48–55 below) make up the four aids to penetrative insight *nirvedhabhāgīya*, the first two being *paryeṣaṇā* and the last two *yathābhūtaparijñāna*; see *Siddhi* pp. 576–578. Compare *MSABh* XIX.47–48 with *BBh* p. 36.

[38] This verse is also found in chapter three of the *MS*.

The investigation of things is fourfold: investigating the name, investigating the referent, investigating ascriptive designations, and investigating descriptive designations. Investigating the name as incidental to the referent is to be understood as investigating the name. Investigating the referent as incidental to the name is to be understood as investigating the thing. The investigation of the ascriptive and descriptive designations as mere designations upon the connection between those two (name and referent) is to be understood as investigating ascriptive and descriptive designations.

Eight[39] verses on the analysis of the thorough knowledge of reality:

> 48. Because of the nonperception of everything, realistic intuition is fourfold; and it arises in the brave (bodhisattvas) on all stages, for their achievement of all their goals.

The thorough knowledge of reality is fourfold, as endowed with the thorough investigations of names, referents, ascriptive designations, and descriptive designations. And it should be recognized (as produced) from the nonperception of all things, names and so forth.

The latter half of the verse shows the greatness and the function of the thorough intuitive knowledge of reality.

> 49. Support, enjoyment, and seed are the causes of bondage; minds and mental functions with their foundations and seeds are bound here.

The supporting cause is the material world; the enjoyment cause consists of the five objects, the visible and so forth. The seed cause is their seed, which is the fundamental consciousness. Here on this threefold causal process minds and mental functions with their foundations are bound, and the fundamental consciousness is that which is their seed. Further, "foundations" are to be understood as the eye and so forth.[40]

---

[39] Eight (Tibetan *brgyad*), not ten (*daśa*, LI, p. 168.24).

[40] Support (*pratiṣṭhā*), enjoyment (*bhoga*), and seed (*bīja*) represent three aspects of the fundamental consciousness in that it serves as the reservoir for the instincts and habits conducive to the false construction of a reality external to consciousness, and the evolution (*pravṛtti*) of the various mental functions. On the fundamental consciousness as seed, see the commentary to XI.32, 44, and surrounding discussion, above.

50.[41] The genius who destroys all causal processes placed in front or standing on their own obtains supreme enlightenment.

The causal process "placed in front" is the imaginatively constructed reality which is taken as an object in the practice of study, reflection, and meditation. The causal process which "stands on its own" is that which is perceived naturally; it is not expressly imaginatively constructed. Their destruction is freedom,[42] the nature of which is nonperception. Its art is nonconceptuality, the remedy for (such) causal processes. The two arise sequentially; first come those placed (in front), later those standing on their own.

The yogi who destroys the causal process of the (habit of) "person" which is endowed with four errors[43] attains the enlightenment of the disciple or the enlightenment of the hermit buddha. If one destroys the causal processes of all (such erroneous) things, one attains the great enlightenment. This elucidates how thorough knowledge of reality realizes the nature of bondage and culminates in liberation.

51. Intuitive wisdom which has suchness for its object abandons the perception of duality; the intuitive experience of the body of negative conditioning is accepted by the genius to effect the termination of such (a bound reality).

This shows that thorough knowledge of the three realities as they are leads to the termination of the (dualistically experienced) relative reality. The actual perception of suchness leads to the thorough knowledge of the perfect reality. The abandonment of dualistic perception leads to the (termination of) the imaginatively constructed reality. The intuitive experience of the body of negative conditioning (leads to the thorough knowledge of) the relative. This leads to the termination of the body of negative conditioning as the fundamental consciousness itself. "To effect the termination" means "for the sake of terminating."[44]

---

[41] Also found in the third chapter of the *MS*.

[42] That is, separation from real existence (*yod pa'i dngos po*); see Sthiramati (P Tsi 243b5; D Tsi 209a6 *ff.*).

[43] The four *viparyāsa*; see XVIII.44–45 (Ms. 43–44).

[44] *Dauṣṭhulyakāya* (LI, p. 169.23). The fundamental consciousness is the "body of negative instincts" as the ground of all addictive and objective obscurations and the basis of all false

(cont'd)

> 52. Meditating the intuitive wisdom which has suchness for its object without any aspect of differentiation, there is direct experience of what exists and what does not exist; such (a person) is called the "master of discrimination."

One meditates without differentiation because no difference is seen between causal process and suchness. This shows the distinctive excellence of the signlessness of the bodhisattva in comparison with the signlessness of the disciple. Those (disciples) see signs and signlessness as different; they do not attend on signs, but attend on the realm of signlessness, and thus absorb themselves in signlessness. But bodhisattvas experience even signs as signlessness by not seeing any sign (of causal process) apart from suchness. Therefore their intuitive wisdom of (signlessness) is meditated without differentiation. "They intuitively experience" "what exists," that is suchness, and "what does not exist," that is causal signs, and they attain mastery over discrimination, in the sense that they can succeed in all their goals according to their discriminating discernment; and therefore, they are called "masters of discrimination."

> 53.[45] For naïve individuals, reality being obscured, unreality appears everywhere; but for the bodhisattvas, having cleared away (unreality), reality appears everywhere.

This shows how just the unreal appears naturally as a causal process to naïve people, but not true reality. Similarly, it is the real itself which naturally appears to bodhisattvas, and not the unreal.

> 54.[46] One should know that (for the realized bodhisattva) the unreal does not appear, and the real appears: this foundational transmutation is liberation, because she (then is free to) act as she wishes.

---

imagination. With the termination of their instinctual propensities liberation is attained; see Sthiramati (P Tsi 244b4–245a3; D Tsi 210b).

[45] This verse is also found in the ninth chapter of the *MS*.

[46] This verse is also found in the ninth chapter of the *MS*.

The non-appearance of the unreal (dualistically imagined) causal process and the appearance of the suchness of the real are to be understood as the foundational transmutation,[47] since through it the one no longer appears, and (the other) appears; and just that is to be known as liberation. Why? Because (such a bodhisattva) acts as she wishes. Being independent at that time she has the power over her own mind, for she naturally does not indulge in causal processes.

> 55. The great object appears everywhere, mutually (evolving with) similar categories; but because it creates obstruction (to the buddhaverse), one should abandon it(s habitual perception) by means of thorough knowledge.

This is the thorough knowledge of reality which is the art of purifying the universe. The material world is the "great object." In mutually evolving, it appears as (containing) similar categories (of things), (which we can identify) as "this is just that." From such (objective) appearance, there is obstruction to the purification of the buddhaverse. Therefore, by means of the thorough knowledge of such obstructiveness one should abandon such perception.

One verse on the analysis of the immeasurables:

> 56. For the geniuses the immeasurables are that to be (evolutionarily) perfected, that to be purified, that to be attained, that to be inspired toward maturity, and that which teaches reality.

These are the five immeasurable things for bodhisattvas. That to be perfected is the realm of all beings without discrimination. That to be purified is the universe included in the material world. That to be attained is the truth realm. That to be impelled toward evolutionary maturity is the realm of disciples. The subject which is taught realistically is the realm of the disciplinary arts.[48]

Two verses on the analysis of the fruits of the teaching:

> 57–58. The fruit of teaching for the dedicated genius is the production of the spirit of enlightenment, the tolerance of creation-

---

[47] See IX.12–17.

[48] The same five immeasurables are discussed at length in *BBh* pp. 200–201. A sixty-four fold classification of the realm of living beings (*sattvadhātu*) is found in *YBh* pp. 48–49.

> lessness, the individual (vehicle) immaculate eye, the termination of the contaminations, the long duration of the holy Dharma, education, resolution, and enjoyment.

The fruit of the bodhisattva dedicated to teaching is recognized as eightfold: among his students, some conceive the spirit of enlightenment, some obtain tolerance of the noncreation of things, some generate the stainless, immaculate truth-vision of things, which is included in the individual vehicle. Some attain the termination of the contaminations.

By (their) maintaining the tradition, the holy Dharma becomes long-lasting.[49] Those who are uneducated become educated about things. Those who doubt have their doubts resolved. And those who have attained certainty enjoy the irreproachable, joyful savor of the feast of holy Dharma.

Two verses on the analysis of the "universality" of the universal vehicle:[50]

> 59–60.[51] The "universal vehicle" is so called because it is endowed with universalities of objective, mutual fulfillment, intuition, creative initiative, skill in liberative art, success, and buddha deeds.

The "universal vehicle" is so called because it is endowed with the seven types of universality. (It has universality) of "objective," being endowed with immeasurable, extensive teachings of the scriptures and so forth. (It has universality) of "mutual fulfillment," as it fulfills both individualistic and altruistic goals. (It has universality) of "intuition," because (it leads to the) realization, at the moment of insight, of the selflessness of both persons and things.

(It has universality) of "creative initiative," because (it enables the bodhisattva to be) dedicated to constant devotion for three incalculable eons. (It has universality) of "skill in liberative art," due to its non-addictedness as it never abandons the cycle of life. (It has universality) of "success," because (it leads one to) achieve the buddha qualities, powers, fearlessnesses, and distinctivenesses. And (it has universality) of "buddha deeds" because (it conveys its bodhisattvas) again and again to manifest perfect enlightenment and universal final liberation.

---

[49] The same five benefits are found in *BBh* p. 201.

[50] Compare *BBh* pp. 201–202 for a different set of seven "greatnesses."

[51] Vs. 60 is quoted in *AAA* p. 321.

Two verses on the analysis of the summary of the universal vehicle:

> 61–62.[52] (The universal vehicle is summarized as) (awakening) the spiritual gene, (having) faith in the Dharma, the conception of the spirit, the practice of generosity and so forth, the advance to predetermination,[53] the evolutionary development of beings, the purification of the universe, the unlocated Nirvāṇa, the supreme enlightenment, and the manifestation (of the buddha-deeds).[54]

The entire universal vehicle is included in ten subjects. "Evolutionary development of beings" should be known as beginning from the entrance upon the stages up to the seventh stage. "Purification of the universe" and "unlocated Nirvāṇa" are on the three nonregressive stages,[55] and "supreme enlightenment" is on the buddha stage. Also there is the manifestation of perfect enlightenment and of universal final liberation. The meaning of the rest is self-evident.

Ten verses on the analysis of the bodhisattva:[56]

---

[52] The Chinese reads (T.31.654c29): "Gene, faith, spirit, action, entering, development, purity, superior enlightenment."

[53] *Nyāyāvakrānti* (LI, p. 171.22). Lévi (LII, p. 281, n. 61.1) emends this to *nyāmāvakrānti*. Sthiramati (P Tsi 253b7–254a1) comments on *nyāma-* as if it were *ni-āma*, or "faultless" (Tibetan *skyon med*) where the fault is attachment to subjectivity and objectivity which is removed on the first bodhisattva stage. However *nyāma* is also a variant of *niyāma*, and *niyāma-avakrānti* refers to the predetermination for certain acquisition of enlightenment in the future. In the individual vehicle the disciple attains certitude at the time of entering the path of insight (*darśanamārga*), but the bodhisattva attains certitude upon attaining the tolerance of the creationlessness of things on the eighth bodhisattva stage. See *VKN* pp. 115–116, n. 64.

[54] The enumeration of "ten" by both Tibetan and Sanskrit commentaries necessitates translating this *darśana* according to Lévi's emendation, as if it were separate from "Nirvāṇa" and "enlightenment." Sthiramati (D Tsi 219a–b) enumerates a total of eight things, counting Nirvāṇa and enlightenment as one. dBal Mang (170a–b), on the other hand, lists them as ten, and considers the "manifestation" of Parinirvāṇa as a further step from the attainments of unlocated Nirvāṇa and perfect enlightenment.

[55] The eighth, ninth, and tenth bodhisattva stages.

[56] On the analysis of the bodhisattva see also *MS* chapter II (*La Somme* II, 34) and references op. cit. p. 24.

63. These five should be known as bodhisattvas on all stages: one possessed of faith, another pure in universal responsibility, those who practice through signs, through signlessness, and without purposeful motivation.

"Practices through signs" (refers to the bodhisattvas) from the second stage up to the sixth. "Through signlessness" (refers to bodhisattvas) on the seventh stage. "Practice without purposeful motivation" (refers to bodhisattvas) on the other (eighth through tenth stages). The rest is self-evident.

64. One is truly a bodhisattva who is unattached to desires, has the three pure actions, has conquered anger, is devoted to supreme good qualities, does not swerve from the teaching, sees profound reality, and longs for enlightenment.

This shows the character of the bodhisattva through the practice of the six transcendences and the vow for the great enlightenment.

65. One is truly a bodhisattva who wishes to help, who does not notice injury, who tolerates harm from others, is brave, vigilant, very learned, and dedicated to the interests of others.

"Brave" means energetic in effort because she is not battered down by suffering. "Vigilant" means she is not attached to the bliss of meditation. The rest is self-evident.

66. One is truly a bodhisattva who understands suffering, is not attached to one's own property and wealth, is without hidden enmity, is a yogi, skilled in signs, is without wrong views, and is inwardly composed.

"Not attached to wealth" (refers to one's) abandoning possessions and renouncing (the mundane). "Skilled in signs" (refers to) being skillful in the three signs of mental serenity and other (meditations). "Inwardly composed" (refers to) not swerving from the universal vehicle. The universal vehicle lies in the interior of the bodhisattvas. The rest is self-evident.

67. One is truly a bodhisattva who is loving, lives in excellence of conscience, willingly endures suffering, is not attached to one's own happiness, who holds mindfulness most dear, whose self is well concentrated, and who does not change vehicle.

"Holding mindfulness most dear" is possession of meditation through the power of mindfulness because the mind has been placed in equipoise. "The self is well concentrated," because such a one is endowed with nonconceptual intuition. The rest is self-evident.

68. One is truly a bodhisattva who clears away suffering, who does not cause suffering, who willingly endures suffering, who does not fear suffering, who is free from suffering, who has no notion of suffering, and who accepts suffering.

"Free from suffering" means she is endowed with meditation; having renounced the desire realm she is free from the suffering of suffering. She "accepts suffering" because she accepts the cycle of life. The rest is self-evident.

69. One is truly a bodhisattva for whom (the transcendent) Dharma is chief, who does not like (material) things (*dharma*s), who naturally enjoys Dharma (things),[57] who dislikes (hateful) behaviors, who is dedicated to Dharma (practice), who has power in (contemplative) Dharma practice, and who sees no darkness in all things.[58]

He "dislikes things," since he dislikes intolerance. "He has power in the Dharma," (due to his mastery of) trance. "For whom the Dharma is chief" means

---

[57] Reading *dharme rato 'dharmaratam̐* with Lévi and the Tibetan (D Phi 248b3) against the Chinese (T.31.655c6) and Sthiramati (P Tsi 260a6–8; D Tsi 225a1) where "enjoys the teachings" refers to enjoying generosity, and "naturally enjoys nothing against the teachings" refers to delight in the non-appearance of any sin reproachable by nature (*prakṛtisāvadyam*). We follow the translation, both verses (D Phi 35b2) and commentary, and dBal Mang (171b–172a).

[58] In order to make this understandable, we have had to lose the play on the multiple meanings of "*dharma*" here, as Truth, thing, practice, teaching, and so forth.

(for whom) great enlightenment is supreme. Here the word "*dharma*" is written "*dharama*" for metrical reasons. The rest is self-evident.

> 70. One is truly a bodhisattva who is mindful about wealth, mindful about rules, mindful about protection, mindful about virtue, mindful about happiness, mindful about truth, and mindful about vehicles.

"Mindful about protection" means being tolerant, because he protects the minds of self and other. "Mindful about the truth" (means that) he realizes things as they are in reality. The rest is self-evident.

> 71. One is truly a bodhisattva who is ashamed of contempt,[59] ashamed of slight faults, ashamed of impatience, ashamed of transgressions, ashamed of distractions, ashamed of narrow views, and ashamed of other vehicles.

"Ashamed of contempt" means he does not despise any suppliant, (and gives him what he asks). "Ashamed of slight faults" means he sees danger even in the slightest transgression. "Ashamed of narrow views" means he has[60] experiential insight into objective selflessness. The rest is self-explanatory.

All these verses illustrate the nature of the bodhisattva with various formulations from the perspectives of the practice of the six transcendences and the great vow for enlightenment.

> 72. One is truly a bodhisattva who engages in helping others in this life and beyond through equanimity, motivated action, attainment of mastery, teaching equally, and the great fruition.

He engages in helping beings through generosity in this life and through morality in the future life, thereby attaining a distinctive rebirth. "Through moti-

---

[59] Sthiramati (D Tsi 226b1) has *sbyin med ngo tsha* instead of *ma gus ngo tsha* which appears in both the verses and the commentary. This seems to fit better with the structure of the verse in terms of the six transcendences, so that the bodhisattva's shame of contempt is rather a shame of being ungenerous.

[60] The Tibetan negative *ma* (D Phi 248b7) seems out of parallel with previous two phrases.

vated action" means action through effort. The "great fruition" is buddhahood. The rest is self-evident.

This (verse) teaches that the bodhisattva acts according to what helps beings by means of the six transcendences and the great vow for enlightenment.

Eight verses on the analysis of the general names of bodhisattvas:

> 73–74.[61] "Spiritual hero," "universal heroine," "genius," "brilliant one," "victor-child," "victor-ground," "triumphant," "victor-sprout," "mighty one," "supreme holy one," "leader," "universally famous one," "compassionate one," "greatly meritorious one," "lord," "truthful one"; (these are the sixteen names of bodhisattvas).

These are the sixteen general corresponding names of bodhisattvas.

> 75. One is called a "bodhisattva" for a (fivefold) distinctive reason: for understanding reality well, for understanding well the universal aim, for understanding everything, for permanent understanding, and for understanding the liberative arts.

One is called "bodhisattva" because of the five types of special understanding; that is: the understanding of the selflessnesses of persons and objects; the understanding of all the aims of self and others; the understanding of all things and all aspects; the understanding of the inexhaustible even when exhibiting total enlightenment; and the understanding of the liberative art of the discipline attuned to the disciple.

> 76. One is called "bodhisattva" for this reason: for understanding the self,[62] for understanding subtle views,[63] for recognizing the

[61] These same sixteen designations of the bodhisattva are found in *BBh* p. 203. In place of the Sanskrit *paramāścaryaṁ*, read *paramaścāryaṁ* with the Tibetan and Chinese (T.31.656a21) which is confirmed by *BBh* p. 203.11, *paramāryaṁ*.

[62] According to Sthiramati, this refers to understanding the fundamental consciousness.

[63] According to Sthiramati, this refers to understanding the nature of the impassioned mentality.

> variousness of ideas,[64] and for realizing the unreal construction of everything.

This (verse) again teaches the special fourfold understanding: through the understanding of mind, mentality, and consciousness, and through the understanding of their unreal construction. Among these, "mind" is the fundamental consciousness; "mentality" is that which, endowed with (passions) such as the self-conviction, takes (fundamental consciousness) as an object; and "consciousness" is the system of the six consciousnesses.

> 77.[65] One is called "bodhisattva" for this reason: for understanding non-understanding, for understanding the well understood, for understanding nonexistence, for understanding production, and for experiential understanding of understanding through non-understanding.

Here, the (verse) teaches the five types of distinctive understanding: the understanding of misknowledge, the understanding of knowledge, and the understanding of the three realities such as the imaginatively constructed. Among them the understanding of the perfect reality should be recognized as the experiential understanding of understanding by means of its non-understandability.

> 78.[66] One is called "bodhisattva" for this reason: for understanding the non-objective, for understanding ultimate reality, for understanding all objects, for understanding the totality of objects, and for understanding the objective, subject, and action of understanding.[67]

---

[64] Sthiramati says this refers to understanding the sixfold consciousness.

[65] The Chinese omits.

[66] In the Chinese (T.31.656b14): "The non-objective, the real object (*zhen yi*), the totally nonexistent, the fulfilled, the inconceivable; (he who has these) five knowledges is called a bodhisattva."

[67] Sthiramati (D Tsi 231a *ff.*) comments on these five in a surprising way. The "non-objective" is the relative reality, as it is not the subject-object-dichotomous realm of objectivity it appears to be; and also, it is not a fit objective, as it is simply filled with sufferings

(cont'd)

Here, (the verse) teaches the distinctive fivefold understanding:[68] the understanding of the relative nature; the understanding of the perfect nature; the understanding of the constructed nature; the understanding of all aspects of all facts; and the understanding of the purity of the three sectors of the understandable, the understander, and the understanding.

> 79. One is called "bodhisattva" for this reason: for understanding perfection, for understanding the station, for understanding the womb, for understanding the display of the (buddha-)procession, and for understanding the powerful resolution of doubts.

"Understanding perfection" is buddhahood. "Understanding the station" enables (the bodhisattva) to enter the station of Tuṣita. "Understanding the womb" enables her to enter the mother's womb. "Understanding the display of the (buddha-)procession" enables her to emerge from the womb, to enjoy sensual pleasures, to renounce the world, to perform austerities, and to achieve perfect enlightenment. "Understanding the powerful resolution of doubts" enables her to turn the wheel of the Dharma in order to resolve the doubts of living beings.

> 80. (A bodhisattva) is a genius, his intellect accomplished, unaccomplished, and present, with realization and understanding, repentant and nonverbally aware, proud and pride-free, and spiritually immature and mature.[69]

Here, "bodhisattva" is elucidated by means of eleven types of understanding, concerning the past and so on. "Accomplished, unaccomplished, and present intellects" relate to the understandings of the past, future, and present, respectively. "Realization" is from his own inner understanding, and "understanding" indicates understanding which comes from another; that is, (the two refer to) internal and external understandings. "Repentant and nonverbally aware" refer to gross and

---

arising from its misperception. The ultimate is of course the perfect. "All things" are constructed as subjects and objects and are in fact identityless, hence this is knowledge of the constructed reality. "Totality" refers to all superficial realities, the realm of speech and thought. And "purity of three sectors" refers to the realm of wisdom.

[68] According to Sthiramati (D Tsi 231a *ff.*), this fivefold division is in terms of the objects of understanding.

[69] *Apakkasaṁpakkamatiḥ* (LI, p. 175.11) is omitted in the Chinese.

subtle (insights into the past). "Proud and pride-free" indicate the inferior and the excellent (bodhisattva stages). "Spiritually immature and mature" refers to being far and near to enlightenment, (respectively).

Chapter XX

Practice[1]

Two verses analyzing the marks (of a bodhisattva):

> 1. The marks of the geniuses are sensitivity, gentle speech, courage, open-handedness, and (skill in) elucidation of the profound intention.[2]
>
> 2.[3] These five marks should be recognized from the (bodhisattvas') ambition and practice, in their helping, inspiring faith, tirelessness, and in their social activism both (with material measures and with the teaching).

The first verse shows the five marks of the bodhisattvas, the second their function and brief summary. (They have) the loving sensitivity to adopt beings with the spirit of enlightenment. (They use) gentle speech[4] to cause beings to gain faith in the teaching of the buddha. (They show) courage[5] not to be exhausted by difficulties such as ordeals. (They manifest) open-handedness and (skill in) elucidation of the profound intention,[6] to bring society together both by (giving) worldly

---

[1] We are separating this chapter, kept together with the next by Lévi, and treating the next one as an epilogue.

[2] These same five *liṅga* form the subject matter of the *Bodhisattvaliṅgapaṭala* of the *BBh* pp. 207–210. In that work the *priyākhyānaṁ*, humane in philosophy, (LI, p. 175.20) and *dhīratā* (courage) of our text are called *priyavāditā* and *vairya*.

[3] The Chinese omits.

[4] *Priyākhyānaṁ* (LI, p. 176.1). One of the four social practices (*saṁgrahavastu*); see XVI.73–79 (Ms. 72–78).

[5] *Dhīratā* (LI, p. 176.2). See XVIII.17–23 (Ms. vs. 16–22).

[6] *Gambhīrasaṁdhinirmokṣa* (LI, p. 176.3). See XII.17–18.

goods and by the teaching, respectively. Among these five marks, sensitivity can be recognized from (the bodhisattvas') ambition, the rest from practice.

Three verses analyzing the roles of householder and mendicant:[7]

> 3. Bodhisattvas always become universal monarchs, and, as householders, accomplish the aims of beings in all their lives.
>
> 4. On all the stages, the geniuses' transcendent renunciation is achieved (either) by taking (vows) or by (understanding) reality, or it is an instructional performance.
>
> 5. The role of the mendicant is endowed with immeasurable excellences, the ascetic (bodhisattva) being superior to the householder bodhisattva.[8]

The first verse shows that the bodhisattva accomplishes the aims of beings while playing the role of a householder; the second (shows how she does so) in playing the role of a mendicant.

In this context renunciation is understood as threefold: as achieved by taking (vows), as achieved by (realization of) ultimate reality, and as an instructional performance by emanation (body bodhisattvas).

The third verse emphasizes the superiority of the role of the mendicant over the role of the householder.

One six-quarter verse analyzing the messianic resolve:[9]

> 6. The brave (bodhisattvas') messianic resolve for beings is considered to consist both of the desire for pleasant results (for them) in

---

[7] *Gṛhipravrajitapakṣa* (LI, p. 176.5). Compare the *Pakṣapaṭala* of the *BBh* pp. 211–213.

[8] *BBh* p. 213 expands upon the superiority of the mendicant bodhisattva to the householder bodhisattva: he is without attachment to parents, children, wives and concubines, is free from the need to earn a livelihood, and is able to practice celibacy.

[9] *Adhyāśaya* (LI, p. 176.15). *Adhyāśaya* is defined in the *Adhyāśayapaṭala* of the *BBh* pp. 214–216 as "conviction" (*adhimokṣa*), "exact knowledge (*pratyavagama*) and certitude (*niścaya*) in the teachings of the Buddha (*buddhadharmeṣu*) preceded by faith (*śraddhā*) and analysis of realities (*dharmavicaya*)." Three types of *adhyāśaya* are distinguished: *vātsalya* (tenderness) which is sevenfold, *āśaya* (disposition) which is fifteenfold, and *kṛtya* (function) which comprises ten of the fifteen *āśaya*.

> future lives and of the (desire to get them) engaged in virtue just in this life, as well as of the desire for (their) Nirvāṇa; on all stages, it is (progressively) impure, pure, and extremely pure.

This briefly shows the fivefold messianic resolve. Messianic resolve for happiness is the desire for pleasant results (for beings) in future lives. Messianic resolve for benefit is the desire to engage (beings) in virtue in this life. It should be understood that the desire for (beings') Nirvāṇa is not another form, but just (the ultimate form of) these two messianic resolves.

(Then) the threefold messianic resolve, the impure and so on, should be understood as referring to (the resolves of) those who have not begun the stages, who have begun, and who have reached the stages of nonregression, respectively.

One verse analyzing the (bodhisattvas') adoption (of beings):[10]

> 7. The geniuses on all stages adopt (all beings) with their vow, with their equanimity, with their mastery, and with their spiritual leadership.

The bodhisattvas' adoption of beings is fourfold. They adopt (them) with a vow, as the spirit of enlightenment adopts all beings. They adopt (them) with equanimity of mind, because at the time of realization they experience the sameness of self and others. They adopt (them) with the mastery of an experienced master, by becoming their teacher. And they adopt them by forming a society, as they bring together a group of disciples.

A verse on the analysis of birth:[11]

> 8. For the geniuses, birth is considered to occur by the power of evolution, by the power of a vow, by the power of meditative concentration, and by the power of lordliness.

The birth of bodhisattvas is fourfold. For those in the stage of action in faith who are born in the happy realms, it is by the power of evolution. For those who have entered the stages who are born in the lower realms such as those of animals, it

---

[10] *Parigraha* (LI, p. 176.22). Compare the *Parigrahapaṭala* of the *BBh* pp. 249–252 which treats six types of assistance.

[11] *Upapatti* (LI, p. 177.2). Compare the *Upapattipaṭala* of the *BBh* pp. 247–248.

is by the power of their vow to develop beings. For those who are born in the desire realm after leaving the contemplation (realms), it is by the power of meditative concentration. Those (who are) emanations manifest birth in places such as Tuṣita heaven by the power of their lordliness.

A summary[12] of the stations and the stages:[13]

> 9.[14] From criterion, person, training, life-system, achievement, sign, etymology, and attainment, station and stage (are to be known) as such.

Five verses on the analysis of the criteria (of the stations and so on):

> 10.[15] Supreme voidness of self; firm persistence in effective action; (willing) rebirth in the desire realm after having dwelt in the fine bliss of contemplations;
>
> 11. then, dedication of the accessories of enlightenment to cyclic life; and the development of beings, without mental addiction;
>
> 12. preserving the passions during voluntary rebirth; combining the totally signless path with the path of the unique vehicle;
>
> 13. the signless, spontaneous purification of the (buddha) field; and then the achievement of the evolution of beings;
>
> 14. and the purification of meditative concentrations, retentions, and the perfection of enlightenment. By these descriptions, the defining criteria of the stages should be recognized.

There are eleven stations and eleven stages.[16] They have (specific) criteria. The defining criterion (of attainment) on the first stage is the realization of supreme

---

[12] Following the Tibetan (D 251a6) *sdom gyi tshigs su bcad pa.*

[13] For a survey of this complex subject see Dayal pp. 270–291 (*Bhūmis*).

[14] The Chinese omits.

[15] In the Chinese (T.31.657b15) vs. 10–14 are summarized in a single verse.

voidness, because (the bodhisattva) realizes the selflessness of subjects and objects. On the second, the criterion is the persistence (in action) without neglect of evolution because she knows the paths of virtuous and nonvirtuous actions and their results. On the third, it is that, having dwelt in the intensely blissful bodhisattva contemplations, she takes birth in the desire realm without any loss of those (contemplations). On the fourth, it is that, even having long dwelt in the enlightenment accessories, she dedicates those accessories to the life-cycle.

On the fifth, the defining criterion is that, having long dwelt in the four noble truths, he can create various arts and sciences in order to develop beings without addicting his own mind. On the sixth, it is that, having long dwelt in dependent origination, he can take voluntary rebirth while preserving the passions. On the seventh, it is that, (he can achieve) the path of exclusive predetermination for signlessness, combining it with the eighth station which is the arrival on the path of the single procedure where all (practices) are totally merged together.

On the eighth, the defining criterion is that, because she stands in the signless without volitional effort, (she can) effortlessly dwell in signlessness and purify the buddhaverse. On the ninth, it is that, by the power of intuition, the evolution of beings is achieved because she is able to develop beings of all forms. On the

---

[16] These are the ten bodhisattva stages plus the buddha stage; see *Saṁdhinir* VIII.35, IX.1; *Laṅkāvatārasūtra* (ed. Suzuki), p. 87.20–25. *MVy* 102 calls the buddha stage the *samantaprabhābuddhabhūmi* (buddha stage of universal light.) The characteristics applied here to the *bhūmi*s resemble those of stations (*vihāra*) 3–13 in the *Vihārapaṭala* of the *BBh* pp. 217–244. The correspondance between the *vihāra*s of the *BBh* and the *bhūmi*s of the *MSABh* is as follows:

VIHĀRA	*BHŪMI*
1. *gotra*	
2. *adhimukticaryā*	
3. *pramuditā*	1. *pramuditā*
4. *adhiśīla*	2. *vimalā*
5. *adhicitta*	3. *prabhākarī*
6. *adhiprajñā* (*bodhipakṣya-pratisaṁyukta*)	4. *arciṣmatī*
7. *adhiprajñā* (*satyaprati-*)	5. *sudurjayā*
8. *adhiprajñā* (*pratītyasamut-pādaprati-*)	6. *abhimukhī*
9. *sabhoganirnimitta*	7. *dūraṁgama*
10. *anābhoganirnimitta*	8. *acalā*
11. *pratisaṁvid*	9. *sādhumatī*
12. *parama*	10. *dharmameghā*
13. *tathāgata*	11. *buddhabhūmi*

tenth, (it is that she can) purify the door of the meditative concentrations and the door of the retentions. On the eleventh, the buddha stage, the defining criterion is that, due to the elimination of every type of objective obscuration, (she can) perfect her enlightenment.

Two verses on the analysis of the person on the stages:[17]

> 15. The bodhisattva (on each stage) has, (respectively): the pure view, extremely pure ethics, equanimity, freedom from Dharma pride, freedom from pride about a distinctive spiritual process, (freedom from pride) about addiction and purification, and instantaneous understanding;
>
> 16. (he has) equanimity, purification of the buddha land, skill in developing beings, great power, physical perfection, skill in manifestation, and true consecration.

Ten (kinds of) bodhisattvas are described as being on the ten stages. On the first, (the bodhisattva) has the pure view, having obtained the intuitive wisdom which remedies (false) convictions concerning subjects and objects. On the second, his ethics are very pure, as his behavior does not transgress into even the slightest sin. On the third, he has equanimity, having obtained unwavering contemplation and concentration. On the fourth, he is free of Dharma pride, having eliminated pride about (mastery of) the variety of the teachings of the scriptures, and so forth. On the fifth, he is free of pride in his spiritual process, having arrived at the equality of all processes through the ten equalities of mind and aspiration.[18]

On the sixth, due to natural purity, she is free of pride from differentiating addiction and purification, since, by long stability in the suchness of dependent origination, she no longer perceives addiction and purification in the suchness of good and evil.

On the seventh, by the power of stability in signlessness, since she practices the thirty-seven accessories of enlightenment in a single instant, she attains the instantaneous understanding. On the eighth, since she stands in signlessness sponta-

---

[17] Compare with *BBh* pp. 222–242 on the aspects (*ākāra*), marks (*liṅga*), and signs (*nimitta*) of the bodhisattvas on the various stations.

[18] For the ten pure equalities of aspiration (*cittāśayaviśuddhisamatā*, LI, p. 178.16) see *DBhS* p. 27.4–8.

neously and her practice is inextricably merged with bodhisattvas on the stage of nonregression, she has equanimity and purification of the buddhaverse. On the ninth, she is skillful in developing beings, as above.

On the tenth bodhisattva stage, having attained great psychic powers, a bodhisattva is established as having great power. Having become saturated with boundless doors of concentration and retention, he is described as physically perfect. Having manifested the emanations of standing in the Tuṣita heaven and so forth, he is described as skilled in physical manifestation. And, having there obtained consecration from all the buddhas, he is described as consecrated in buddhahood.

Five verses on the system of education:

> 17. Having realized the nature of reality in this life, (the bodhisattva) continues to educate herself in supreme morality, supreme mind, and supreme wisdom; but wisdom has a double domain.
>
> 18. The thatness of things, and the functions which proceed from the misknowledge and knowledge of that, constitute the domain of wisdom, thus classified as on two stages.
>
> 19. There are also four other results of the educations and their meditations. The first result is the station of signlessness with volitional effort.
>
> 20. The same station without volitional effort, involving the purification of the (buddha) land, is accepted as the second result.
>
> 21. The actual achievement of the evolutionary maturity of beings, and the achievement of concentrations and retentions, constitute the supreme results. These four types of results are manifested on the four stages.

Having understood reality on the first stage, (the bodhisattva) is educated in supreme morality on the second; on the third, in supreme mind; on the fourth, fifth, and sixth, in supreme wisdom.

On the fourth stage, wisdom is included among the accessories of enlightenment. Again, on the (next) two stages, (wisdom) has two domains, one being the reality of things such as the truths of suffering and so on, and one being the forward and reverse processes of dependent origination which derive from realizing and not realizing that (reality, respectively). The process which emerges from such ignorance is misknowledge and so forth (the twelve links in forward order), and the process which comes from such realization is the intuitive knowledge (of wisdom). Therefore supreme wisdom is divided into two stages.

Following them, one should recognize the four results of the educations, based on the four stages, respectively. The first result is the station of signlessness and volitional effort. The second result is the station of signlessness without volitional effort, and of the total purification of the (buddha) land.[19] The meaning of the rest is self-evident.

Two verses on the system of (pure) systems:

> 22. Having gained insight into reality here, the system of morality becomes purified, and after that the systems of meditative concentration and wisdom are purified as well.
>
> 23. In the other (stage)s, liberation and the intuition of liberation are purified, free from the fourfold hindrance[20] and the obstruction of impenetrability.

On the other (stage)s from the seventh up to the buddha stage, there is purification of both liberation and intuition of liberation. Liberation (on these stages) is to be understood (as liberation) from the hindrance of the fourfold result. On the buddha stage, (it should be understood as liberation) from the obstruction of impenetrability, since, while the intuitions of others are obstructed by objects, the buddhas, because they are liberated from that, have an intuition which finds no obstruction anywhere. The meaning of the rest is self-evident.

Three verses on the system of achievement:

> 24. All the stages are to be known as unachieved and achieved; although achieved, they are unachieved and also achieved.

---

[19] According to Sthiramati (D Tsi 244a6 *ff.*; P Tsi 294a4–5) the third result (on the ninth stage) is the maturation of living beings through the four intellectual knowledges, and the fourth result (on the tenth stage) is immeasurable meditation and retention.

[20] The Chinese (T.31.658a13) has: "is free from the five hindrances."

> 25. Achievement should be understood through a systematically trained attitude, through knowing it as construction, and through its nondiscrimination.
>
> 26. Meditative practice and achievement are inconceivable on all stages because they are individually intuited and because they are the object of the buddhas.

In this context the stage of action in faith is unachieved, and the others are achieved. This is for all stages. Among those achieved, seven are also not achieved; the others are achieved because their process is effortless.

The stage of the joyous has been previously explained as achieved, which achievement involves a mental process systematically trained for the stage. Therefore, (this stage) can be understood (as "achieved") when (the bodhisattva) knows that the stage system is a mere construction, and (as "unachieved") when he does not discriminate any (stage system). When the stage system is understood as mere construction and he no longer makes conceptual discriminations about that mere construction, then, as he has attained the wisdom of the nondiscrimination of subject and object, it is said that the stage is fully achieved.

In addition, both the meditative practice and the achievement of the stages are inconceivable on all stages, since they are to be individually intuited by the bodhisattvas and are the object of the buddhas and of no one else.

Two verses analyzing the signs of those on the stages:

> 27. Faith with clarity is everywhere accepted as a sign (of a bodhisattva on the stages); (additional signs are) non-discouragement, irrepressibility, independence of others,
>
> 28. universal realization, universal equality of mind, unexcitability, detachment, knowledge of liberative art, and birth in the (buddha) circle.[21]

The signs of a bodhisattva who has entered the stages are to be known as tenfold on all stages. She has clarity about that stage where she has entered and she has faith about that (stage) where she has not entered. That is one sign. (She is) not

---

[21] The Chinese (T.31.658b14) adds: "Thus these ten signs are fulfilled on each stage."

discouraged about teachings which are supremely profound and magnificent, not cowardly in ordeals, and not dependent on others on the same stages for realization. She has realized all stages because she is skillful in achieving them. (She is) equal-minded toward herself and all beings, unexcited by praise or blame, and without attachment even to the excellences of such as universal monarchs. (She is) skilled in liberative art because, having attained ultimate nonperception, she knows the liberative art of buddhahood. When born, she is always born in the circles of the buddhas. These are the other signs of the bodhisattvas on the stages.

Two verses on the analysis of the signs of having achieved the transcendences while on the stages:

> 29. Not without will-power, with heart free of greed and fickleness, free of anger and laziness, free of unloving and callous thoughts, the intellect undisturbed by negative notions and discriminations,[22] the mind free from distraction, not overcome by happiness, not daunted by suffering, relying on the spiritual friend, (the bodhisattva) seeks learning, and strives to honor the teacher.
>
> 30. Knowing supreme liberative art, having put together an enormous store of merit, he shares it with all, and dedicates every day to perfect enlightenment. Such a buddha-child is born in excellent realms, always does good, enjoys the excellences of the psychic powers, excels all others, and is a treasury of good qualities.

This shows the sixteen signs of the bodhisattva who has achieved the ten transcendences. These sixteen signs are (the following): He never lacks the will to attain the transcendences. He is always free of the resistance to each of the six transcendences.

(Then, there are) the signs of (the attainment of) the transcendence of skill in liberative art:[23] He is not distracted by concern for other vehicles. He is not attracted even to consummate happiness. He does not give up a course of action

---

[22] Tibetan (D Tsi 254a5) *blo gros rnam rtog ngan rtog 'phrogs pa med* translates a Sanskrit something like *na matiḥ kukalpairvikalpairhataḥ*, instead of Lévi's *na kumatiḥ kalpairvikalpairhataḥ* (LI, p. 180.23). This Tibetan slight change in the Sanskrit verse is not reflected in either the Tibetan or Sanskrit version of the commentary.

[23] This phrase is not in the Sanskrit. See the Tibetan (D Tsi 254b1).

just because he suffers hardships and failures. He relies on spiritual friends and earnestly seeks learning. He puts priority on worship of the teacher. He dedicates all virtues to unexcelled enlightenment.

(Then) through the transcendence of vows, he is born in excellent places, for he is born in the realms which lack neither buddhas nor bodhisattvas. Through the transcendence of power, he always acts virtuously, because he is not contaminated by any resistant tendencies. And through the transcendence of intuitive wisdom, he plays with the excellences of the psychic powers. Here, love, the remedy for malice, is the ambition to bring happiness (to others). Compassion, the remedy for violence, is the ambition to eradicate (their) suffering. Mental construction is the construction of an intrinsic nature. Discrimination is to be understood as the construction of distinctions.

A verse on the analysis of the benefits (of attaining the transcendences):

> 31.[24] For the geniuses, the benefits throughout the stages are considered fivefold in relation both to serenity and insight.

When the transcendences have been achieved, the bodhisattvas have all kinds of benefits which should be understood to be fivefold on all stages. At every moment, she causes the foundation of all negative conditionings to be destroyed. She enjoys the pleasure of the Dharma, free from notions of plurality. She recognizes the light of the Dharma which is everywhere indivisible as well as immeasurable. Without being conceptualized, the signs of purification present themselves to her. In order to perfect the fulfillment of the truth-body, she creates an assemblage of causes which always increases from ultimate to more ultimate.

The first two (of these benefits) are to be understood as relating to serenity, the third and fourth to transcendent insight, and the last to both.

Nine verses on the analysis of the etymology of the stages:[25]

> 32. Seeing the approach of enlightenment and the accomplishment of the aims of beings, intense joy arises (in the bodhisattva); thus, (the first stage) is called "joyous."[26]

---

[24] The Chinese (T.31.658c21) has: "Advancing higher on each stage, each transcendence has five benefits; two and two and one should be understood (as applying to) serenity, transcendent insight, and both together."

[25] On the etymology of the *bhūmis* see *Saṁdhinir* IX.4 and *Siddhi* pp. 613–619.

Here there is nothing to be explained.

> 33ab. Because it is free from the stains of immorality and (misdirected) effort, (the second stage) is called the "stainless."[27]

Because it is free from the stain of immorality and beyond the stain of concern for other vehicles it is called the "stainless." As it is said:[28] "Thus I must apply myself to realize equality, to realize purification in all its aspects."

> 33cd. Because it produces the great light of Dharma, (the third stage) is called the "illuminating."

On this stage, by persisting in the examination of the immeasurable Dharma by the power of meditative concentration, (the bodhisattva) creates a great light of the Dharma for others.[29]

> 34. The accessories of enlightenment are like the light of a blazing fire; such a (fourth) stage, which burns up both (obscurations), is called the "radiating."

Wisdom, by nature the accessories of enlightenment, comes close to burning up almost all two (obscurations). Here the two are known as the addictive and objective obscurations.[30]

---

[26] According to *MS* 35a3 the first stage is called the joyous "because for the first time the ability is acquired to achieve the aims of self and other."

[27] Chinese (T.31.659a5).

[28] The Chinese (T.31.659a21) has: "according to the *DBhS*"; see *DBhS* p. 16.30.

[29] According to *MS* 3524: "As it is the basis (*gnas*) of incorruptible (*nyams pa med pa* = *acyuta*) meditative concentration and absorption, it is the support (*gnas su gyur pa*) of the great light of Dharma." *Madhyamakāvatāra* p. 39 (Louis de La Vallée Poussin ed.) explains the name of this stage as follows: "This stage is called the illuminating because at that time there appears the peaceful light (*zhi ba'i bdag nid can gyi 'od*) of the fire of intuition which entirely consumes the fuel of knowable objects (*shes bya*)."

[30] *Madhyamakāvatāra* p. 53 explains: "Then, the light which is born from the extreme cultivation (*lhag bsgoms pa*) of the accessories of enlightenment which have been perfected (*rdzogs pa*) in the child of the Tathāgata exceeds that of the light of copper (*zangs*)."

35. The development of other beings and the protection of their own mind are conquered with difficulty by the geniuses; thus (this fifth stage) is called "hard-to-conquer."

There, although (the bodhisattva) is engaged in the development of beings, he is not defiled by their perverseness. Both (tasks) being hard to accomplish, it is the hard to conquer.[31]

36. Because here reliance on the transcendence of wisdom confronts both the saṁsāric life-cycle and nirvāṇic freedom, this (sixth) stage is called "confrontation."

Relying on the transcendence of wisdom, one faces the (bondage of the) life-cycle and the freedom of Nirvāṇa, settling down neither in cyclic life nor in Nirvāṇa.[32]

37ab.[33] Because it is related to the unique path, (the seventh stage) is called the "far-going."

The unique path has been indicated previously.[34] Because it is linked to it, it "goes far," for it goes to the culmination of practice.

---

[31] *MS* 35a5–6: "It is difficult to achieve (*sgrub*) due to the mutual incompatability (*phan tshun mi mthun pa*) between knowledge of the truth (*bden pa*) and worldly knowledge (*'jig rten pa'i shes pa*)." *Madhyamakāvatāra* p. 57: "The bodhisattva who stands on the fifth bodhisattva stage cannot be conquered even by the heavenly Māras, not to speak of others such as those who follow Māra's orders, etc. (*bdud kyi bka gnyan la sogs pa*). Therefore the name of the stage is the 'difficult to conquer.'"

[32] *MS* 35a6: "It is the place of understanding relativity (*rten cing 'brel 'byung ba shes pa'i gnas*), as it realizes the arrival in transcendent wisdom (*shes rab kyi pha rol tu phyin pa la gnas pa mngon du byed pa'i phyir*)." *Madhyamakāvatāra* p. 61: "Because they understand that the nature of things (*chos nyid*) is like a reflection, because bodhisattvas on the sixth bodhisattva stage perceive (*dmigs pa*) the truth of the path, and because they confront (*mngon du phyogs pa*) the truth of perfect buddhahood (*rdzogs pa'i sangs rgyas kyi chos*), this stage is called 'confrontation.'"

[33] The Chinese (T.31.659a12) reads: "(Because it) is not shaken by ideas with signs (*xiang si*) (or) ideas without signs (*wu xiang si*), (it is called) the 'unshakeable stage.'"

[34] See XX.12.

> 37cd. Because it cannot be disturbed by the two types of conceptualization, (the eighth stage) is called the "immovable."

(It is called "immovable") because it is not disturbed by the two types of conceptualization, signifying volitional conceptualization and signless spontaneous conceptualization.

> 38ab. Because it has benevolent intellectual knowledge, this (ninth) stage is called "benevolent intelligence."

"Because of the benevolence of (its) intellectual knowledge" means "because of its priority" (in enabling the bodhisattva to exercise his benevolence).

> 38cd. (This tenth stage is called) "Dharma-raincloud," because it is like a raincloud in the sky of the Dharma, pervading both (concentrations and retentions).

"Because it is" (up to) "pervading both" means that, because the Dharma – permeating the foundational (consciousness), and attained by means of the doors of concentrations and retentions – is like a raincloud (pervading) the sky-like (Dharma-realm), it is called the "rain-cloud of Dharma."[35]

> 39. The bodhisattva stages are considered stations, because (bodhisattvas) always stand joyously on them for the sake of the various accomplishments of virtue.

The bodhisattva stages are called "stations," because (bodhisattvas) always stand joyously on them in order to accomplish all manner of good.

---

[35] This metaphor seems confused, the Tibetan and Sanskrit differ markedly, and there is no help from Sthiramati and dBal Mang. The Sanskrit would literally translate: "because of the pervasion by doors of contentration and retention, like by a cloud (there is pervasion) of the sky-like, foundational (consciousness) permeating, attained Dharma...." The Tibetan: "because of pervasion of the sky-like attained Dharma, existing in the foundational, by the door(s) of contentration and retention, like a cloud."

The solution comes from recognizing, somewhere in between the two versions, two "Dharmas," an "attained Dharma" (*śrutadharma*), which is like a cloud, and a "sky-like" (*ākāśasthālīya*) Dharma, which we are comparing to the Dharmadhātu.

40. They are considered "stages," because (bodhisattvas) strive to ascend higher and higher on those immeasurable (stages), in order that numberless beings may become free of fear.

The stations are also called "stages" because (bodhisattvas) strive to ascend higher and higher in those immeasurable (realms), in order that beings without number may become free of fear. The ten stages are called "immeasurable" because each of them is without measure. "Because they strive to ascend ever higher" means because they strive to reach a higher stage. "In order that numberless beings may become free of fear" means for the sake of eliminating the fear of numberless beings.

A verse on the analysis of the station of realization:

41.[36] The stages are attained in four ways: by faith, by engagement in practice, by penetrating realization, and by fulfillment.

The attainment of the stages is fourfold. Attainment by faith is by the faith already described as pertaining to the stage of action in faith. Attainment by practice is on that same (stage), by engaging in the ten Dharma practices.[37] Attainment by penetrating realization is (the bodhisattva's) realization of the ultimate at the time of entering the stages. And attainment by fulfillment occurs at the time of attaining the stage of nonregression.

A verse of six quarters on the analysis of practice:

42. The fourfold practice of the brave bodhisattvas has been taught according to the (universal vehicle) scriptures for the sake of beings who have faith in the individual vehicle and in the universal vehicle, to attract and to tame them both.

The practice of the transcendences was taught for the sake of those who have faith in the universal vehicle, and the practice of the accessories of enlightenment

---

[36] This verse is found in the fifth chapter of the *MS*.

[37] *Daśadharmacarita* (LI, p. 183.12). The Chinese (T.31.659c14) gives the same list as *MVy* 903–910: 1) transcribing (*lekhanā*), 2) worshipping (*pūjanā*), 3) circulating (*dānam*), 4) studying (*śravaṇam*), 5) reciting (*vācanam*), 6) memorizing (*udgrahaṇam*), 7) elucidating (*prakāśanā*), 8) rehearsing (*svādhyāyanam*), 9) contemplating (*cintanā*), and 10) meditating (*bhāvanā*) the scriptures of the universal vehicle. See *SN* VII.19, and *MAV* V 9cd–10ab.

was taught for those who have faith in the vehicle of the disciples and hermit buddhas. The practice of the superknowledges was taught for those who have faith in both the individual and universal vehicles, in order to attract them by their power. And the practice of developing beings was taught in order to develop both (kinds of persons). Here, "development" means "discipline."[38]

[38] The same fourfold practices form the subject of the *Caryāpaṭala* of the *BBh* pp. 256–258.

Chapter XXI

Epilogue – Culmination

There are a number of verses on the analysis of the qualities of a buddha. As a hymn to the Buddha, a verse on the analysis of the immeasurables:[1]

> 43.[2] O You who are love for beings,
> O will to (their) union with happiness,
> O will to (their) freedom (from suffering),
> O will to (their) nondeprivation (of joy),
> O will to help and happiness –
>
> Homage to You!

(The buddhas') love for beings is shown by their will to help and happiness. Again, the will to happiness is: love, which wants to unite (beings) with happiness; compassion, which wants to free them from suffering; joy, which wants (them) not to be deprived of happiness; and equanimity, which wills the benefit (equally of all). This (love) should be recognized as the mark of a will totally pure of addiction.

A verse on the analysis of liberation, sphere of sovereignty, and sphere of totality:[3]

> 44. Released from all obscurations, O Sage,
> You have sovereignty over all the world!
> Your wisdom pervades all knowables!
> Homage to You, whose mind is free!

---

[1] On the immeasurables see XVII.17–28.

[2] Vs. 43–61 are found in the tenth chapter of the *MS*.

[3] See VII.9.

The distinctive liberation of the Lord is shown through his freedom from the addictive and objective obscurations. His distinctive sphere of sovereignty (is shown) by his sovereignty over all the world, since, due to his sovereignty over his own mind, he has mental power over things, emanations, and transmutations. He has a distinctive sphere of totality, because there is no impediment to his intuition of all knowables. And since he is free from the resistances to the virtues of liberation, his mind is free.

A verse on the analysis of immunity:[4]

> 45. Compassionate to the impassionate!
> Total tamer[5] of all passions of all beings!
> Passion-conqueror!
> Homage to You!

Here, the distinctive immunity of the Lord is shown through his compassion for impassionate beings, because for all beings he tames the addictive passions (yet to arise), and activates the remedies of those addictive passions already arisen. Others who stand in immunity to passions eliminate merely some conditions for the arising of just certain passions experienced by some beings, but they do not cause the eradication of passions already arisen[6] within beings' mental processes.[7]

A verse on the distinctive intuitive wisdom of the (buddha) vow:[8]

> 46. Effortless and unattached,
> You are unobstructed!
> Ever balanced in concentration,
> You resolve all questions!
> Homage to You!

---

[4] *Araṇā* (LI, p. 184.14). For references see *La Somme* p. 53 and *VKN* pp. 154–155, n. 1 on the traditional interpretations of this term.

[5] The Tibetan *'dul* reads a Sanskrit *vināyaka* for Lévi's *vināśaka* (LI, p. 184.15).

[6] Reading with the Tibetan *skyes pa*.

[7] That is, only buddhas have fully purified the subconscious instincts for the passions, and hence can influence the instinctual propensities within other beings.

[8] *Praṇidhijñāna* (LI, p. 184.20). For references see *La Somme* p. 53.

Here the Lord's distinctive intuitive wisdom (arisen) from his vows is shown with five aspects. He has directly realized the spontaneous. He directly realizes non-attachment. He is without obstruction in knowing all things. Always in equanimous concentration, he resolves all beings' doubts.

Others who attain wisdom from a vow do not directly realize intuitively through their vow, as it lacks effortless spontaneity. They are not without attachment because they are dependent on concentration in equanimity. They are not without obstruction because their intuition is partial, and they are not always concentrated in equanimity and do not resolve all doubts.

A verse on the analysis of intellectual knowledge of teaching:[9]

> 47. Your intelligence is always unimpeded
> About the ground and the grounded,
> About spoken teaching and intuited teaching!
> O best of Teachers! Homage to You!

Here the Lord's four intellectual knowledges are shown in brief by constant unobstructedness about what is taught and the means of teaching. In this context two things are taught, the Dharma which is the ground and the meaning grounded upon it. It is taught in two ways, by speech and intuition. "Best of Teachers" indicates their activities.

A verse on the analysis of the superknowledges:[10]

> 48. Keeping track of beings (by teleportation),
> (Hearing) their words (by clairaudience),
> (Knowing their minds by telepathy),
> You know their past and future deeds
> And also their way out (of the life-cycle)!
> O best of Instructors! Homage to You!

Here the Lord's instruction is indicated (to be) authentic, with reference to the six superknowledges. Having followed the disciples with the superknowledge of teleportation, knowing their mental activity by the superknowledge of telepathy and their speech with the superknowledge of the divine ear, and, with the other

---

[9] *Pratisaṁvid* (LI, p. 185.4). See XVIII.35–38 (Ms. vs. 34–37).

[10] *Abhijñā* (LI, p. 185.10). See VII.1, its commentary, and its notes.

three superknowledges respectively,[11] knowing how they have come from the past down to the present, what is their future destiny, and how they will transcend the life-cycle, he gives the best instruction.

A verse on the analysis of the signs and marks:[12]

> 49. When all beings see You
> They recognize a Holy Being!
> You create faith from just a glimpse!
> Homage to You!

This shows that the mere glimpse of the Lord's body, with its auspicious signs and marks, creates great faith in others, due to their confidence in his Holy Being; such is their function.

A verse on the analysis of purification:[13]

> 50. O You who have gained mastery
> Of assuming, enduring, and abandoning (life-forms),
> Of emanating and transforming (objects),
> And of contemplative concentration and wisdom!
> Homage to You!

Here the four universal purifications are explained by the four masteries of the Lord: purification of the foundation (as explained) by his mastery in assuming, maintaining, and abandoning the body; purification of objects, by his mastery of incarnation and transmutation; purification of the mind, by his mastery of all aspects of contemplative concentration; and purification of wisdom, by his mastery of omniscience.

A verse on the analysis of the powers:[14]

---

[11] Lévi's Sanskrit puts this important phrase at the end of the paragraph; better order is picked up from the Tibetan (D Tsi 257b2).

[12] *Lakṣaṇānuvyañjana* (LI, p. 185.17). For a list of the thirty-two major and eighty minor marks of the great person (*mahāpuruṣa*), see *HTV* pp. 156–157. See also the *Lakṣaṇānuvyañjanapaṭala* of the *BBh* pp. 259–264.

[13] *Pariśuddhi* (LI, p. 185.21). Compare *BBh* p. 265.

[14] *Bala* (LI, p. 186.3). See *La Somme* p. 59 and *HTV* p. 154. They are treated in extensive detail in *BBh* pp. 265–277.

51. Who crushes the devils who deceive beings
About methods, refuges, purification,
And about transcendence in the universal vehicle!
Homage to You!

Here, the devils who deceive beings in four areas are crushed by the Lord. This shows the activity of the ten powers of the Lord. (One devil) deceives (beings) about the methods of going to a good rebirth and avoiding a bad rebirth and so on; about refuges, one deceives by (promoting) refuge in worldly gods and so forth; about purification, one deceives by (offering) a contaminated purification; and one deceives about transcendence in the universal vehicle.

In the first context, the buddha crushes the devil by the power of knowledge of proper and improper. In the second, he crushes the devil by the power of knowledge of the fruition of evolutionary actions. In the third context, he crushes the devil by the power of knowledge of contemplation, liberation, concentration and entrancement. And in the fourth, he crushes the devil by the power of his knowledge of superior and inferior faculties, because he eliminates the inferior faculties and so forth and puts (beings) in touch with (their) superior faculties.

A verse on the analysis of fearlessness:[15]

52. You who teach the wisdom and the abandonment,
And the transcendence and the prevention,
(Required) for both individualism and altruism,
Are never disturbed by religious fanatics!
Homage to You!

Here, the teaching of wisdom and abandonment is for the sake of the individual's own interest, and (the teaching) of transcendence and its prevention is for

---

[15] *BBh* pp. 277–278 explain the four conditions (*sthāna*) of a Tathāgata's fearlessness: 1) full understanding of all phenomena in all their aspects, which is not common to the disciples, through liberation from objective blocks (*śrāvakāsādhāraṇo jñeyāvaraṇavimokṣāt sarvākāra-sarvadharmābhisaṁbodhaṁ*); 2) liberation from the affective blocks, which is common to the disciples (*śrāvakasādhāraṇaśca kleśāvaraṇavimokṣaṁ*); 3) the liberational path to transcend the suffering of living beings who are desirous of liberation (*vimokṣakāmānāṁ ca sattvānāṁ duḥkhasamatikramāya nairyāṇiko mārgaṁ*); and 4) abandonment of the impeding factors which are hinderances toward attainment of that path (*tasyaiva ca mārgasya prāptivibandhabhūtā ye āntarāyikā dharmāṁ parivarjayitavyāṁ*). The teaching of these four constitute the *vaiśāradya* of a Tathāgata.

the sake of others' interest. Since rival religious teachers, the fanatics, do not disturb him, the fourfold fearlessness of the Lord is manifested in due order.

A verse on the analysis of invulnerability and the foci of mindfulness:

> 53. You teach open-handedly in the assemblies!
> You are free from the two defilements!
> You are invulnerable and not unmindful!
> You attract a retinue! Homage to You!

This clearly shows the Lord's three invulnerabilities[16] and three foci of mindfulness.[17] Their function is the attraction of a retinue. Concerning them, respectively, he speaks open-handedly in the assemblies, because he is not vulnerable; he is free from the two defilements, because he is free of indulgence and revulsion; he is always mindful, because he is without unmindfulness.

A verse on the analysis of the complete conquest of the instincts:

> 54. Moving or at rest, everywhere and always,
> You have no non-omniscient action!
> O Omniscient One, Your aim is reality!
> Homage to You!

While moving or at rest, always and everywhere, the Lord has no action which is not that of an omniscient being. This shows that he has conquered all the instincts for the addictions.[18] One who is not omniscient, although his addictions be destroyed, since he has not conquered their instincts, still performs actions which are not that of an omniscient being, such as encountering a mad elephant or a runaway chariot,[19] and so forth. As it says in the *Māṇḍavya Sūtra*: "Because of

[16] *Ārakṣa* (LI, p. 186.16). *DN* III.217 and *AN* IV.82 enumerate four *arakṣyāṇi*: purity of body, speech, mind, and livelihood. See *MVy* 191–195, *BBh* p. 278, and *La Somme* p. 59.

[17] According to *M Vy* 187–190 the three *smṛtyupasthāna* special to a Tathāgata are: 1) equality of thought towards those who wish to listen (*śuśrūṣamāṇeṣu samacittatā*); 2) equality of thought towards those who do not wish to listen (*aśuśrūṣamāṇeṣu*); and 3) equality of thought towards those who do and those who do not wish to listen (*śuśrūṣamāṇāśuśrūṣamāṇeṣu*). See *BBh* p. 278 and *Kośa* VII pp. 76–77.

[18] Compare *BBh* p. 279.

[19] This is an interesting remark in light of the well known story of Gautama's encounter with the mad elephant.

omniscience concerning reality, the Lord does not encounter any such (untoward events)."

A verse on the analysis of non-confusion:[20]

55. In accomplishing the aims of all beings
You do not waste time! Your work is never futile!
You are always unconfused!
Homage to You!

This shows that whatever aim there is to accomplish, for whatever being, at whatever time, the deeds of the Lord are always fruitful because he does not waste time. The characteristic of non-confusion is shown in its nature and activity.

A verse on the analysis of great compassion:[21]

56. You survey the whole world
Six times in a day and a night!
You are endowed with great compassion!
You have the good heart! Homage to You!

Here the great compassion of the Buddha is explained in its nature and activity. With great compassion the Lord surveys the world six times each day and night, seeing who is deteriorating and who is developing and so forth. Through such dedication, the Lord always wills the benefit of all beings.

A verse on the exclusive qualities:[22]

57. You surpass all disciples and hermit buddhas
In practice, realization, wisdom, and activity!
Homage to You!

---

[20] *Asaṁmoṣatā* (LI, p. 187.4). See *BBh* p. 279. It is the proper performance of whatever has to be done without loss of attention (*smṛtyasaṁpramoṣatā*).

[21] *Mahākaruṇā* (LI, p. 187.9). See XVII.43.

[22] According to the *Kośa* VII p. 66, the eighteen qualities exclusive to a Tathāgata are the ten powers, four fearlessnesses, three foundations of mindfulness, and great compassion. For a different list see *MVy* 787–804 translated in *HTV* p. 158. See also *Le Traité* pp. 1625–1628.

The Lord surpasses all beings because he surpasses the disciples and hermit buddhas who surpass all others; with six exclusive buddha qualities included in practice, six included in realization, three included in wisdom, and three included in activity. The Transcendent Lord makes no mistakes, he does not hurry, his mindfulness does not fail, his mind is not unconcentrated, he has no notions of plurality, and he indulges in no inconsiderate equanimity. These are the six exclusive buddha qualities included in practice, among buddhas but not among others.

He never suffers the loss of either will-power, energy, mindfulness, meditative concentration, wisdom, or liberation; these are the six included in realization. The Transcendent Lord's intuitive wisdom is not impeded or obstructed about anything in the past, present, and future; these are the three included in wisdom. All physical activities of the Tathāgata are preceded by wisdom and are accompanied by wisdom, and the same is true for all verbal and mental activities; these are the three included in activity.

A verse on the analysis of omniscience:[23]

58. You attained the universal great enlightenment
By means of the three bodies!
You resolved the doubts of all beings everywhere!
Homage to You!

This explains the Lord's omniscience, since universal enlightenment is realized with the three bodies by means of the omniscience about all knowable objects. The three bodies are the natural (truth) body, the beatific body, and the emanation body. The omniscience of all knowables is shown here as an activity which consists in resolving all the doubts of all beings such as gods and humans.

A verse on the analysis of the fulfillment of the transcendences:

59. You do not take,
You are free of faults,
Free of disturbance,
You do not stand,

---

[23] According to *BBh* p. 280–281 a Tathāgata has fully awakened (*abhisaṁbuddha*) to three topics: 1) with import (*arthopasaṁhitā*), 2) without import (*anartho-*), and 3) neither with nor without import (*naivārtho-*, *nānārtho-*). Knowledge (*jñāna*) of the first is called omniscience (*sarvākārajñāna*), of the second, best knowledge (*varajñāna*), and of the third, best omniscience (*sarvākāravarajñāna*).

Unagitated,
You fabricate nothing anywhere!
Homage to You!

The Lord in being free from all resistances to the six transcendences has fulfilled the six transcendences. It should be understood that he does not take, because he has no interest in wealth. He has no fault, as his physical activities and so forth are immaculate. He is undisturbed, as neither worldly concerns nor suffering disturb his mind. He does not stand, since he does not dwell in small or trifling understanding. He is not agitated, as he is not distracted. He makes no fabrications, because he does not engage in any discriminatory fabrication.

Two verses on the analysis of the character of the Buddha:

60. You have achieved the ultimate!
You have transcended all the stages!
You have become the chief of all beings!
You are the liberator of all beings!

61. Endowed with endless, peerless excellences,
You manifest to the worlds and also in Your circles!
Yet You are totally out of sight of gods and humans!

The buddha character is explained here under six headings: nature, cause, result, activity, endowment, and function.

The ultimate achieved is pure suchness, which is the natural reality body[24] of the buddhas. The transcending through all the bodhisattva stages is the cause. The achievement of supremacy over all beings is the result. The liberation of all beings is the activity. Possession of endless, peerless excellences is the endowment. He is seen in the various world systems by means of the emanation body, and in the circles of (heavenly) assemblies by means of the beatific body. Yet he is entirely beyond being seen in his body of truth. Thus his function has this threefold distinction.

(A final verse (from the verse translation):[25]

---

[24] Following the Tibetan (D Tsi 260a3).

[25] Tibetan (D Phi 38b7–39a1): */ de lta na yang de yi mthus / / gdul bya'i skal ba ji bzhin du / / srid pa ji ltar gnas kyi bar / / de yi mdzad pa rgyun mi chad /.*

62. Nevertheless, by the power of those (bodies,)
According to the destiny of the disciples,
As long as the world exists,
Your activity is uninterrupted!)[26]

Among the (chapters of the) *Mahāyānasūtrālaṁkāra*, taught by the great Bodhisattva Vyavadātasamaya,[27] this (concludes) the twenty first chapter, "Practice and Culmination."

The *Mahāyānasūtrālaṁkāra*(*vyākhyā*)[28] is concluded.[29]

---

[26] The colophon of the Tibetan verse version continues: "This is the twenty first chapter of the *MSA*, "Practice and Culmination." This completes the *MSA Verses*, writted by the Holy Maitreya. It was translated, copied, and edited by the Indian master Śākyasiṁha and the Zhu Chen gyi Lo Tsva Ba Ban De dPal brTsegs and company. Later, it was slightly corrected and edited after critical elucidation by the Paṇḍit Parahita, the Great Brāhmin Sadjana, and the Translator Bhikṣu bLo lDan Shes Rab. This final verse was written to increase the benefit to beings and to accord with the tradition of other treatises. */ / Maṅgalaṁ / / / / Ye dharma hetu-prabhāvā hetūn teshān tathāgato hyavadāt / teshāñca yo nirodha evam badi mahāśramanaḥ / /*"

[27] Ui (p. 623) conjectures that the *Mahāyānasūtrālaṁkāreṣu* of the colophon is incorrect in light of the *Mahāyānasūtrālaṁkāre* which appears at the conclusion of every chapter, and that the *ṣu* is actually a mistake for *su* which belongs to the following *vyavdātasamaya-*. However, notwithstanding what might appear as an aberrant locative plural, the form *vyavadātasamaya* is attested to by both the Tibetan and Chinese.

[28] Following the Tibetan.

[29] The Tibetan colophon of the commentary (D Tsi 260a6–7) continues: "…translated, copied, and edited by the Indian master Śākyasiṁha and the Zhu Chen gyi Lo Tsva Ba Ban De dPal brTsegs and company. The measure of this commentary on the *Ornament of the Scriptures of the Universal Vehicle* is known as 3650 *ślokas*."

Abbreviations

AA	*Abhisamayālaṁkāra*. Maitreyanātha/Āryāsaṅga. In *AAA*. See *AAA*.
AAA	*Abhisamayālaṁkārāloka* of Haribhadra. In *Aṣṭasāhasrikāprajñāpāramitā*, P. L. Vaidya, ed., Darbhanga, Mithila Institute, 1960.
AAV	*Abhisamayālaṁkāravṛtti of Ārya Vimuktisena*. Corrado Pensa, ed., ISMEO, Roma, 1967.
AMN	**Akṣayamatinirdeśasūtra*. Peking 843.
AN	*Aṅguttaranikāya*. 5 vols., Pali Text Society, 1885–1900.
AS	*Abhidharmasamuccaya of Asaṅga*. Pralhad Pradhan, ed., Viśva-Bharati, Santiniketan, 1950.
Asvabhāva	**Mahāyānasūtrālaṁkāraṭīkā* by Asvabhāva. Peking 5530.
BBh	*Bodhisattvabhūmi* ascribed to Asaṅga. Nalinaksha Dutt, ed., K.P. Jayaswal Research Institute, Patna, 1966.
BBS	**The Buddhabhūmi-Sūtra and the Buddhabhūmi-Vyākhyāna of Śīlabhadra*. 2 vols., Kyō Nishio, Nagoya, 1940.
BCA	*Bodhicaryāvatāra* of Śāntideva. P. L. Vaidya, ed., Darbhanga, Mithila Institute, 1960.
Chin.	Chinese
Dayal	Dayal, Har. *The Bodhisattva Doctrine in Buddhist Sanskrit Literature*. Motilal Banarsidass, Delhi, 1970.
DBhS	*Daśabhūmikasūtra*. P. L. Vaidya, ed., Darbhanga, Mithila Institute, 1967.
dbYangs-can	dbYangs-can dGa-ba'i bLo-gros. *Theg pa chen po mdo sde'i rgyan gyi gzhung 'grel kun bzang mchod sprin zhes bya ba*. Losaling Press, 1965.
DDV	*Dharmadharmatāvibhaṅga*. Maitreyanātha/Āryāsaṅga. Peking 5523.

DN	*Dīghanikāya*. 3 vols., Pali Text Society, 1890–1911.
Edgerton	Edgerton, Franklin. *Buddhist Hybrid Sanskrit Dictionary*. Motilal Banarsidass, Delhi, 1972.
Histoire	Lamotte, Étienne. *Histoire du Bouddhisme Indien*. Louvain, 1967.
HTV	*The Holy Teaching of Vimalakīrti*. Robert A. F. Thurman, tr., Pennsylvania State University Press, University Park, 1976.
Kārikā(s)	*Mahāyānasūtrālaṁkārakārikā*. Maitreyanātha/Āryāsaṅga. Peking 5521.
Kośa	*L'Abhidharmakośa de Vasubandhu*. Louis de la Vallée Poussin, tr.; 6 vols., Paris, 1923–1931.
La Somme	*La Somme du Grand Véhicule*. (*Mahāyānasaṁgraha* by Asaṅga; see *MS*). Translated by Étienne Lamotte, Louvain, 1938.
Le Traité	**Mahāprajñāpāramitāśāstra*. Nāgārjuna. Translated by Lamotte as *Le Traité de la Grande Vertu de Sagesse de Nāgārjuna*, 5 vols., Louvain, 1944–1980.
LI	Lévi, *MSA* vol. I. See *MSA*. Also referred to as "Ms." ("manuscript").
LII	Lévi, *MSA* vol. II. See *MSA*.
MAV	*Madhyāntavibhāgaśāstra* of Asaṅga. R. C. Pandeya, ed., Motilal Banarsidass, Delhi, 1971. Edition of the Sanskrit, usefully printed together with the *MAVBh* and *MAVT* (*ṭīkā*).
MAVBh	*Madhyāntavibhāgabhāṣya* by Vasubandhu. See *MAV*.
MN	*Majjhimanikāya*. 3 vols., Pali Text Society, 1887–1902.
MS	*Mahāyānasaṁgraha* by Asaṅga. Peking 5549. Translated by Lamotte as *La Somme du Grand Véhicule*. See *La Somme*.
Ms.	Lévi's Sanskrit manuscript of the *MSA*. See LI.
MSA	*Mahāyānasūtrālaṁkāra*. Maitreyanātha/Āryāsaṅga, with *Bhāṣya* by Vasubandhu. Ed. and trans. by S. Lévi, Paris, 1907, 1911. See also LI and LII.

MSABh	*Sūtrālaṁkārabhāṣya*. Vasubandhu. Peking 5527.
MVy	*Mahāvyutpatti*. R. Sakaki, ed., Tokyo, 1962.
Nagao	Nagao, G. M. *An Index to the Mahāyānasūtrālaṁkāra*. Parts I, II, 1958–1961.
Prasannapadā	*Prasannapadāmūlamadhyamakavṛtti* by Candrakīrti. P. L. Vaidya, ed., Buddhist Sanskrit Texts, vol. 10. Darbhanga, 1960.
PTSD	*The Pali Text Society's Pali-English Dictionary*. T. W. Rhys Davids, William Stede, eds., London, 1972.
RGV	*Ratnagotravibhāga Mahāyānottaratantraśāstra*. Maitreyanātha/Āryāsaṅga. E. H. Johnston, ed., Bihar Research Society, Patna, 1950.
Ruegg	Ruegg, David Seyfort. *La Théorie du Tathāgatagarbha et du Gotra. Études sur la Sotériologie et la Gnoséologie du Bouddhisme*. Paris: Adrien-Maisonneuve, 1969.
s.v.	*sub verbo*, *sub voce*, under the word
Saṁdhinir	**Saṁdhinirmocanasūtra*. Tibetan text ed. and tr. by Étienne Lamotte, Louvain, 1935.
ŚBh	*Śrāvakabhūmi*. Asaṅga. Karunesha Shukla, ed., K. P. Jayaswal Research Institute, Patna, 1973.
Siddhi	*Vijñaptimātratāsiddhi: La Siddhi de Hiuan-Tsang*. Louis de la Vallée Poussin, tr., Paris, 1928–1929.
Skt.	Sanskrit
SN	*Saṁyuttanikāya*. 5 vols. Pali Text Society, 1884–1898.
Sthiramati	*Sūtrālaṁkāravṛttibhāṣya*. Sthiramati. Peking 5531.
T	*Da-cheng zhuang-yan jing-lun*. Taisho 1604.
Tib.	Tibetan
TOSN	**Tathāgatotpattisaṁbhavanirdeśa*. Chapter 43 of the *Avataṁsaka-sūtra*. Peking 761.
Ui	*Daijō Sōgenkyōron Kenkyū*. Japanese translation of *MSA* by Hakuju Ui, Tokyo, 1961.

VKN	*L'Enseignement de Vimalakīrti*. Étienne Lamotte, tr., Louvain, 1962.
VS	*Viniścayasaṁgrahaṇī*. Asaṅga. Peking 5539.
vs.	verse(s)
YBh	*Yogācārabhūmi*. Asaṅga. Peking 5536. Partial Skt. edition (part I) ed. by Vidushekhara Bhattacharya, University of Calcutta, 1957.

Bibliography

Anacker, S. *Seven Works of Vasubandhu: The Buddhist Psychological Doctor.* Delhi: Motilal Banarsidass, 1984.

Batchelor, S. *A Guide to the Bodhisattva's Way of Life [by Shāntideva].* Dharamsala: Library of Tibetan Works and Archives, 1979.

Berzin, A. "Lam Rim Man Ngag: A Standard Intermediate Level Textbook of the Graded Course to Enlightenment: Selected Materials from the Indo-Tibetan 'Mahayana' Buddhist Textual and Oral Traditions." Ph.D. dissertation, Harvard University, 1972.

Bhattacharya, V. *The Catuḥśataka of Āryadeva.* Calcutta: Visvabharati Books, 1931.

Bhattacharya, K. *The Dialectical Method of Nāgārjuna (Vigrahavyāvartanī).* Delhi: Motilal Banarsidass, 1978.

Chang, G.C.C. *The Buddhist Teaching of Totality: The Philosophy of Hwa Yen Buddhism.* University Park: Pennsylvania State University Press, 1971.

———. *The 100,000 Songs of Milarepa.* Boulder: Shambala, 1977.

Chattopadhyaya, A. *Atiśa and Tibet.* Calcutta: R.D. Press, 1967.

Chattopadhyaya, A., and L. Chimpa. *Tārānātha's History of Buddhism in India.* Simla: Indian Institute of Advanced Study, 1970.

Cleary, J.C., and T. Cleary. *The Blue Cliff Record.* Boulder: Shambala, 1977.

Conze, E. *Abhisamayālaṁkāra.* Serie Orientale Roma VI. Rome: Istituto Italiano per il Medio ed Estremo Oriente, 1954.

———. *The Large Sūtra on Perfect Wisdom.* Berkeley and Los Angeles: University of California Press, 1975.

———. *The Perfection of Wisdom in 8,000 Lines and Its Verse Summary.* San Francisco: Four Seasons, 1973.

Dalai Lama, H.H. *The Buddhism of Tibet and the Key to the Middle Way.* London: Allen & Unwin, 1974.

Dasgupta, S.B. *An Introduction to Tantric Buddhism.* Calcutta: University of Calcutta, 1950.

de Jong, Jan W. *Cinq Chapitres de la Prasannapadā.* Paris: Geuthner, 1949.

Dhargyay, G.N. *Tibetan Tradition of Mental Development.* Dharamsala: Tibetan Library, 1978.

Dutt, N. *Bodhisattvabhūmi.* Patna: K.P. Jayaswal, 1966.

Eckel, D.M. "A Question of Nihilism: Bhāvaviveka's Response to the Fundamental Problems of Mādhyamika Philosophy." Ph.D. dissertation, Harvard University, 1980.

Fa Tsun. *Leau Yi Bu Leau Yi Fen Bye* (Chinese translation of *Essence of True Eloquence*). Microfilm copy made available by Dr. R.S.Y. Chi, Indiana University, Bloomington.

Gokhale, V. "Fragments from the Abhidharmasamuccaya of Asaṅga." *Journal of the Royal Asiatic Society* (Bombay) 23 (1947): 13–48.

Griffiths, P.J. "Painting Space with Colors: Tathāgatagarbha in the Mahāyāna-sūtrâlaṅkāra-Corpus IX.22–37." In *Buddha Nature: A Festschrift in Honor of Minoru Kiyota*, ed. by Paul J. Griffiths and John P. Keenan. Tokyo: Eikyoji Institute of America, 1990.

Hattori, M. *Dignāga on Perfection.* Harvard Oriental Series. Cambridge: Harvard University Press, 1971.

Hopkins, P.J. "Meditation on Emptiness." Ph.D. dissertation, University of Wisconsin (Madison), 1973.

Hopkins, P.J., Kensur Lekden, and Tsong-ka-pa. *Compassion in Tibetan Buddhism.* Valois, N.Y.: Snow Lion, 1981.

Hsuan Tsang. *Vijñaptimātratāsiddhi: La Siddhi de Hsuan Tsang.* Trans. by Louis de la Vallée Poussin. 3 vols. Paris: Geuthner, 1928–1948.

Hurvitz, L. *Chih I.* Brussels: Institut Belges des Hautes Etudes Chinoises, 1962.

Iida, S. *An Introduction to Svātantrika-Mādhyamika.* Ph.D. dissertation, University of Wisconsin (Madison), 1968.

Inada, K. *Mūlamadhyamakakārikās of Nāgārjuna.* Tokyo: Hokuseido, 1970.

Ingalls, D.H.H. *Materials for the Study of Nāvya-Nyāya Logic.* Harvard Oriental Series. Cambridge: Harvard University Press, 1951.

Jamspal, V.L., Samten Chopel, and P. Della Santina. *Nāgārjuna's Letter to King Gautamīputra.* Delhi: Motilal Banarsidass, 1978.

Jayatilleke, J.N. *Early Buddhist Theory of Knowledge.* London: G. Allen & Unwin, 1963.

Jha, G. *Tattvasaṁgraha with Pañjikā.* 2 vols. Baroda: Gaekwad, 1937.

Johnston, E.H. *Ratnagotravibhāga-Mahāyānottaratantraśāstra.* Patna: Jayaswal Institute, 1950.

Kaschewsky, R. *Das Leben des Lamaistischen Heiligen Tsongkhapa Blo-Bzaṅ-Grags-pa (1357–1419).* Wiesbaden: Otto Harrassowitz, 1971.

Kato, B. *The Threefold Lotus Sutra.* Tokyo: Weatherhill, 1975.

Komito, D. "Nāgārjuna's Śūnyatāsaptatī." Ph.D. dissertation, University of Indiana, 1980.

Lamotte, E. *Explication des Mysteres.* Louvain and Paris: Maisonneuve, 1935.

———. *L'Enseignement de Vimalakīrti.* Louvain: Muséon, 1962.

———. *La Somme du Grand Véhicule.* 2 vols. Louvain: Muséon, 1938–1939.

———. *Le Traité de la Grande Vertu de Sagesse de Nāgārjuna.* 5 vols. Louvain: Muséon, 1944–80.

La Vallée Poussin, Louis de. *L'Abhidharmakośa de Vasubandhu.* 6 vols. Paris and Louvain: Institut Belges des Hautes Etudes Chinoises, 1923–1931.

———. *Madhyamakāvatāra par Candrakīrti.* Edition of Tibetan. Bibliotheca Buddhica IX. St. Petersburg: Academie Impériale des Sciences, 1907.

———. *Madhyamakāvatāra de Candrakīrti.* Partial translation: VIII, pp. 249–317; XI, pp. 217–358; XV, pp. 236–328. Paris: Muséon, 1907–1911.

———. *Mūlamadhyamakakārikās de Nāgārjuna avec le Prasannapadā commentaire de Candrakīrti.* St. Petersburg: Academie Impériale des Sciences, 1903–1913.

Lévi, S. *Mahāyāna-Sūtrālaṁkāra: Exposé de la Doctrine du Grande Véhicule.* Paris: Librarie Honoré Champion, 1907 (Sanskrit); 1911 (French).

Lhalungpa, L. *Life of Milarepa.* New York: Dutton, 1977.

Limaye, S.V. *Mahayanasutralamkara.* Bibliotheca Indo-Buddhica, no. 94. Delhi: Sri Satguru Publications, 1992.

Maxwell, N. *Great Compassion: The Chief Cause of Bodhisattvas.* Ph.D. dissertation, University of Wisconsin (Madison), 1975.

Mullin, G. *Lives of the Six Ornaments.* Mundgod: Drepung Monastery Press, 1979–1980.

Murti, T.R.V. *The Central Philosophy of Buddhism: A Study of the Madhyamika System.* London: George Allen & Unwin, 1955.

Nagao, G. *A Study of Tibetan Buddhism.* Tokyo: Iwanami Shoten, 1954.

———. *Mādhyamika and Yogācāra: A Study of Mahāyāna Philosophies.* Ed. and trans. by L. Kawamura. Albany: State University of New York Press, 1991.

———. "The Bodhisattva's Compassion Described in the *Mahāyānasūtrālankāra.*" In *Wisdom, Compassion, and the Search for Understanding: The Buddhist Studies Legacy of Gadjin M. Nagao*, ed. by Jonathan A Silk. Honolulu: University of Hawai'i Press, 2000.

Nāgārjuna. *Precious Garland.* Trans. by P.J. Hopkins. London: Allen & Unwin, 1975.

Nagatomi, M. "The Pramāṇavārttika of Dharmakīrti." Unpublished manuscript.

Obermiller, E. *Analysis of the Abhisamayālaṁkāra.* London: Luzac, 1933.

———. *Buston's History of Buddhism in India and the Jewelry of Scripture.* Tokyo: Suzuki Research Foundation, 1975.

———. *Doctrine of Prajñāpāramitā as Exposed in the Abhisamayālaṁkāra of Maitreya.* Heidelberg: Acta Orientalia, 1932.

———. *The Sublime Science of the Great Vehicle to Salvation, Being a Manual of Buddhist Monism.* [A study and transaltion of the Ratnagotravibhāga/ Uttaratantra] Acta Orientalia, vol. 9. Leiden: Apud E. Brill, 1931.

Pandeya, R.C. *Madhyāntavibhāgaśāstra.* Delhi: Motilal Banarsidass, 1971.

Pasadika, B. "Nāgārjuna's Sūtrasamuccaya." *Journal of Religious Studies* (Patiala, Punjabi University) 7, no. 1 (1979): 19–44.

Pradhan, P. *Abhidharmasamuccaya.* Santiniketan: Visvabharati Press, 1950.

Rahder, J. *Daśabhūmikasūtra.* Louvain: Institut Belges des Hautes Etudes Chinoises, 1926.

Rahula, W. *Le Compendium de la super-doctrine.* Paris: L'École Française d'Extrême-Orient, 1971.

Roerich, N. *The Blue Annals.* Delhi: Motilal Banarsidass, 1976.

Ruegg, D.S. *Life of Bu Ston Rinpoche.* Serie Orientale Roma, XXXIV. Rome: Istituto Italiano per il Medio ed Estremo Oriente, 1966.

———. *La Théorie du Tathāgatagarbha et du Gotra: Études sur la Sotériologie et la Gnoséologie du Bouddhisme.* Paris: L'École Française d'Extrême-Orient, 1969.

———. *Le Traité du Tathāgatagarbha de Bu Ston Rin Chen Grub.* Paris: L'École Française d'Extrême-Orient, 1973.

Schayer, S. *Ausgewahlte Kapitel aus der Prasannapadā.* Krakow: Polska Akademja Umiejetności, Prace Komisji Orjentalistycznej, 1931.

Shastri, D. *Abhidharmakośabhāṣya.* Varanasi: Bauddha Bharati, 1973.

———. *Pramāṇavārttika.* Varanasi: Bauddha Bharati, 1968.

———. *Tattvasaṁgraha.* Varanasi: Bauddha Bharati, 1968.

Shastri, N.S. "Madhyamakāvatāra VI" (Sanskrit restoration). *Journal of Oriental Research* (Madras): IV (1930); V (1931); VI (1932).

Sprung, M. *Lucid Exposition of the Middle Way.* Boulder: Prajñā, 1979.

Stcherbatski, T. *Buddhist Logic,* vol. II. New York: Dover, 1972.

———. *The Conception of Buddhist Nirvāṇa.* Leningrad: USSR Academy of Sciences, 1927.

———. *Discrimination between Middle and Extremes.* Calcutta: R.D. Press, 1971. (Reprint Bibliotheca Buddhica XXX.)

Streng, F. *Emptiness, A Study in Religious Meaning.* New York: Abingdon, 1967.

Suzuki, D.T. *Laṅkāvatārasūtra.* London: Routledge and Kegan Paul, 1956.

Takasaki, J. *A Study on the Ratnagotravibhāga.* Serie Orientale Roma, XXXIII. Rome: Istituto Italiano per il Medio ed Estremo Oriente, 1966.

TAKEUCHI Shōko. "On Māhāyānasūtrālaṁkāra—brought by Ōtani Mission" (in Japanese). *Ryūkoku Daigaku Ronshū: Journal of Ryūkoku University* (Kyōto) 352 (August 1956): 72–87.

Thurman, R.A.F. *Tsong Khapa's Speech of Gold in the "Essence of True Eloquence".* Princeton: Princeton University Press, 1984. (Reprinted in paperback as *The Central Philosophy of Tibet: A Study and Translation of Jey Tsong Khapa's Essence of True Eloquence.* Princeton: Princeton University Press, 1991.)

Indexes

The following indexes to the translation are provided below:

Index of Texts Cited

Acintitasutta of the Aṅguttaranikāya, 62

Akṣayabodhisattvasūtra, 38

Amarakośa, 117

Ārya-varmavyūha-nirdeśa (Dkon brTsegs P.760:7 Tshi 144b7–145a5), 100

Bhārahāra Scripture, 290

Discourse on the Ten Stages (*Daśabhūmikasūtra*), 58, 176, 266

Dialogue with Brahma Sūtra, 150, 154

Former Life Tales, 92

Gayāśīrṣasūtra, 32

Heap of Faculties Scripture (*Bahudhātukasūtra*), 23

Jñānālokālaṁkārasūtra, 74, 80

Kāśyapaparivarta, 45, 173, 300

Kṣāranadī Sutra, 181

Lalitavistara, 112

Laṇkāvatārasūtra, 323

Mahāyānasūtrasaṁgraha, 166

Maṅgalasutta, 168

Māṇḍavya Sutra, 340

Pañcaka-nipāta (Discourse) of the Aṅguttaranikāya, 199, 289

Pañcaviṁśatiśāhasrikāprajñāpāramitā, 38, 127

Parijñā Scripture, 290

Purity of the Realms Scripture (*Gocarapariśuddhisūtra*; *spyod yul yongs su dag pa'i mdo*), 47

Ratnameghasūtra, 137

Saddharmapuṇḍarīkasūtra, 75, 88

Śatasāhasrika-prajñāpāramitāsūtra, 127, 169, 170

Scripture on the Five Points (*Pañcasthānasūtra*), 199

Sāgaramatisūtra, 86

Śrīmālā Sūtra, 141

Tathāgatācintyaguhyanirdeśa, 100

Author-Text Index (Sanskrit)

Author-Text Index (Tibetan)

Subject Index